THE
TWO
HUNDRED
YEARS WAR

MICHAEL LIVINGSTON

THE
TWO HUNDRED YEARS WAR

THE BLOODY CROWNS
OF ENGLAND AND FRANCE,
1292-1492

An Apollo Book

ALSO BY MICHAEL LIVINGSTON

The Killing Ground: A Biography of Thermopylae
Agincourt: Battle of the Scarred King
Origins of the Wheel of Time
Crécy: Battle of Five Kings
Never Greater Slaughter: Brunanburh and the Birth of England
Medieval Warfare: A Reader

FICTION

The Seaborn Cycle:
Seaborn
Iceborn
Stormborn

The Shards Series:
The Ark and the Empire
The Spear and the Storm
The Ring and the Ruin

This book is dedicated
to Kayla

First published in the UK in 2025 by Head of Zeus Ltd,
part of Bloomsbury Publishing Plc

9 7 5 3 1 2 4 6 8

A catalogue record for this book is available from the British Library.

ISBN (HB): 9781035906369
ISBN (E): 9781035906345

Typeset by Siliconchips Services Ltd UK
Maps © Jeff Edwards

Printed and bound in Great Britain
by Clays Ltd, Elcograf S.p.A.

MIX
Paper | Supporting
responsible forestry
FSC
www.fsc.org   FSC® C018072

Bloomsbury Publishing Plc
50 Bedford Square, London, WC1B 3DP, UK
Bloomsbury Publishing Ireland Limited,
29 Earlsfort Terrace, Dublin 2, DO2 AY28, Ireland

Head of Zeus Ltd
5–8 Hardwick Street
London EC1R 4RG

To find out more about our authors and books
visit www.headofzeus.com
For product safety related questions contact productsafety@bloomsbury.com

Ten thousand bloody crowns of mothers' sons
Shall ill become the flower of England's face,
Change the complexion of her maid-pale peace
To scarlet indignation, and bedew
Her pastures' grass with faithful English blood.

— Shakespeare, *Richard II*

It is the magic of nationalism to turn chance into destiny.

— Benedict Anderson, *Imagined Communities*

Contents

List of Maps

Preface:
A New History, a New War

Labelling History | Keystones of History |
Names in This Book

Henry V at Agincourt. Edward III at Crécy. The Black Prince at Poitiers. Joan of Arc at Orléans. The Hundred Years War is a generational conflict bursting with some of the most famous figures and fascinating fights in history. Across this age of war, England and France bore witness to uncountable deaths, unbelievable tragedy and uncompromising glory. It's the stuff of remarkable movies and some of the best damn lines in Shakespeare.

And no one knows what it is.

The traditional definition is clear enough: The Hundred Years War was a 116-year period of conflict between England and France that began in 1337 and lasted until 1453. Trouble is, no one at that time believed they were engaged in a 'Hundred Years War'. No one declared it begun. No one declared it ended. No one who fought and died in the Hundred Years War would have even *called* it that. The label 'Hundred Years War' didn't exist until it was coined for a chapter heading in a French textbook in 1823, some 370 years after the struggle's supposed conclusion.[1]

Modern historians typically date the start of the war as 24 May 1337. This is the day on which King Philippe VI of France declared that English-held lands in France were forfeit to the French crown. Three years later, King Edward III of England responded by declaring himself, rather than Philippe, to be the rightful king of France, going so far as to quarter the English royal coat of arms with the *fleur-de-lis* of France to show how serious he was.

Starting the war in 1337 also roughly fits a statement from Jean de Rinel, a Frenchman in the service of the English king, who said in 1435 that 'for one hundred years, by battles and other deeds, evils and irreparable damages have continually multiplied both by sea and on land', in a war fought 'over the right and title to the crown of France'.[2]

But the fighting wasn't over in 1435. Historians typically mark the end of the Hundred Years War almost two decades later, on 19 October 1453. This was the date when French forces seized control of the city of Bordeaux, the last major English holding in the French region called Gascony, after a massive French victory at the Battle of Castillon that summer. Yet if we accept this as our end point, then not only was Jean de Rinel wrong about the war's end date, he was also mistaken in thinking that it was fought over the crown of France. The English claim to the throne of France didn't technically end until the start of the nineteenth century. It was in 1800 – eight years after the French Revolution violently ended the monarchy of France – that King George III had the *fleur-de-lis* at last removed from the royal arms.

If we accept the traditional dates, in other words, the only thing the longest military conflict in the history of Europe can coherently be said to be about is the physical presence of English administrators in Gascony. That is what started it. That is what ended it.

But this would be a strange way to understand a violent age that tore Europe apart. Blood was spilled far beyond the borders of England and France. The Low Countries (in particular those parts constituting modern Belgium) became war zones. Italy was swept up. So, too, the Holy Roman Empire, the Iberian peninsula, Scotland and Wales. We may think of the Hundred Years War as a fight between two crowns, but the reality is much larger, much more complicated and infinitely more interesting. These years of conflict drove enormous leaps forward in military technology and organization. They helped build political systems and national identities. They forged myths and fundamentally shaped multiple modern states. Few periods in history have done so much to create our world.

Labelling History

If you've heard of anything associated with the Hundred Years War, odds are that it will be related to its four most famous military engagements: Edward III's victory at Crécy in 1346, the Black Prince's victory at Poitiers in 1356, Henry V's victory at Agincourt in 1415 and Joan of Arc's victory at Orléans in 1429. Three won by English leaders. One by a French girl who heard voices. It's telling, in that regard, that three of the four are England's greatest victories in the war. And the fourth, while an English defeat, is generally remembered outside France not for its role in an English loss, but for what it says about gender, faith and hope.

It's natural that English speakers, raised and educated in England or in countries historically tied to England (as mine is), should have an England-centred view of the past. It surely helps explain why so many have understood the conflict as reflecting English interests alone, like Edward III's claim to be the rightful king of France. But when we step back and try to see the bigger picture of what was happening, one of the first things we notice is that the English did not start the fight. The French did.

The events that we have collectively labelled the Hundred Years War are best seen as a sequence of steps in France's struggle to define itself: its borders, its powers, its place in the world. For much of this period, France's primary obstacle to growing and coalescing as a state was indeed England. But this was by no means its only rival. Burgundy stood in the way, too. So did Brittany. The king of England wasn't even the only sovereign at the time who argued he had a better claim to the throne of France than the French king did. Around the same time the king of Navarre (a region of modern Spain) said the same thing and probably had a better case.

Recognizing France as the engine driving the war – and recognizing that the war was about far more than just control of Gascony – also requires us to take a wider view of when the conflict began and ended. By my reckoning, the war didn't last 116 years, 4 months, 3 weeks and 4 days. The Hundred Years War as I will define it actually lasted two full centuries – from 1292 to 1492.

Not a Hundred Years War, but a *Two* Hundred Years War.

I do not make this claim lightly. I am not trying to be bold. My redefinition of one of the most famous periods in history simply follows from the facts as I see them, and a recognition that *any* after-the-fact label we put on history says more about the interests of the person (or persons) doing the labelling than it does about the period being labelled. Our attention to the present fundamentally shapes our definition of the past. As we change, as our interests change, so does our understanding of our history.

The Middle Ages themselves are a case in point. This historical label has roots in fourteenth-century Italy, where figures like the poet Petrarch saw themselves as rebirthing (this is what the word *renaissance* means) 'proper' culture into a world that had lost its way after the 'fall' of the Roman empire. For Petrarch and others of like mind, the period 'in the middle' between Rome and their own modern age was quite literally the Middle Ages, and it was not looked upon favourably. It's easy to see Petrarch's vested interest in defining history in ways that made him and his country the centre of things, but the basic implication of his idea has been hard to shake. People still use the word *medieval* (which comes from the Latin *medium aevum*, meaning 'Middle Ages') to refer to things they think are dirty, backward or just plain wrong. Meanwhile, the larger periodization of human history into the categories of ancient, medieval and modern has stuck, too, despite the fact that there's no agreement at all on just how *any* of these periods ought to be defined.

It would not be fair for me to speculate too much on the intentions of those who created our old definition of the Hundred Years War in the nineteenth century. What I can do, though, is lay my own cards on the table as I propose a definition for the period I'm about to study.

The best way to do that is with a story.

On 22 July 1274, the king of Navarre and count of Champagne died – somehow choked on his own fat, so the stories said – leaving his titles in the hands of his one-and-a-half-year-old daughter.

Her name was Jeanne, and she and her mother, who was acting as regent for the little girl, immediately found themselves under attack from those who wished to take advantage of Navarre's perceived weakness. Jeanne's mother hurried her daughter into the protection of her cousin, King Philippe III of France. Navarre was made safe with French support, and in return France negotiated for a treaty. It ensured that the child-queen of Navarre would marry one of Philippe's two sons when she was older.

It was a shrewd political move.

On 16 August 1284, the terms of the treaty that Navarre had signed at last were met. The eldest surviving son and namesake of the king of France married Jeanne, the queen of Navarre and countess of Champagne. The groom was sixteen. The bride a mere eleven. On that day, the young man taking his vows married into the rule of both her kingdom of Navarre and her county of Champagne.

Only a few decades later, the poet Dante Alighieri, in the second of the three books of his *Divine Comedy*, describes meeting two rulers in Purgatory. Both of them, he says, are for ever fixed in abject grief, because as

> Father and father-in-law to the plague of France,
> They know his foul and filthy life.
> Thus are they saddled with sorrow[3]

The two men are King Philippe III of France and King Henry the Fat of Navarre. The plague that they lament setting upon France – and, by Dante's thinking, upon the world – is Jeanne's husband, who, less than fourteen months after becoming king of Navarre and count of Champagne, succeeded to his father's throne and took the crown of France as Philippe IV in 1285.

Philippe IV managed to do a lot during his subsequent 29-year rule as king of France. Dante despised him for causing the movement of the papacy from Rome to Avignon – and all the political and religious turmoil that resulted from it. Philippe opened up major, bloody conflicts against both England and Flanders as he tirelessly centralized power to the French throne. In so doing he became one of the people most responsible for the cruelties and calamities of the centuries of war to come.

So, as I define the war he did so much to birth, I could pick any number of dates as its start. Is it the year Philippe IV became king in 1285? Or would it be better to pick his marriage to Jeanne the year before, since that was the moment he first pulled new territory into the French domain? Or, given that their marriage hinged on the treaty that was signed when Jeanne had to flee her home, should *that* be the start date? Every happening relies on what happened before.

To define a war, we surely ought to seek a particular flashpoint. Human history is marked by seemingly endless competitions for power – whether that power is political, economic, cultural or something else – but *wars* happen when that existing struggle for power breaks into active, violent conflict at scale, as one group or state tries to wrest power from the hands of another that tries to claw it back. The moment can be small, if what follows is large. The First World War, for example, is often said to begin with a single death: the assassination of Archduke Franz Ferdinand of Austria in Sarajevo on 28 June 1914.

In the case of the Two Hundred Years War, I don't see the beginning in a royal court in 1337. Instead, it starts with a murder during a chance encounter between mariners seeking water on a desolate island in 1292.[4] That first killing fed generations of death that only ended with the Peace of Étaples in 1492.

Keystones of History

This book is a traditional narrative history, recounting the events and characters of the story in chronological order.[5] But which events, and which characters?

We often talk about history as a chain of events, in which every action depends upon the action or actions that came before it. Since one cannot recount every event like this, we might do better to think about history in the image of an architectural feature that would have been very familiar to the people living in the Middle Ages: the stone arch.

Each block of an arch is held in place by the blocks around it. For all its graceful beauty and remarkable ability to support a structure, an arch is only as strong as those individual blocks, and they all need to be there: pull just one out and the entire arch will collapse. Unlike a chain, in which the links are truly all the same, there is one block in an arch that is different from the rest: the keystone. A wedge slotted between the curving uprights to either side, the keystone sits at the apex of an arch. The keystone does not need to be the strongest of the stones. It can actually be the weakest, since it bears less weight than any other piece in an arch. But what it *must* be is a perfect fit. When an arch is being built, external supports hold up the two sides as the blocks are stacked one upon another, slowly curving inward. Throughout this process, an arch-to-be is in constant danger of collapse. Once the perfect keystone is slipped into place, however, those delicate, unstable stacks of stone become a single, stout structure. The scaffolding that supported the construction can be pulled away. Put simply, the keystone defines the arch.

It is the essential job of those who study the past – from archaeologists working in the field to archivists working in the library – to find as many stones as possible, to touch and catalogue them, preserving every possible sliver of history's graceful arc. No discovery is too small. The historian then sifts through the incomplete set of interconnected stones that remain – the myriad bits of data about the events in question – in order to determine the shape of the arch that they create. This shape allows us to re-create the missing pieces that must have been there to make it complete. And that shape, as I've said, is ultimately defined by the keystone, the single piece that makes the whole thing click into place.

This would be a very long book if we were to look at *every* stone. Of necessity, we must focus largely on the keystones, those events that, establishing one arch after another, can ultimately hold up the edifice of the story we are trying to understand. But we will also take moments to dive into the details – not just to explain how we know what we know, but also to help us understand the realities of this war. The casualties of the Two Hundred Years War are quite literally uncountable. The majority of them were innocents.

In the years of writing this book, I've studied that violence and horror. I've lived with it as best I can. The blood spilled and the lives shattered are heart-breaking and mind-boggling. I will have failed if I do not share this, too.

Names in This Book

I am writing this book in English, but I am *not* writing an English-centred history. I'm not interested in writing a book favouring *any* identity. I am presenting a story of these years as they would have been known to those who lived them in England, in France, in Spain and elsewhere.

Some of the differences will be obvious. Others will be subtle, like a small but important shift in how I will talk about the key players of our story: I may not use their names as you know them. Already I have called the king of France Philippe VI, not Philip VI. He was French, and I use his name as he would have known it. This may make things a little harder for you if you are an English speaker, but I hope you understand why this is important.

That said, this is a guideline and not a rule. Looking back, you can see that I've referred to the amazing young woman who lifted the siege of Orléans as Joan of Arc, when by my guideline I ought to have written Jeanne d'Arc. Rightly or wrongly, I feel like her identity is so deeply engrained in popular culture that to force a linguistic adjustment in her case would interrupt the flow of the story. For similar narrative reasons, I also generally refer to dukes, earls and the like by their titles or nicknames rather than their given names. Likewise, I've done everything I can to streamline the events and the cast in this story. For instance, I might refer to 'the English' in a battle, even though the force in question might hold Gascon, Castilian and other unit components.

There has also been a question of how to refer to the names of places that have changed over time. When there is a difference, I have opted for modern names. Though these may not be the names familiar to the people in the story, they are the names that we will find on maps today, and I strongly believe in using the present landscape to bring us into contact with the past. Henry V spoke of the castle at Agincourt, but I'll be referring to the town as Azincourt since that's where you'd go to see it today. That said, I'll still call the *battle* Agincourt for the same reason that Joan is Joan. Thus the Battle of Agincourt in 1415 took place near today's town of Azincourt.

Introduction:
The Wars Before the War

Early France | Of Insurance and Kingship | Enter the Vikings |
England, France and the Oriflamme | Rise of the Angevins | First
Hundred Years War | Bouvines | Treaty of Paris | Stage Set

Joyous, curious, in some parts rapturous, the crowds in the streets on this cold Christmas Day in 508 strained to glimpse the king who strode up the wide steps of the cathedral of Reims.[1] Those who managed it would have seen a middle-aged man, his beardless face framed by long locks of hair freshly combed and oiled for the occasion. His crimson cloak, adorned with golden bees, was clasped at his right shoulder in the style of a Roman military commander, and in the masses there were some who saluted him as citizens once did for the emperors of old.[2]

But little about the man was truly Roman.

The Romans had first encountered his forebears on the northern frontier of their empire, around the lower reaches of the Rhine. Though these Germanic peoples were not a single tribe or a unified group, the Romans collectively called them *Franks*, which may derive from the Proto-Germanic word for 'javelin' or 'spear'. This man's name, in that same language, was probably pronounced something like Chlodovech, but the history books record it as Clovis.

Through bloody battles and tense alliances, Frankish leaders before Clovis had steadily unified and expanded their territory south and west from the mouth of the Rhine. Much of this expansion was likely driven by a particular group of Franks called the Salians, a name we will hear again in the story of the Two

Hundred Years War. By the time Clovis became king, the extent of their territory was something close to today's modern Belgium.

Clovis outdid them all. Just a year and a half before this cold day, sometime in the spring of 507, he had beaten a rival Visigothic army in the Battle of Vouillé, not far from the city of Poitiers. His victory opened the doors to a Frankish take-over of the massive region in the southwestern corner of today's France that the Romans had called Gallia Aquitania – or, more simply, Aquitaine – and won him such renown that the Byzantine emperor in distant Constantinople had named Clovis an honorary consul.[3] By the time he was done, the borders of the Frankish kingdom had expanded to encompass even more of what would become modern France. Brittany was still largely outside his control, as was the immediate coastline along the Mediterranean, which was split between the kingdoms of the Visigoths (largely in what we now call Spain) and the Ostrogoths (largely in Italy). Caught between them, also outside Frankish control, were the Burgundians, a rough bubble of non-Frankish people centred on Lyon, taking up parts of modern France and Switzerland. Because he held just about everything else that is today considered France, Clovis is called by many the 'first king of France'. Whether or not that's an apt descriptor, he came to loom over how France defined itself.

And this day in Reims was central to that perception.

According to one story of what happened that day, the cathedral of Reims was ablaze with colour and the splendours of earthly riches that promised heavenly rewards. The air was thick with lustrous perfumes. Everything had been prepared in advance. The bishop, a man named Remigius, led the king to the waiting baptistry. Prayers were said. The queen, already a devout member of the church, wept. Clovis professed himself a Christian, and the bishop duly baptized him into Christianity's Nicene faith.

In another, more detailed, story the bishop – now *Saint* Remigius, or Saint-Rémi in French – looked up to heaven just before he baptized the king. As he did so, a white dove descended, a vial clasped in its beak. When the bishop took it, the dove disappeared. Astonished, he uncorked the small glass bottle, and the sweetest, most splendid scents arose from the oil within, washing out over the gathered throng and filling them with gladness. Clovis bowed down before the miracle, and the bishop anointed him with the holy oil.

It was this second story that became standard belief across the coming centuries. It made Clovis into a consecrated king, chosen and affirmed by God. Little wonder, then, that it became necessary for the kings of France to be crowned in Reims and there anointed with this same oil: doing so marked *them* as consecrated kings.

Just as importantly, though, the story also marks his *kingdom* as one chosen and affirmed by God. The borders of what Clovis had built had divine sanction, making this moment the origin for a definition of 'France' that would not only lead to the Two Hundred Years War, but also make Reims itself a vital location in that conflict.

Early France

When Clovis died in 511, his kingdom went to his sons. They and their descendants ruled the Merovingian dynasty, named after Merovech, a supposed Salian progenitor of Clovis.

In time, the Merovingians managed to fold the Burgundians into their rule, and they pushed further into the central reaches of modern Germany. But more land meant more administration and more complexity. The power of the kings was increasingly decentralized, and their dynasty steadily weakened until it was at last supplanted by a family called the Carolingians. Their most famous member was Charlemagne, who began his reign as king of the Franks in 768. Over the course of his long and remarkable career he managed to unify almost the entirety of western Europe, along with a good part of Central Europe. On Christmas Day 800, the pope crowned him emperor of the West (meaning the western part of the old Roman empire). The political entity that would eventually descend from this title – what we call the Holy Roman Empire – would be one of the powers against which France would need to define itself in the Two Hundred Years War.

At this point, though, all was unity. Even after Charlemagne's death in 814, the realm remained whole: the emperor had only one surviving son to succeed him, so Louis the Pious – his name the French version of Clovis – ruled over a unified Carolingian empire.

When Louis died in 840, however, there were *three* sons – and civil war broke out over who would get what.[4] It took three years of fighting for the three sons to agree to break the empire into three pieces: West Francia, Middle Francia and East Francia. Alas, the Treaty of Verdun, which codified this agreement, purchased an immediate peace at the cost of long-term conflict.

The main problem was Middle Francia. This comprised the Frisian coast in today's Netherlands, as well as a narrow vertical stretch of lands situated between the Rhine and Scheldt rivers. The eastern half of the old Burgundian kingdom was included, along with Provence and essentially all of northern Italy. So, unlike the kingdoms of East and West Francia to either side of it, Middle Francia lacked geographical cohesion. Quite to the contrary, it was split in two by the Alps. The relative stability of West Francia allowed it to directly evolve into France. East Francia, albeit less directly, evolved into Germany. But Middle Francia didn't evolve. In part due to its geographical disunity and in part due to the unexpected early deaths of several of its princes, Middle Francia *de*volved into smaller bits and pieces of states and cities. These inevitably squabbled with each other while the more powerful kingdoms to east and west eyed them hungrily. We can still see the vestiges of this disunity in the stack of middle European states on a modern map: Italy, Switzerland, Liechtenstein, Luxembourg, Belgium and the Netherlands. The jumble of these regions was, we'll see, actually far messier for much of the Middle Ages.[5]

Still, we need to be cautious in terms of how much political cohesion we attribute to West Francia. Yes, it had enough cohesion to hold together and become France, but it would be *very* misleading to imagine the kingdom of West Francia as anything

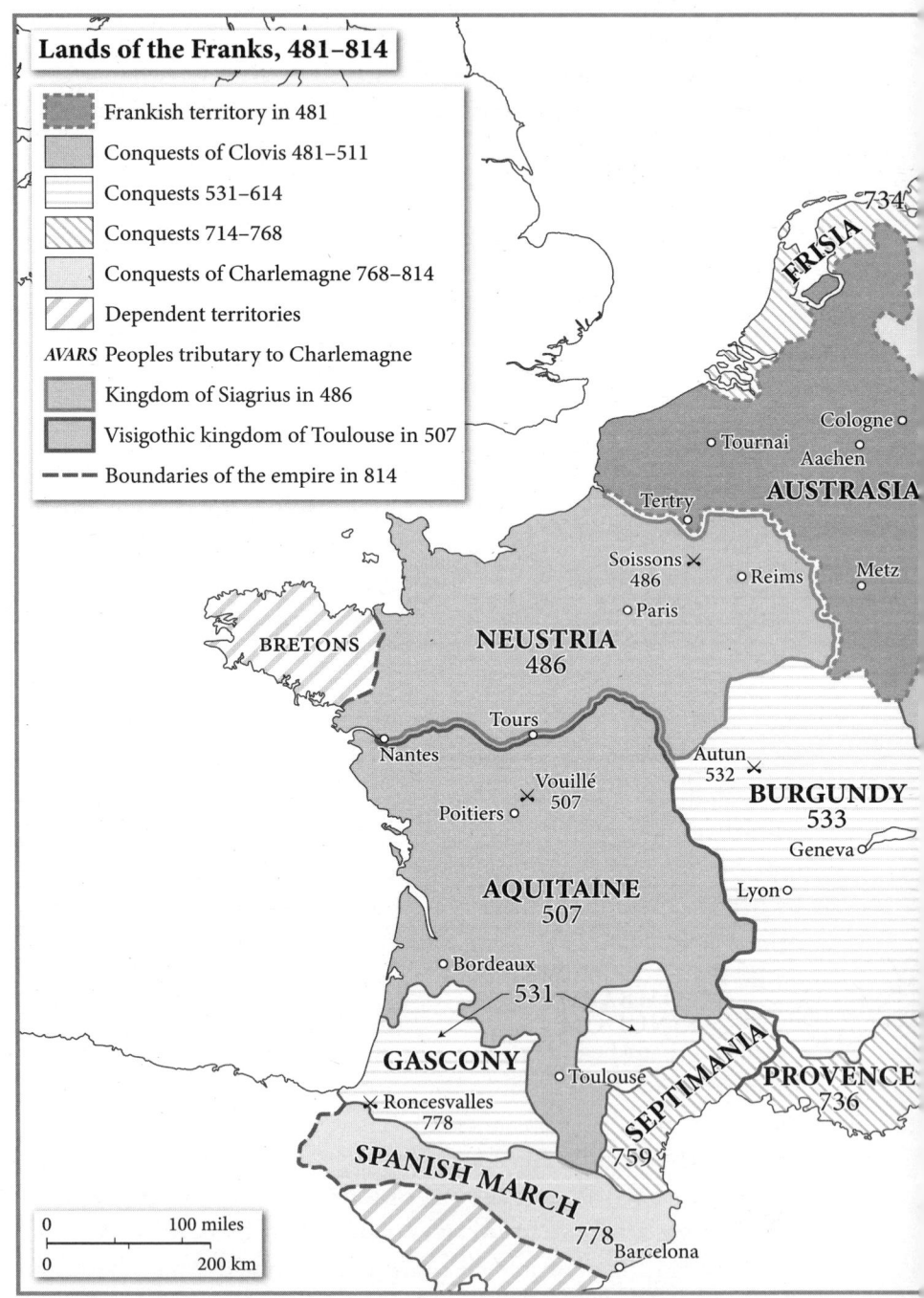

Lands of the Franks, 481–814

- Frankish territory in 481
- Conquests of Clovis 481–511
- Conquests 531–614
- Conquests 714–768
- Conquests of Charlemagne 768–814
- Dependent territories
- *AVARS* Peoples tributary to Charlemagne
- Kingdom of Siagrius in 486
- Visigothic kingdom of Toulouse in 507
- – – – Boundaries of the empire in 814

734

FRISIA

Cologne
Tournai
Aachen
AUSTRASIA

Tertry

Soissons
486
Reims
Metz

Paris

BRETONS

NEUSTRIA
486

Tours

Nantes

Autun
532

BURGUNDY
533

Vouillé
507

Poitiers

Geneva

AQUITAINE
507

Lyon

Bordeaux

531

GASCONY

Toulouse

SEPTIMANIA

PROVENCE
736

Roncesvalles
778

759

SPANISH MARCH

778
Barcelona

0   100 miles
0   200 km

N

810

OBOTRITES

SAXONY
777–97

Süntel ✕
782

VELETI

531

SORBS
805

Fulda ○

THURINGIA
774

CZECHS

MORAVIANS

SWABIA
502

Strasbourg ○

Regensburg ○

BAVARIA
788

Salzburg ○

CARINTHIA
788

AVARS
796

536

Milan ○
Pavia ○

Venice ○

Ravenna ○

CROATS

SERBS

**LOMBARD
KINGDOM**
533

Spoleto ○

CORSICA

Rome ○

Carolingian Empire, 814–43

West Francia
Middle Francia
East Francia

like a unified state in the way modern France is today. The difference has everything to do with what it meant to be king.

Of Insurance and Kingship

Most of us imagine kings as absolute authorities. But the truth is that while monarchies *can* be one-ruler-above-all, they don't *have* to be. The king of the Franks in this period more often than not held a lofty title but surprisingly little central command.

In the early Middle Ages, becoming king required more than just a bloodline: it required the support of rich and powerful people. Without that, all one had was a fancy chair and hat. So one way to understand kingship at this point in history is to ask what's in it for those other people. Why would they even want a king?

A king was something like an insurance policy. He received the support of his lords, who swore to provide service if called upon. Whether that service was military support or money or some other kind of duty, they promised to give *something* to the king. The king then agreed to provide support in return. If, say, a lord's lands were attacked, then the king promised to marshal the pooled resources of the kingdom to bear in his lord's defence. For most of the lords, having a king was probably something of a bad investment: if nothing went wrong, they were doing little more than subsidizing the king's living. But on balance they believed that the potential benefits of the king's help outweighed the cost of keeping him around.

In the Middle Ages, this basic concept of taking an individual oath to ensure collective benefit established a series of relationships between a lord and his vassals (the people agreeing to serve the lord). These oaths of fealty lie at the centre of what we call *feudalism*, which appears in recognizable forms in the Carolingian period: at this point, a major part of the benefit to the vassal was not just the promise of mutual military aid in time of need, but a grant to use an area of land called a fief (in Latin, a *feodum*). Whether what was being granted was the land itself or only the right to collect revenues from it, the point was the same: collection of resources gave the vassal the ability to maintain a sufficient base from which he could meet his duty to the lord.

Feudalism has something of a bad name among many historians of the Middle Ages. They worry that it suggests a more standardized system of political governance and social organization than it really was, and they're right. Feudalism evolved in different ways across different places and times: because it was based on individual relationships surrounding wants, needs and capabilities, it never could be a one-size-fits-all system. These details of difference matter.

Even within narrow slices of time and place, we still need to take care with the term: feudalism does not organize full social systems. For one thing, it was not equally distributed across the haves and have-nots. A person who cannot afford a car has little part to play in the collective-benefit system of car insurance. Likewise, a person with nothing to offer a lord might be said to have little part to play in the feudal relationship-making of medieval kingship.

That said, generalities like feudalism nevertheless provide a framework we can use to better recognize individual differences, and even those who were in no position to make oaths of their own could nevertheless have their lives and fates bound by the oaths of others.

Those oaths are essential to our story. Though the Middle Ages had legal contracts and some basic mechanisms of contract enforcement, the primary glue that bound society together was trust that these feudal agreements would be upheld – that people would maintain fealty to what they said they would or would not do. In this world, follow-through was not just expected, it was a matter of quasi-religious importance. The word *fealty* derives, in fact, from the Latin *fidelitas*, meaning 'faithfulness'.

Medieval people were perfectly capable of lies and deceit, of betrayal on the grandest of scales. We will see plenty of it all in the course of the Two Hundred Years War. But it was nevertheless the social norm that most people would do what they said they would do, because a mutual delivery on agreements enabled the cohesion of the community itself.

We will talk a great deal about 'honour' in the course of this book. It's an amorphous concept, but a vital one. In the Middle Ages, oaths weren't something you merely said, they were something you almost always definitively *meant* – because it would be dishonourable if you did not.

Dishonour, of course, is a social problem. If you do something dishonourable and no one knows about it, it's of little impact. What matters is when dishonour is known and becomes a matter of identification within the larger community. So oaths of fealty were not just heavy with symbolic gestures to signify their social importance, but they also tended to involve public declarations in what were called acts of homage: ceremonial public pledges that the vassal would be the lord's man (Latin *homme*, from which the word *homage* derives).

These oaths of fealty, and the feudal structures upon which they were built, would actively tear lives and kingdoms apart in the centuries of war ahead.

Enter the Vikings, 845–1066

In the year 845, just two years after the treaty splitting the empire into thirds, the people of Paris awoke on Easter Sunday to find the Seine filled with over a hundred ships carrying thousands of men. The Vikings had come.

The sack of Paris was devastating, and the king of West Francia, Charles the Bald, was only able to end it by paying off the invaders with roughly 2.6 tons of gold and silver. It was a steep price for peace, especially as it informed future raiders of just how wealthy West Francia was. More attacks inevitably followed.

The most important of these raids for our present purposes is that of a Viking the history books usually name Rollo – he probably called himself Hrólfr – who had seized Rouen in 876 and used it as a base for further attacks. In 911, the king of West Francia – by now it was Charles the Simple – decided that the best way to defend his lands from the invaders was to welcome them. If he gave lands to some of the Vikings, the king reasoned, then they would defend those lands as his subjects. And so the Treaty of Saint-Clair-sur-Epte was signed, giving

Rouen and its surrounding lands at the mouth of the Seine to the Normans – that is, the 'Northmen' – who counted Rollo as their leader. Rollo was named the count of Rouen, but his descendants expanded their holdings in northern France beyond that city and gave their name to the region: the duchy of Normandy.

The cleric Dudo of Saint-Quentin, writing around the year 1000, tells us that after the treaty's terms were decided, Rollo 'put his hands into the hands of the king, which his father, grandfather, and great-grandfather had never done to any one'.

So far, so believable. It was common, in making homage, for the vassal to place his hands into those of the lord in order to mark submission. None of Rollo's Viking predecessors had done this, but now Rollo had. It was a big deal.

For Charles and his fellow Franks, though, it was expected not only that the vassal would put his hands into the hands of his lord, but that he would kneel or bow in order to do so – furthering the symbolism of submission. More than that, it was expected that the vassal would go so far as to kiss the lord's foot. 'But Rollo was unwilling to kiss the king's foot,' Dudo tells us, 'even though the bishops told him that a man who receives such a gift must do so':

> 'I will never bend my knees to anyone else's,' Rollo replied, 'nor will I kiss anyone's foot.' Compelled by the entreaties of the Franks to do something, though, he commanded a certain soldier of his to kiss the king's foot instead. The man immediately seized the king's foot, brought it to his mouth, and, standing up, planted a kiss upon it. This made the king fall over, and all the people laughed.[6]

It makes for a wonderful scene: the king's pride colliding with the Viking's pride, and the king heaved over on his ass. Whatever the slapstick humour in the moment, one doubts that Charles found it amusing. The symbolism of the act was quite literally flipped on its head. And that symbolism mattered.

Alas, we have no idea if the scene really happened. It appears only in Dudo's book, which we cannot take at face value. Dudo tells us that he wrote it at the behest of Rollo's grandson, which must surely leave us wondering how much pro-Norman 'spin' the cleric gave to the stories he chose to record and how he recorded them. At the same time, his access to the Norman court might mean that he had access to stories otherwise unavailable. We often face this tension when it comes to our sources: because none of them are free from bias, we must weigh all of them with careful consideration – while accepting that without them we know close to nothing.

Whether the king-flipping bit is true or not, though, the rest of the story accords with the expectation of a public act of homage to accompany the oaths of fealty. The terms of the treaty itself are likewise correct insofar as we can check: the king was giving lands that at that moment he either could not adequately control (Normandy) or did not control at all (Brittany). To him, the technicality of physically possessing the ground didn't matter. He believed he had the right to give these lands away because they had belonged to his forebears and therefore belonged to him. Though it was gone, the idea of France still existed in the shadow of what it once had been.

This was a fundamental truth of France as it formed out of West Francia: it wasn't 'what we would call a state, but, rather, a collection of lands, rights, and claims'.[7] To the point, the personal lands of the king of the Franks were relatively small. As a result of a weakening in the Carolingian line, a man named Hugh Capet took control of the realm in 987, beginning what we call the Capetian dynasty. Through its main line or its cadet branches, descendants of the Capetians would rule France until the French Revolution.[8] But for all of that, Hugh's royal domain – the land under his direct control, like the Île-de-France and Orléans – totalled only a few hundred square miles. His possessions were veritable islands in a sea of lands under the control of other Frankish lords. These lords could work closely with the king of the Franks or almost completely independently from him. What they held in common, to one degree or another, were the bonds of collective memory, tradition and oaths. Among these semi-autonomous lands were duchies and counties that will play major roles in the Two Hundred Years War: Normandy, Brittany,

Flanders, Burgundy, Aquitaine and Gascony, to name a few. Complicating things further, the internal rule of these lordships often mirrored that of the kingdom itself: the duke or count might rule in name, but he did so over an often unruly sequence of sub-domains as lordships broke governance down into smaller and smaller manors and estates. Insofar as it was a 'system', it was one that favoured those strong enough to enforce their claims upon those who were weaker.

As a result, the next centuries were stretched to breaking by the persistent tension between the perceptions that individual leaders had of themselves as independent actors and the king's perception of them as players within his greater domain. The heart of this tension was the symbolism in that act of homage, the submission that supposedly affronted Rollo.

England, France and the Oriflamme, 1066–1124

Of all the intense bloodshed that would result from these com-peting interests, none is more famed today than the terrible con-flict between England and France that is the subject of this book. Their violent trajectory was arguably set from the moment Duke William of Normandy killed King Harold of England in the Battle of Hastings on 14 October 1066.[9] After a couple of months cam-paigning through the south of England, William was crowned king in Westminster Abbey on Christmas Day 1066: good for him, obviously, but profoundly problematic and undeniably untenable on a larger scale.

In England, King William was a head of state who humbled himself to no man.

In France, Duke William was a man who knelt to put his hands in those of the king of France.

William recognized the strange position of being both a duke and a king. He resolved it by dividing his Norman and English lands between his heirs. His eldest son, Robert, became the duke of Normandy. His second son, William Rufus, became king of England.

In 1100, William II died in a hunting accident, and the

Conqueror's youngest son claimed the throne of England as Henry I. The eldest brother, Robert of Normandy, tried to claim it for himself, but they eventually made peace, only to have Henry I turn around and invade Normandy. After Robert's forces were defeated at the Battle of Tinchebray in 1106, the lands of England and Normandy were once more united.

Unfortunately for Henry, his only legitimate son died when the *White Ship*, sailing from Barfleur in Normandy to England, sank in 1120. With no clear heir to his throne, rivals began looking for ways to weaken and potentially replace him. Among them was Louis VI of France, who saw a chance to push the English king out of Normandy and replace him with William Clito, the well-respected eldest son of William the Conqueror's eldest son. William Clito had a strong claim to the duchy of Normandy and the kingdom of England. He was also, without question, allied with French interests. The plan failed in 1123, with a furious Henry subsequently pushing his son-in-law – who just happened to be the Holy Roman Emperor – to invade northern France from the east while he threatened it from the north. The emperor hoped this might expand his reach into the Lorraine and the Low Countries – we will hear more of them soon enough – but there can be no question that he probably also had an eye towards the potential benefits of being the avenger of his powerful but still heir-less father-in-law. In 1124, the army of the Holy Roman Emperor prepared to march. Its destination was the city of Reims.

The invasion was to be a dagger thrust at the symbolic heart of France, and Louis VI would have to parry it or perish. After calling the country to arms, he headed to the abbey of Saint-Denis north of Paris: Clovis was buried there, as were most of France's subsequent monarchs, and Denis was one of the kingdom's most important patron saints.

After taking communion at the altar, Louis retrieved the standard of the abbey, a triple-pointed banner depicting a golden sun on a blood-red field. It was called the *Oriflamme* (from the Latin *aurea flamma*, meaning 'golden flame'), and it was the duty of the count of Vexin to carry it. Retrieving it now established the

Oriflamme as the battle standard of France, and the tradition that the French king would signify the onset of war by retrieving the banner from Saint-Denis. Time and again throughout the Two Hundred Years War we will see the Oriflamme fly: by that point, it had become understood that if it was raised in a given battle, no prisoners were to be taken.

That Louis's use of the Oriflamme had such lasting impact says much about how well things went for the king in 1124. With the army of the Holy Roman Emperor on the march, Louis raised the Oriflamme and 'powerfully called upon all of France to follow him', as the eyewitness Abbot Suger later wrote.[10] The response was far greater than anyone would have thought possible. A truly massive French force mustered in Reims:

> The fighting spirit of France was spurred in every direction, and the best knights were sent with the strongest forces and men of high valor and veteran, victorious experience. These gathered in great strength in Reims. So massive was this army of knights and infantry that they seemed to devour the surface of the earth like locusts, not only along the banks of the rivers, but also in the mountains and plains.

Previously, the 'French army' often consisted of a small circle of the king's immediate, loyal lords, who kicked enough of their underlings into action to form a host. The good abbot, with an eye towards history, was eager to emphasize the difference in this unprecedented coalition: in 1124, Louis managed to draw his support from nearly every corner of the realm. This time, the French army *was* France. Blois was there. So was Burgundy. And while Anjou and Aquitaine didn't make it, Suger claims this was due to the speed of events.

The Holy Roman Emperor was close to Metz when he received word of the French host gathering to oppose him. Rather than face it in battle, he turned around. 'At that point,' Suger tells us, 'the French returned home, having won such a magnificent and celebrated victory, which was as great or greater than if they had triumphed upon the battlefield.'

This event rarely gets much attention in most history books, but it should not be forgotten. That Louis had forged such a unity among the many dukes and counts of France speaks volumes about not just his personal prestige, but also the growing strength of the French crown. It was a moment of special significance, a fact not lost on Suger, who recalled it in the most hyperbolic terms he could manage: 'Not in our modern age, not even in ancient times has France ever witnessed a more glorious moment – uniting the strength of its members, displaying the glory of its powers – than when, at the same time, it triumphed over the Holy Roman Emperor and the king of England.'

Rise of the Angevins, 1125–54

The Holy Roman Emperor was dead the next year, and his widow, Henry I's daughter, Matilda, returned to her father in England. The death of his son-in-law had taken another of Henry I's potential heirs off the board, and the matter of his succession was an increasingly central concern. At a Christmas gathering of his barons in 1126, Henry made them swear to recognize Matilda as his heir. The following year he arranged for her to wed Geoffrey, the eldest son and heir of the count of Anjou.

Despite the public show of oath-taking in Matilda's favour, many of the ruling elites were utterly opposed to her succession. And while the complexities of alliances meant that there could be additional reasons, there can be little question that her gender was the central problem. For a woman to be declared heir in this way was highly unusual.

Something of this gender imbalance is visible in the fact that although the powerful family of her descendants would come to rule England, the dynasty would be named after Geoffrey's side: theirs would be the house of the Angevin (French for 'from Anjou'), or, more famously in England, the House Plantagenet, an epithet that Geoffrey had been given.

Unsurprisingly, when Henry died in 1135, there were a wide number of people who considered a claim upon the throne of England or the duchy of Normandy. None of them moved faster than Stephen of Blois, the Conqueror's grandson. Reaching England first, Stephen orchestrated his own rapid coronation.

Matilda refused to drop her claim, though, and her husband – by now the count of Anjou, Touraine and Maine – backed her up with an army, sparking a civil war. The subsequent period of English history, from 1135 to 1153, is now known as the Anarchy.

The Anarchy is tremendously fascinating in and of itself, but what matters for *our* story is the eventual settlement of this civil war. Stephen would rule as king, but his own son would not succeed him. Instead, his successor would be Matilda's son by Geoffrey, also named Henry, who had already been made duke of Normandy after she and her husband had wrested those lands from Stephen's side in the tumult. The reason this is so important to our story is simple: the future Henry II married *very* well.

Eleanor of Aquitaine was born into a staggering degree of wealth and power. She was the daughter and heir of the duke of Aquitaine – one of the largest and wealthiest regions of the kingdom now called France. She was still a teenager, perhaps fifteen years old, when her father died. If she wasn't already one of the most sought-after brides in Europe, the moment she became duchess of Aquitaine in 1137 she jumped to the top of the list.

Marriage for those of such station typically had little to do with love. Rather, it was centred on diplomacy and politics – the business of securing estates and titles for future generations of one's house.

If we judge her match by these terms, her first marriage was a good one: just three months after she became duchess of Aquitaine, she married the heir to the throne of France. Weeks later, after his father died, her new husband became King Louis VII, and Eleanor became a queen.

The marriage started well, but in time it became strained. Among other difficulties, Eleanor had borne the king two daughters but no sons. In 1152, their marriage was annulled, leaving Eleanor once again a most eligible bride. On her way back to Poitiers, the capital of Aquitaine, multiple lords attempted to kidnap and marry her by force.

She made her own match instead: she would wed Henry,

the duke of Normandy and count of Anjou, son of Matilda and Geoffrey. They were married just two months after the annulment of Eleanor's marriage to King Louis VII.

Two years later, in 1154, King Stephen was dead. And by the terms that had concluded the Anarchy, Eleanor's husband was accordingly crowned King Henry II of England – the first of its Plantagenet kings. Eleanor was again a queen. Less than two years later Henry II made a move to expand his holdings on the Continent by seizing the viscounty of Thouars.

At home, Eleanor and Henry's marriage was tempestuous but fruitful. She bore him eight children, including five sons. Their union also created what has been popularly, but poorly, termed the Angevin empire: none of its rulers styled themselves – or were styled by others – as 'emperors', and the administrative cohesion of their lands was shaky at best. But the Angevin holdings were nevertheless geographically significant: adding up their duchies of Normandy and Aquitaine and the other regions that they managed to control, Eleanor and Henry held roughly half the lands in France – plus, of course, the whole of England.

However awkward it had been for William the Conqueror to be king of England while also holding lands in France, this was arguably worse. Henry II of England held almost as much French land as the rest of the French lords combined. This made him a rival to King Louis VII of France not just in international terms, but in domestic terms, too.

Eleanor's first and second husbands were on a collision course.

First Hundred Years War, 1159–1259

What happened next is sometimes called the Capetian–Plantagenet rivalry, the Angevin–Capetian struggle or even the First Hundred Years War.

It began when, in 1159, Henry II invaded the county of Toulouse, and King Louis VII of France had no choice but to defend it. Its count was his brother-in-law, but more importantly he had to do something to check Henry's power before it overwhelmed his own. The Capetians had come to power when Hugh Capet took advantage of a weakening Carolingian dynasty. If Louis wasn't careful, Henry might do the same to him.

Henry backed off from Toulouse, only to make a push in the opposite direction. By the mid-1160s he was making an open play for the duchy of Brittany: after orchestrating the marriage of the duke's daughter to one of his own sons, Henry forced the duke to abdicate, leaving his son as duke and the duchy in Angevin control.

Much as this was a gain for the son, though, it wasn't enough to sate his or his brothers' desires to have a larger slice of their father's vast lands. For his part, Louis was only too happy to stoke this family heat into destructive flame. He knew that if each son took his part, the whole would be weakened. This was exactly how the once great Carolingian empire had been broken to create the realm he now ruled as king.

Everything boiled over in 1173, when three of Henry's sons – and Eleanor, who at this point was feuding with her husband – joined with Louis and several other regional powers to try to topple him. The enterprise ended in disaster after a mere eighteen months. Henry was triumphant.

Louis VII died in 1180, and his son took the crown as Philippe II. He would become the first monarch to style himself 'king of France' rather than 'king of the Franks', and within ten years of his coronation he was being called 'Philippe Augustus' in honour of his accomplishments. What he had done to be associated with the great Caesar Augustus was to expand the royal domain – those lands that belonged to the king directly – and in the process check the power of his most threatening rivals, the Angevins.

When Henry died in 1189, only two of his sons had survived him: Richard, who inherited the crown of England and control of most of the Angevin lands, and John, who inherited so little that he was given the epithet 'Lack-land'.

Meanwhile, the Kingdom of Jerusalem had fallen to the Ayyubid sultan Saladin after the Battle of Hattin two years earlier. Both Richard and Philippe made vows to reconquer the Holy City – an externally devotional act but perhaps an internally political one – and in 1190 they set out for the Third Crusade with much

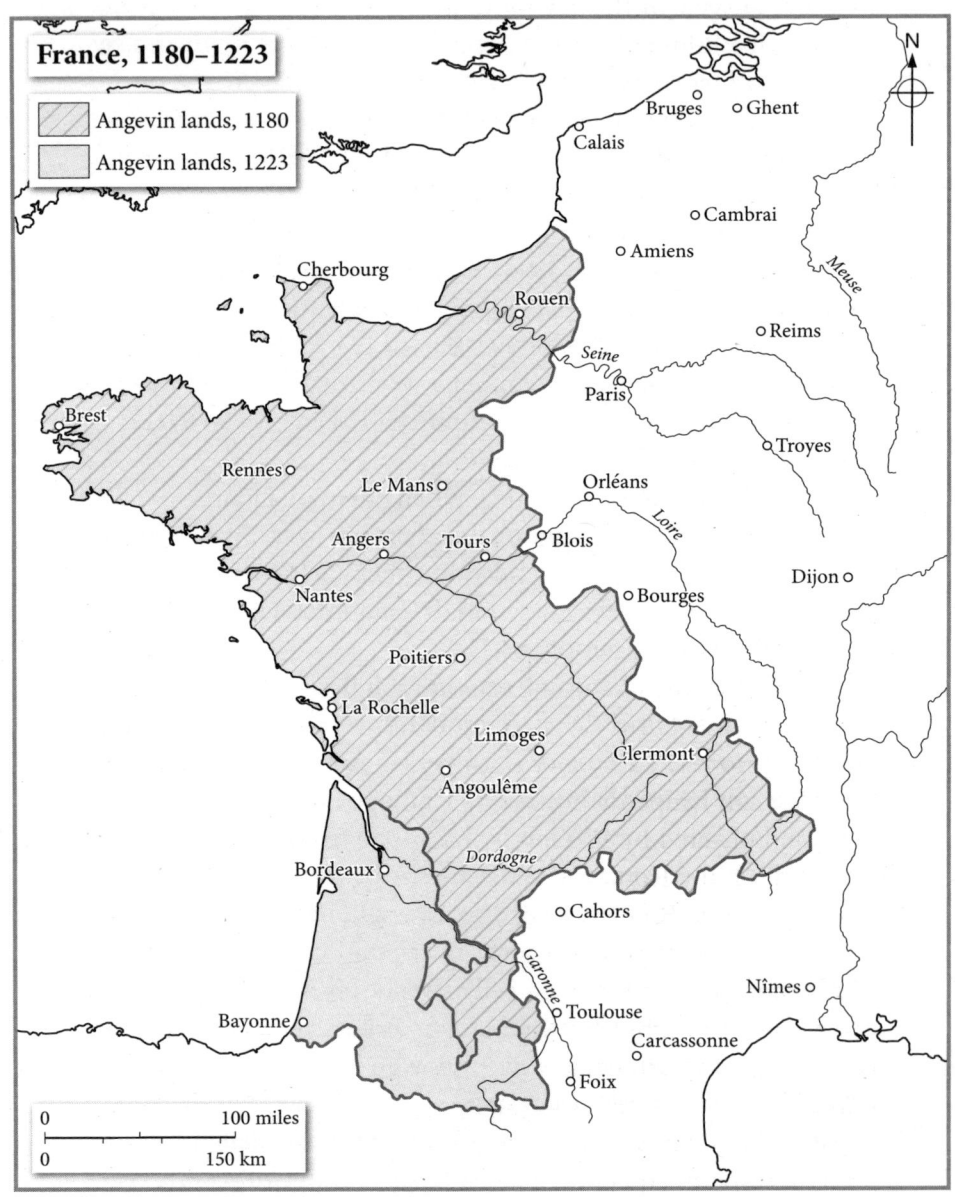

France, 1180–1223

Angevin lands, 1180
Angevin lands, 1223

N

Bruges
Ghent
Calais
Cambrai
Amiens
Meuse
Cherbourg
Rouen
Seine
Reims
Brest
Paris
Troyes
Rennes
Le Mans
Orléans
Loire
Angers
Tours
Blois
Dijon
Nantes
Bourges
Poitiers
La Rochelle
Limoges
Clermont
Angoulême
Dordogne
Bordeaux
Cahors
Nîmes
Bayonne
Toulouse
Garonne
Carcassonne
Foix

0   100 miles
0   150 km

fanfare. Their routes were indirect, to say the least, so it wasn't until May and June of the following year that the two kings arrived at an ongoing siege of the key port city of Acre in the Holy Land.[11]

Though Philippe had worked hard to befriend Richard when he was a prince, now that he stood as the head of the Angevins their interests were increasingly at odds and their relationship accordingly strained. When Acre fell in July, Philippe abandoned the crusade. He claimed to be too ill to continue – he was suffering from a disease that made his hair and nails fall out and his skin peel off in strips – but he also appears to have been increasingly suspicious of Richard's motives and making plans of his own.[12] The count of Flanders had died during the siege of Acre, and the French king was anxious to see the situation there turned to his advantage. He was also well aware that with Richard away in the Holy Land he could land significant blows against the Angevin holdings in France. Not long after he'd returned to France, Philippe was urging Richard's brother, John, to make up for the lands he lacked and rise up in rebellion. As his father had, Philippe recognized that driving a wedge into his rival's family could be an effective way to crack the Angevin base of power.

When Richard wrapped up his time in the Holy Land – the crusade having failed to retake Jerusalem – and headed home, he was shipwrecked en route and ultimately imprisoned by the Holy Roman Emperor. John was by now in outright rebellion, his position bolstered by Philippe seizing Angevin holdings directly. When the Holy Roman Emperor asked for a massive ransom in order to release Richard, Philippe shrewdly offered him an even greater sum to keep the Angevin king in prison.

Eleanor eventually scrounged up enough money from family and friends to outbid Philippe's attempts to keep her eldest son imprisoned. In early 1194, over a year after he was shipwrecked, Richard was at last released. On hearing the news, Philippe wrote to John 'that he must take care of himself, for the devil is loose'.[13] John, in response, quickly made peace with his brother, who then began clawing back the lands that Philippe had taken from him.

Richard did well at first. There's no question that the legend of the Lionheart's military superiority has long outpaced the actual reality, but he was nevertheless a capable commander. With enough time, he might well have rewound the clock on Philippe's gains.

But time was not on his side. In 1199, while besieging one of his own vassals at the relatively insignificant castle of Châlus-Chabrol, the Angevin king was struck in the shoulder by a crossbow bolt. The wound became gangrenous, and in a matter of days the king of England was dead.[14] His brother, John 'Lack-land', now became king.

The French kings had worked hard to shake the great mountain of Angevin lands. Richard had for a moment arrested the erosion of its slopes, but under John whole stretches of it slipped and slid loose. His reign was a disaster for the Angevins, and a time of glory for their rival Capetians in Paris.

It didn't happen overnight, but in retrospect we can see the seeds of John's failures from the beginning: unlike his brother and their father, who had both been ready to fight for their rights at the drop of a hat, John seemed most interested in cutting deals to keep what he had. In a different time and place, this might not have been a problem. But in a rivalry with the clever and ruthless Philippe, the new king of England was out of his depth.

Philippe had, on Richard's death, supported the claims of John's nephew, Arthur of Brittany, over those of John. Many of the French lords had followed suit. To get Philippe to back off this support and thus secure his new position, John agreed to sign the Treaty of Le Goulet with the French king in 1200. By its terms, John accepted Philippe as feudal lord over most of the Angevin lands on the Continent: only Gascony, that part of Aquitaine between the River Garonne and the Pyrenees, remained an independent entity.

This was a staggering win for Philippe and the Capetian dynasty. John agreed, publicly and formally, that most of the English lands outside England weren't English at all. They were French.

When I say that the First Hundred Years War was about the definition of England, this is the point. Since 1066 the kings of England had struggled with what it meant to be lords in France. The Angevins had very nearly broken this model by force of arms. At the height of their power, they'd likely had a shot at toppling

France entirely, as the Capetians had done to the Carolingians, and the Carolingians to the Merovingians before them. John had undone this dream with a stroke of a pen. It earned him the enmity of English lords who aspired to full sovereignty over their lands in France. To them, John was no longer 'Lack-land'. He was 'Soft-sword'.

Things got worse a couple of years later, when in 1202 Philippe declared John in violation of the terms through which he held his lands in France. The French king offered many of these lands to Arthur of Brittany, and once again the Angevins and Capetians were marching to war. John managed some initial victories, including a win at Mirebeau, where he captured Arthur. But soon enough he was getting the worst of it. Philippe took Normandy, and then his armies started rolling up the rest of the Angevin lands.

John was losing badly. But the next decade revealed he wasn't the only ruler fearful of Philippe. The king of France had other enemies, and, in desperation, they might well become allies.

The result would be a massive battle that changed the course of history in Europe.

Battle of Bouvines, 1214

Every story has its main characters, and there is no question that England and France are those standing centre stage for the subject of this book. But the reality was exceedingly more complex. The tensions between England and France touched every single one of their neighbours – sometimes affecting them in extraordinarily important ways, and sometimes being affected by them, in turn. So while our story may have its two main leads, it also has a terrific cast of supporting characters who, at moments, take centre stage.

The Battle of Bouvines, fought near a small town between Lille and Tournai on 27 July 1214, is just such a moment. One of the most important but least-known battles in history, Bouvines had extraordinary international impact.

Even briefly told, the story of the battle offers a prime example of the essential interconnectedness of the medieval world. In 1212

Emperor Otto IV of the Holy Roman Empire was reeling. His hold on the empire was in doubt. He needed a way to strike back at his French-supported rival for the throne of the empire, the king of Sicily, who claimed the title under the name Frederick II. He found it thanks to a crusader count who had become an emperor in Constantinople.

The crusader in question was Count Baldwin IX of Flanders, who had departed for the Fourth Crusade in 1202. Although aimed at the Holy Land, this crusade instead conquered Constantinople. Baldwin became its emperor, but he was captured by Kaloyan the Romanslayer, emperor of the Bulgarians, and died in captivity sometime afterwards. As Baldwin's wife had died during her journey to join her husband in the east, this meant that the county of Flanders – and the sizable riches that flowed into its prosperous ports – fell to Joan, the eldest of their two orphaned daughters. As she was only around seven years old at the time, Joan and her county were placed in the care of her uncle, the count of Namur, another of the Low Countries, which had only recently fought for its independence from neighbouring Luxembourg. Namur needed allies, and Philippe Augustus was more than happy to take advantage of the situation. The French king arranged for one of his daughters to marry the count of Namur in exchange for custody of Joan and her sister. They would be raised in Philippe's household, giving him a chance to keep Flanders in the French sphere of influence.

Everyone knew Joan was an enormous prize, and substantial sums of money were offered to the king of France to wed her. In the end, Philippe Augustus chose a Portuguese prince named Ferrand. On paper, it seemed a solid choice. Ferrand was royalty. He was thought potentially acceptable to the people of Flanders – he was the nephew of the widow of Joan's granduncle, who had been count of Flanders until his death in 1191. He also came with 50,000 livres to secure Joan's hand.

The two were wed in January 1212, but en route to Flanders they were captured by the eldest son of Philippe Augustus. His mother had been countess of Artois – yet another of the Low Countries – but Joan's father had seized it and now the French prince (and future King Louis VIII) wanted recompense. To secure their release, the young couple was forced to sign the Treaty of Pont-à-Vendin, which surrendered substantial lands and several rich towns.

Joan and Ferrand were furious, and as soon as they were free they began looking for ways to strike back against the French prince and, by extension, the king of France.

Otto was looking for his own chance to strike at France, which was supporting the rival claimant for the Holy Roman Emperorship. And John, who had lost so many of the Angevin holdings, wanted the same thing. It turned out there were a lot of people who may not have liked each other but were more than willing to set aside their differences for the chance to push back against Philippe Augustus: in the end, a number of additional rulers in the Low Countries joined the coalition, and John ponied up great piles of cash to help fund the endeavour. It was money that, if they won, he surely thought would be repaid in a restoration of former Angevin lands.

The plan was for John to threaten the king of France from the west, drawing Philippe and his army away from Paris, which would then be attacked from the northeast by the rest of the coalition forces. It was a solid plan, and in 1214 they put it in motion. John landed on the west coast at La Rochelle in February, and Philippe began mustering forces in response. But John's allies in the northeast were unable to take immediate advantage of the situation. Their army was coming together too slowly, and it was nearly impossible to coordinate action over the long distances between their forces and those commanded by John. By the summer, John had spent his momentum in the west and was forced to pull back to safer positions, leaving Philippe free to turn most of his attention to face the coalition army that was at last beginning to threaten from the northeast.

The armies that now approached each other in July were substantial.[15] Philippe had perhaps as many as 6,000 fighters on foot and 1,400 on horseback – the vast majority of them knights. The coalition army was likely of similar size, but due to its international nature it was inherently less cohesive. The trouble they'd had in organizing for the invasion would have been repeated on smaller and smaller scales as the groups tried to take actions in the field.

At first, the allies seemed to have the upper hand.

We will see at multiple points in this book that topography is one of the greatest determinants of conflict: as I shorthand it, *a battle is its ground*. A ditch can undo a charging line. A hedge can hide an ambushing force. A forest can stand athwart an invasion.

For the battle we are about to see, the main topographical feature we need to know is the River Marque. It's not a massive river today, but in the Middle Ages it was likely a little wider and for certain it was far marshier upon its banks. For a man crossing the river on foot it would be a soggy, muddy effort, with a good chance of a boot or two left behind. But an army is a much bigger and complex entity. It is many thousands of soldiers, every one of them churning the banks with each footfall, some of them flailing, perhaps even drowning in the muck. It is thousands of horses, huge numbers of carts filled with precious supplies. It is herds of livestock (often called 'meat on the hoof') that are used to feed the army. It is the enormous number of non-combatants – merchants, family members, specialist professionals providing critical services – who accompany the men to war both to support them and to make money off them: the 'teeth' of any army, its combat personnel, is typically far smaller than its non-combat 'tail'.

So when Philippe, marching his army to Lille, needed to cross the Marque, he wasn't going to do it just anywhere. He was going to use a bridge. Specifically, he was going to use the bridge at Bouvines.

In modern military terms, any linear obstacle to an army's advance is a 'gap', and it needs to be crossed. Philippe, in 1214, was thus conducting what we call a 'wet-gap crossing', which is among the more dangerous military operations to undertake if the enemy is nearby. As Flavius Vegetius Renatus, a late fourth-century writer whose book *De re militari* became one of the most widely read military manuals in history, cautions: 'When crossing rivers careless armies often get into serious difficulties [...because] the enemy often launches rapid ambushes or raids [there].'[16] It's easy to understand why. Because a bridge can only handle so many men at a time, it functions as a bottleneck for any army trying to cross it. The army is slowed as it crawls across the wet gap, which allows an opposing force to catch it. And if that opposing force should attack while an army is, for instance, halfway through its crossing, then the river has effectively cut the army's strength in half.

For his part, Philippe was clearly hoping to use the river to his advantage. Once he moved across the Marque, the coalition army would be in a bind: his enemies would have to decide how to conduct their own wet-gap crossing with the French in a perfect position to pounce upon them.

He almost pulled it off.

When he learned that his enemies were bearing down on his position, Philippe had managed to get the vast majority of his army across the river. Only he and his mounted men – most of them his knights and lords – were still on the 'wrong' side.

At a glance this might seem no bother at all. Though he was apparently having a leisurely lunch when the scouts sounded the alarm that the enemy vanguard was quickly approaching, they were still a mile or two away. And he had a horse. He could ride over the bridge, then turn around and hold it. He'd be fine.

But there was no way to get all his remaining men across. And whoever was left behind faced certain slaughter. So when Philippe jumped onto his horse, he didn't ride west to safety across the Marque. He rallied the men around him and turned east, towards the danger.

The vanguard of the coalition had surely hoped to meet with a scene of chaos at the river. Instead, it was met with the sight of perhaps a thousand cavalry, bristling with weapons that shone in the sunlight, their colourful banners held high and flapping in the breeze.

Philippe's gamble was a bold one, and it worked. Knowing that they'd lost the chance of surprise, and not knowing what strength lay behind the gathered French cavalry, the coalition vanguard pulled up and waited for the rest of the army to catch up and organize. This process took some hours, and all the while Philippe had the rest of his army streaming back over the Marque as quickly as they could manage so that he could even the odds.

The battle opened with a cavalry attack on the southern side of the field. Ferrand seems to have been in charge of the allies on this side, though command and control of so many men from different regions would of necessity been delegated down to officers in charge of smaller units of manoeuvre. After repulsing an initial French probe, Ferrand made his own attack, which led to a back and forth of mounted actions. Several lords fell or were captured. Unhorsed and surrounded, Ferrand himself eventually surrendered. The Flemings broke and scattered.

Meanwhile, Philippe had taken his position in the centre of his lines, in front of the bridge, and Otto sent a massive line of men on horse and foot hurtling towards him. Their aim was the king's banner. If it came down, it likely meant the king was dead or captured. His army would collapse.

The fighting was vicious. For a time, everything was in doubt. One of Philippe's own royal knights was unhorsed and killed: 'before the eyes of the king, Stephen Longchamp, an honest and faithful soldier, was slain, with a knife thrust into his head through the slits of his helmet'.[17] But steadily the tide turned. With the Flemings in retreat on the south side of the field, the French could push more strength into the centre. Otto's advance was stopped and then turned. Under duress, he withdrew and was nearly captured. Those of his allies still in the fight, seeing his banner pulling back, followed suit. Soon, nearly the whole side was in rout, running in hopes of living to fight another day.

Philippe, who had nearly been undone at lunchtime, found himself the winner of a near-total victory by dinner. It was an extraordinary win with enormous impacts that would be felt for generations. In the Holy Roman Empire, Otto's crushing loss did nothing to improve his political struggles. The next year, he was deposed and Frederick II became the undisputed Holy Roman Emperor. After his death, though, the electors once again could not agree on who should take over. This began what we call the Great Interregnum, during which time there were many rival claimants for the title. It would last into the next century. Without a centralizing authority, the cohesiveness of the Holy Roman Empire weakened considerably, with the result that lordships on the margins – like those in the Low Countries – saw avenues to greater autonomy.

And this wasn't the only impact in the Low Countries. Whole swathes of the nobility of several counties died on the field at Bouvines. Others survived but faced crippling ransom costs to secure their release: Ferrand would spend the next dozen years in prison, with Joan trying desperately to raise the ransom for his release. The Low Countries had already been under threats both internal and external, and these many losses blew enormous holes in their ruling structures. The gaps in governing power and feudal relationships had to be filled with a new class of leaders, and many of those who moved into these positions did so not because they were 'old money', but because they were 'new money': their power was built not on their names but on the massive urban wealth that they were generating through the wool trade with England. Though in the moment Philippe was able to grip more tightly to the region, the connection these new leaders had to the English would mean a great deal to the course of the coming Two Hundred Years War.

Meanwhile, though John had not been on the field at Bouvines, the efforts of the coalition that he'd helped finance and oversee were a military disaster so total that he not only lost any chance of restoring Angevin power on the Continent but also saw his authority in England compromised. The next year, facing a rebellion of barons, the king was forced to sign the Magna Carta.

On the flip side of all this, Philippe held more power than ever. As an anonymous chronicler in Béthune observed, 'After this, no one dare wage war against him, and he lived in great peace and the whole of the land was in great peace for a long time to come.'[18]

Philippe II died in 1223. His son, who had done so much to cause the crisis by his actions against Ferrand and Joan, was crowned Louis VIII. He lasted only three years (1223–26), but during this time largely continued the success of his father. He wrestled back even more Angevin domains, including the great port city of La Rochelle in 1224, which left the English only the major ports of Bordeaux and Bayonne in the south of France.

Beginning in 1230, the son of Louis VIII, Louis IX – later

canonized Saint Louis – faced multiple attempts by King John's son, Henry III, to reinvigorate the Angevin cause. But none were successful. After a final, major Capetian victory at the Battle of Taillebourg in 1242, it was all over.

Monarch by monarch, nail by nail, the coffin of the so-called Angevin empire had been hammered shut. All that remained would be the paperwork.

Treaty of Paris, 1259

The outcome of this First Hundred Years War was made official with the Treaty of Paris, which Louis IX and Henry III ratified on 13 October 1259. We have seen several treaties to this point in the backstory, but if you're going to remember any of them moving forward, *this* is the one. Because the Treaty of Paris made no one happy.

To set the stage, it should be said that Henry was not in a good position to make a deal. His futile efforts to reclaim Angevin lands had been expensive and unpopular at home. His barons were discontented, his coffers nearly empty. And then in 1258 England was savaged by what chronicler Matthew Paris called 'an awful and intolerable pestilence' – a weather-related famine – that sent food prices soaring and left 'numberless dead bodies' in the streets.[19] At that year's Parliament the pressures came to a head, with Henry powerless to stop his barons from asserting their rights. The result was the Provisions of Oxford, a reformation of the government that greatly diminished royal authority.

Across the Channel, Louis was in no such straits. His coffers were full, and his authority was unquestioned at home and respected abroad. He was, in fact, widely regarded as the ideal Christian prince. Supposedly, his mother had told him, when he was still a child, that she'd rather stand over his corpse than see him commit a mortal sin. If true, the lesson clearly stuck: as king, Louis often had the church at the forefront of his mind. Something of his religious ambition – not to mention his wealth – can be seen in the most cursory visit to the extraordinary Sainte-Chapelle, which he built as a royal chapel on the Île de la Cité in the heart of Paris.

He was so secure in his realm, in fact, that he personally led the Seventh Crusade, which attacked the seat of Mamluk power in Egypt in 1248. Although the crusaders managed a few early victories in the siege of Damietta in 1249 and the Battle of Mansurah in 1250, they were almost completely wiped out in a disastrous defeat that April in the Battle of Fariskur, in which Louis was captured. Added to the enormous expense of the crusade itself – an estimated six times the king's annual revenues in addition to the economic losses resulting from having so much of France's manpower abroad – the royal treasury now had to pay a massive ransom to secure his release. It was a hard blow, but it did little to stem the king's fervour for the cause. By the time he returned to France in 1254, he had an eye towards unifying Christendom in the West as a way of reinvigorating the crusades.

There were also familial reasons to want peace with England. Louis had married Margaret of Provence in 1234. Her sister Eleanor had married Henry in 1236. This made the children of the two kings first cousins.

In 1259, the terms of what would be called the Treaty of Paris were drawn up. Louis offered Henry an enormous sum of money that he'd gathered from his people – coin that the English king needed quite desperately – and he also offered to allow him to retain the title of duke of Aquitaine. It was hardly the once vast holding of Eleanor of Aquitaine, however. The English would have control only of the smaller region of it called Gascony, along with the dioceses of Limoges, Périgueux and Cahors closer to the middle of France. If Louis's vassal Alphonse of Poitiers died without an heir, Henry would also acquire bordering lands in the Agenais, Quercy and Saintonge. Finally, the English king was allowed control of the Norman islands in the English Channel.

And that was it. The Treaty of Paris codified the Angevin loss of Normandy, Maine, Anjou, Touraine and Poitou… and did so via renunciation. Henry affirmed that neither he nor his heirs could lay claim to them. Those fights were finished. It also dictated that the English king would have to do homage to the French king to hold *any* of the lands on the Continent – this time it included all the lands to the Pyrenees. All of these would henceforth be hereditary fiefs of the French crown.

As punishing as the treaty was to English interests, there were many in France who thought it far too merciful. Jean de Joinville, who had accompanied the king on crusade, recorded in his *Life of Saint Louis* that many on the French king's own council objected to giving the English anything at all. The king responded:

> as for the land I am giving him, I do not regard it as something I am bound to surrender either to himself or his heirs, but rather as a means of establishing a bond of love between my children and his, who are first cousins. Moreover, it seems to me that what I give him is to good purpose, since he has not hitherto been my vassal, but will now do me homage as his lord.[20]

French nobles weren't the only ones who objected to the Treaty of Paris. Henry's eldest son and heir, Edward, was incensed by the hand the English had been dealt. As he saw it, his father was signing away his birthright: a painful ignominy atop the calamity of the Provisions of Oxford. Edward had previously been given control of Gascony, even styling himself as its 'prince and lord',[21] but his father doing homage for the lands meant they were his, not Edward's. And both of them, in any case, were now under Louis.

From one perspective, we could say that the discontent on both sides means that this was a fundamentally good treaty. Everyone had to compromise. No one had won everything.

Alas, it also meant that everyone felt like they'd lost something. That gave them reason to fight again.

The Stage Set

The Treaty of Paris illustrates the stakes of the centuries of war that lay ahead. No one disputed that lands on the Continent were in the possession of the kings of England. The question was the degree to which those lands ought to be considered part of a whole with France (as the Capetians believed) or part of a whole with England (as the Angevins desired). Richard the Lionheart, in his captivity, had supposedly refused to render respect to the Holy Roman Emperor, proclaiming rather famously that he was 'born of a rank that recognizes no superior but God'. And later, in 1198, he took the motto – still used by the crown of England today – *Dieu et mon droit* [God and my right]. In his view, there was no overlord, there was no Philippe, between him and his ultimate authority. This was the Angevin cause in a nutshell.

The fact that the Angevins, fighting against the Capetian kings in Paris, held court more often in France than in England *matters*. England, for the Angevin dynasty, wasn't home. They had the English crown and the lands that came with it, but their heart and their eyes remained fixed on the Continent. Despite being the most famous of its Angevin kings, Richard the Lionheart spent less than a single year in England during his decade of rule. He was engaged in a great many events on the Continent – including his imprisonment there! – but from an Angevin perspective, his time away from England wasn't something that needed to be excused. It was how things ought to be: the Continent was where things mattered most, because the Continent was where the things that were most important were at stake. England, for the Angevins, was an extension of a Continental base of power. We think of this relationship the other way around – that the Angevin kings were English first and Continental second – because we regard the crown of England as a greater claim than a duchy in France. But by all appearances, Richard's lands in England mattered most to him as a means to achieve his goals on the other side of the Channel. *That* was home.

To the point: Richard is buried in three places. His heart was taken to Rouen, the great city of Normandy. His entrails were buried in Châlus, the place of his death. The rest of him was entombed at Fontevraud Abbey in Anjou, alongside the remains of his father, Henry II, and, after her death in 1204, his mother, Eleanor of Aquitaine. The Lionheart may have marvellous statues in England – including his equestrian statue in front of Parliament – but nothing of the man himself is left there.

Even if we nevertheless think of Richard's 'home' as being in

England – and I see no reason why we should – we ought to think of him as a superstar footballer who uses the support of his home club to pack his bags for the brighter lights of another city in the Premier League. Put simply, Richard *used* England.

The Treaty of Paris had put an end to all this. Any sense that England by definition stretched across the English Channel was finished. The king of England's home was in England, not France. This was the outcome of the First Hundred Years War.

Accordingly, on 4 December 1259, Henry knelt and put his hands in those of Louis. It was a momentous occasion, meant to bring a lasting peace. And, in fairness, the relationship between England and France remained relatively stable and quiet for the remainder of their reigns.

Henry III died in 1272. His eldest son, Edward, who had already been given the title of duke of Aquitaine, was returning from a crusade – variously called Lord Edward's Crusade or the Ninth Crusade – when he heard the news. He wouldn't be crowned Edward I until 1274, but there was no question of his succession to the English throne.

Louis IX had died on the Eighth Crusade in 1270 and was followed to the throne by his son, Philippe III, who was in turn followed by *his* son Philippe IV in 1285. It is *this* man, Louis IX's grandson, whom we met in the Preface: fourteen months before receiving the crown of France he had married Jeanne of Navarre, thereby becoming king of Navarre and count of Champagne. He is, as I said earlier, the man most responsible for the fact that thirty-three years after the Treaty of Paris ended the First Hundred Years War, the Two Hundred Years War began.

The seeds of the fighting were in the making of the peace.

How was it supposed to work? Was the king of England to be treated as merely another vassal in France? What would happen if the interests of one crown didn't align with the interests of the other? Could the king of France long allow the English hold on Gascony, just on principle?

And while Henry and Louis might have engaged in their acts of homage as co-rulers and brothers-in-law who respected one another, these close ties were not necessarily shared by all at court.

They were certainly not shared by those further down the food chain. As one historian has noted, 'a community of interest was forming between the ruling houses' thanks to the Treaty of Paris, but this goodwill had little reflection within 'the community of interest between ruler and ruled'.[22]

After all, the Angevin losses had been Capetian gains. Henry's position in England was so weakened that he had to call on the support of Louis against his own barons in 1264. The crown of France, on the other hand, was increasingly strong, increasingly powerful and increasingly interested in centralizing its authority. The Carolingian power of West Francia, unified as it had been of old, was not forgotten. It might have felt as close to becoming as real as the Oriflamme standard hanging in the abbey of Saint-Denis – a sacred banner that was increasingly believed to have been carried by Charlemagne himself.

It is this expansionist French perspective that propelled the two states headlong into the next phase of conflict. The First Hundred Years War had established that England's foothold on the Continent was subject to France. The Two Hundred Years War was an attempt to remove that foothold permanently.

The first war had defined England. The second would define France. And it would begin, simply enough, with a murder.

I

The Years of the Beginning,
1292–1303

*Pirate War | Forfeit of Gascony | Wine, Wool and War |
Auld Alliance | Golden Spurs | Treaty of Paris*

Brittany juts into the Atlantic Ocean like a shelf hanging
from the northwestern corner of France. Anyone making
the journey between the English Channel and ports to the south
has to get around it. In the age of sail this was far more difficult
and dangerous than it is today. Here the Gulf Stream frequently
whipped up sudden storms that hurtled wood-hulled ships against
the boulder-strewn coast.

Salvaging these shattered hulks was a decent source of income
for the counts of Léon – not to be confused with the similarly
named kingdom of León in northern Spain – who controlled
the ports of the mainland around the point of Brittany. Another
money-maker was their system of taxing the ships that made
stops in those safe harbours to seek shelter from the elements or
to take on much-needed provisions for their journeys across the
inhospitable sea.

Thrifty mariners might avoid the tax by attempting to sail further out at sea, around the Molene Archipelago, a stretch of rocky
islands and islets that reaches from Brittany into the Atlantic,
framing the westernmost reach of the English Channel. Already
dangerous, this run very often required a short stop on one of the
islands to take on fresh water for the crew.

Low and rocky, pounded by waves and wind, the mile-long isle
of Quéménès offered one of the few sources of sustenance. On a

day close to Lent in 1292, two ships dropped anchor at this tiny island to get it.[1]

One of the ships was from Normandy, up the English Channel to the east, a region ultimately governed by the king of France. The other was from Bayonne, down the coast to the south, which was ultimately governed by the king of England in his role as duke of Aquitaine. The Bayonnais could have been bringing Gascon wines to England's markets. The Normans could have been hauling Flemish textiles the other way. We don't know.

Out on the open water, such crews might have waved to each other as they passed by. There was more than enough room to share the sea. But once they were ashore on Quéménès, the two crews were anxious to use the single freshwater source on the island. No one wanted to be there a minute longer than needed. If a storm arose, it would be ruinous. The faster they could take on the water, the faster they could be safe.

An argument broke out over who would get to draw water first. Words flew. Then fists.

Then someone drew a blade.

Who brandished the weapon is difficult to say. Writing in England not long afterwards, a monk named William Rishanger claimed that the guilty party was a Norman, who bared steel with the intention of killing one of the mariners from Bayonne. The Norman's wrist was grabbed before he could strike, and in the struggle he was killed. Other sources, however, claim that it was the man from Bayonne who died, or that the parties should be flipped around entirely. We may never know the truth of it.

What's certain is that a man was dead, and killing begat killing.

Pirate War, 1292–93

Across the spring and through the summer, ships from Normandy and Gascony attacked each other in a series of ferocious reprisals. Ships were plundered. Crew were slaughtered and cargoes stolen. The line between vengeance and piracy blurred, then disappeared. In just one incident, ships sailing out of Winchelsea and Hastings were struck. Some forty people were killed, and goods and treasures worth 500 pounds were stolen. Those killed 'allegedly had their feet, hands and finally heads cut off in Dieppe'.[2]

Traders soon began hauling half-cargoes in order to attack or escape potential enemies, further piling up the economic losses on both sides. In the spring of 1293, the escalation gave way to an outright battle between English and Norman ships in the waters off Pointe Saint-Mathieu. The Normans got the worst of it, supposedly losing 200 ships. Flush with victory, the English launched a devastating attack on the important port of La Rochelle.

Most historians have shrugged off this chain of events, seeing it as a minor footnote of little consequence to the great actions that surround it.[3] But even accounting for exaggeration on the part of some of our eyewitnesses – several of our primary accounts are clear efforts to paint both their own side as horrifically abused and the other side as the 'bad guys' who started it – the violence was quickly metastasizing. More importantly, stories were circulating that there was more to the struggle than random reprisals and piracy. More and more people believed that states were behind the fighting.

Between 1304 and 1307, for instance, a man named Guillaume Guiart composed a poem for the king of France. It was no small effort: Guiart's work is more than 20,000 lines of poetry, detailing the eighty-year history of his kingdom from the reign of Louis VIII to his present day. The *Branche des royaux lignages* [*Branch of Royal Lineages*], as it is titled, is not highly regarded in literary circles, but it is nevertheless important for those of us interested in the history of the period: Guiart was a soldier from Orléans who had turned to the poetic life after suffering a wound on campaign in Flanders in 1304. He was eyewitness to many important events, and his poem provides us with a great many details not found elsewhere.

As it happens, Guiart has a lot to say about the events of 1292. He begins by pointing out that King Edward I had dutifully come to France in 1286 and – as Henry III had done before him – given homage to the king of France for the title of Aquitaine and the lands of Gascony. This was what the Treaty of Paris demanded of him, and the fact that Edward had acted in fealty with that accord was important. This was the rough equivalent of signing a rental agreement: it was an essential part of the contract through which the English could hold the lands in France (the bank owning the rental property in this analogy).

At that point, Guiart claims, everything was on the up and up. In 1292, however, Edward was up to no good, for he had built

> A great multitude of ships
> Beautiful and strong,
> And he filled them with armors
> And with vigorous, loyal men
> From his kingdom and from Bayonne.
> Wise men and fools alike say
> That he pretended (a lie of malice)
> That all these with great expense
> Were intended to go to the Holy Land,
> Where God took death so we might live.
> Instead, he directed the ships
> (If they wanted to get French coins)
> Towards the islands of Guernsey,
> Which can be reached in the deep waters
> Off the coast of Normandy.[4]

At Guernsey, Guiart says, the English fleet encountered ships from Normandy. These ships were heavily laden with wine and other goods from Gascony, all of it being transported north and east through the English Channel. The English attacked them. 'Many were killed or wounded', he claims, as every one of the innocent trader ships was seized. In a poignant image, he likens the violence to the wine in the cargo holds: 'All are harvested and pressed.' The English ships returned to England with their gains, but Guiart says that Edward soon had them on the move again, sending them to the coastal port of La Rochelle – the attack we've already noted – where 'they would burn the harvests and the towns… killing many women'.

This account paints the English as the sole aggressors, with Edward himself ultimately calling the shots. Several other French sources agree: the greedy king of England had shattered the Treaty of Paris.

Unsurprisingly, the English sources describe the events in quite the opposite terms. They pin the blame on the king of France or, more often, his brother, Charles of Valois, who 'persecuted the English with inveterate hatred', perpetrating 'intrigues and evils', as the Annals of Dunstable Abbey put it. The opinion was shared by many: one or both of these French royals had secretly broken the Treaty of Paris.[5]

To be clear, we have no firm evidence that the royals on *either* side were masterminding these events. Quite to the contrary, we know that throughout 1292 and into 1293 both kings were making public pronouncements telling their vassals to stand down. What is fascinating is that despite these open declarations, writers and their audiences in both England and France were more than willing to believe that there were deeper conspiracies afoot.

Forfeit of Gascony, 1293–94

For all that's uncertain about the events leading up to it, we have sharp clarity on what happened after La Rochelle was stormed and sacked by forces allied with the English in 1293. We know, because La Rochelle had recently become a personal domain of the French king, making this a direct attack on the king's own lands.

Philippe responded by writing to Edward, accusing him of being in league with those who

> with wicked intent, had invaded our men and subjects of Normandy and certain other parts of our kingdom, both by land and by sea, in places even subject to our own jurisdiction, and inhumanely murdered and massacred innumerable of our subjects. Others were seized, taken away as captives. And the invaders, driven by an ancient wickedness, plundered ships and inestimable numbers of goods, and after breaking into many of the ships sank them.[6]

Initially, Edward had agreed to a temporary removal of his garrisons from the fortified towns of Gascony, handing over control to the French in February 1294, but this hadn't been enough to stop the escalation. So Philippe now summoned the king of England, in his role as the duke of Aquitaine, to appear before him to answer charges on behalf of his vassals. Rather pointedly, he refused to grant safe conduct for Edward's coming to France.

Whether either of the kings had been secretly plotting to this point, there is no question that at this pivotal moment it was Philippe who was pushing the action. As one historian observes, 'he was ultimately the only one of the actors in this drama who had the power to stop the escalation of events'.[7] Perhaps the French king recognized that a failure to react aggressively to an attack on La Rochelle would be read by French magnates as weakness on the part of the crown. Or perhaps he refused to pull back because he recognized how easily he could use the attacks to support his growing political ambition to heave the English out of Gascony – as one historian puts it, the 'complete dispossession of Edward as duke of Aquitaine was a major objective of French activity from the outset'.[8]

What mattered most in this moment was the fact that the French king had left no diplomatic way out of the problem. Edward would either answer for what had transpired or he would lose Gascony.

It's hard to imagine what happened next as anything less than Philippe's intention. Though Edward had previously performed homage for his lands in accordance with the Treaty of Paris, he now refused to appear in answer to Philippe's summons. For the king of England to submit to the judgement and potential punishment of the king of France would be to acknowledge the French king as his superior. From the English perspective, this simply could not be. From the French perspective, of course, it *had* to be: no matter his kingship in England, Edward was a mere duke in France, with the French king his sovereign, as the Treaty of Paris and Edward's own act of homage had previously confirmed.

After seeing that Edward wouldn't come forth to be judged, Philippe declared Gascony forfeit in May. Guillaume de Nogaret, keeper of the seal of Philippe IV, made clear the position of the monarchy in France in 1294: 'the king of France is subject to no one', he wrote.[9]

The forfeiture of Gascony wasn't just a matter of paperwork. A French army prepared to march in and expel the English from the area. Edward, in response, renounced his homage to the French king. We might think of this rather like someone who quits their job when they know they're about to be fired, except for a key difference: Edward wasn't walking away from Gascony and his other French holdings. He was preparing to shed blood to keep them.

Wine, Wool and War

The immediate conflict that resulted between England and France – sometimes called the Gascon campaign – lasted until 1303. By that point, the fight had embroiled other realms: likely more destruction took place in Scotland and Flanders across these years than in either England or France. But wherever it happened, the horrors of war served to pile kindling to ignite future conflict. All the later, more famous fires – like Crécy and Agincourt – can trace back to this moment.

The murder of a man on the forgotten isle of Quéménès in 1292 had, in just two short years, set in motion a war that would last two centuries. Why this happened is complicated.

As we begin our journey through a fight crossing two centuries among a great many players in multiple countries, we need to be clear that not everyone who engaged in the Two Hundred Years War did so for the same reason. Even those who were on the same side at the same time on the same field may not have been fighting for the same causes. Nor would rationales remain constant: the hungry engines of war run on many different fuels.

We have already seen in 1292 and 1293 how quickly and easily events shifted from defensive to offensive actions, from vengeance to pillage and plunder, from personal squabbles to political movements. Philippe declaring Gascony forfeit was the product of multiple influences. From Philippe's position, there was a pride in his kingdom, laden with both historical memory of past glories and a future hope of seeing Gascony united with it. From Edward's position, there was the individual friction of having the English king answer to the French king for Gascony. Monarchs are rarely recognized for their humility, and Edward was by no means an exception to this rule. These same frictions spread heat across the ruling classes, making the status of Gascony a broader political issue on both sides of the English Channel. Honour was at stake. In time, this would evolve into a religious conflict in which salvation competed with pride, ambition and so much else to drive men to the battlefields.

Amid all of this – arguably the one constant, common cause of violence in any age – was a desire for profit.

What constitutes profit is as varied as our desires, but the focus here is on substantive gains – or the preservation of existing gains – in land, resources and, of course, money. Countless conflicts have been driven by the desire to protect economic interests, to expand them or to seize them from others. And all conflicts, to one degree or another, also *rely* on money, because war-making is expensive. Often massively so.

At the beginning it cost money to gather an army. Even if you pressed men into service, you incurred the cost of their lost production in doing whatever work they would have performed in times of peace. If you needed to pay them wages, these costs multiplied. And once gathered, an army needed to be armed, supplied, housed and fed. Unless you were fighting literally for hearth and home, the army and all its needs had to be transported, man by man and ton by ton, to wherever it needed to fight. In war, every day was another fortune spent.

All this is to say that if we want to understand what fuelled the Two Hundred Years War, we need to understand the economics of England and France. This will mean talking about wine and wool.

And Charlemagne, as he often is when it comes to medieval Europe, is a good place to start. According to his biographer, Charlemagne enjoyed wine but 'rarely' had more than three cups in the course of his dinner.[10] Though meant to illustrate the king's temperate personality, this tidbit tells us something about the popularity of wine: it had a place on the king's table in the greatest court of northern Europe at the start of the ninth century.

Though wine had a long history of production around the Mediterranean, the extensive vineyards required for its production simply couldn't grow – much less flourish – across the majority of the north. So for a number of centuries the drinking of wine was far less common than the drinking of mead or ale, both of which could be sufficiently produced on a local level.

Yet as Christianity spread through Europe, wine-drinking spread with it. The faith was founded and centred in a Mediterranean climate, and wine played an integral role in the celebration of Mass. So in an increasingly Christianized Europe, wine became something of a sacred necessity, no matter the climate. This popular need for wine inevitably drove up prices in places where it had to be imported, and that increasing cost helped cement the drink's value as a marker of economic and cultural status. It's no wonder Charlemagne wanted it on his table.

In time, those who wanted to show off their high status were aiming to procure not just wine, but the *best* wine. The idea of wine as a status symbol spread beyond the regions where it was in short supply, and in time the wines from southern France came to be regarded as the best of all.

These lands were blessed with a combination of fertile soil and mild climate that was ideal for growing the finest grapes. Even better, the same broad and slow-rolling rivers bringing nutrients down from the surrounding mountains served as ready transport corridors between farmlands and the sea. There, on the Atlantic coast, bustling ports like Bordeaux, Bayonne and La Rochelle transferred barrels of wine from river barges to trading ships that plied an international market on routes that ran up and down the Atlantic seaboard from the British Isles to North Africa, and at either end meeting routes running eastward. In the south, trade routes extended into the Mediterranean; in the north, they reached into the Baltic.

The traders running these waters were central to the evolving conflict between 1292 and 1294. That a murder among them could lead to an international geopolitical crisis lasting generations is a testament to just how much money was being made where Aquitaine's rivers met the sea.

Barrels of fine wine floated by barge down the Garonne to the port of Bordeaux. Here, the barrels were loaded onto ships bound northward. Many of these ships, perhaps the majority, put into English ports, where they sold the wine for a high price: England's own wine production was essentially nil. Empty holds were then filled back up with loads of English wool bound for the ports and ultimately the mills of the Low Countries. These mills produced finished woollen products, which a trader could sail back down to southern France to sell and start the whole cycle over again.

Routes like this one would have been exceedingly profitable – and not just for the merchant captains. Just to keep our focus on the wine industry in southern France, this trading cycle meant money being made by vintners and barrel-makers, barge operators and ship-builders. There were secondary sources of wealth in lodging, retail, and other services and industries that grew as the port cities expanded.

Above it all was a ruling class that skimmed off the top in the form of customs and other duties that enabled, at least in theory, more security and trade infrastructure that could produce more and more profit for everyone involved. In such ways, a land rich in resources begets cities rich in, well, rich people with rich tastes for the better wines or the better woollen textiles that could further extend the cycle.

By 1250, three-quarters of the wine imported into England for the use of the royal family was coming from its port at Bordeaux, and that number would only increase in the coming years. In 1307, preparing for his wedding to Princess Isabella, Edward II ordered the equivalent of 1 million bottles of the city's wine. Tax records show that in 1308 Bordeaux exported over 26 million gallons of it, with the vast majority going to England. Each barrel and bottle was taxed coming and going, amplifying the wealth of southern France.

It's no wonder that the English wanted to keep control of Gascony, nor that the French were more than ready to take it for themselves.

Yet wine-making was only one part of the financial engine that was churning in the waters of the Atlantic. Another vital part of it – the reason England could afford all that wine in the first place – was wool. In the Middle Ages, sheep were the living backbone of the English economy.

Exactly when the British Isles became known for its wool production, we can't be sure. One of the early signs of it, though, returns us again to the court of Charlemagne. Around the year 796, the king of the Franks sent a letter to King Offa of Mercia, one of the early English kingdoms. It was, judging by its contents, a response to a letter the Mercian king had sent him regarding, among other things, the movements of pilgrims and merchants between their two realms. Charlemagne informs Offa that he will once again encourage the export of some particular milling stones from Francia to Mercia, just as Offa had requested.[11] In return, however, Charlemagne has a request of his own, regarding woollen garments that would be imported from Mercia to Francia:

> But just as you intimated your desire regarding the length of the stones, we likewise have a desire for the length of the cloaks: that you may order them to be made such as they used to come to us in ancient times.[12]

Charlemagne, it seems, enjoyed a longer, fuller cut to the garment that was, to his eye, more traditional in appearance. Charlemagne's fashion sense aside, this exchange tells us much about the state of English wool. Even in these early years, there was an ongoing, active trade that aimed to get it into the hands of those at the highest levels of society.

To be clear, there were sheep in Charlemagne's fields. The king could have had a cloak of any length he desired made from Frankish wool. But he wanted *English* wool because he thought it was superior.

Probably it was. While sheep can survive just about anywhere in Europe, the amount of wool they produce – and its quality – varies according to climate. In warm regions, their wool grows slow and thin. In cold regions, it grows fast and thick. So if you want to get rich in the wool business, you want a climate that is cold enough to encourage rapid growth of the densest wool but also mild enough to provide suitable grazing for many sheep to thrive. In other words, the climate that made England such a poor producer of wine made it a perfect producer of wool.

This is why those barrels of wine flowing into England from Gascony would be met with sacks of wool. The English wool industry was by that point sustaining not just its own internal systems of wealth – as with the wine getting from the vineyard to the port, there was an elaborate system of middlemen making a profit by funnelling the wool from the shepherds to the ships – but also a massive export business that, through heavy taxation, filled the king's coffers. When Eleanor of Aquitaine needed to pay a literal king's ransom for the imprisoned Richard I, she was finally able to do so with wool taxes. By the end of the thirteenth century, wool production, trade and taxation were responsible for half of the wealth generated in England.

Many things can turn the engine of war. But when it comes to the Two Hundred Years War between England and France, wine and wool should be foremost in our mind.

And that *also* means the Low Countries must never be far from our mind. On the other side of England's wool trade stood the waiting looms of urban cloth-makers, nowhere stronger and more profitable than in the Low Countries, which was blessed with excellent ports in close proximity to England and its abundance of fine wool. We will eventually encounter a number of the individual regions in the Low Countries, but for the moment the most important to know is Flanders, whose count and countess played an important role in the coalition that was destroyed at Bouvines.

Flanders was one of the most prosperous regions in Europe thanks to the thick English wool that arrived by the shipload in its ports. Textile industries in Flemish cities like Ghent, Bruges and Ypres dyed and tailored this raw material into fine cloth, and the wealth poured in. The cities of Flanders blossomed into massive and bustling economic centres of international mercantilism. The sheep of England were making people on both sides of the Channel very rich indeed.

Trouble was, since the ninth century Flanders had been a nominal county of France, owing allegiance to the French kings. This meant that its political interests were not necessarily in line with its economic interests. And while the French kings may have allowed Flanders to enjoy a relatively autonomous existence for long periods of its history, its booming economy stressed this relationship.

We hinted at this when we talked about the Battle of Bouvines, but it is worth emphasizing. We may think of England and France as the key players, but places like the Low Countries played a vital role in the centuries of war to come. Flemish prosperity depended upon English exports of wool, and English prosperity depended on Flemish imports of the same. Yet the richer the Flemings became, the more the French kings wanted a piece – and the more the rising classes of Flemings wanted independence. The victory of Philippe Augustus at Bouvines had wiped out many of the 'old money' leaders who were at least traditionally tied back to France. The leaders who took their place were mainly from the 'new money' classes whose prosperity was directly tied to England. This further widened cracks between those Flemings who were pro-English and those who were pro-French.

In light of all this, it should hardly come as a surprise that almost as soon as the king of France had declared Edward forfeited of his Continental holdings in May 1294, the English king turned his eyes to Flanders.

Edward knew everything I've just told you. He knew the importance of Flanders to his own economy, and he knew that many there would readily cast their fortunes with the English rather than the French – because those fortunes depended on England's wool. And he knew Flanders was a great way to hurt Philippe. He began sending men and materiel to help the count of Flanders push back against Philippe's taxation practices. Even more importantly, he sent the bishop of Durham to negotiate a marriage between the count's daughter and the Prince of Wales, the future Edward II.

It was a bold stroke. The marriage, which was agreed upon in principle by the end of August 1294, could have set the stage for eventually ripping Flanders out of French hands and into those of England.

Even if that didn't come to fruition, though, Edward recognized the opportunity that an uprising in Flanders would provide by splitting the attention of Paris. So in October of that year, Edward's army set sail for the Continent to press the French in the south. En route to Gascony, they attacked Pointe Saint-Mathieu. This was the port whose duties the men who had put in at Quéménès had been trying to avoid, and where one of the subsequent naval battles had taken place in 1293. Sailing on, the English army then made their entry on the Garonne and took the town of Castillon.

The French forces that had moved into Gascony after the temporary English withdrawal were unable to prevent a string of English victories over the next days and weeks. Bordeaux managed to hold out, but by the new year the English had taken Bayonne and seemed poised to sweep up what French resistance remained.

Philippe, however, had not been standing idly by. When he learned of Edward's plan to marry an English prince into the family of the count of Flanders, Philippe captured and imprisoned the count and his daughter, named Philippa. She was then perhaps eight or nine years old, a pawn in a political game she likely did not understand. Negotiations for the count's release in February 1295 included his public renouncement of the marriage agreement. This got the count out of prison, but he was forced to leave Philippa behind. She died in 1306, having never left French custody.

With the Flemish front at least temporarily settled, Philippe's attentions were no longer divided. He was able to push more of his forces towards Gascony, under the command of his brother, Charles of Valois – who was, as we've seen, thought by some to have masterminded the conflict from the beginning. The French flooded down the Garonne, taking back towns through the spring and into the summer.

Auld Alliance, 1295

Meanwhile, far to the north, there was another player about to enter the stage. Many in Scotland were anxious for a way to push back against the English themselves. Watching what was unfolding between England and France, they saw their chance.

In light of all that would transpire between Scotland and England in the centuries ahead, an attempt by the Scots to take advantage of English distraction overseas might seem expected, but it was novel at that time. Aside from a few tense periods, like the participation of King Constantine II in the grand alliance of Scots, Vikings and Britons that was defeated by King Athelstan of England at Brunanburh in 937, relationships between the two great kingdoms of Britain had been relatively peaceful and productive for the couple of centuries leading up to our story.

But history changed in 1286, when King Alexander III of Scotland defied his advisors' guidance, rode out on a chilly, wet night in March, fell out of his saddle and rolled down a rocky coastal slope, breaking his neck. His two sons having predeceased him, his designated heir was his granddaughter, named Margaret, who was three years old and living in Norway. In 1290, negotiations got underway to marry her to the Prince of Wales. The fact that this same young man would later be in negotiations for the hand of Philippa of Flanders says much about how this went. With some fanfare, the 'Maid of Norway' set sail for Scotland at the age of seven. Tragically, she died in Orkney along the way. No one knows why.

With no clear heir left, thirteen men made a claim to the throne of Scotland, raising the threat of a kingdom-rending civil war. Thinking that a third-party arbitrator with clout might resolve the issue, the leading men of the country asked Edward – now king – to head a feudal court that would determine who had the best claim. The king of England was only too happy to help, but he did so on one condition: he wanted the Scots to accept England as Scotland's overlord. The Scots danced around the issue with political skill, many of them agreeing to view Edward as their personal overlord while also insisting that since none of them were king, none of them could speak for Scotland. It was enough to get Edward to do what they wanted, though in retrospect we can see that these diplomatic subtleties set the stage for future conflict.

For the moment, the court went ahead. Edward played a leading role, but the decision was made by a vote meant to represent all parties. In November, a man named John Balliol was chosen to be the new king of Scotland.

Over the next couple of years, the English king treated Balliol as the subordinate subject he believed him to be, and the Scots predictably rankled at what they believed to be mistreatment of their king and their sovereignty. When Edward insisted that the Scots – being, in his eyes, vassals – should provide men to support the English fight against the French, the Scots were determined to better their position by making contact with the enemy instead. An embassy sailed from Scotland to Paris in October 1295, and the following February they had a treaty in hand. The terms were simple: if the English invaded either country's territories, the other country would invade English territories in order to weaken their mutual enemy. It would become known as the Auld Alliance.

Agreement in hand, Balliol renounced his homage to Edward.

Scotland paid the price almost immediately. Edward headed north with speed, putting the major port of Berwick to a brutal sack that may have cost thousands of civilian lives. Pushing onward, on 27 April 1296, English forces crushed a Scottish force at the Battle of Dunbar, and from that point forward the coming weeks were filled with a veritable tour of Scotland in which its lords submitted, castle by castle, manor by manor, valley by valley, to the English king. A fragment of a journal recording Edward's movements gives us a taste of it:

> On Wednesday [1 May], the eve of the Ascension, the king went to Haddington; on the Sunday after to Lauder; on Monday to Roxburgh, to the Friars Minors; on the Tuesday to the castle, and the king tarried there fourteen days. On the fifteenth day, being Wednesday, he went to Jedborough; on the Thursday to Wyel; on the Friday to Castleton; on the Sunday afterwards back to Wyel; on the Monday to Jedborough; on the Friday afterwards to Roxburgh; the Monday afterwards to Lauder; the Tuesday to the abbey of Newbattle; the Wednesday to Edinburgh to the abbey, and caused to be got ready three [siege] engines casting [stones] into the castle day and night. On the fifth day they treated of peace. On the eighth day the king slept at Linlithgow,

and left the engines under good guard throwing before the castle. On the Thursday he went to Stirling, and they who were within the castle fled, and none remained but the porter, who surrendered the castle, and there came the earl of Strathern 'to the peace', and there tarried the king five days.[13]

And so it went. Day after day. Family by family. With the great castles of Edinburgh and Stirling in Edward's hands, resistance was broken. Balliol surrendered himself and his kingdom, and Edward, who was never one for subtlety, went to Scone and dug up the stone upon which the kings of Scotland had been crowned. He transported it to England, where it was eventually placed beneath the coronation chair of England. The symbolism was a double insult: Scotland was below England, and all future English kings would be simultaneously crowned upon the rock.

Back in France, Philippe tried to take advantage of Edward's Scottish sojourn by once again countering English interests in Flanders. French officers took control of many of the county's cities, and the count himself was pushed to submit to French authority once and for all.

As the Scots had done earlier, the count of Flanders responded to the pressure by trying to make friends with the enemy of his king: he contacted Edward and began negotiating an alliance. This move went no better than the Scots' Auld Alliance had: Philippe was livid at the news and declared Flanders a royal domain of the king of France. In the summer of 1297, a French army crossed into Flanders to make good on the claim. Under the command of the count of Artois, they defeated a Flemish army at the Battle of Furnes on 20 August. The victory came at a heavy cost for the count: his son was badly wounded in the battle and would die of his wounds a year later.

That same month, Edward tried to respond with a Flemish expedition of his own to counter Philippe, but matters in Scotland once more pulled him away. In May 1297, William Wallace, a lesser Scottish nobleman, had attacked and killed an English sheriff in Lanark. Exactly why he did so is unclear, but soon enough his actions had thrust him into a prominent role among those resisting

English control in Scotland. That September, Wallace helped lead an outnumbered army to victory over English forces at the Battle of Stirling Bridge,[14] and it wasn't long before the Scots had regained control over most of Scotland and were preparing to raid across the English border.

Battle of the Golden Spurs, 1302

All the while, fighting continued in Gascony. With neither side any closer to victory, the pope began mediating serious negotiations for a peace between Edward and Philippe. Neither man wanted to back down, but both recognized that the fight was costing them dearly. Edward needed time and space to confirm his control of Scotland. Philippe needed time and space to confirm his control of Flanders. As one historian has observed, if this era of fighting 'proved anything, it was that neither side could hope to emerge victorious from a conflict fought exclusively in the duchy of Aquitaine'.[15] The final war to come would be waged upon a much larger map.

October 1297 brought a truce allowing a more formal treaty to be negotiated. The following March, Edward withdrew from Flanders, leaving its count to fend for himself. Eventually, discussions between England and France would lead to agreements for two marriages. Edward, whose first wife had died in 1290, married Philippe's sister, Marguerite, in 1299. That same year it was agreed that his son – first betrothed to the Maid of Norway, then to Philippa of Flanders – would in the future marry Philippe's daughter, Isabella, who at the time was perhaps four years old.

With the needed time and space secured, both kings set about securing their gains.

Almost as soon as he returned to England, Edward set off for a second invasion of Scotland. This time, his forces faced not minor resistance but a fully fledged Scottish army under the command of Wallace. On 22 July, they met in the Battle of Falkirk. It was over almost as soon as it began. Wallace survived the disaster, but his cause was devastated.

For his part, Philippe invaded Flanders again in 1299, ultimately capturing the count and his sons. He punished the population with new taxes and restrictions that swelled his treasury and took more and more control out of the hands of the people and placed it in the hands of royal officers, who cracked down on dissent with military strength.

On 18 May 1302, the oppressed Flemings of Bruges – triggered in part by a dispute over the rights to trade in English wool – vented their fury in a bloody massacre. Some 300 members of the French garrison were killed. The hunt then began for anyone who had supported Philippe. To the Flemish, it was a righteous act. On a human scale, it was a night of horror. The Matins of Bruges, as it came to be known, took as many as 2,000 lives.

Philippe sent in the army to quash the spreading revolt, once more under the command of Artois. The Flemish rebels quickly drew together an army of their own from their town militia. On 11 July, the opposing forces met outside the walls of Kortrijk, which had held out for the king of France.[16] The Flemish forces, almost entirely on foot, were backed up against a river below the city's fortifications. They might have numbered close to 10,000. The vast majority were militia. The French likely had a smaller total number, but not by much. Among them were at least 2,000 of their finest armoured cavalry, ready to ride down upon the townspeople and peasants on the other side. On paper, it seemed a lopsided fight. But the rebels knew their ground, their strengths and their enemy. Backed against the water, they also had literally nowhere to go. A great many of them wielded a weapon of their own design: a five-foot shaft of wood topped with a single deadly spike that they called the *goedendag* ('good day'). Perhaps originating as a tool used in the wool production process, it functioned as both a short pike and a club. With these and other weapons, the Flemings held their ground against the French charge. A prepared field of pits and other ditches in front of them took down horses and men. Those French who got through either met the spike of the planted *goedendag* or the weight of its blunt side as it was swept through the air. The Flemings were prepared to fight to the death and had the same expectation for their enemy. They gave no quarter.

It was a French disaster. Artois tried to mount a second attack after the first was obliterated, but it fared no better. He lost his life in the effort. Afterwards, the Flemings collected hundreds of pairs of spurs from the knights they'd slain. They hung them in a church in Kortrijk. What others called the Battle of Kortrijk became, for them, the Battle of the Golden Spurs.

Treaty of Paris, 1303

The loss of so many fighting men in Flanders brought Philippe IV to the table to negotiate a peace with Edward. In it, the agreement that the future Edward II would marry his daughter Isabella was confirmed, and France affirmed it would do more than merely break its commitment to the Auld Alliance. It would also end the fighting in Gascony and hand the seized castles and cities there back to England. For their part, the English would return to paying homage for these lands.

In other words, the 1303 Treaty of Paris essentially restored the status quo of the 1259 Treaty of Paris.

The underlying problems that had caused the fight were *still* completely unresolved. The fire was out, but the embers remained smouldering. When in 1337 a later king of France named Philippe again declared Gascony forfeit, it was a blast of oxygen bursting it once again into white-hot flame.

The events that followed 1292 had initially escalated as mariners in the Atlantic traded blows in an evolving tit-for-tat of increasing violence, but it was Philippe, the man who could have most easily put an end to the crisis, who pushed it to outright war. He had not only demanded Edward's appearance to answer charges in Paris, but he also took the most extreme action he could by confiscating his lands when Edward predictably didn't show up.

The war that Philippe had instigated was at base about expanding the borders of the French kingdom to what were believed to be its historical extent and, correspondingly, bringing the lands within those borders under more centralized control.

This is not meant to accord blame. It takes two to fight, and Edward's attempt to wrest Flanders away had been a shrewd, opportunistic move that nearly paid enormous dividends. Nevertheless, as long as France allowed England its holdings in Gascony – and didn't stand in the way of the free flow of trade that monetized those holdings – the English seemed content with the status quo.

Understanding this helps make sense of two things.

First, it is why, for the next twenty years, there would be relatively little direct conflict between England and France. Philippe had recognized how difficult it would be to dislodge the English from Gascony, and the important thing was that the sovereignty of these lands was settled: the lands were French, and the English were merely holding them.

Second, it explains why this period of peace between the two nations does not mean that the Two Hundred Years War wasn't still ongoing. Philippe had by no means ceased his efforts to expand his kingdom's borders and centralize his authority within them. To that end, the most immediate item on his to-do list at this point was to take his vengeance on the Flemings for the Battle of the Golden Spurs and re-establish what promised to be the very lucrative control of Flanders.

It was time for vengeance.

The Years of Philippe, 1303–14

*Practice of Ransoms | Armies on Campaign | Mons-en-Pévèle |
War in Wales | Murder in Scotland | Marriage of Edward II
and Isabella | Iron King | Pope vs King | Affairs of the Crowns |
Bannockburn*

Guillaume Guiart frowned. The water-filled ditch that he and his men needed to cross looked to be 40 feet wide, more or less. And once they were across that – if they got across that – they would need to somehow get over the palisade wall protecting the manor.

Then, of course, the real fight would begin.

But the Orléanais sergeant didn't see any other options. He'd been ordered to seize La Haignerie from the Flemish loyalists within, to plant the flag of Orléans upon its gate and scour it for supplies. So that's exactly what he would do. He had no intention of heading back to the French king's encampment near Orchies empty-handed. And now that he'd scouted it all out, he had no better plan than to swim, climb, then fight.

Guiart tried to project confidence for the benefit of his men. They were not professional soldiers and such armour as they wore had been scrounged from the dead. The same was true of the battered weapons in their hands. Few wore helmets, and none bore the livery of a lord. If they followed him, it wouldn't be for duty or honour, but because they thought there was something worth looting on the other side of the walls.

So as he unstrapped his helmet and dropped his shield onto the grass, he assured them that they'd all have far better ones soon enough. Nor would he object if a few bottles of wine happened not to make it back to the camp.

Then he picked up the banner of Orléans and jumped into the water. The men, no doubt to their sergeant's relief, followed.

It's uncertain how long it took Guiart to breach the palisade and take the manor. But we know that he did it. We know that none inside were worth taking for ransom. The inhabitants were rounded up and slaughtered. Everything that couldn't be carried off was put to the torch.

We know all this because Guiart took two wounds in the assault: one to the right foot and one to the left arm. Sent to Arras to recover, he found himself reading a Flemish book describing recent events that he found so wholly inaccurate that he resolved to correct the record. His first attempt at such a history was, he admits, based too much on hearsay rather than genuine research. He burned it and, in late April 1306, blended information from the great French library at Saint-Denis with his own memories. The result was a chronicle in poetic form about the history of the French monarchy.[1]

Guiart was among those who recorded rumours about the fighting that followed the murder on Quéménès in 1292. But his poem is particularly useful when it comes to the French invasion of Flanders in 1304: as a participant, he shows us the reality of life on a medieval campaign on the precipice of two centuries of war.

Practice of Ransoms

One of the first insights Guiart provides is a description of how a ninety-man unit of Orléanais – probably his own unit – was dressed when they were sent to secure the town of Pont-à-Vendin between Lens and Lille while the army was gathering. In the Middle Ages this small community was a more important location than it is today because it was where a bridge crossed over the River Deûle. Guiart is clearly full of pride as he describes his fellow Orléanais, who set out

> Armed with their trimmed coats
> And with good hauberks of mail,
> With strong gauntlets and tight coifs,
> Gorgets and swords.

And each of them, as was appropriate,
Had a crossbow or a spear.
And all were dressed, in this crowd,
In their attire of black coats,
Which is like nothing else worn in the army.
Because each one of these is made to look
Like two fully formed shields,
One in front, the other behind:
The shields are solid red,
Set with three silver shells.[2]

Though many people imagine medieval armies as a jumble of men in drab, colourless garments, the reality was more often a riot of colour. Guiart's companions, for instance, wore the coat of arms of the city of Orléans: a red shield adorned with three silver pebbles in silver shells. This heraldry enabled them to find and recognize each other in the inevitable chaos of battle. It also meant that anyone else with knowledge of heraldry would be able to recognize them, too.

Identification could be a matter of life and death, not just in terms of maintaining command and control within the army by knowing who was fighting where, but also in terms of saving lives if anything went wrong. Heraldry made for fancier clothing, and wearing fancier clothing meant a person either had money or meant something to someone else who had money. The fact that someone might pay to buy their freedom could mean the difference between being captured or killed in battle. The amount of money exchanged – the ransom – was negotiated based on a number of factors, but one of the biggest was social standing. The higher the status, the higher the ransom.

The practice of ransom was normalized in the Middle Ages – we'll see it again and again as we move forward through the Two Hundred Years War – because the idea of attaching a negotiated price to a human being's life was widely accepted. So many social and political structures were founded upon relationships of exchange that the line between social and monetary debt often blurred. Furthermore, within the highly interconnected wealthy classes of medieval Europe in which marriage was used to resolve or prevent rivalries between competing interests, capturing an enemy satisfied the needs of war, while ransoming them maintained familial social bonds that killing them would have severed.

Plus there was good money to be made, if you captured prisoners of sufficient value. We will see many more lords and even kings captured and redeemed for coin in the centuries ahead. But we will also see its indirect effects, like lives squandered in senseless attacks that can only be explained – inasmuch as anything senseless can ever be explained – by the existence of ransom. While chance events could bring death to anyone on the field, a commander believing his own life to be reasonably safe no matter the carnage around him was a commander more willing to throw other lives into peril.

It's this last point that returns us to Guiart and the Orléanais. The experience of medieval battle – in the moment and in the aftermath – could differ wildly depending on who and where you were. Yet most of our sources from the period come from the upper reaches of society. If the chronicles, poems and letters we have weren't written by the nobility themselves, they were usually written by those whose livelihoods depended upon the generosity of that class: monks, secretaries, administrators and so forth. Not surprisingly, these accounts often disregard what was going on outside their own social spaces as not worth the time it would take to write about them. And because the work of historians relies heavily on these sources, our history is heavily – alas, inevitably – skewed.

This is among the things that makes Guiart such an interesting voice. Though he was affiliated with a unit that was close enough to power to be wearing the coat of arms of Orléans, Guiart was a soldier of no particular status or renown. At the time he headed to Flanders in the army of the king of France, he had no pretence of being a recorder of events, either. He was an ordinary man at war.

Armies on Campaign

After gathering its strength in Arras, the French army of an estimated 3,000 cavalry and 10,000 infantry prepared to march north towards the Flemish frontier in 1304. Guiart was one of those men, and he tells us much about what it was like.

Eight days after the Feast of Mary Magdalene, Guiart says, the king's order was cried out across Arras. The army would take the road northward out of the city, to cross the River Deûle at Pont-à-Vendin – the very bridge that the Orléanais had earlier secured.

The following dawn, men reported to their companies in the army, directed by constables,

> Where each man is assigned and situated,
> In order to move against their enemies;
> And they pack the road tightly,
> All of them following in an orderly manner
> The marshals and their banner-bearers
> Who go in the first position in front of the army.[3]

The largest divisions of men in a typical medieval army are called battles, and the first of them on the march was called the vanguard. It was a matter of pride to be placed here. Not only was the vanguard likely to be the first to make contact with the enemy, it was also generally far more pleasant to march up front. As anyone who has been forced to make a long slog en masse will tell you, the air is cleaner and every step easier where the road is untrodden. Those further back eat the dust of the thousands ahead, while stumbling along a road churned up by the passing of countless feet and hooves and wheels.

All morning the army streamed out of the city following the vanguard. The men were hounded out of their lodgings and onto the road by sergeants who did their best to keep everyone organized. Guiart was just such a sergeant, so his own voice would have been among those shouting to be heard over the discordant din of everyone trying to get onto the road, including the enormous supply train that would be needed to keep the massive army going.

> You would see the harnessing of carts with arms,
> And the saddling of prized horses,
> The loading of victuals on wheelbarrows,

And you would hear the rattling of carts,
The neighing of horses and blaring of trumpets,
The boys, who could not keep quiet,
Shouting and singing with joy.

Hours passed and the rearguard – the last battle in an army on the march – was still issuing out. The scale is something to remember. When we're told that an army moved from one location to another, we should not imagine a single mass of men marching in a unified block. Instead, it would have been something like the movement of an inchworm, which stretches forward to a spot, then waits while the rest of its body catches up. A medieval army marching down the road in column could be miles long from tip to tail. It was a cumbersome thing to manoeuvre, and highly vulnerable to attack at any point along its length.

While the last of the men were still extricating themselves from Arras, word came that the Flemings had retaken Pont-à-Vendin and were holding the line of the Deûle in force ahead of them. Guiart implies that Philippe IV might well have pushed his army to assault the wet-gap crossing anyway, but other commanders in the army convinced him this would not be wise:

For this reason the king decided, without delay,
To turn his army in a completely different direction.
The people who had already left Arras
Were stopped by a soldier,
Re-routed to the countryside of Fampoux.

To have any hope of reconstructing medieval warfare we have to pay attention to the roads. An army on the march – all those feet, all those hooves, all those wheels – cannot go just anywhere it pleases. To make any kind of speed it must follow roads, use existing paths and bridges. Guiart concurs: with Pont-à-Vendin held, the army had little choice but to abandon one road and take another in hope of crossing the Deûle to reach the enemy. Those still in Arras now headed eastward on a road towards Douai. Those who had only recently departed would have backtracked to do the same, while those in the vanguard, now well out of town, had to seek other local paths across the countryside to get to the new route.

An army on the march can only move as fast as its slowest units, which is often very slow indeed. Delayed by the change of plans, the army was only two leagues out of Arras when it needed to settle in for the night. Once again, Guiart provides us a rare view not only of the fine field accommodations for the rich commanders, but also the meagre arrangements that many of the rank and file had for the night:

> With shovels and buckets
> They deploy tents and pavilions,
> As if in strong houses and halls,
> Furnished with trunks and luggage.
> Those on foot who do not have revenues,
> Not a penny do they have for tents,
> So they search out the limbs of trees:
> There would you see little branches cut
> And the sergeants dragging these
> And bending them towards little saplings,
> To make lodges and lean-to shelters
> From the branches they have gathered up.

Guiart describes the encampment as having a perimeter more than a league in length, centred on the 'pleasing, welcoming and beautiful' pavilions of the king. The closer one lodged to that beating heart of France, the more authority one had.

Guiart also tells us about the non-combatants within the army. These, too, are something many of us ignore. How many they were in comparison to the fighting force – in military jargon, what the army's tooth-to-tail ratio was – we aren't sure, but there can be no doubting both their presence in great numbers and their importance to the army's survival. Many of them, Guiart explains, were selling food and drink to the men:

> In the host here and there, by the roads,
> Are the diverse good people,

Who live by the work of their hands,
And who, for profit, accompany the army.
Here they make little furnaces and ovens
In ditches near the crossroads;
Many are there to make spits;
There they cook tarts and pastries.
Barkeeps, to whom so many are in debt,
Bring barrels of wine in wagons,
Which to the soldiers who demand it
Watered down, even the dregs, they sell.
Others cry for their beers
Which are from Arras, as they say.
Here and there the aged ones echo,
Cry out their diverse calls,
The ones to sell cheeses,
Others white bread hard or tender.
These cooks set aside their pots;
Everyone's tents are filled with smoke.

So it went for a medieval army on the march, day after day, until the enemy was found and monotony erupted into battle.

Battle of Mons-en-Pévèle, 1304

After being wounded at La Haignerie, Guiart was for a time still in the camp of the army before being sent back to Arras. He was there in mid-August, when the Flemish army encamped nearby at a small town called Mons-en-Pévèle. The Flemings had something of a high ground on the relatively flat landscape. 'Fight from the high ground' is arguably the most famous and true adage in military history, something we learn even in school-yard games like 'king of the hill'. For several days, skirmishes were fought between the two forces, but no major action was taken. After that, several more days were taken up by negotiations that bore no fruit.

By 17 August, it seems, Philippe was done waiting. He'd come for vengeance upon the Flemings for the disaster at Kortrjik and the thought of all those knightly spurs hanging from the church rafters.

He ordered the attack.

The Battle of Mons-en-Pévèle was a day of intense but unusually inconclusive fighting. Medieval engagements were usually quick, bloody and horrible. Men will line up to fight, but courage is never uniformly shared. Panic can burn through the lines of otherwise brave men like a wildfire through dry grass. It only takes a handful of men turning in flight to put a unit into retreat, then multiple units. As the panic spreads, a whole army is likely to break. No one wants to be the last to leave, after all, because once retreat turns into rout, the slowest to run will be the first to die.

But at Mons-en-Pévèle neither side broke, and by the end of the day each seemed content to retire. Whether there was a formal agreement that the fighting was done isn't clear. But certainly most of those on both sides thought it finished. The way these things tended to go, after darkness fell, the armies would head back to their encampments and the leaders on both sides would spend the night exchanging messengers in negotiations.

Sometime in the early evening, though, things went very differently than they usually did. Earlier in the day, a small part of the French force had made a flanking attack that had pillaged part of the Flemish camp. The Flemings had repulsed it, but remained infuriated by what they perceived to be an act outside the realm of proper conduct. In response, they now made a precipitous attack of their own: the right wing of their army descended on the French camp as it was settling down for the night.

Thanks to Guiart's description we know that the pavilion of the king sat at the camp's centre. So sudden and so fierce was the Flemish assault that they plunged all the way to those royal lodgings. Philippe himself would have been overrun and taken for a literal king's ransom had a group of his knights not bought his escape at the cost of their lives.

The next minutes were chaos as both sides scrambled for control of the encampment. Many died. But the French horsemen regained their mounts, wheeled around and counterattacked. The Flemings withdrew, which gave Philippe the chance to claim the victory, but when his pavilion was attacked one of the enterprising Flemings had stolen the sacred Oriflamme banner, which gave the Flemings the chance to claim the victory.

Because the battle hadn't been decisive, the Franco-Flemish war would continue for nearly another year. Philippe largely had the upper hand, but the war cost him great sums of money to execute. So in June 1305 he cut a deal. With the signing of the Treaty of Athis-sur-Orge between the two sides, Philippe gained the cities of Béthune, Douai and Lille for France, as well as a yearly Flemish payment to the French crown.

War in Wales

All the while, the English had kept the peace with France. A key reason was King Edward I himself, who was in his mid-sixties when he made peace with Philippe in 1303. The years he'd spent campaigning had not been kind to his body, and he was ready for a break. His kingdom needed it even more. Waging war is expensive, and England had waged an awful lot of it.

Flanders and Gascony had been costly. Scotland, even after the victory he'd managed over the Scots at Falkirk, continued to siphon off funds. And then there was Wales. If each of the campaigns Edward began had burned a hill of cash, then what he'd spent on the conquest of Wales must have seemed a mountain.

Though it has often been strangely neglected in histories of the time, Wales plays a fascinating role in the Two Hundred Years War. Among other things, it was one of the major reasons that England's coffers were too bare to keep up an endless fight in France.

In the early Middle Ages, Wales had been splintered into many territories, each ruled by their own king. As time passed, these smaller kingdoms had merged to form larger and larger ones, until, around 1057, Gruffudd ap Llywelyn was able to unite them into a recognizable kingdom of Wales. It didn't long outlast him, however, as native rule was destabilized by a series of internal conflicts combined with external invasions from England. At that point, the partial conquest of Wales by the Normans after 1066 set up a series of what were called Marcher lordships along the tense and heavily militarized frontier between England and Wales.

In 1267, Henry III signed the Treaty of Montgomery, acknowledging Llywelyn ap Gruffudd as Prince of Wales. It was, in many respects, a treaty much like the Treaty of Paris that Henry had signed with the king of France to bring peace across the English Channel in 1259, just with the roles reversed: in that treaty, Henry had agreed to do homage to the French crown to continue to hold Gascony; in this treaty, Llywelyn agreed to do homage to the English crown to continue to hold Wales.

The relationship between the crowns went sour after Henry died and his son Edward took the throne. For a variety of reasons, Llywelyn refused to do homage to the new king, and Edward soon marched into Wales. The Marcher lordships expanded. More blood was spilled. And in 1282, Llywelyn the Last, as he thereafter came to be known, was killed at the Battle of Orewin Bridge.

All this had been expensive enough. But Edward was intent on solving the uprising in Wales once and for all. Through a combination of fortified towns and castles, the English would control the landscape and shift the populace. It was conquest and colonization.

The man the king hired to oversee his vision was Master James of Saint George, an architect and master mason from Savoy who'd worked on the castle of Saint-Georges d'Espéranche in southeastern France. In June 1273 Edward had met the count of Savoy at the castle, and its formidable architecture clearly made an impression on him: just a few years later, Edward had summoned Master James to England and directed him to construct a sequence of new strongholds in Wales.

The strength of this ring of stone, as the final project came to be called, is clear enough today in its great castles like Conwy, Harlech and Caernarfon. The birth of Edward's son at the last of these in 1284 led to the tradition that the crown prince of England would be the Prince of Wales: for the English, an honour; for the Welsh, a reminder of what had been taken from them.

Though what Master James managed to build is stunning, for the medieval treasurer, the project was a staggering nightmare. The costs of a medieval military campaign, if successful, could in the short term be offset by pillaging, the taking of ransoms and other potential war-booty. But the costs of building fortified towns and castles could only pay off as a long-term investment in future tax income.

During the first twenty years of his reign, Edward had only needed to levy a tax subsidy on his realm three times. During the first three years of his Gascon campaign, from 1294 to 1297, however, he'd needed to do it four times. This led to resentment among his people, including significant opposition in Parliament. The costs of war were adding up far too fast.

The peace with France in 1303 thus came as a well-earned break from war-making and war-spending.

It wouldn't last long.

A Murder in Scotland

Five years earlier, in the summer of 1298, Edward must have thought he had peace sewn up in the north. The truce he'd signed with Philippe in January had given him the space and time to march his army into Scotland, and he had crushed the army of William Wallace at Falkirk. While the Sottish leader had survived, he was on the run. That winter, Wallace resigned his position as Guardian of Scotland and sailed for the Continent in the hope of winning back French support.

In his place, the Scots chose two of the men who had strong rival claims to the throne upon which John Balliol would have sat if he wasn't a prisoner of the English: Robert the Bruce and John Comyn.

Bruce and Comyn didn't like each other one bit, but amid their squabbles the Scots had enough success – including the retaking of Stirling Castle – that Edward again felt it necessary to march his army north in 1300. A few skirmishes occurred as the army campaigned, but after Falkirk the Scots were in no position to take the English on in a pitched battle. After some months, the English withdrew, regrouped and then came back in 1301. It was largely as before: whenever the English marched about the countryside, the Scots retreated further into it. The English could take positions but could only hold them if they stayed in force. With no great victory in sight, Edward resolved to winter over in Linlithgow.

Sometime that winter Bruce bent the knee to Edward. Why he did so is much debated, but he had probably come to believe the cause lost, and the sooner he was on the winning side, the better. The last men standing on the Scots side would no doubt be destroyed, but the first men to leave might well be rewarded for the transference of their allegiance.

Other nobles joined Bruce in making peace with the English. Comyn was not among them, though he resigned his position as Guardian, handing it over to John de Soules.

Though Scotland was not entirely conquered, Edward must have thought the tide had turned. He was winning, and the 1303 Treaty of Paris struck another devastating blow by tearing up the Auld Alliance.

The English hit the Scots again in 1303 and 1304. At this point, Edward, in increasingly poor health, was no longer accompanying his army on its campaigns. He also didn't seem to see the Scots as dangerous enough to warrant his own presence and guidance.

In February 1304, Comyn at last offered terms. He would surrender if he and the other nobles could keep their properties. Edward agreed. Wallace and de Soules were now among the last holdouts.

The next spring, Edward took them on. When a small group of Scots held Stirling Castle against him, he ordered his master craftsmen and engineers to build one of the largest siege engines in history. A trebuchet they named the Warwolf took more than two months to complete the project, during which time the Scots sued for peace. They were running out of supplies inside the castle and could well see the extraordinary engine of war that the English were threatening to unleash upon them. Edward was so incensed that he refused their surrender until the Warwolf was operational and began battering Stirling's walls. Only *then* did he consider his point made.

Wallace was captured near Glasgow on 3 August 1305. The English paraded him south to London. There, just twenty days later, after a brief trial, he was publicly and gruesomely executed at Smithfield. His head was put on a spike on London Bridge. His body was quartered, and the four parts were sent north to Berwick, Newcastle, Perth and Stirling.

The dismemberment of Wallace was a warning, and Edward surely thought it the last one he'd ever need to send. Resistance in Scotland was broken. There was no one left to organize against him.

But Scotland was at peace for only months. On a cold February night in 1305, Bruce murdered Comyn in the church of Greyfriars in Dumfries.

Stories abound about why. In most of the tales, we hear that the two rivals got into a heated argument, perhaps because Comyn had informed the English king that Bruce was preparing to renew his claim on the throne of Scotland. Angry at this betrayal, Bruce pulled a knife and plunged it into his betrayer.

What we *know* is this: the two chief claimants to Scotland's crown walked into a church to talk, and only Bruce walked out again. Not only had Comyn been murdered, but the deed had been done on hallowed ground.

Bruce bolted for Glasgow, where he secured absolution from the bishop. That put him right with his heavenly Lord, but he still had to deal with his secular lord. If Comyn had indeed told Edward that he was planning to rise up, then Bruce needed to throw himself on the mercy of the English king or else declare his rebellion outright.

He chose rebellion.

On 26 March, Bruce journeyed to Scone to be crowned king of Scotland – albeit without the coronation stone that Edward had confiscated.

Back in England, the English king was livid. Too ill to lead his army himself, he dispatched subordinate commanders northward to root out the rebels. A year later, on 19 June 1306, the English army under the leadership of the earl of Pembroke met Bruce's army near Perth. The forces were only a few thousand on either side, but the Battle of Methven, as it came to be called, made up for a lack of numbers with a stunning amount of drama. Pembroke made the unusual decision to attack his enemy's encampment at dusk. Many of the Scots were out of their armour. Countless Scots were slain, and Bruce – thrice unhorsed in the chaos – only barely escaped with his life.

With Bruce in hiding, the English took out their wrath on anyone left behind. They targeted his family, along with anyone else suspected of supporting him. The suffering was intended to pound the Scots into submission, but it achieved the opposite. Anti-English sentiment grew, and Bruce managed to raise a new army. On 10 May 1307, at a place south of Glasgow called Loudoun Hill, he met Pembroke in battle once more.

This time, the Scots won a shocking victory. The English had significant superiority of numbers, perhaps as many as five to one. They also had veteran leadership and well-armed heavy cavalry, whereas many of the Scots were fresh-faced and armed with spears and scrounged armaments. But Bruce fought on ground of his choosing. More than that, he fought on ground of his own making: the Scots identified a place where the road by which the English would approach him ran along a low ridge through a bog. Taking the high ground at the far end of this approach, Bruce could be assured that only a small number of Englishmen would face him at any given moment: Pembroke wouldn't charge through a bog, so the width of his attack was limited by the dry ground. The Scots then furthered the strength of their position with trenching that would slow and funnel the enemy into killing zones.

It was, in many interesting respects, a battle akin to the Battle of Golden Spurs just five years earlier in Kortrijk. There, too, an army of new recruits and militia was able to destroy a more veteran, cavalry-heavy force by a combined effort of field preparation and the ability to hold in the face of a charging force.

His army's loss at the Golden Spurs had brought the French king to the field in pursuit of victory and vengeance. Loudoun Hill did the same for the English. Despite having been in ill health for several years, Edward, now sixty-eight, roused himself to once more climb into the saddle and ride north to war.

He made it as far as Hadrian's Wall. Weakened by what we believe to be dysentery, he died at Burgh by Sands on 7 July.

Marriage of Edward II and Isabella

Edward I towered over the thirteenth century. His grandson, Edward III, would tower over the fourteenth. Between them was a king who towered over very little at all: Edward II.

We've already briefly met Edward: there had been talks that he would wed Margaret, the Maid of Norway, before she died in 1290 at age seven. Just four years after that, there had been talks that he would wed Philippa, the daughter of the count of Flanders, before she was imprisoned by the king of France at age eight or nine. Then the Treaty of Paris in 1303 had stipulated that he would instead marry Isabella, the daughter of that same king, who at the time of the engagement was age seven or eight.

Amid it all, in 1300, a lesser Gascon nobleman named Piers Gaveston joined the household of the young Prince of Wales. He and Edward were roughly the same age, and the two men very quickly became very close.

Exactly *how* close they were has been a subject of much lurid speculation. Many over the centuries have concluded that their relationship was sexual in nature, and that Edward was therefore homosexual. Sexual their relationship may have been, but both men had children with their wives in the years to come, and any attempt to explain this away simply as 'doing their duty' despite their own needs certainly doesn't fit well with Edward: it appears he had another child with one of his multiple mistresses. So *if* he and Piers were lovers, Edward was bisexual. But there's no evidence available to us now to prove or disprove the notion that they were thus engaged with each other.

Their relationship absolutely troubled the kingdom, as we will see, but no one at the time tied those troubles to anything happening in the privacy of Edward's bedroom. The troubles were about access to power and money.

Before he died, Edward I had clearly recognized the close connection that Gaveston had with his son. He had twice banished him from the kingdom, but he'd also used him: in 1306, between those banishments, the king had knighted Gaveston just a few days after knighting the prince in a grand ceremony called the Feast of the Swans. Part of the preparation for the campaign that followed news of Comyn's murder, this event began with Edward I knighting his son at Westminster Abbey. The son then knighted 266 more men, an act that was meant to position the Prince of Wales at their head now and in the future.

Exactly why Gaveston was exiled after this is uncertain, but there are stories that one of the king's final instructions to his men, in the moments before he died on the way to bring royal vengeance upon Bruce, was that they not allow the prince to end the exile.

If he truly asked it of them, I've no doubt that they would have promised the dying king that Gaveston would never again set foot on English soil. Perhaps some of them would have meant it.

But if Edward I's word was that of a king, so was Edward II's. One of the new king's first acts was to recall Gaveston from exile to his side. His father hadn't been dead a month when Edward named his friend the earl of Cornwall – a positively dizzying rise in station. Less than half a year on from that, Edward gave Gaveston the power to act as regent when he left England for France to get married. The rest of England's magnates were hardly pleased.

Edward was twenty-three when he arrived on the Continent to fulfil his part in the 1303 Treaty of Paris by marrying Isabella of France. His bride-to-be was twelve.

Her age is a disturbing idea for us today, but within the moral landscapes of the time this was a political marriage. It wasn't about affection. Once she was old enough, it was expected that they would have sex and produce children whose parentage would help ensure continued peace between the rival houses of their parents. *That* was the point of their union.

This helps explain why our sources don't tell us much about how Isabella felt about marrying Edward. They instead tell us that her father had misgivings about her marrying Edward.

His hands were tied, though. The treaty not only ensured peace in France, it also ensured that the definition of France included those lands held by the English. So while there were negotiations over exactly how much dowry Philippe would pay Edward to take Isabella's hand, things were bound to go forward.[4] On 25 January 1308, the two were married in Boulogne-sur-Mer. Six days later, Edward did homage to his new father-in-law for Aquitaine and Gascony. Shortly afterwards, the newlywed couple sailed for England and their coronation.

The English king's heirs, when they came, would be Philippe's grandchildren. From the perspective of the French, this could only add up to good things. The conflict between the kingdoms, begun in 1292, was surely finished. France had, in effect, won.

No one could have foreseen the improbable truth: the fact that Isabella's children would be Philippe's grandchildren would soon enough add a new wrinkle to the French crown's ongoing efforts to unify its lands and leadership. Through a chance series of tragedies that we'll look at in the next chapter, those children would instigate a bitter, lasting struggle for the crown of France itself.

Iron King

By the time his daughter sailed away with her new husband, Philippe had already done much to centralize the power of the French throne. Philippe was at that time no doubt pleased to be known as *le Bel* – the Handsome, the Fair – but it should never be forgotten that he had another epithet, too: *le Roi de fer*, the Iron King.

To understand Philippe's work, we need to rewind a bit to how his father had run the kingdom. Philippe III had been the one to arrange the betrothal of his son and heir to Jeanne of Navarre, after the three-year-old inherited the kingdom of Navarre and the county of Champagne when her father died in 1274. The move wasn't surprising. We've seen many other instances of political marriage with land or power dynamics behind them. The arranged marriage of Edward II and Isabella of France was just such an event. As young as she was, in fact, Jeanne of Navarre had already been betrothed to another prince: one of the other sons of Edward I.

Sometimes these political marriages resulted in peace. Other times they resulted in war.

Philippe III's sister had been married off to the heir of the kingdom of Castile in modern-day Spain. In 1275, that heir to Castile died, and the inheritance soon started to get messy. So the next year the king of France sent an army in that direction, aiming to shore up his sister's position. On the way, it crushed a revolt that had sprung up against the French administrators that Philippe had forced upon Navarre – foreshadowing the role that the kingdom would play in the coming decades of the Two Hundred Years War – but this was the extent of its successes. The army was turned back before it could affect anything in Castile.

Then, in 1282, a bloody rebellion broke out against its king, the French-born Charles of Anjou, the son of Louis VIII. It came to be called the Sicilian Vespers, and the costly War of the Vespers that followed kept Philippe heavily engaged in the Mediterranean for over a decade.

Events following on from the Vespers led to the excommunication of the king of Aragon. Philippe convinced the pope to proclaim a crusade against the kingdom, the result of which would be the throne going to one of his own sons. The Aragonese Crusade in 1285 was enormously expensive and an even greater failure than the earlier effort in Castile. After some initial successes in the field, the king's army was run through with dysentery. Philippe himself was stricken. Already limping back over the Pyrenees, the French were soundly defeated by the Aragonese in the Battle of the Col de Panissars on 1 October. Four days later, in Perpignan, Philippe was dead.

None of these fights involved traditionally French lands. The kingdoms of Navarre, Castile and Aragon were three of the largest principalities of what we call Spain today. (The other main players on the Iberian peninsula at this point were the kingdom of Portugal and the emirate of Granada.) And the kingdom of Sicily stretched westward from there across the Mediterranean. France's efforts to influence or outright subsume these southern realms can be summed up as both expansionist and supportive of papal policies. They were *external* in focus. They'd also been costly failures: in money, in morale and in men.

For Philippe IV, the lesson was clear. The power and security of the French monarchy was paramount. His reign would be *internal* in focus.

So it's no surprise that Philippe responded the way he did to the events on the Atlantic coast in 1292. Though the English saw his actions in Gascony and Flanders as expansionist, from Philippe's perspective these were internal to his borders. He could not concede any diminishment of the crown's authority there. If it meant a war, so be it.

We've noted how the fighting that followed was enormously expensive for the English crown, and it was much the same for the French. Philippe was still dealing with the costs of his father's southern expeditions in support of papal policy. Both he and Edward needed money, and both sought it from the same place: the church.

This wasn't the first time that kings had levied taxes on rich church properties, but it was usually done with the agreement of the pope. Such an arrangement had been in place for Philippe III's Aragonese Crusade, for instance. But this time, neither king asked permission.

Pope vs King

Pope Boniface VIII was indignant. He issued a bull (a papal declaration) called *Clericis laicos*, which didn't call out Edward and

Philippe by name but was *absolutely* aimed at them. Anyone who taxed the church without the pope's permission could be excommunicated. Philippe responded with a proclamation that bullion could no longer be exported from France. Like *Clericis laicos*, his move did not outright proclaim its target, but Boniface's financial ledgers in Rome relied on church incomes in France, and the import of bullion was how he got it.

After more tit-for-tat proclaiming, Boniface backed down and Philippe got his money. But the underlying contest wasn't finished. In November 1302, Boniface issued his bull *Unam sanctam*, which concluded with a line that became famous – at least in terms of ecclesiastical documents. 'Furthermore, we declare, say, define, and pronounce that every human being is subject to the Roman Pontiff, and that this is necessary for their salvation.'[5]

To be fair, this was hardly a new position.[6] But *Unam sanctam* was a big deal then and is still remembered as a big deal today because of *who* was being addressed and *why*: Boniface was, in effect, telling Philippe that secular power was subordinate to ecclesiastical authority, always.

Similar conflicts between church and state had taken place over the centuries, but with the promulgation of *Unam sanctam* Boniface wasn't backing down. He was confident he had a winning hand.

He did not.

Philippe and his advisors viewed this external threat to the king's internal authority in the gravest of terms. Matters escalated quickly. Boniface threatened Philippe with excommunication if he didn't fall into line. In reply, Philippe's keeper of the seals, Guillaume de Nogaret, denounced Boniface as a heretic. Then, on 7 September 1303, Nogaret took the extraordinary step of leading a small army into the town of Anagni in Italy, where they seized the 73-year-old pope. The townsfolk arose in anger, forcing the French to withdraw, and the pope excommunicated Nogaret and his king. The following month, Boniface was dead. Of shock, some said. Of physical harms he'd suffered, others claimed. We probably won't ever know.

His successor, Benedict XI, was in part chosen to smooth things over with the French king – he was quick to rescind Philippe's excommunication, for instance – and to restore the status quo in Europe. To that end, Benedict was instrumental in brokering the ceasefire between England and France that was formalized in the 1303 Treaty of Paris. Then, after a few months, he died.

What happened next would have lasting implications for Philippe and the course of the Two Hundred Years War. The College of Cardinals could not agree on the next pope. Half the conclave wanted someone favourable to the French king. Half did not. It took until June 1305 for them to choose the new head of the church, and when they did, it was something of a surprise. Rather than choosing one of their own, the cardinals selected the archbishop of Bordeaux, who became Pope Clement V.

As archbishop of Bordeaux, Clement had owed loyalty to its English lord, but as a pope he had no such obligation. His French leanings quickly became clear. He rolled back *Unam sanctam* and other provocations against Philippe. At Philippe's request he even went so far as to subject Boniface to a posthumous trial for heresy. But Clement's most famous move was to make Avignon, not Rome, the seat from which he would oversee the church. Thus he began a run of Avignon popes in what many called the 'Babylonian Captivity of the Papacy', equating it with the biblical story of the Jewish people being exiled from Jerusalem to Babylon. In the eyes of detractors, popes in Avignon were slaves to the kings of France.

It's often said that Clement was a mere puppet of the French king, but that's far from clear. Clement was hardly the first pope not to reside in Rome, for instance. Thirty years earlier, Pope Gregory X had governed from Lyon, and there were others before him. Clement initially stayed for health reasons, and in choosing Avignon he chose a city held by a papal vassal rather than one like, say, Paris, which would be directly under the control of the king. By the time Clement was in a position to head to Rome, the Italian states were a mess of political problems. Clement's stay in Avignon has the look of complacency rather than the look of conspiracy. Certainly, he never ordered an official move of the papal court to France. That didn't occur until 1339, when Pope Benedict XII had the records of the papal court moved to Avignon and installed in a brand-new papal palace constructed for his use.

On the whole, then, Clement is guilty of pliability more than of puppetry. He wasn't a man to stand up to the power of Philippe at the start, and each time the French king 'won' something the power differential between them grew. Nothing better shows this than the suppression of the Poor Fellow-Soldiers of Christ and of the Temple of Solomon – a military order of the church more famously known as the Knights Templar. The group began in 1119 as an organization dedicated to the protection of pilgrims making the journey to the Temple Mount in Jerusalem, which had been captured in 1099 at the conclusion of the First Crusade. Their numbers grew rapidly, as did their iconic status as battle-hardened troops. Money poured in, and it wasn't long before there were more Templar accountants than fighters. This was especially true after the collapse of the Crusader states in the Holy Land with the loss of Acre in 1291. At this point, the Templars were more of an international banking network than a military order. Their treasure was their power.

In retrospect, it's hardly surprising that Philippe would come after them. Many European monarchs were uncomfortable with the degree to which the Templars, operating under direct papal authority, functioned as a powerful and influential 'state within the state', but Philippe was especially zealous in his dedication to centralizing state authority in himself as monarch. In Clement he also had a pope who seemed likely to dance if the king pulled the strings. And, as it happens, he also owed a great deal of money to the Templars.

On 13 October 1307, Philippe ordered the simultaneous arrests of Templars throughout his kingdom, including the order's leader, Grand Master Jacques de Molay. The official charge was a vague hand wave at heresy, but the arrested Templars were tortured by French authorities into confessing that the organization was dedicated to all manner of heretical sins. Historians don't think there was much, if any, truth to it all – torture anyone long enough and they'll confess to anything – but Philippe wasn't after truth.

Clement protested to the French king that it was the church's responsibility to investigate and punish heresy, but Philippe's propagandists only used this to begin rumours of the pope's complicity. In 1312, Clement had little choice but to sign off on the suppression of the Templars. Many of its members who hadn't already been killed were shuffled off into other arms of the church. A select few remained in prison, still loudly protesting their innocence and no doubt hoping for the winds to change. But Philippe was simply too powerful. When, after years of imprisonment, Jacques de Molay appeared before the French court in March 1314 to declare his innocence, Philippe ordered him promptly burned at the stake. In the end, most of the Templar treasures went to the rival military order of the Knights Hospitaller, but the French authorities collected heavily from the transferral.

Philippe was now in his mid-forties. With his victory over the Templars, his power within his kingdom was verging on absolute.

The next month, the Iron King's family was in tatters.

And a key player in what had happened was Isabella, the daughter who'd sailed to England with Edward II in 1308. Like her father, she, too, would have a nickname: the She-wolf of France.

Affairs of the Crowns

History is full of remarkable coincidences.

On 31 January 1308, the same day that Edward II paid homage to Philippe for Aquitaine and Gascony, a number of English nobles signed what we call the Boulogne Agreement. The text, preserved in a copy made before its disappearance in the eighteenth century, says that the men agreed 'to guard the king's honour and the rights of the crown', and to combat 'those things that were done against that honour and those rights', including 'the oppressions' of the king's loyal subjects, past and present.[7] The signatories swore to uphold this mission at peril of excommunication if they failed.

The text doesn't identify the specific problems that merited this act, but all evidence points to the baronial desire that the royal administration undergo some reform to prevent the kind of problems – many of them financial – that had plagued the end of Edward I's reign. It's also likely that the concerns these men had about the abuse of royal powers would have been made exponentially more urgent by the king's favourite, Gaveston, who'd been recalled from exile, elevated to an earldom and then given the regency of the kingdom while the king was in France.

If the nobles who signed the Boulogne Agreement had Gaveston in mind, they were not left hopeful by what happened after they all returned to England. While the arranged celebrations that welcomed them were ostensibly meant to honour the young king and his new wife, Edward sat next to Gaveston, not Isabella.

Day by day the situation deteriorated. Philippe had given his new son-in-law treasures at the time of the marriage, and rumours flew that Edward passed many of these almost directly on to Gaveston, along with other royal gifts.[8] England's nobility began calling for Gaveston to once more be sent into exile.

Watching it all, Isabella and the French diplomats surrounding her had reason for concern. When word of the situation reached France, Philippe left no question that he was profoundly disturbed that his daughter was being neglected by her new husband. He threw his weight behind the barons against Gaveston. Forced to exile his favourite, Edward did his best to soften the blow by granting him rich lands in Gascony and appointing him to command in Ireland.

The exile lasted only a year, with Gaveston returning to England and his old position in the summer of 1309. Within weeks it was clear that Gaveston was now even more eager to take advantage of his access to the king.

Edward tried to distract everyone by declaring a campaign against Scotland, where Bruce had been free to manoeuvre and secure his gains since the death of Edward I. Many of the barons, though, refused to lend much support for the effort. As far as they were concerned, the most urgent need was the removal of

Gaveston. By late November 1311, Edward was once more backed into a corner. Gaveston was exiled again.

This time, it lasted only weeks. Gaveston was back with the king in mid-January, and Edward back-pedalled on all the promises he'd made to the barons about change.

In March 1312, the same month that the king of France boxed the pope into the suppression of the Templars, the king of England was facing the very real threat of a baronial revolt that could tear his kingdom to pieces. All because he refused to be rid of Gaveston, who holed up in Scarborough, busily fortifying its castle in anticipation of an attack. Soon enough, Gaveston was indeed besieged, and he was forced to surrender on 19 May.

On 19 June, on Blacklow Hill, Gaveston was beheaded. A distraught Edward swore vengeance.

Spending her teenaged years in this dysfunctional, foreign court, Isabella had done her best to play the queen, even trying to work with Gaveston to maintain stability. Now seventeen years old, though, she was thinking more and more about her own security. Part of that security lay in providing an heir. On 13 November, she did just that in giving birth to Edward, named after his father. Eventually, ruling as Edward III, he would reignite the open conflict between England and France. The child's importance stemmed from the fact that he was, through Isabella, the grandson of the king of France. And because of events that were about to unfold, that relationship was going to mean more than anyone ever thought it would.

Tensions, meanwhile, had continued in Gascony. Edward II and his advisors well knew that as difficult as his reign had been, an outbreak of fighting would make things worse by orders of magnitude. So in order to stave off bigger problems, Edward and Isabella journeyed to Paris in the summer of 1313.

Philippe was at the apogee of his royal power. His position could hardly have been more different from Edward's, and he was more than happy to show it off. The royal visit was one grand spectacle after another, including a ceremony at Notre-Dame in which the two kings joined together in knighting Philippe's sons. Both kings also made declarations that they would mount a new crusade. And in the middle of it all, Isabella and Edward enjoyed a puppet show.

Under normal circumstances, this bit of entertainment would have been inconsequential. In this case, though, the show was put on by Isabella's newly knighted brothers, Louis and Charles. And Isabella enjoyed it so much that she gifted beautiful purses to them and their wives. So it was very strange, Isabella thought, that when she and her husband had French visitors for a dinner held in London later in the year, the purses that she'd given to her sisters-in-law were being carried by two brothers, the Norman knights Gautier and Philippe of Aunay.[9]

The next spring, Isabella travelled to France alone, her primary aim being the continued stability of Gascony. She arrived in Paris on 16 March 1314, and she probably met with her father that same day.[10] Jacques de Molay, the grandmaster of the Templars, had been burned at the stake in the heart of Paris the previous month. The whole business of the suppression of that order had been a shocking affair. But what Isabella now told her father was a shocking affair of an altogether different sort.

Philippe the Fair had three surviving sons, all older than Isabella. All of them, as she was, were married with political aims. The wives of her eldest and youngest brothers, Isabella claimed, were having an ongoing affair with the two Norman brothers whom she'd seen with the purses in London. The wife of the middle brother, named Philippe, was either likewise involved with another man or knew about the illicit activities of her fellow princesses but had kept silent about them. When it broke, the scandal took the name of the old guard tower in Paris in which much of the adultery had supposedly taken place: the Tour de Nesle.

Isabella suspected the affair because of the purses, but she and the king knew this wasn't proof positive. Philippe resolved to have the knights watched, and it wasn't long before he had the evidence he felt he needed. In the third week of April, he ordered all involved arrested, and there was a public confrontation at Pontoise. While the arrests were being made, Isabella was in residence only a couple of miles away – though pointedly not at the court itself.

The knights proclaimed their innocence, but after three days of torture they admitted to *lèse-majesté* – a crime against the crown – by conducting affairs with the princesses. The two men were hideously executed, probably on 19 April. The two princesses who'd been with them were found guilty at trial and sentenced to life imprisonment. The third princess was imprisoned while a debate raged over whether she, too, had been having an affair or had merely known of what was happening and said nothing. Her husband was vocal in her defence, though, and the next year she was free.

As for Isabella, she was on the move once the confrontation in court had happened and the brothers were under arrest. It seems reasonable that her actions throughout were being guided by her father. The king wanted her close by while the arrests were being made, both to support him and also perhaps to tell the court what she knew if required. But he also wanted to protect her from being tarnished by the whole sordid business. Over the next week she journeyed north to Boulogne-sur-Mer, where she'd earlier married Edward. We know that a flurry of letters were sent out as she travelled. Many of these, no doubt, informed the nobility of what had happened, while also reassuring them that her father was very much in control of the situation and, if anything, ought to be held in higher esteem for having publicly confronted a scandal that threatened to hurt his own family.

Historians have a great many questions about the Tour de Nesle affair that are unlikely to ever be answered. One of them is why Isabella had informed her father of the affair. The simple truth is that we don't know. It may have been as straightforward as familial love: she could not abide her sisters-in-law making fools of her brothers.

For many, there's a desire to believe that something darker was at work: if the reputations of her brothers' wives were ruined – along with their marriages and any offspring from them – then Isabella's son was in a better position to have a claim on the crown of France himself. Thinking in such terms would be deeply nefarious on Isabella's part, but it would be equally impressive. A claim to France is exactly what Edward III would soon be able to make.

From Isabella's perspective, though, this would have been exceedingly unlikely. She had three brothers. And while their marriages were presently in shambles, it would be reasonable to assume that they would remarry and that these marriages would, in time, be fruitful. All three would have to die without heirs for her son to become next in line.

That those small odds came true is among the more extra-ordinary and tragic rolls of the dice in all the history of the Two Hundred Years War.

Battle of Bannockburn, 1314

From the port of Wissant, on 27 April, Isabella took ship to England. The kingdom behind her was reeling from the shock of the Tour de Nesle affair. The kingdom ahead of her was preparing for outright war. Edward II had decided to march north against the Scots.

It's hard not to see his decision to march north within the context of his strained relationship with England's nobles and his experience of witnessing Philippe's powers the previous year. Among the many complaints of the nobles had been the fact that the king was taxing their wealth as if he was his warlike father, yet never actually going to war. There were surely some who were glad that Edward I's constant campaigning was over. But if taxes were being raised for a march, they ought to be spent on one, especially as Bruce's grip on Scotland grew tighter and tighter. The Scots had besieged Stirling Castle, and an agreement had been made that if its English defenders weren't relieved, they would surrender the fortification.

The loss of Stirling would be a major embarrassment for the English – and its corresponding gain a major win for the Scots – because the castle was in a remarkably important strategic location.

In the Middle Ages, a great proportion of Scotland's popula-tion lived in communities surrounding the Firth of Forth. As a result, any army that needed to control Scotland needed to be able to access both sides of that water, something that could be man-aged either with a navy big enough to ferry thousands across the firth – exceedingly rare and difficult – or with a bridge to march over it.

The mouth of the firth was much too wide for a bridge at Edinburgh, but the water narrows as it pushes inland and becomes a river. Today, the first bridges cross at Queensferry, but these are feats of modern engineering: the crossing is roughly a mile in length, and it was previously served by a ferry said to have been established by Queen Margaret in the eleventh century (from which the town gets its name). In the Middle Ages, an army needed to go as far inland as Stirling before it would find a bridge over the Forth. Here, the still-tidal river narrowed enough that a wooden bridge was put in place in the distant past, roughly 150 yards north of where the beautiful stone arches of the 'Old' Bridge still cross the river today. As the first crossing of the Forth, Stirling was bound to show up repeatedly in history. We have already seen it once in this book: it was on the plain east of this bridge, where the road ran along raised ground towards the aptly named Causewayhead, that William Wallace had won his major victory over the English in the Battle of Stirling Bridge in 1297.

But Stirling was far more than just its important bridge. Looming over the crossing stands a steep-sided crag, which dominates the plains around this important waterway and provides a ready control for the bridge at its feet. It was probably fortified from the earliest days of habitation in the region, and by the time of our story its heights were crowned by Stirling Castle. The combination of this formidable construction and the bridge made Stirling the gateway to Scotland.

Edward II's father had well understood the importance of Stirling. He had, in 1301, tried to build a new bridge over the firth, closer to Edinburgh, that would bypass the control of the Stirling bottleneck. When this failed to materialize due to a lack of funds, he had a pontoon bridge constructed to aid his attack on Scotland in 1303: this prefabricated bridge was sailed up the east coast in parallel with his march and then put in place either at Alloa or Kincardine.[11] He'd then built his Warwolf trebuchet in order to take Stirling itself.

The old man had shed a lot of blood to secure the great castle and keep the gate to Scotland open. Edward II did not want to be the man to lose it.

And so the king marched north in the early summer of 1314, at the head of a truly massive army said to have numbered more than 20,000 men. He followed the main road to Edinburgh, then west to Falkirk and Camelon. Here, the road ran northwest, passing over the small stream of Bannockburn at Milton Ford and then bending around the hills to reach St Ninians. From there, it ran north to the castle and the bridge.

By the time Edward and his army had reached Falkirk, Robert the Bruce knew he was outnumbered significantly. Depending on our reading of the sources, the disparity in men was at least two to one, but it may have been even more dire. Bruce was also well aware that the last time the armies of England and Scotland had met in a large, pitched battle the result had been the disaster at Falkirk in 1298. He was hardly eager for such a fight, but he knew he had the significant advantage of being able to fight on ground of his choosing.

The Scots took position upon the wooded hills south of St Ninians. We remain uncertain where Bruce's encampment was, but there's little reason to doubt that as the English approached, the man himself would have been reconnoitring the position on horseback, probably not far from the triumphant monument depicting him that stands beside the battlefield visitor centre today. From here, on the relative safety of the treed high ground, he could overlook the road up from the south and its ford over the Bannockburn. He also could have looked northward towards the castle that he hoped would soon be his.

The Battle of Bannockburn was a two-day affair.[12] The action began on 23 June when advanced units of the English, marching at speed, crossed over the Milton Ford below Bruce's position. If the stories are to be believed, this has to be considered a remarkable failure of the Scots: not only was the crossing unopposed, but the English stumbled upon Bruce himself, who was not yet prepared to fight. Recognizing the king of the Scots, a fully armoured Henry de Bohun charged him with a lowered lance. Bruce, dodging that killing blow, instead struck one of his own: as the English knight rode by, he caved his skull in with an axe. Around this single combat, the Scots poured down upon the English, who were forced to retreat at great loss.

Meanwhile, another advanced contingent of the English army was attempting to swing northeast around the hills via the open ground down towards the Forth. Whether they meant to encircle Bruce's position from the north or simply run past it in order to blast through to reach Stirling Castle is not now clear. They were, in any case, spotted. Bruce's nephew led his division out and attacked them, probably northeast of St Ninians. Once again the English got the worst of it and were forced to retreat.

By now, the rest of Edward's army had reached the area, and the king or his lieutenants decided to pull off the main road in order to make their encampment for the night. Exactly where they did so is uncertain. Our lack of knowledge here is unfortunate, since the encampment would help us narrow down the location of the next day's fighting – the English disaster that people refer to when they talk about the Battle of Bannockburn.

Recent archaeological work gives us hints, though, and at present the clues point us towards the encampment and the subsequent day of fighting being located in the fields called the Carse, over a mile northeast of the visitor centre. The finds recovered thus far are not yet a smoking gun, but they certainly fit with what our sources tell us about the English crossing over the Bannockburn out into the open fields. If so, then the men who were repulsed from St Ninians fell back directly into the main bulk of the English army.

That night, we are told, was a miserable one for the English. Edward had pushed them hard on the march north, trying to reach Stirling Castle before the appointed deadline came and went. So they were exhausted and now, given the events of the day, dispirited. And as if things weren't bad enough, the Carse was a boggy landscape. The Bannockburn wandered its way through the ground, as did the Pelstream Burn just north of it. Likely the English thought these could serve as natural defences to make their position more secure for the night, but the ground between was hardly comfortable.

When word of the pitiful English morale reached Bruce, he

made the bold decision to attack the enemy despite his fewer numbers. At daybreak, the Scots marched down from the hills and into the Carse. What followed was an enormous triumph for Bruce. The surprise assault caught the English off guard. Where they managed to organize, they were ground up by the pikes of the advancing Scots. And the winding courses of the two streams now hemmed them in and prevented the English from making many of the manoeuvres that they could have used to keep the Scots at bay.

For the English, the Battle of Bannockburn was a slow-rolling horror. For the Scots, it was a relentless march towards glory.

With all hope for victory lost, Edward was led from the field. He first tried to find refuge in Stirling Castle, but he was turned away: the men there knew that they'd have to surrender the fortification, and they certainly didn't want the king to come with the keys. So Edward fled east, pursued by Scots. He eventually took ship and sailed south for England.

Edward is often chided for moving his army into the difficult terrain of the Carse. It's an easy accusation to make considering the disastrous and unexpected outcome of the move. Yet we should be careful that hindsight doesn't blind us to the possibility that there might have been good reasons for what turned out to be a bad move.

I suspect that Edward moved into the Carse because he was attempting a surprise of his own. Cambuskenneth Abbey sat at a bend in the River Forth a mile east of the castle, just downstream of Stirling Bridge. There was, at low tide, a ford to the abbey's east, called the Abbey Ford, which connected to a road called 'the abbot's great carriage road' in a charter from around the year 1200.[13] This road ran to Throsk, where the abbots were said to have lodgings.[14] Recognizing that the Scots were in force along the main road south of Stirling, Edward may have been attempting to move towards this road, in hope of getting enough men across the Abbey Ford to seize Stirling Bridge from the north via Causewayhead. If successful, such a manoeuvre would have cut the Scots off from the Highlands and put them in a perilous bind.

But it didn't happen. *If* that was the intention, it was a plan that was torn up along with the English army when Bruce and his Scots pre-empted the surprise with one of their own.

Whatever Edward's plans, Bruce was triumphant in the battle. Bannockburn rightfully holds a central place in the history of Scotland. And for England, the fight is a distinguishing marker in the life of a most undistinguished king.

The full extent to which the loss damaged Edward's reputation moves us into the next phase of the conflict.

3

The Years of the Successions,
1314–30

*Salic Law | Homage for Gascony | Despenser War | War of
Saint-Sardos | Isabella in France | The She-wolf Invades |
Weardale Campaign | Stanhope Park | Lessons of War |
Succession Crisis | Cassel*

On a crisp November morning in 1314, Philippe IV awoke in his
rooms at Pontpoint in northern France. If it took him some
time to get going, no one could blame him. Fights with England
and Flanders. Struggles with the church. And just months earlier
the family-shattering trauma of the Tour de Nesle affair. But get
up he did, dressing in a clean tunic and high leather boots before
donning wool overgarments, likely in the green and grey appropriate for a day of hunting in the forest of Halatte.

For men of high station, hunting was about more than the
challenge of tracking and killing wild game. In the practice of
weaponry, horse-handling, communication, bravery and much
else, it was training for war. But there was also release in it, the
chance to be away from the bustle of court. So for most of his
life he'd been coming here to escape the grind of Paris, to enjoy the
chase through the old-growth trees of oak and beech. He'd built
the fortified manor at Pontpoint for just this purpose.

Given the time and the place, the king was likely in pursuit of
deer. Whether he succeeded in finding one is unknown. But at some
point, the king fell from his saddle and broke his leg. Some would
say it was a simple accident. Others would say he'd had a stroke.

His men rushed the king to Paris, then on to the royal castle at
Fontainebleau. In the coming years, many would claim that God

had struck him down to avenge his killing of the Templars. But whether in those last days and hours he himself had memories of the flames consuming the men he'd put upon the stake – or whether he glimpsed the fires of Hell to which Dante would condemn the 'plague of France' – we just don't know.

When Isabella and Edward II had married, her father had been expected to have many good years ahead of him. And her three older brothers would have had all that time to sire healthy heirs to the throne. But when Philippe IV died on 29 November at the age of just forty-six, the timeline was accelerated. His eldest son took the throne as Louis X, but who might rule after him was for the moment unclear. And because any child of Isabella and Edward II could potentially be on that list, the matter of succession could conceivably tear the kingdom apart.

Salic Law

For the moment, at least, there were no immediate worries. As Philippe IV's eldest son, Louis was the natural choice to take the crown when their father died. This was how things had been done in Capetian France for generations. No one disputed it.

It was, in fact, his second crown. He'd also been heir to the crown of Navarre, which he'd received when his mother, Jeanne, had died in 1305. So now, with his coronation at Reims, Louis was the king of France and Navarre. Assuming his own heir inherited these titles at his own death, the two kingdoms might yet be unified, giving France all the more reason to expel the English from Gascony at last.

On the day the crown of France was lowered onto his head in Reims, Louis X had an heir in place. His wife Margaret, the second daughter of the duke of Burgundy, had borne him a daughter, also named Jeanne. Through her father, Jeanne stood to inherit France and Navarre, and through her mother, she was a more distant heir to Burgundy. Trouble was, Margaret was now in prison after the Tour de Nesle affair, and Jeanne's legitimacy had become an open question.

With the College of Cardinals utterly deadlocked over the next leader of the church, there was no pope to annul Louis's marriage to Margaret and allow him to move on. At the moment of his coronation, she therefore became the queen of France in spite of her incarceration.

A year later Margaret died in prison, and Louis moved as quickly as he could to rectify his situation: in August 1315 he married a Hungarian princess named Clémence. She was twenty-two. The king was twenty-five. As soon as the young couple produced a son, Jeanne's ambiguous paternity would be resolved by default. By spring 1316, the new queen was pregnant, but by June, Louis had followed his father's example by dying shockingly young.

According to contemporary writers, it happened when, after a rousing game of tennis, the king drank a copious amount of chilled wine. Somehow, this put him on his deathbed. There were some who have speculated that the wine might have been poisoned. On his deathbed, he managed to declare that Jeanne was his legitimate daughter. In theory, that made her the heir to France and Navarre, though hope remained that Clémence would give birth to a boy: as the son of a crowned king, there'd be little question about his taking the throne. But when Clémence's newborn son died just five days after his birth, the problem of Jeanne's birthright could no longer be avoided.

The family attempted to simply bypass her. Philippe IV's middle son, the brother of Louis X, seized the crown, becoming Philippe V. When Jeanne complained, her uncle and his allies claimed that a woman could not inherit the crown, and they pointed to the Salic Law, named after the Salian ancestry of the first king of France, Clovis. One of many legal codes in the realm, this ancient directive read as follows:

1. If a man dies without sons, then his father or mother shall inherit.
2. If he has neither father nor mother, then his brothers or sisters shall inherit.
3. If there are none, then it shall be his father's sisters.
4. If there are none, his mother's sisters.
5. If there are none, the nearest relatives on his father's side.

6. But no portion of Salic land shall be inherited by a woman; the inheritance of the earth belongs to men.[1]

While it clearly favours men over women from top to bottom, the law very clearly allows members of both sexes to inherit property if it falls to them – just not any 'Salic land'. This is why Jeanne couldn't inherit the kingdom, some said, because that would mean inheriting the *land* of the kingdom, which had been part of the 'Salic land' in the time of Clovis.

No one had ever applied the centuries-old Salic Law in quite this way. But Philippe V pushed matters even further: not only could she not inherit France, since it was 'Salic Land', he held that she couldn't inherit Navarre either, even though it wasn't Salic Land at all.

Jeanne was left empty-handed, and Philippe was secure in his reign – for now.

Homage for Gascony

According to the agreement made in the Treaty of Paris, to hold Gascony, the English king was required to perform homage to the French king. Edward II had failed to fulfil this obligation to Louis X, though the king's early death was perhaps a suitable excuse. But when the English king didn't perform homage to Philippe V, and the months turned into years, it was beginning to look like Edward was refusing to do his required duties altogether.

To be fair, Edward was quite busy at home in England. His campaign into Scotland in 1314 was meant to rally his kingdom into unity, but his disastrous defeat at Bannockburn had achieved just the opposite: the nobles who'd tried to force reform upon the crown found renewed strength for their cause. Many of this party had opposed Gaveston's influence and even cheered his death, which added a dangerous personal dimension to the already difficult political division.

As bickering among the nobles threatened to erupt into open war across England, the Scots were happy to press their advantage after Bannockburn by raiding over the northern border. At the same time, angry riots popped up across Edward's realm, each a potentially destabilizing rebellion. And from 1315 to 1317, England suffered from the debilitating losses of the Great Famine, in which vast numbers of people starved to death.

Bad as things were, though, if the English wanted to keep holding Gascony – and they very much did – the king needed to perform homage for it. But when Edward finally complied in 1319, he did so by proxy: by sending an emissary to do homage in his name, an English knee bent, but it wasn't the king's. Philippe accepted the effort as a temporary remedy, but he told Edward in no uncertain terms that he had twelve months to come to France and do the deed himself.

So Edward sailed for the Continent in 1320. He went to Amiens, as had been arranged. He prepared to do homage for Gascony. But when he got there, he was stunned to learn that Philippe also wanted him to swear a personal oath of loyalty to the French king. There were negotiations and recriminations from both sides, and though Edward performed homage for Gascony, he refused to provide the oath of loyalty.[2]

The bare requirements of the treaty may have been met, but no one left happy.

Despenser War, 1321–22

By this time, Edward had a new favourite: Hugh Despenser the Younger. The heir of the earl of Winchester – Hugh Despenser the Elder – he'd worked hard to ingratiate himself with the king and then take advantage of his position to enrich himself and his father at the expense of the other barons and members of the court. He was, essentially, a new and – in the eyes of many who opposed him – worse version of Gaveston.

Opposition to the Despensers took root in the Welsh Marches, where the powerful earl of Lancaster, the earl of Hereford and Lord Roger Mortimer in 1321 led attacks on Despenser lands in Wales. Edward gathered forces, demanding that the lords, who styled themselves 'Contrariants', appear before him to answer charges. They refused. As their attacks grew fiercer, Edward retreated to

London, and the growing forces of the Contrariants began what could be described as a low-scale siege there. It was the start of an outright rebellion that we now call the Despenser War.

Isabella also hated the Despensers, and she saw in the armed resistance of the Contrariants a means to be rid of her husband's latest favourite. She knelt before the king in a public display, pleading with him to send the son and his father into exile for the safety and security of the realm. By forcing Edward to make a public declaration for or against the Despensers, Isabella had deftly given him a way to do the right thing in a show of benevolence to his queen and his kingdom. The Despensers were exiled.

Ironically, though, it was Isabella who inadvertently enabled their return only months later. When she was refused entry to the castle of one of the Contrariants, her husband cried havoc against all of them anew – and then recalled the Despensers to his side for the fight.

Edward's royal army dove into the Welsh Marches, seeking a killing blow against the Contrariant leaders. Mortimer surrendered and was taken to the Tower of London, while Hereford and Lancaster marched north hoping to find safety in Scotland.

On 15 March 1322, the Contrariants were trapped between Edward's pursuing army and a second royalist force on the north bank of the River Ure at Boroughbridge.

The Battle of Boroughbridge did not favour the rebels. The royalists had the better position and perhaps four times as many men as Hereford and Lancaster. Hereford was killed trying to smash his way across the bridge. Lancaster, after failing to force a nearby ford, surrendered and was beheaded. The rebellion was over. Edward and the Despensers stood victorious. But Edward's domestic triumph would soon be overshadowed by international concerns.

War of Saint-Sardos, 1324

Though we tend to think of territorial rule as a political matter, *judicial* power was every bit as real and, arguably, far more present in the day-to-day lives of medieval people. The 1259 Treaty of Paris gave Edward authority in Gascony, but it did so in his position as a duke under the sovereignty of the French king. In practice, this meant that French justice was supreme, even in English-held Bayonne, deep in the heart of Gascony. Final appeal to any legal disputes – the literal court of last resort – was in the Parlement of Paris.

What made French judicial sovereignty over the English untenable was the fact that while a case was in appeals, the French king could take possession of the land. Many judicial systems still do something like this today, as when a court takes temporary authority of disputed property to prevent either party from using it until the dispute over ownership is settled. But in medieval Gascony, the justice system was not an objective third party – particularly when it came to land ownership disputes between the English and French. The king of France might encourage litigation in Gascony, for example, because he himself could take temporary possession of the land while the case was heard. And if the results didn't favour the French, an appeal would keep the land under the French king's protection until the case was heard by the Parlement in Paris, which was likely to favour the French side.

The slow-burning war between the English and French had moved from battlefields into the courts, and the English were losing badly. It was little surprise, then, that in 1324 this judicial problem rekindled physical conflict anew, in what we call the War of Saint-Sardos.

The seed was planted by a court case that began in 1318. The abbey of Sarlat was in an area that was subject to local French jurisdiction, but a priory under its control was located in Saint-Sardos, in an area subject to English jurisdiction. The abbot petitioned the courts to allow the priory in Saint-Sardos to be exempted from English oversight. This would have placed both ecclesiastical houses in French control and simplified the abbot's life considerably. Mindful that Saint-Sardos was in a strategic location, the good abbot offered to fortify his part of it for the French.

In December 1322, the abbot's petition was granted, and the following October a French sergeant showed up in Saint-Sardos, declaring it royal land. The next night, a local English lord responded by raiding the place. The French garrison was wiped out. The royal sergeant was hanged.

Calls for vengeance and reprisals were swift. Saint-Sardos was Quéménès all over again: a killing that could beget killing in a rising, red tide of violence.

The king of France – now Charles IV, the third and last of the sons of Philippe IV, his brother Philippe V having died of an unexpected illness – demanded an apology from Edward and insisted that he perform the necessary homage for Gascony. Edward had not yet performed it for Charles, so it was necessary in any case, but the act would have been an excellent way of publicly quashing the rumour that the killing at Saint-Sardos may have been sanctioned by the English crown. Edward swiftly apologized, but he delayed the homage.

By August 1324, Charles was done waiting. A French army, under the command of his uncle, marched into English-held lands and immediately began rolling up villages and towns. Many fell without a fight. The English proved shockingly ill-prepared for war. By the time a temporary ceasefire was called in September, all the English had left was a strip of coastline and the prize cities of Bayonne, Bordeaux and Saintes.

Though the French were tantalizingly close to sweeping the English off the Continent completely, Charles knew that seizing those remaining cities would be a daunting task. All three were well fortified, and their defenders could afford no retreat. Though literally against the sea, their backs were metaphorically up against a wall. Recognizing the potential cost in both money and men, the French king informed the English that he was willing to make peace. Edward would need to perform his overdue homage and cede some of the captured lands to France. But Charles was displeased with the diplomats who'd been negotiating for England. If there was to be a final deal, he wanted to settle the terms with someone he could trust.

Luckily, Edward's queen happened to be Charles's sister.

Isabella in France, 1325

As far as we know, Isabella arrived in Paris with every intention of negotiating a lasting peace between her husband and brother that would benefit England. By the last day of March 1325, she had cut a deal to do this: both sides could keep what they had, but Edward would pay France's war costs and perform his homage.

The French figured that the English were getting off easy. As duke of Aquitaine, Edward had failed to obey his lord; that he would walk away with his title intact and any lands at all was nothing short of mercy. But the English, already reluctant to perform homage to the French in peaceful times, were furious at these terms. From their perspective, the French had invaded their lands and now demanded to be paid to give them back.

More determined than ever to avoid personally performing homage, Edward decided to grant Gascony to his teenaged son, the future Edward III, then sent the boy to his mother in Paris.

Whatever Isabella's intentions had been before she came to Paris, the situation in front of her now was *very* different. The hated Despensers were entrenching themselves in England, but she now held possession of the heir to the kingdom. And the boy – after he dutifully performed homage in September 1325 – held Gascony.

That Christmas, Isabella met up with Mortimer, one of the chief leaders of the Contrariants during the Despenser War. After his capture he'd managed to escape the Tower of London and flee to France. There are theories that he'd had an affair with the queen back in England before his exile, but more likely it began not long after they connected in Paris. Together they began to plot an attack on England to take the throne from Edward.

What Charles personally felt about what Isabella was doing – and when he was aware of it – would be interesting to know. Isabella had been central to the Tour de Nesle affair in 1314, which had seen the three princesses of France – including his own wife and mother of his two children – exposed to charges of adultery and the ridicule and imprisonment that followed. So his sister's involvement with Mortimer must have wounded him. At the same time, he would have recognized the singular opportunity that her actions presented.

It is an unlikely coincidence that in January 1326 the king of France wrote to his regional administrators, instructing them to begin gathering men and materiel for 'our war in Gascony'.[3] Whatever agreements he had made with Isabella and her son – his sister and nephew – Charles understood that if England's throne was destabilized, then he might have a chance to seize Gascony in total and complete the work of removing England's foothold in France.

Why he didn't follow through with such a plan might be explained by a document found among the papers of one of his counsellors, Miles de Noyers. Though undated, it fits well with the royal order in January since it presents, as it says, 'an estimation of the potential costs of the war, supposing it is made'.[4]

The individual calculations that this document presents are thorough and fascinating. Taken as a whole, they perfectly illustrate the French awareness that getting the English out of Gascony was going to be devilishly difficult. The plan estimates the cost of a multi-phased fifteen-month campaign, involving 20,000 infantry officers and 5,000 men-at-arms in full military gear.[5] Just how many additional common foot soldiers would serve beneath these men goes unnoted, a fact that has its own implications about the degree to which such men were expected to fend for themselves. Calculations encompassed the cost of wages, gear, transport, supplies and an itemized lists of foodstuffs, including 'approximately 2,000 barrels of wine'. The total estimated cost, it says, came to 843,900 *livres tournois*. In silver content alone – 150,475 pounds of it – this would be worth over $48 million today. More importantly, it was roughly three times the crown's annual income in 1326.[6]

The She-wolf Invades, 1326

Meanwhile, Isabella and Mortimer went forward with their plan to dethrone her husband and replace him with her young son. They raised a small army, and Isabella cut a deal with the Flemish count of Hainaut. In exchange for enabling their passage across the English Channel, she promised that young Edward would marry the count's daughter, Philippa.

Isabella and Mortimer landed in England on 24 September 1326. The king had ordered thousands to resist any such invasion, but the Despensers were so thoroughly loathed that the invaders found more reinforcements than resistance. Within a fortnight, Edward was on the run. In November, he and Despenser were captured in Wales. Isabella and Mortimer had the king sent to Kenilworth Castle for safekeeping while they figured out what to do with him.

They already knew what they wanted to do with Despenser. After a quick trial, he was dragged naked through the streets of Hereford to a gallows. He was hanged, cut down while still breathing, then tied to a ladder and hoisted high so that the gathered crowds could see. According to the chronicler Jean le Bel, his genitals were then cut off and burned on a fire in front of him. He was disembowelled and had his heart cut out – all these being fed to the flames 'because it was a false and treacherous heart'[7] – before he was beheaded and his body cut into quarters.

Edward II, we are told, agreed that he was not a good king, and understood that he and his son would both be disinherited unless he agreed to abdicate the throne in favour of his fourteen-year-old heir.[8] Whether the old king was truly so compliant, we cannot know. Our sources here all come from the subsequent regime. Regardless of the old king's willingness to give way, his reign was over, and his son would take the throne as Edward III. Most believed that the young king would be little more than a puppet for Isabella and Mortimer. But his education in wielding power and waging war began immediately

Weardale Campaign, 1327

Among the first orders of business that lay before this strange triumvirate of Isabella, Mortimer and Edward III was pacifying Scotland. The Scots had rung in Edward's coronation day, 1 February 1327, with a raid across the border.

The Scots, to be sure, had done well after their victory at Bannockburn in 1314. Bruce had grown in strength, and the cause of Scotland had grown with him. The Scots had made an important claim of independence from England in 1320 – the Declaration of

Arbroath – and by 1323 Edward II had agreed to a truce that was meant to last for thirteen years.

It lasted only four.

Why Bruce was willing to break the truce by mounting a raid on the coronation day of Edward III in 1327 seems clear enough. A truce was by definition only a temporary peace, and what he wanted instead was a permanent peace: one in which England acknowledged Scotland as independent and himself as its rightful ruler. To achieve this, he needed to bring the English back to the negotiating table, and he wanted to be in the strongest position possible when this happened. This was the reason that he'd renewed the Auld Alliance with France through the Treaty of Corbeil in 1326.

Bruce knew that additional political insecurity was about the last thing that Isabella and Mortimer needed. Edward II hadn't been a popular king, but he had been a consecrated one. His ouster was upsetting to many. With Isabella and Mortimer facing the prospect of internal unrest, Bruce clearly thought they'd be more liable to cut Scotland loose than to shed blood for it.

But Bruce had bet wrong. After he followed up his February attack with a larger raid through the northeast in June, Isabella and Mortimer responded by gathering a major army in York and placing young Edward at the army's head. What better way to galvanize loyalty to the throne than by having the new king ride to defend his kingdom?

What followed that July and August of 1327 is usually called the Weardale campaign. Although the teenaged Edward III was mostly along for the ride – the man calling the shots on the campaign was Mortimer – it was the young king's first real taste of war. Decades more of it lay ahead for him.

Robert the Bruce was himself ill and couldn't lead the raid, so the key leader of the Scots army was Sir James Douglas, often called the Black Douglas. Against his forces, the English had brought with them a sizable contingent of men from Hainaut – the county in the Low Countries that had given Isabella and Mortimer ships and men when they'd crossed the English Channel to dethrone her husband. The Hainauters that gathered with the English army in 1327 were led by the veteran Jean de Hainaut, and among his troops – quite fortunately for us – was a man named Jean le Bel, who in coming years would write a remarkable chronicle that we will return to again and again as we move through this book.

Le Bel says that the Scots he encountered, who were 'exceedingly bold and fearsome fighters', could 'cover twenty or thirty leagues at a stretch, by day or night'. The main reason for this was their mobility:

> The fact is that when they invade they're all mounted, except for the rabble who follow them on foot… And because of the mountainous terrain in those parts they have no baggage train and carry no supplies of bread or wine; when they go to war their custom is such – and their abstinence so great – that they make do for long periods with half-raw meat (and no bread), and plain river water (no wine). And they don't bother with pots or pans: they cook their meat in leather – even in a beast's own new-flayed hide.[9]

It wasn't until 29 July – four weeks after setting off from York – that the English and their Hainauter allies finally located the Scots. This was not unusual in a pre-modern world without satellite and aerial reconnaissance. Even the best scouts cannot escape the confines of hills, trees and hedges, and the Scots made the effort to find them more difficult: theirs was an agile force, intended to be fast-moving over irregular, little-trodden ground.

Still, a better leader would have devoted ample resources to scouting and reconnaissance in order to increase the odds of finding and tracking the enemy. As far as we can tell, Mortimer did not gather this data, nor did he prepare for the campaign in the most basic ways. Investigations into his logistical efforts for transporting supplies into the field have revealed his repeated organizational inadequacies[10] – problems systemic enough for at least one historian to suggest that Mortimer was making an elaborate show of war in accordance with a previous deal he'd made with the Scots during his French exile.[11]

More probable than conspiracy is incompetence. When he

took the reins of government Mortimer would have sidelined a number of administrators who had loyally served the previous administration. Whatever positives this would have brought to him personally would have been more than offset by the significant negatives it brought to the kingdom at large: men of the old regime might well have been men of experience who would be of great value in making preparations for war. It's an old adage that sergeants, not generals, run the army, but the truth more often than not is that it's the accountants, the procurement officials, the transportation specialists and all the rest of the logistics corps that make military operations a reality. An army simply isn't of much use unless it can get to field.

When the English *did* finally find the Scots, the invaders were encamped close to Stanhope, on a hillside above the River Wear. We've talked before about the danger that a wet-gap crossing could pose for an army, and here that danger would have been particularly acute: the enemy had the high ground on the slopes overlooking the river, with the English on the other side.

Jean le Bel tells us that the English sent messengers to the Scots, requesting free passage over the river and free movement to form up ranks for a battle. Either that, or they'd give the Scots the chance to come down and cross over themselves to do the same. One way or another, the English were asking for a pitched battle on even ground. The Scots scoffed, replying that 'they would do nothing whatever', and that 'it should be plain to the king and his lords that they [the Scots] were in his kingdom and had burnt and ravaged it, and if he didn't like it he'd have to come and sort it out, for they'd be staying as long as they wished!'[12] In other words, the Scots had little interest in making the fight easier for the English.

The English were frustrated. They complained that it wasn't honourable for the Scots to insist on keeping their advantage – though for their part, they weren't about to give up that advantage. Leaders will talk a great deal about the importance of honour when it is to their advantage, but they rarely bring it up when it isn't: and it would have been a disadvantage indeed for the English to fight their way across a river and then uphill at the enemy. They'd have been fools to do so.

For three days the two armies faced each other across the Wear. On the fourth day, the English awoke to find that the Scots had moved west during the night. They were now encamped in an even more defensible position within the bishop's hunting grounds of Stanhope Park. The English moved their encampment to once more face them across the river, and the stalemate resumed.

Battle of Stanhope Park, 1327

Some days later, under the cover of darkness, Douglas set out with a contingent of a few hundred Scots and crossed the river. Because Jean le Bel writes a complaint about the price-gouging on the bread and wine that the English were getting from Newcastle, which would be reached via roads downstream of the armies,[13] my bet is that Douglas made his crossing further upstream – which is also where the river is more easily forded.

Remarkably, whatever pickets the English had set out failed to notice this little force until its attack on the camp was already underway. Jean le Bel claims that 300 English were killed in the strike, and that a number of the ropes holding up the king's pavilion were cut through. If his eyewitness account is true, then the Battle of Stanhope Park was nearly a major disaster for the English. The Scots had penetrated all the way to the king's pavilion, no doubt intending to capture the young man. Had they succeeded, Robert the Bruce would have had a strong hand indeed when he next came to the negotiating table.

But even as the heavy tent came down upon their terrified king, the English managed to organize a response. Mindful that his few hundred men were a mere raiding party, Douglas wisely withdrew without the king, but having suffered minimal losses.

The whole thing worked so well that one can almost suspect that an attack like this was Douglas's plan from the beginning: he'd let the English find him at Stanhope and then track him upstream to where he could spring the trap. A few days later, the Scots repeated their feat of moving camp during the night. This time, they managed a complete withdrawal. They crossed a bog that the English had thought uncrossable, bypassing the force between them and home. Once they were ahead on the roads, there was no catching them. Douglas returned to Scotland with little loss in men and a great gain in plunder.

For the English, the Weardale campaign was a debacle in every way. Their army dispersed, having done little besides spend money that the king could little afford. The service of the men from Hainaut cost more than the crown's typical annual income – and the damage from the raid was sure to put a dent in that.

Lessons of War

For the fifteen-year-old Edward III, the miserable failure of the Weardale campaign would have provided many lessons. Stories said that the young king, when he knew the Scots would get away, cried in anguish. No doubt he wanted to do everything possible to make sure he wouldn't feel *that* again.

Another lesson from the Weardale was the power of a superior position. The Scots had made superb use of the natural terrain by taking high ground behind a frontage of river. Their leaders had also maintained superb command and control over their troops, even managing an impressive night-time shift of their encampment. In the hours before his greatest victory – the Battle of Crécy in 1346 – Edward surely remembered what he'd learned here.

Another lesson he might have learned in the Weardale was the power of the longbow, in particular its ability to surprise the enemy. According to Jean le Bel, the English actually did try to cross the river to assault the Scots at one point, but they were ambushed by archers that Douglas had hidden among the trees and brush near the river. This, too, would be echoed at Crécy and elsewhere.

Edward also learned the need for reconnaissance about the enemy's location and intent to manoeuvre. An enemy that could not be found could not be fought. Similarly, it was essential to understand the enemy's *ability* to manoeuvre upon the landscape, which in the Weardale meant paying attention to the key differences between the road-bound English and the off-road Scots.

But more than anything, the Weardale campaign taught Edward III not to wait for his enemies. The English had been largely passive once they had made contact with the Scots, responding to the actions of the enemy instead of dictating those actions. The Scots, in contrast, had taken a strong defensive position, but they'd also been keen to take an offensive action when an advantageous opportunity presented itself, as they had when Douglas struck the English encampment.

Edward III must have told himself that when he took control, things would be different – and soon enough, he'd get that chance.

Succession Crisis, 1328

As for the king of France, Charles had to be feeling good as the calendar ran out on 1327. Under Isabella's guidance, Edward III had agreed to perform homage for Gascony and consented to cede several English territories and pay a vast sum of money to France. The borders of France had just expanded, and his wife was pregnant with their first child. But Charles died on the first day of February 1328. And two months later, his widow gave birth to a baby girl.

Improbably, unimaginably, all three of Philippe IV's sons were now dead. They had ruled for a mere fourteen years combined and left behind a pool of daughters, but no immediate male descendant to continue the family line.

There were now two options for succession.

The first option was to move one branch over on the family tree. Just as the crown had passed from one brother to another among Philippe IV's sons, so could it pass from one brother to another among Philippe III's sons. Tracing from there, the eldest male descendant whose claim to the throne entirely passed through men was Philippe of Valois, first cousin of the recently deceased king. During the two months waiting to see if the widowed queen would give birth to a son, the 35-year-old had acted as regent for the realm.

The second option was to allow land inheritance to pass *through* a woman even if she couldn't inherit the land herself. This wasn't explicitly contrary to Salic Law as it had been applied for the last twelve years. By this reckoning, the next in line for the throne of France would be the oldest son of Philippe's daughter, Isabella. That, of course, was young King Edward III of England.

Unsurprisingly, few magnates in France were excited about *that* prospect. A party of English bishops journeyed to France in May 1328 to press Edward's claim to the throne. No one was in the mood to hear it. Edward was English, and a teenager at that: to give him the throne of France not only threatened to destabilize the balance of powers, it also meant a regency under his mother, who had few remaining friends in France. In addition, there was a legitimate concern that if Isabella could pass the right of inheritance to her son, then any son from any of the pool of daughters in the Capetian line could do the same. *That* could get messy quickly.

The great men of France gathered, and clarified Salic Law to exclude any claim to Salian Lands passing through a woman at all.

Here at last we return to Jeanne, the daughter of Louis X who had been passed over the first time Salic Law was dusted off to keep a man on the throne of France. She'd been the heir to both France and Navarre, but her uncles had taken both crowns in turn: though Navarre wasn't Salian Land and thus wasn't really subject to Salic Law, they had made a secondary claim to Navarre and used the power of the state behind them to enforce it.

The same could not be said of the new king. Being from the house of Valois, he had *no* right comparable to Jeanne's when it came to Navarre. So it was that at the end of May, Philippe of Valois was crowned Philippe VI of France, but not of Navarre. The council of the great men resolved that the Pyrenean kingdom would instead revert to Jeanne. The other Capetian princesses were awarded significant payouts as compensation for the fact that they would receive no land.

The fact that the soon-to-be Jeanne II of Navarre was inheriting land at all raised the question of what to do about her corresponding claim to Champagne, which *also* came to her through her grandmother. Eventually, an agreement was made: she gave up her old rights to the lands of Champagne, thus handing them over to Philippe VI, and she was given new rights to lands in Normandy. This would be important in later years.

Battle of Cassel, 1328

Meanwhile, the newly crowned Philippe almost immediately had a problem that he hoped to turn into an opportunity: the count of Flanders needed his help.

In many respects, the Flemish troubles led back to the Battle of Bouvines in 1214. Back then, the French victory had wiped out huge swathes of 'old money' leaders in Flanders, who were replaced by 'new money' leaders whose fortunes were largely tied to the wool trade in England... but who were under the thumb (and the taxation schemes) of the French-allied counts of Flanders. The century and more that had passed since then had done little to resolve this fundamental disconnect between Flemish political and economic interests, so it couldn't have been a great shock when, in 1323, a peasant uprising erupted largely under the leadership of a farmer named Nicolaas Zannekin. Though the Flemish Peasant Revolt is far less known than the later, similar revolts in France and England – in 1358 and 1381, respectively – it was much larger and arguably had a greater impact.[14] Such was the revolt's early success, in fact, that the rebels in 1325 captured the count, Louis of Nevers.

In early 1326, Louis was released after promising concessions to the rebels, but the French were in no mood to be lenient. And the count certainly had no intention of making any changes that would kick out the stool upon which his own high station balanced.

So by 1328, the revolt was back on. And this time, when Louis of Nevers sought help, he did so at the coronation of the new French king, Philippe VI. It can hardly have been a coincidence. Louis knew that he needed French support to defeat Zannekin and the Flemish rebels for good. He also knew that Philippe was anxious to prove that he was a legitimate and worthy heir to the throne of France. They could hardly have been a better match.

That summer, the French army gathered in Arras just as they had during Guiart's campaign into Flanders twenty-four years earlier. The result would be another French victory: the Battle of Cassel.

The town of Cassel crowns a high hill above fertile plains. And high ground, as we know, tends to be defensible ground. This particular hill has been fortified since at least the Iron Age. Its name even comes from the Latin word for a fortification – *castellum*, from which the English word *castle* also derives – thanks to Roman development after Julius Caesar seized the place during the Gallic Wars. It was up here that Zannekin and the Flemish rebels dug in when the French army went on the march.

Philippe, once he knew where they were, marched his army up to the base of the hill and made camp. He knew it would be foolish to send his forces charging uphill into the teeth of the rebel defence, so he bided his time. Both to supply his army and goad his adversary, he sent forces out to the surrounding farms and villages. They pillaged what they could take and burned everything they could not.

The rebels, with the advantage of their elevated position, could see it all. This might be why, on the second day after the French army arrived, Zannekin sent men down to negotiate with Philippe. Their intention was to set a time and place for battle.

But the king wouldn't even give them the time of day. He and his knights were relaxing in camp, not even bothering to put on their armour. Perhaps Philippe was trying to send a message about the relative status of himself and these common folk – that they were beneath his notice. Or perhaps it was a gesture of his confidence – that they were no threat to him. Or perhaps it was simply the heat of the late August day.

Zannekin's rebels responded by launching a downhill assault on the relaxed French camp. The Flemings might have been remembering what happened at Mons-en-Pévèle – only some 40 miles away – when the Flemings came downhill to strike at King Philippe IV, captured the Oriflamme and nearly took hold of the French king himself. They might also have heard of Robert the Bruce's extraordinary victory over Edward II at Bannockburn when the Scots rolled down into the English encampment in the lowlands near Stirling.

The Flemish attack shocked the unprepared French, who at first scattered pell-mell. Many in the French army simply bolted. French officers found some of them the next day in the safety of the walled city of Saint-Omer, about 15 miles away. As the onslaught was slowed by tents, wagons and pockets of men, Philippe VI and his dispersed knights managed to reorganize themselves amid the chaos. Taking horse, they looped around the side of the Flemings and charged into them from the flanks and rear.

Philippe does not fare well in the annals of military history, almost entirely due to his failures at Crécy, which are yet to come. Here, though, it must be said that he performed courageously under extremely adverse conditions, his tactical manoeuvring was spot on and he inspired his men by leading the charge.

The energy of the rebels was spent. Now cut off from the heights, French knights were riding rampant among them. On foot, they circled up and bravely repelled a number of mounted attacks before their ranks at last broke. When the end came, there was nowhere for them to go. A contemporary French accounting of the Flemish dead, assembled to allow the crown to confiscate rebel properties in Flanders – a matter calling for the utmost precision – concluded that 3,185 Flemings were killed in the battle. The French reportedly lost a mere 17 knights.[15]

The Battle of Cassel was a staggering victory for the French. For all intents and purposes, the revolt was crushed. Though he owed his throne to the other magnates of France in a way that would have been quite foreign to his Capetian predecessors, the first of the Valois kings had reason to feel increasingly secure about his hold on power.

Philippe now turned his attention to Gascony: in February or March 1329, he ordered the calculation of an estimate of costs in preparation for its invasion.[16] Like Charles IV had found when he did the same thing two years earlier, Philippe recognized the financial toll necessary for delivering a decisive military blow. In wages alone, the cost was suggested to run to 435,000 *livres tournois*. This would pay for three months of service from 16,000 infantry as well as 1,000 mounted men-at-arms from Languedoc, plus another 4,000 mounted men-at-arms from greater France who would serve for a total of five months. This was a gigantic cost, but on 25 March Philippe nevertheless prepared to levy a war tax to pay for it. Knowing that the other peers of the realm who had put him on the throne might be concerned by his attack on one of their number – which, as duke of Aquitaine, Edward was – Philippe reassured them that the offensive action was necessary because Edward had not performed homage as king.[17] This was true, but no doubt the real reason was that Philippe believed Gascony ripe for the taking.

Fully aware that Gascony was for the moment indefensible, Edward III agreed to perform homage as soon as it could be arranged. On 6 June 1329, the two kings met in Amiens Cathedral. Edward tried to do homage for both the lands he currently held and those that the French had taken during the War of Saint-Sardos. Though he was in no position to fight France to regain them, it was certainly an indicator of his intentions. Philippe would have none of it. As far as the French were concerned, the territory they had gained was permanently acquired. Isabella counselled her son to be satisfied with the lodging of protests about the seized lands. It was the best they could do.

A tournament was held after the official business was concluded. By all accounts, everyone played nice. But the old wounds from the 1259 Treaty of Paris still festered: when it came to the homage ceremony, Edward refused to place his hands between those of Philippe. This may seem a little thing, but it was of grave importance: by his words the king of England had acknowledged the French king as the rightful holder of the Gascon lands (this was called *simple* homage), but by his actions the English king had refused to acknowledge the French king as his personal lord (*liege* homage).

The French noted it, but for the moment they did not press the matter. The sixteen-year-old king of England was, for them, a weak adversary.

He did win the tournament, though, and soon he would win far more.[18]

4

The Years of Edward, 1330–47

Edward's Homage | Robert of Artois | Dupplin Moor | Breaking Points | Costs of War | Sluys | War of the Breton Succession | Chivalry and the Round Table | Aiguillon | Crécy Campaign | Crécy | Neville's Cross | Siege of Calais

The moon was only the faintest crescent amid the stars, hardly enough for William Montagu and the other conspirators to see the thin, hidden path carved into the stone below Nottingham Castle. If he wanted to curse the dark, he wanted to bless it, too: it was one more veil to hide them from the many guards lurking above. Some of those might be loyal to their cause, but this wasn't the time for blind trust. Too much was at stake.

When they found the narrow, rock-hewn stairs, the two dozen men crept up the steps as quickly as they dared, taking care to keep their weapons from rattling. Nerves were high. The question of whether this October night would end in triumph or with their heads on spikes now depended on the locked gate ahead.

It had been Montagu who had learned of the postern gate and conceived a plan to infiltrate the castle through it. All he needed was someone on the inside to ensure that it was left unbarred.

As it happened, the king of England himself was inside: Edward III, a month shy of eighteen, father to a four-month-old prince, was a virtual prisoner under the ever-watchful eye of Roger Mortimer, the man who had stolen his crown in all but name. Claiming to be under the weather, the young man had retired to his rooms early, then used the same dark that covered the conspirators' passage to slip back out into the night.

The gate on the little passageway was unlocked. Montagu and the others slipped into the heavily guarded castle sight unseen.

Though most of the guards looked outward from the walls, the conspirators still moved from shadow to shadow lest anything give them away before they reached the queen's chambers. Mortimer was there, they knew, discussing plans with some of his key allies. Catching them all at once, all in one place, was essential. Montagu's little company would never make it if they had to fight their way in.

The men had reached the hallway just outside the queen's chamber when they were spotted by Sir Hugh of Turplington. An old friend of Mortimer's, it took him only an instant to recognize what was happening. 'Traitors!' he cried out. 'Traitors!'

One of the conspirators plunged a blade into him, cutting his words into screams. The others rushed for the queen's door, which Mortimer's squire and another man were desperately trying to bar. Montagu and the others shouldered the wood, burst through. The two men on the other side were quickly slain.

The queen shielded her lover, first screaming and then pleading. 'Dear son!' she cried out in French. 'Dear son, have pity on gentle Mortimer!'

Rough hands separated the two. The queen was whisked away. Mortimer was put in chains. One of his last key allies was found in the queen's latrine, trying to wedge himself to freedom through the shit-smeared chute. He, too, was arrested.

In minutes, it was over.

Edward III had completed a *coup d'état* against the very people whose *coup d'état* had made him king.

The events of 19 October 1330 had been a long time coming. We don't know exactly what Edward III's relationship with Isabella and Mortimer was like at the start of his rule, but there's little question that it had steadily deteriorated over time. While the Scots were thrilled by the results of the Weardale campaign, for the English it had been a disaster. The failure in battle had led nearly directly to the likely murder of the imprisoned Edward II. Just months after that, in the spring of 1328, a peace was struck affirming Robert the Bruce as the rightful king of an independent Scotland and stipulating that Robert's four-year-old son, David, would marry Edward III's little sister, the six-year-old Joanna. It was a near-total loss for England's aspirations in Scotland. Many in England called it 'the shameful peace'. The authors of this capitulation were Isabella and Mortimer, and by all accounts Edward was furious.

Meanwhile, the fact that Mortimer was increasingly taking on the trappings of a king himself – something that he very much was not – further worsened the situation as the actual king grew closer to his age of maturity. Mortimer took steps to keep the young king under control, including planting informants within the household. The king likewise paid off informants within the entourage of Mortimer and Isabella.

The birth of Edward's son may have been the trigger for the king and his allies to act. They had to wonder, after all, if Mortimer might conspire to push him out of the way in favour of the infant – thereby buying himself eighteen more years of power.

Montagu and the other conspirators would be heavily rewarded for their aid in arresting Mortimer. Many of them would become forceful and steady allies during Edward's long, remarkable reign. A month after that dramatic night, Mortimer was found guilty of treason and executed, his naked body left hanging on the gallows for days. As for Isabella, she was put under house arrest for a few years before Edward phased her into what can best be described as a forced retirement. She would die a nun in 1358.

It is with Edward's self-rule that many books on the so-called Hundred Years War start. Instead, we're already four decades into a much larger picture of a Two Hundred Years War – the story of a far more complicated struggle between England and France.

Up to this point, the French had been largely (but hardly exclusively) on the offensive. Bit by bit, they had been expanding their lands and consolidating their power. France now stretched north to south from the English Channel to the Pyrenees, and east to west from the Holy Roman Empire to the sea. They had moved against English interests in the Low Countries and, through the Auld Alliance, in Scotland. Progress hadn't always been easy, but it had been more or less steady. The biggest difference between France in 1330 and France now is that the lands east of the Rhône had not yet been integrated into the realm. Other than that, at least on paper, the king of France held sway over something that at least in its borders was approaching both the West Francia of old and the state of France of today.

But the fact that it was on paper *mattered*.

The French kings had worked hard to centralize authority, and the area of the lands under their direct control had grown. But even so, much of what was 'France' remained an interlacing of agreements, treaties, relationships and traditions, an assemblage of duchies and counties that could and would take independent actions if it suited local interests.

It's an uncomfortable truth that *most* societies are held together far more loosely than those living within them care to recognize: apply enough pressure, and the cracks in any community will quickly show. More troubling, no single thing functions as the lever to apply that pressure. For one society, it could be a natural disaster that destroys a harvest. For another, it could be an unprecedented pandemic that carves through the social strata. It could be an economic calamity, a political tragedy, a military defeat… almost anything can destabilize a community.

Edward's Homage, 1330–31

From 1330, Edward ruled as his own man. Traumatic as his actions were in securing his autonomy, many in his realm were relieved to have the government restored to some sense of normalcy. A monarchy led by a king, his mother and her lover was hardly bound to work like a well-oiled administrative machine.

Alongside this streamlined state, though, greater responsibilities fell to the king. With his French mother, Isabella, out of the picture, Edward was increasingly under French pressure to demonstrate that the terms of the Treaty of Paris in 1259 were upheld. Since Edward held Gascony not as the king of England but as the duke of Aquitaine, whether the English liked it or not, the French king was still sovereign in Gascony.

In the wake of the War of Saint-Sardos, those obligations rankled. Though peace had been proclaimed, a great many Gascon nobles had lost their lands and properties during the fighting. In case after case, they appealed to the English king-duke, demanding restoration or, barring that, restitution for their losses. These losses could not be simply ignored or swept under the rug. Yet the French king wasn't likely to uphold the return of seized lands to the Gascons, since this then transferred the loss to his own people, who would demand restoration or restitution in turn.

For many on the English side, the answer to these problems was to end French sovereignty in Gascony. At the heart of the duchy, the English had been in local control for generations. To make England's lords, courts and king the final authority, the 1259 Treaty of Paris needed to be undone. This would mean war, though, and Edward still wasn't able to wage it.

For many on the French side, the answer was to ensure that Edward knew his place. If, as duke, he was dutifully loyal to the French king in the same way that any other peer of France ought to be, then all could be resolved without a costly war.

At this point Edward had twice performed homage for Gascony, so it might seem that this box had been checked. But the particulars are important. The first time he'd done it, in 1325, he'd been a child-prince of England. On the next occasion, in June 1329, he'd been England's king, but still a young man under his mother's influence. More troubling, Edward had bristled against some of the oaths that the French had wanted him to make, particularly by refusing to perform *liege* homage.

This detail – small though it might look – mattered. The simple homage that Edward had performed in 1329 had prevented an immediate invasion by asserting that he held Gascony under the sovereignty of the king of France. It did not say that he, Edward, was himself under the sovereignty of the king of France: that would be liege homage.

Month after month, as the squabbles over restitutions grew, the tensions between the two kingdoms grew more and more untenable. Finally, on 30 March 1331, Edward took the action that many hoped would defuse the potentially explosive situation. In an open letter, he proclaimed that although what he had performed 'to the king of France' at Amiens in 1329 was an act of simple homage, 'it was, is, and should be understood as liege homage, and that we should give him [i.e. Philippe] faith and loyalty as a duke of Aquitaine and peer of France'.[1]

He had bought himself time to prepare, but the slightest disruption could set things off again. Within just a few short years, a new and terrible round of violence would commence. The trigger was the exile of a nobleman from France. Like the murder at Quéménès in 1292 that had set so much of this in motion, it was an act that had staggering repercussions far beyond what anyone could have imagined at the time.

Robert of Artois, 1331

Just over the border from France, stretching up to Calais, was the county of Artois. Running up the coast, from Gravelines to the river Scheldt, was the county of Flanders. Heading up the coastline from there: the counties of Zeeland and then Holland. Further north was the See of Utrecht centred on that city. The county of Guelders was built around Arnhem and Nijmegen, with the county of Cleves just beside it. The duchy of Brabant had the great cities of Antwerp and Brussels. Valenciennes was the centre of the county of Hainaut. Tournai was an island amid it all, called the Tournaisis. Lille and Bouvines stood in Walloon Flanders. Namur had its own county, and so did Luxembourg; between them, punched up to include Liège, was the county of Loon. Beside it, Maastricht and Valkenburg were within the duchy of Limburg.

Though a few of these regions eked out some measure of independence, the Low Countries were mostly carved up between the surrounding rival powers of France, England and the Holy Roman Empire. Ties of marriages, treaties, economics or even cultures made for highly complicated relationships. The county of Hainaut, for instance, was a feudal lordship of the Holy Roman Empire for much of its history. Most of its populace, however, was linguistically and culturally tied to France. At this point in our history, its count was married to the sister of Philippe VI, one of their daughters was married to the Holy Roman Emperor and the other daughter was married to Edward III. He had, we might recall, given Isabella and Mortimer the fleet they had needed to cross the Channel and depose Edward II. The interconnection of these crowns, combined with the extraordinary wealth that moved through these lands, made the Low Countries a potent front in the Two Hundred Years War.

All of which is background to our exiled nobleman who arguably restarted the timer counting down to war. He did it by claiming to be the count of Artois.

Artois had been formed as a French vassal state in 1237, led by Robert I, brother to Saint Louis. After the death of this first count of Artois at the Battle of Mansurah during the Seventh Crusade, rule had passed to his posthumous son, Robert II, who was a loyal soldier for France until his own death leading a French charge at the Battle of the Golden Spurs in 1302. His son had predeceased him in 1298 from wounds received fighting against the Flemings at the Battle of Furnes in 1297, so Robert II's grandson – also named Robert and for our purposes *the* Robert of Artois – thought the county of Artois ought to be his. Instead, it went to the eldest surviving heir, which was Robert's aunt. He was fifteen at the time, scarcely in a position to do anything about it, but over the years he very clearly came to believe he'd been wronged. He just needed some way to press his claim.

He got the chance thanks to two unrelated events. The first was his marriage, in 1320, to Joan of Valois, whose half-brother became Philippe VI in 1328. The second was the death of Robert's aunt in 1329. Combined, these gave him the means and the opportunity to try to take Artois.

Hoping to ensure that his claim would be irrefutable, Robert hired a woman named Jeanne de Divion to help him create a fake will from his father, naming him the heir. This deception was remarkably bold, but it also went against every foundation upon which medieval society rested: it was an act of perjury and dishonour meant to change a noble inheritance. When the forgery was discovered, condemnation was swift. Philippe exiled Robert and confiscated his lands. Jeanne was burned at the stake.

Robert then made his way to England, and Edward III welcomed him. Because Robert knew the French court well – and talked up his knowledge quite beyond this – the English king saw him as a military asset. Edward was also aware that Philippe had come to despise the would-be count. Giving him protection was thus an easy way for Edward to thumb his nose at his counterpart across the Channel.

For his part, Robert seems to have early on decided that his best way forward was to encourage Edward to make war on France. If the English king took on such a fight and won, Robert thought, he'd surely carve Artois off and give it back to him. So even as early as his arrival in England in 1331, Robert was piling the tinder for the fire to come. And of course the French king's personal hatred of Robert played no small part in his decision to throw a match at that pile only five years later.

Battle of Dupplin Moor, 1332

Edward III had never been pleased with the agreement to end hostilities in Scotland, and he was hardly alone. So when Robert the Bruce was succeeded in 1329 by his five-year-old son David II, the English king took the opportunity to revisit the situation in the north.

His way in was Edward Balliol, whose father, John, had been the candidate chosen by Edward I and the great council of Scots magnates to become king in 1292. The way Edward Balliol figured it, that meant he had the better claim to the throne than young David. What's more, the 'Disinherited' – a group of English-friendly Scots who'd had their lands confiscated by Bruce – agreed on the point, and they were willing to fight to see David pulled down from the throne and Balliol raised in his place.

With the support of Edward III – secretly, since the two kingdoms were officially at peace – the Disinherited raised a small army and sailed for Scotland in the summer of 1332. It was, though no one would have known it yet, the start of the Second War of Scottish Independence, which would last for just over twenty-five years.

On 6 August, the Disinherited managed to disembark on the north shore of the Firth of Forth. It was not easy, as the Scots attacked while the army was making its landing. But the attack was repulsed, the Scots retreated and the Disinherited marched northward to Dunfermline. The goal of the invaders was to get to Scone, where Balliol could be crowned king of Scotland.

Gathering in their way, however, was a much larger army that was loyal to the boy-king, David. They were under the leadership of the earl of Mar. Exactly how many men Mar commanded is not known, but it has been estimated that the Scots outnumbered the invaders by as many as ten to one. They had a good notion where the Disinherited wanted to go, and a corresponding notion of how to keep them from getting there.

Mar set a defensive line along the River Earn, which ran west out of the Firth of Tay just south of Perth. The most direct route from Dunfermline to Perth – and thence to Scone just beyond it – would cross the Earn at the aptly named town of Bridge of Earn. So the Scots, no fools, made the bridge unusable.

The Disinherited moved upstream on the Earn's south bank, looking for a way across. The Scots paralleled opposite them on the north bank. But by 10 August, Mar knew that a second force of Scots was on the approach under the command of the earl of March. That day, Mar ordered most of his army to march east, back towards Bridge of Earn. Likely he planned to cross over to the south bank to position himself where the Disinherited would be caught between the two armies and the river. At that point, March's army was at Auchterarder, some eight miles west of the Disinherited encampment, which was just east of the small village of Forteviot.

The Battle of Dupplin Moor would be fought the next day. Though little remembered, it played a vital role in the development of what we might call an English way of war.

That night, the Disinherited managed to cross the Earn by a local ford. They pounced upon a poorly protected encampment that the Scots had left behind. News of the crossing reached Mar, who now ordered an immediate turn back along the roads they had just taken. The hastiness of this march left the Scots in some disorganization, though it also nearly caught the Disinherited flat-footed: Balliol and his men were stunned to see, by the light of dawn, that the Scots were nearly upon them. In response, the Disinherited formed up in what would become a standard English formation for many fights to come. In field command for the

Disinherited was the highly experienced Henry de Beaumont, who had been a key figure at the Battle of Boroughbridge in 1322. His tactics at Dupplin Moor seem to be an extension of lessons learned in that earlier fight.[2]

First, Beaumont picked a location that had a relatively small frontage to defend and could not be easily outflanked. This helped negate the numerical advantage of the enemy while also funnelling them into a predictable approach of attack. Across this frontage he set out his available men-at-arms, all of them dismounted and prepared to receive a charge. The Disinherited lords would have been in this mix, with bright banners declaring their presence. To either side of this, protected by the terrain – hills, trees or perhaps both – Beaumont established lines of archers.

The Scots, seeing the Disinherited, came in a rush, hoping to break through the dismounted centre and send it into rout. As they came on, the archers on either side loosed ruinous volleys into them. Men were struck down in waves, and the living in-stinctively shrank away from the attack, thereby creating a tighter mass for the archers to target with their next shots. Withering as it was, many Scots got through and struck the Disinherited centre. Beaumont's men bent back – 20 or 30 feet, according to the *Chronicle of Lanercost*. In this crucial moment, the earl of Stafford shouted out: 'Englishmen! Put your spears to your chests, not your shoulders!'[3] In other words, don't disengage. Put the bloody points to the enemy and *hold*. They did just that.

The next line of the Scots was already coming in, making its own headlong charge for glory. It stumbled through the killing zone, organization crumbling as it crashed into the remains of the bogged-down first line. 'Thousands of horses and men fell,' according to the chronicle we call the *Brut*, 'piling up, bodies on top of bodies'.[4] Few escaped the massacre that followed when the collapsing lines of the Scots broke and were chased down in a merciless rout 'until night fell'.

Locating the fight would do much to help us understand any details beyond this, but there is at present no confirmed location for the battle. The name it carries in most of our sources is either Dupplin or Gask, and tradition locates the fight near the Dupplin

Estate today, placing it not far from an old stone cross (dated to the ninth century) on the slopes just southwest of the castle proper. Another position that has been suggested is roughly a mile and a half further west, near the intersection of the A9 and B934 today. I find neither convincing and would posit a site further upland, probably somewhere along the line of the Roman road that ran towards Perth.

One of our only other clues to help narrow the search is the *Brut*'s claim that the fight occurred in a 'strait passage' near 'a deep bend in the moor'. This 'deep bend' has been interpreted to be a sharp slope at the moor's edge by many historians, but the meaning more directly refers to a sharp turn in the landscape: my guess is that it refers to a pronounced bow of the Earn, which itself defines the course of the moor. The course of the river has shifted in the modern era, but a look back to our eighteenth-century maps reveals a dramatic, deep double-bend of the river immediately west of the town of Broom of Dalreoch. The remains of the old route can still be seen on the fields today, including on satellite imagery. Settlement patterns in the vicinity suggest the likelihood of a medieval ford across the river near this same bend. A working hypothesis would be that this is the 'deep bend' to which the *Brut* refers, and that the English made their crossing close to the location of the current Dalreoch Bridge. Moving uphill from here, the Scots encampment that the Disinherited surprised could have been located at the old Roman fort at Gask, though we can't know without archaeological finds. The same is true when it comes to locating the climactic fight itself, which would likely be eastward of wherever that initial ambush happened, following the 'strait passage' of the Roman road in the direction of Dupplin. Perhaps it would have been near the Midgate Roman fortlet, which is almost dead centre between Gask and Dupplin, or a little further east towards Crossgates, near Westmuir Roman signal station. The Scots, for their part, would have gone north from Bridge of Earn towards Perth before moving west up these same roads. This wasn't the straightest route to the enemy's location, but it was the route that would ensure they were positioned between the Disinherited and Perth. This had to have been the first priority.

This neglected fight, though relatively small, had an outsized role not just within the context of Scotland's history but also within military history more generally. Beaumont's arrangement of men – a dismounted centre, with protected ranks of archers to either side that would funnel an attacking enemy into destruction – became standard operating procedure for generations of medieval English armies. We will see these tactics in France at Crécy. We will see them at Agincourt. But first, the Auld Alliance would ensure that the French would not stand by and let the Scots face English attacks alone.

Breaking Points, 1336–37

The bickering between the French and English kings over jurisdiction in Gascony was growing more and more heated. And with the Scots facing devastating losses on the battlefield at Dupplin Moor, then at the Battle of Halidon Hill a year later, Philippe encouraged the piracy of English ships to support the Scots' cause.

Dominoes fell fast, one into another, and starting in 1335 both kings were working hard to put themselves onto a ready war footing in the region, while bringing the rest of Europe along for the ride. The count of Flanders, for instance, was Louis of Nevers, who owed his power to Philippe's victory at the Battle of Cassel. He was steadfast in his support of the French crown, so when the French king asked him to crack down on English interests, he did it. Edward responded by shutting down the export of wool to Flanders in August 1336. Flemish textile production ground to a halt, with crushing economic results: as this key industry faltered, so did dozens of other industries and services that relied upon it. Incomes plummeted. Unrest grew.

On the day after Christmas in 1336, Philippe demanded that Edward return the exiled Robert of Artois to France. The request was at least partially personal: we know that Philippe had a real loathing for the man and was anxious to see him in fetters. But more was afoot.

Philippe sent his demand not to Edward personally but to one of his underlings – a hardly subtle sign of the French king's superior position. Even more, the demand went so far as to quote back at Edward the 1331 letter in which the English king had pronounced that as the duke of Aquitaine he owed personal 'faith and loyalty' to Philippe as king of France.[5] Philippe was using Robert to directly engage with Edward's word, thereby directly testing Edward's status as a French vassal: if he refused to obey, Edward was no vassal at all, and a liar to boot. Gascony could be forfeit and the game they were playing would turn quite deadly serious indeed. It was a bold move.

Edward refused to hand Robert over. The following May, Philippe responded by declaring that – since Edward had broken faith with his liege – his lands in France were forfeit.

This moment may mark the traditional start of the Hundred Years War, but it was only the latest flare-up in decades of ongoing friction. After all, Philippe was making the same move that had eventually brought Edward II into line during the War of Saint-Sardos. The difference this time was that Edward III was not his father. Rather than backing down, he renounced his oaths to Philippe.

These latest flames spread fast. In Flanders, many citizens were incensed that Louis had favoured French interests over their own. The destabilization of the wool trade had already severely damaged the economy, and the rift between Edward and Philippe meant worse was likely to come. At the end of 1337, these resentments erupted in outright insurrection, led by Jacob van Artevelde, a leading citizen from Ghent whose wealth was tied to the wool trade and England. As soon as he took control of the rebellion, he entered into negotiations with the English to declare Ghent, Bruges and Ypres as neutral parties in the hostilities. In return, Edward agreed to reopen the wool trade. Beyond the economic benefits, this gave the English a pivotal launching point against the lands of France.

Costs of War, 1338–39

For all Edward's bravado, the French attacked across the Channel first. In March 1338 a group of ships arrived in Portsmouth harbour.

It would later be said that they did so under the disguise of flags of England. Once the ships were tied off to the docks, Frenchmen poured out of them, pillaging goods, burning buildings and killing those who resisted. They then sailed out to sea, attacking the Channel Islands and capturing Jersey.

Edward swiftly renewed his claim to the throne of France, and he swore to defeat 'Philippe of Valois', as he addressed the man who wore the crown. But directly taking the fight to Philippe was beyond his means. Already fighting in Scotland, Gascony and the Low Countries, he now faced a need to rapidly defend England's ports and trade routes: news of the successful Portsmouth raid brought pirates and other independent raiders hoping for their own easy coin.

None of this was an accident. In a letter, Philippe's admiral, Nicholas Béhuchet, described the French strategy as nothing less than a campaign to cripple the English ability to wage war, not only by devastating England's fisheries and its trade routes but also by forcing its crown to spend money on ships it did not yet have.[6] And if English riches were also stolen en route to these ends, all the better.

On the morning of Sunday, 4 October, the French hit Southampton, another major English target. They spent hours in the town pillaging and burning, raping and killing. As much as a third of the town's population was lost, and the ships sailed out of the harbour heavy with wine, wool and wealth. English records hint that what was left was then further looted by the English themselves.[7]

Soon enough Harwich and Hastings were hit. Plymouth, Sandwich and Rye, too. The coasts of Devon, Sussex and Kent were fair game for the enemy. Nowhere seemed safe.

Already in danger of losing the war, Edward needed help and a means to take the fight to France. He found both in the Low Countries. Hainaut had long been a supporter. Edward owed his crown to his Hainauter father-in-law. That count had died in 1337, right when Edward most needed him again, but the dying man had made his son and heir swear an oath to support England over France. This and a £15,000 sweetener were enough to get

Hainaut on Edward's side. Guelders came for the same payment, and Brabant followed: the duke was Edward's cousin, but more importantly he was interested in how his port city of Antwerp could take advantage of the profitable wool trade with England. That and a £60,000 payment were sufficient.

The neutrality of van Artevelde's Flemings already ensured that Flemish ports would no longer be staging grounds for French attacks on English interests at sea, and the Flemings would not resist the English king if he sailed up the Scheldt. With the Low Countries as another front to worry about, Philippe could not put all his strength into Gascony.

What Edward needed to be sure of was the Holy Roman Emperor, Louis IV. His influence in the rest of the Low Countries meant that he could make English efforts there difficult if not impossible. Edward needed him on side or effectively neutral to keep the Low Countries corridor open at all costs.

And it *did* cost. Louis supported Edward in return for around £45,000.

The king was bleeding money he didn't have.[8] For all that he needed it to attack the French, he also needed coin to scrape together coastal defences – walls, ships, warning systems – to keep safe his people and keep open his means to even get at the enemy. And his alliances were now multiplying his costs considerably. To make up for his shortages, he borrowed considerable amounts of money from anyone who would lend it to him – including massive sums from Italian bankers. The interest owed on these loans made his finances even more perilous in the long term. Without a victory, as he himself noted on 6 May 1339, he faced the 'dangerous and humiliating' prospect of bankruptcy.[9]

That autumn, Edward finally made his move. He marched out with an army built from all these allies, targeting the region around Cambrai in northern France. Historians call it the Thiérache campaign.

Philippe mobilized an army of his own, which he joined at Péronne on 10 October. The English were only 18 miles away, but Philippe made no move in that direction. He seemed content to continue to strengthen his forces, knowing that Edward

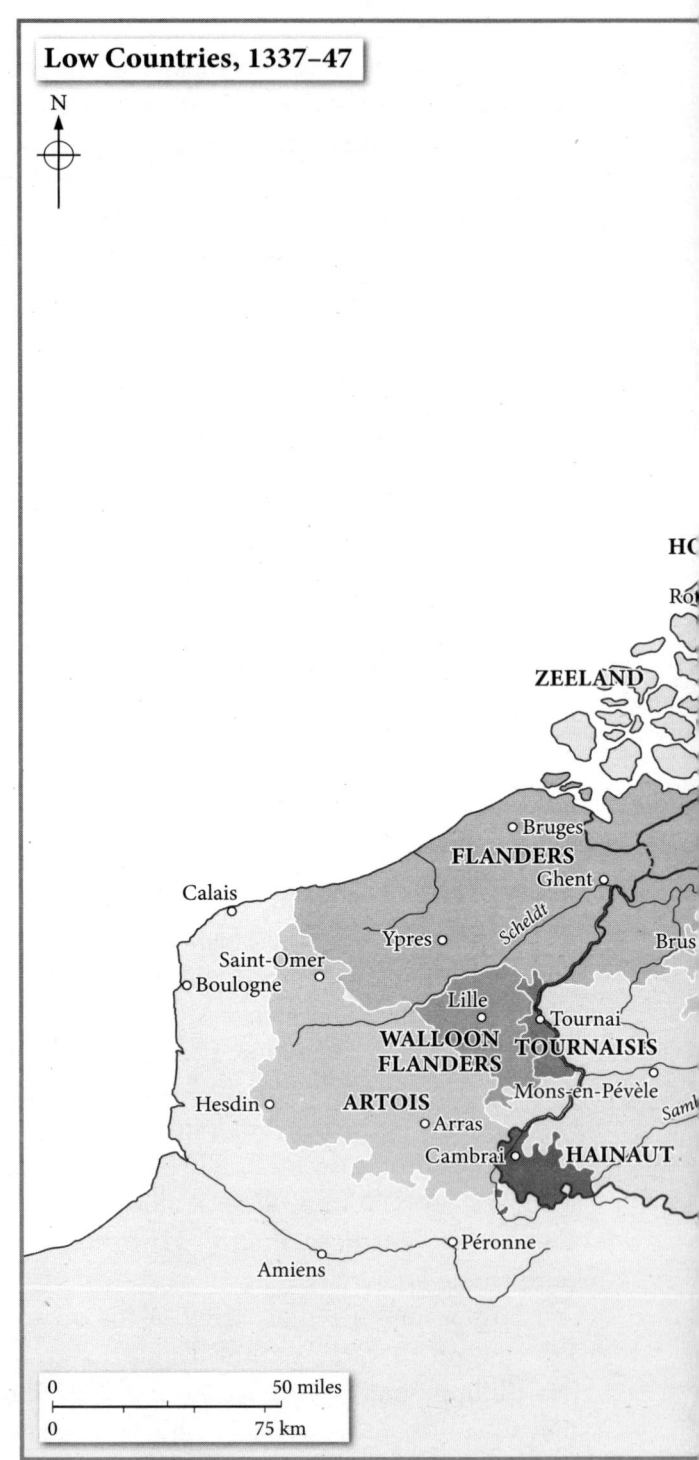

Low Countries, 1337–47

N

HO[...]

Ro[...]

ZEELAND

Bruges
FLANDERS
Ghent

Calais

Ypres
Scheldt
Brus[...]

Saint-Omer
Boulogne

Lille

Tournai
WALLOON
FLANDERS
TOURNAISIS

Mons-en-Pévèle
Sam[...]

Hesdin
ARTOIS

Arras
Cambrai
HAINAUT

Péronne
Amiens

| 0 | | 50 miles |
| 0 | | 75 km |

– in foreign territory, haunted by creditors – would continue to weaken.

By 13 October, Edward had moved within a few miles of Péronne, clearly itching for a fight. But just when it seemed Philippe was planning to give him one – he and his council had decided to strike the next morning[10] – Edward retreated to Origny-Sainte-Benoite.

The English king had clearly recognized that the conditions made a victory unlikely. On 22 October, after arrangements had been made for the two armies to engage in battle near La Flamengrie, the situation reversed: Philippe recognized that the conditions made a French victory unlikely and so withdrew.

Accusations of cowardice were thrown about, as we would expect. But these were propagandistic spins upon the basic truth that the two kings were trying to fight on the best terms for their sides because they wanted to win.

In the end, Edward could stay in the field no longer. Low on food and money, he retreated. From across the border in Avesnes he made a show of challenging the French king to come and fight, complaining about Philippe's unwillingness to fight like a man. Philippe wisely ignored it.

Battle of Sluys, 1340

Edward's first campaign in France had ended. It had accomplished nothing of substance. But on 26 January 1340, Edward outright declared himself the king of France.

He might have been pushed to do it for legal reasons. If Philippe was king, and Edward his duke, then Edward was fighting against his sworn liege lord. This would be highly ignoble. Edward might have solved this problem by renouncing his homage to Philippe, but that could have made some in Gascony and elsewhere wonder whether he was still *their* liege or not. More importantly, his allies in Flanders would be going against their own oaths to the French crown if they supported him – except that by declaring himself king they could now say that they were doing exactly what they were supposed to do.

Yes, this meant ignoring the English king's previous oaths, but Edward probably thought those mistaken anyway. He'd *always* had a claim to the crown, Salic Law be damned.

The French, in response, prepared to take action. Philippe ordered the creation of a 'Great Army of the Sea' – a fleet comprising over 200 vessels – to prevent the English from crossing the Channel, while land forces prepared to move against the Flemings, who'd already declared their support for the English and sent their Francophile count fleeing to Paris. In England, Edward knew that if he wanted to move his army to Flanders to support his allies, he would need to do it as soon as possible. As if he needed another reason to go, he'd also left his pregnant queen in Ghent at the end of his previous foray into the Low Countries. In March she'd given birth to his third son, John. He would come to be known by his foreign place of birth: John of Ghent. Or, as the English pronounced it, John of Gaunt. Like the previous two sons of Edward – Edward, who had just turned ten, and Lionel, who was not yet two – John of Gaunt would play a major role as the larger war rolled on.

But the English would lose the race to Flanders. It took until 20 June for Edward to assemble the necessary fleet to move his army over the sea. Near as we can tell, everyone – English or French, friend or foe – knew where he was going: the port of Sluys, on the River Zwin. From here he could disembark his army and join forces with his allies and his queen. And because everyone knew this was the king of England's intention, the king of France's Great Army of the Sea had been at anchor in the waters off Sluys for at least a dozen days at this point.

Edward knew this, and on 22 June, he sailed anyway.

A battle is its ground – that is, if there *is* a ground. The Battle of Sluys, fought on 24 June, had none.

Worse, even the waters upon which it was fought are gone. To travel to the location of the battle today is to stand in fertile fields, miles away from the sea. The inlet of the Zwin where the English and French fought has long since silted up. Any attempt to reconstruct the fight requires a lot of imagination.

Our sources claim that Edward delayed his arrival until late in the day, so that the English could attack with the sun at their backs, its light blinding their enemies. I doubt this. 'The sun at their backs' is said so often about winning fighting units in the Middle Ages (and long before and after) that it has the ring of a literary conceit rather than an astronomical truth. The north–south orientation of the inlet in which the battle was fought doesn't align with the east–west journey of the sun: the late-day light would have been off the beam of the ships on *both* sides.

But while it has nothing to do with blinding light, I think the idea that Edward delayed his attack might nevertheless be the key to understanding why the English won.

In the centuries before gunpowder artillery, many early naval battles were something like land battles on the water: ships would manoeuvre close, grapple together and then melee fighters would board and attempt to seize control of the decks while missile fighters shot into the crowds from perches in the rigging above. Anticipating such an action, the French had tied their ships to one another, forming great, blockading lines. This might have been an advantage in an immediate fight, but each hour that passed without fighting would have turned it into a disadvantage. In the relatively close confines of the inlet, the accumulating drift of tidal movements, wind and wave would have pushed the ships into one another, entangling both the anchor lines and the lines that bound them to each other.

So by the time the English ships arrived, moving under independent sail and probably riding the tide, I suspect the French lines were in disorder. Their commanders tried to disengage their lines and re-establish the ships for the fight, but they found themselves corralled up against the eastern side of the inlet.

Already holding the advantage of manoeuvrability, the English now unlimbered the weapon that had so recently proved itself in Scotland. The longbow had a longer range and a faster rate of reload than its French counterpart, the crossbow. More than that, a crossbow bolt flies with a fairly flat trajectory, making it hard to strike targets behind a wall or, in this case, a ship's railing. An arrow's arcing trajectory can literally get around this problem. Put together, this meant that the English arrows could safely rain down upon the men on the jumbled French ships before they had any hope of a response.

Naval battles tend to have high casualty rates. When the metaphorical tide turns in a battle on land, there are usually places to hide and routes of escape. In a battle at sea, there are few options. To flee the killing on the deck is to chance survival in the waves – a slim chance for the swimmer, much less the warrior weighed down with weapons and armour, exhausted from fighting, and surrounded by enemy ships or crushed between the colliding hulls of his own.

Of the roughly 200 ships in the Great Army of the Sea, perhaps a couple of dozen made it out. The English captured 166. The rest sank to the bottom of the sea. Many thousands of French died on the decks and in the waters. Those who managed to make it out alive to the surrounding shorelines found Flemish locals waiting for them with whatever weapons they could lay their hands upon.

Back in Paris, a jester was reportedly tasked with bringing the bad news of the slaughter to the king. He asked if the French could walk on water, because the English had made them try. In the years that followed, Flemish fishermen would quip that their fish spoke French.

Sluys was an undoubted disaster for the French, a major win for the English. All those French ships in the Channel had been a major impediment to the wool trade. Even their partial removal was an economic win.

But the military implications were more significant. If Edward had lost, the war would have looked very different. Instead, he was now free to land in Flanders and support his allies. This he did, bolstering Flemish defences considerably and then using this base to launch an attack on France. His target was Tournai.[11]

As before, Philippe brought his army close enough to keep the English on their toes, but he refused to charge headlong into a battle. Edward, meanwhile, was having difficulty keeping his alliance in one piece. In the end, both armies withdrew, and on 25 September 1340 the Truce of Espléchin was signed. Nothing was resolved. Nothing was settled. But both kings were more or less out of the money needed to keep fighting at these scales. They needed time to replenish, restock and then re-engage.

War of the Breton Succession

What happened next returns us to Brittany, where the Two Hundred Years War started on the isle of Quéménès in 1292.

The duchy of Brittany had passed the decades since that inciting incident largely at peace. Though historically linked to the British people, Brittany had in the meantime submitted as a vassal state to the French. This split history returned in force when, in 1341, John III, the duke of Brittany, died childless.

John III's father, Arthur II, had married twice. John himself was the first of three children from his first marriage. So one option for the duchy, and the one that John had favoured for most of his life, was that it pass to Jeanne of Penthièvre, the daughter of John's deceased younger brother, who had married Charles of Blois – whose uncle was Philippe VI. But Arthur's second marriage had been fruitful, too, producing a son, Jean de Montfort, who had married the daughter of the count of Flanders, named Joanna. Shortly before his death, John III had decided that the duchy should pass to this half-brother instead.

Jean de Montfort, recognizing that the king of France would likely support the claim of his nephew's wife, made an appeal to Edward III for help, which brought Philippe's attention to the issue. The king of France put the question of the succession to the leading magnates of his realm, and they declared that the duchy should pass to Jeanne of Penthièvre and thus to his own nephew: Charles of Blois was made duke, and he was given the military support he needed to attack Jean de Montfort's holdings. At Nantes, Montfort was captured.

The succession dispute might have ended then and there, if not for Joanna of Flanders. Jean le Bel describes her as 'a lady with the heart of a man and indeed of a lion'.[12] She took up arms to defend the claim of her husband and her son – who was also named John. Besieged by Charles of Blois at Hennebont, she performed what

Le Bel calls 'the boldest and most remarkable feat ever performed by a woman':

> Know this: the valiant countess, who kept climbing the towers to see how the defense was progressing, saw that all the besiegers had left their quarters and gone forward to watch the assault. She conceived a fine plan. She remounted her charger, fully armed as she was, and called upon some three hundred men-at-arms who were guarding a gate that wasn't under attack to mount with her; then she rode out with this company and charged boldly into the enemy camp, which was devoid of anyone but a few boys and servants. They killed them all and set fire to everything: soon the whole encampment was ablaze.[13]

Joanna's efforts bought the time needed for English forces to begin arriving in support of the House of Montfort against the House of Blois. This shifted the War of the Breton Succession from a local dispute into an international incident.

By a remarkable coincidence, Edward, who was otherwise fighting for a claim to the kingdom of France that passed through the female side, was now engaged in Brittany fighting for a claim that passed through the male side – with France oppositional to both. But consistency didn't matter. Strategic advantage did. Edward recognized that Brittany was a means to open both another front against the French and another base from which he could launch attacks. It was also, given its place between England and Gascony, a region he did not want to see in hostile hands.

Significant English forces under the command of the earl of Northampton and the earl of Salisbury reached Brest in August 1342, where Joanna was once more besieged by the forces of Charles. The Franco-Bretons retreated, and the Anglo-Breton force under Northampton pressed inland and was soon besieging the Blois stronghold of Morlaix.

Charles of Blois, fearing the loss of the town to the English army, marched to relieve the siege. The English moved to intercept.

The forces met on 30 September in what is now called the Battle of Morlaix.

About all we can say with certainty is that the Anglo-Bretons took a prepared defensive position: they deployed on foot with their backs to a wood, and they dug trenches and pits – though whether across their full frontage or only part of it is unclear. The Franco-Bretons attacked this position in waves. The first was a cavalry force led by Geoffroi de Charny.

The grandson of Jean de Joinville – the biographer of Louis IX, the revered saint-king who had made the Treaty of Paris in 1259 – Charny was in his mid-thirties and already one of France's greatest warriors. Gilles li Muisit, an abbot who had probably seen Charny in action during the siege of Tournai in 1340, described him as 'a vigorous soldier' who was 'an expert in the use weapons and was greatly famed at home and abroad, having fought in many wars and in many mortal conflicts, in all of them bearing himself properly and nobly'.[14] The youngest of three sons of a minor lord, Charny decided to make his way in the world by dedicating himself to becoming a great knight. From a relatively humble start, he was soon winning fame in tournaments while seemingly taking every chance he could to prove his worth on the battlefield. He was among the leaders in that successful defence of Tournai, but a year later he was in front of the first charge at Morlaix when it foundered. Many of the knights he was leading died, but he was captured. It would not be his last appearance in the unfolding war.

Although the second wave of Franco-Bretons met with no greater success than the first, Northampton sized up his odds and withdrew into the woods. This protected him from further cavalry charges, but it also made it difficult for him to engage in any himself.

The Franco-Bretons, recognizing that the route to Morlaix was now open, withdrew from the battle and marched towards the town. They'd lost a few hundred men, certainly more than the Anglo-Bretons had, so by that token it was a victory for the English side. At the same time, the English side had to lift their siege of Morlaix, which was the whole point. By that token it was an English loss.

On 19 October, Edward himself landed in Brest. He made some quick gains and laid siege to Vannes, but a victory wasn't immediately forthcoming.

With no great gains being made on either side, the kings of England and France were both hesitant to commit to the massive expense of deploying more forces into the peninsula. On 19 January 1343, all sides agreed to the Truce of Malestroit. A key clause stated that the current status quo would be temporarily upheld while representatives worked out something longer-lasting. It's doubtful any of the signatories of the truce thought a permanent peace was possible. It was an obvious play for time.

The Truce of Malestroit was supposed to put an end to the fighting in Brittany until September 1346. Among its provisions was an agreement that the two sides would temporarily set aside vengeance for what had happened to this point. But on 2 August 1343, only months after it went into effect, Philippe broke the truce by executing a man in Paris.

The man was a Breton lord, Olivier IV de Clisson, who had fought for Charles of Blois and the side of the king of France in Brittany. When the English had besieged Vannes in 1342, he had been one of the two men in charge of its defence. Both were captured and brought to Edward, but only Clisson was released.

This raised some eyebrows, as did the fact that he was released for what was – in French eyes – a lesser ransom than ought to have been expected. Suspicions grew that he might have secretly cut a deal of some kind with the English.

After the Truce of Malestroit was in place, Clisson was invited by Philippe to participate in a tournament in France. As soon as he arrived, he was arrested and shipped off to Paris to be tried for treason. He was found guilty and beheaded in 1343. His head was placed on a pike in Nantes as a warning to any Bretons thinking of aiding the enemy. What remained of his body was hung by its armpits on the highest level of the Gibbet of Montfaucon: sixteen stone columns atop a hill outside Paris, with at least two tiers of beams for hanging victims between them.

We cannot be sure if Clisson really did commit treason. And *if* he did, exactly how Philippe found out about it is also unknown. The trial records no longer exist.[15]

What we do know is that Clisson *was* executed, violating the Truce of Malestroit just months after it was signed.

Also not in doubt is the fact that his son, named after his father, was just seven years old at the time: he would become Olivier V de Clisson. His mother took him and his younger brother to Nantes to see their father's head rotting in the sun. She made him swear his personal vengeance against France. He did so. But, as we'll see later on, it wasn't France that would learn to fear 'the Butcher', as he'd grow up to be called.

It was England.

Chivalry and the Round Table, 1344

In January 1344, at the conclusion of a week-long, high-style royal tournament at Windsor Castle, Edward announced that he would re-establish King Arthur's Order of the Round Table. What's more, he would build an enormous House of the Round Table in which the order's 300 knights would gather at Windsor.[16]

From some small, debated seed of semi-historical reality, the legend of King Arthur exploded in popularity in Europe following the completion of Geoffrey of Monmouth's imaginative *History of the Kings of Britain* in the late 1130s.[17] This legendary past provided convenient leverage for Europe's nobility as they sought to bolster their power. Not surprisingly, the kings of England were particularly keen to utilize this connection.

Edward I, who worked so hard to enforce English hegemony across the whole of Britain, was especially keen to utilize the Arthurian legend for his own ends. Among his many efforts to connect himself with Arthur was the construction of a literal Round Table – 18 feet in width – that can still be seen hanging high on a wall in the Great Hall at Winchester. In 1278, he also travelled to the abbey of Glastonbury in order to oversee the re-interment of King Arthur's remains, which had supposedly been found buried on its grounds in 1184. That 'discovery', during the reign of Henry II, probably owes a great deal more to Henry's efforts to end Welsh resistance to his rule than it does to any arch-aeological fact: many Welsh believed that Arthur would 'return' to save them, so finding him good and buried was rather lucky for the English king! For Edward I, too, a confirmed-dead Arthur allowed him to further his own attack on Welsh patriotism while also positioning himself as Arthur's imperial heir by ceremonially reburying his forebear.

Edward III no doubt had his grandfather in mind when he proclaimed the re-establishment of the Order of the Round Table. It connected him with these past glories, showed his own strength as a leader, and marked his court as a place where warriors could gather and win renown. Such was the perceived threat that the king of France was provoked to proclaim his own, rival Round Table, 'so that he might attract the knights of Germany and Italy to himself, rather than see them hasten to the Table of the king of England'.[18]

These moves were all rooted in a proclaimed dedication to the code of chivalry.

The word itself comes from the Old French for someone who fights on horseback: the English words *cavalry* and *chivalry* are cousins. But whereas *cavalry* refers to pretty much any mounted fighting force, *chivalry* has a more particular meaning. For most of us, it calls to mind knights and some set of principles about fighting for honour and the acknowledgement of ladies – or, as it is often shorthanded, following a code of chivalry.

The development of chivalry is enormously complicated. Historically, it begins coming into focus during the infighting that followed the collapse of Charlemagne's empire, as warriors recognized in themselves a shared identity that transcended pol-itical borders. The fact that part of this identity was a shared Christian faith meant that chivalry was from its beginning rooted in something of a paradox: the Christian precept to react to a strike by 'turning the other cheek' ill suits a battlefield on which the enemy will happily strike that one, too, before slitting the throat between. Theologians correspondingly developed theories of 'just war': times when the violence normally abhorred by God would be welcomed by God's warriors, such as when the church itself was under assault. Christianity also shifted behaviours upon the battlefield itself: fighters could be praised for offering clemency to those they defeated, rather than outright death. This itself depended on changing social practices and the stabilizing systems of economic exchange that were necessary to carry out, for example, the payment of ransoms between different communities. The crusades crystallized these various creative streams by further organizing the fighting class and giving their violence a direction. This itself was a result of the church's political aims, of course, but it also owed much to the rise of primogeniture, which resulted in many non-firstborn sons – who'd been trained for war in case their elder siblings died – finding their future in a correspondingly well-funded church.[19]

By the thirteenth century, chivalry had become a system influencing nearly every aspect of life in the Middle Ages. And more often than not, the idealized vision of the system was held to be the 'Golden Age' of King Arthur and his Round Table.[20]

In its broadest terms, chivalry was a social code of conduct that stands at the intersection of military engagement (in the form of martial prowess), Christian religiosity (in the form of personal piety) and social class structures (in the form of largesse and nobility). It sanctified and made acceptable the inherently sinful and social-fracturing act of not just engaging in violence, but having a lifelong dedication to getting good at it. For many in the Middle Ages, war and violence were perceived as inevitabilities, and chivalry made safe the necessary evils to respond to it. It legitimized killing, while also putting fetters on when and how killing could be committed. In the times between fighting, it offered a way of organizing the behaviour of the martial class.

As a code of conduct, however, chivalry wasn't universal. Though we often talk as if there is a single 'code' of chivalry, the truth is that what it means to be chivalrous depends a great deal on who is talking about it and when. We don't often make laws to enforce what everyone is already doing. Instead, we make laws to stop people from doing something we don't want them to do.

When Edward proclaimed his chivalrous Order of the Round Table in 1344, the very idea was flush with a vision that was both idealistic and imperialistic, aiming to serve the interests of his own rule. Work on the House of the Round Table began soon after Edward announced it, and by November the shell of the structure, which was 200 feet in diameter, was likely complete.[21]

But it was never finished. It was already clear that the fighting on the Continent was about to begin again. The future wouldn't be mock fights and pageantry – it would be ashes and blood.

Aiguillon, 1345–46

The 1343 Truce of Malestroit more or less held until the summer of 1345, when Edward shattered it by attacking France on three fronts. He himself would travel with a force to Flanders, to pressure France's northeastern border. The earl of Northampton, meanwhile, would apply pressure on the northwestern border using England's new bases in Brittany. At the same time, Henry of Grosmont – the earl of Derby, but soon to be the duke of Lancaster – would sail for Gascony and attempt to retake what the French had seized in the War of Saint-Sardos. To that end, the directive that Edward gave Grosmont on 13 March was exceedingly open-ended: 'If there is war,' Edward wrote, 'do the best that you can.'[22]

Philippe, warned of the three attacks through intelligence channels – spycraft is as old as warcraft – decided to concentrate his defence on the border with Flanders, guessing that the largest army would accompany Edward.

He was right. Edward's force was indeed the biggest threat on paper. But in practice things went quite differently. Edward sailed to Sluys, but rather than disembarking in Flanders and marching inland – as he'd done twice now – he sailed westward into the English Channel. We think he was headed for the shores of Normandy. We can't be entirely certain, however, since he never managed the landing: his fleet was scattered by storms and limped back to English ports.

Back down in Gascony, though, Grosmont had extraordinary success. A later French chronicler would call him 'one of the finest warriors in all the world', showing how highly even his enemies regarded him.[23] It was a deserved reputation. Knowing that the

French army could gather far greater numbers than he ever could, Grosmont aimed to attack fast and defeat the French before they could coalesce their strength. Almost as soon as he landed, Grosmont was on the offensive.

The results were impressive. Issuing out of the English stronghold of Bordeaux, he pushed east and rolled up the French forces he met. In late August, Grosmont ripped through a French command near Bergerac, chasing them all the way back to the gates of the city, which was soon sacked. Grosmont next set his sights on Périgueux, which he besieged.

By this point, French strength was indeed coalescing. Multiple armies many times larger than Grosmont's were in the field. One of the armies was laying siege to the English-held city of Auberoche, less than ten miles from Grosmont's position. The other, perhaps twice in size, was closing in.

Grosmont could have retreated and taken a static, defensive position. Instead, he chose a dynamic offence. Though significantly outnumbered, he made a night march in order to attack the first French army in the Battle of Auberoche on 21 October. Catching his enemy unawares, he smashed them in a victory so demoralizing that it made the other French army in the field skitter away.

The victory was a massive morale boost for the English and Gascons both, and Grosmont exploited his new freedom in the field by targeting key strategic positions along the roads and waterways that led to Bordeaux.

Among them was Aiguillon, which commands the confluence of the rivers Garonne and Lot. The French knew they had to retake it if they had any hope of moving downriver to Bordeaux. In March 1346, the eldest son of the French king, Jean, the duke of Normandy – who would later come to rule as Jean II – brought perhaps 15,000 men to lay siege to the Anglo-Gascon garrison that Grosmont had installed at Aiguillon, which may have numbered as few as 1,000 men. Week after week, the beleaguered men at Aiguillon held out despite the enormous odds against them.

Worried that they could not hold out for ever, though, no matter the exploits they managed, Grosmont sent urgent word back to England, asking Edward to come to their aid.

That help arrived, though not where Grosmont expected it. On 20 August, the French abandoned the siege of Aiguillon and hurriedly marched north because on 12 July, Edward had landed a massive army on the Cotentin peninsula in Normandy.

No one knew it yet, but five kings were marching to meet at Crécy.

Crécy Campaign, 1346

Though Crécy is very rightly held to be one of the great battles of history, we should be clear about a few things at the start. First is that no one intended for it to happen. Despite what many people like to think, the king of England did not land at Saint-Vaast-la-Hougue on 12 July planning to fight a battle over 200 miles away at Crécy on 26 August.

Second, the extraordinary event of Crécy rather unfairly overshadows an extraordinary campaign. Had the battle not ended as it did, the preceding six weeks of Edward's campaign in France would still be a marvel.

Third, the Crécy campaign and its culminating battle were rapidly and very intentionally mythologized within England. Henry V's Agincourt campaign in 1415 was quite consciously modelled after Edward III's campaign in 1346 because Crécy was held as the very pinnacle of military achievement. Astounding as the campaign and its culminating battle were in their own rights, the process of mythologization detached them from their own marvellous reality and, stripping them of flaws, created inhuman perfection out of them.[24]

We don't know if the English army that came ashore in Normandy was meant to come ashore in Normandy. Though Philippe's informants kept him well informed about the English invasion force, Edward kept his exact plans very close to the vest. When the fleet set sail, it may be that many of its captains were not fully informed of the destination.

The presumed ports of call would have been the previous year's Low Countries, Brittany or Gascony. So when Edward landed instead in Normandy – by preplanning or perhaps simply due to

Crécy Campaign, 1346

Edward III's march:

12 July: Saint-Vaast-la-Hougue	11 August: Épône
18 July: Valognes	12 August: Ferelaguillon
19 July: Saint-Côme-du-Mont	13 August: Poissy
20 July: Carentan	16 August: Grisy-les-Plâtres
21 July: Pont-Hébert	17 August: Auteuil
22 July: Saint-Lô	18 August: Troissereux
23 July: Sept-Vents	19 August: Sommereux
24 July: Torteval-Quesnay	20 August: Camps-en-Amiénois
25 July: Fontenay-le-Pesnel	22 August: Airaines
26 July: Caen	23 August: Acheux-en-Vimeu
31 July: Troarn	24 August: Blanchetaque
1 August: Léaupartie	25 August: Sailly-Bray
2 August: Lisieux	26 August: Crécy site
4 August: Duranville	28 August: Valloires Abbey
5 August: Le Neubourg	29 August: Maintenay
7 August: Elbeuf	30 August: Saint-Josse
8 August: Le Vaudreuil	31 August: Neufchâtel-Hardelot
9 August: Longueville	2 September: Wimille
10 August: Freneuse	4 September: Calais

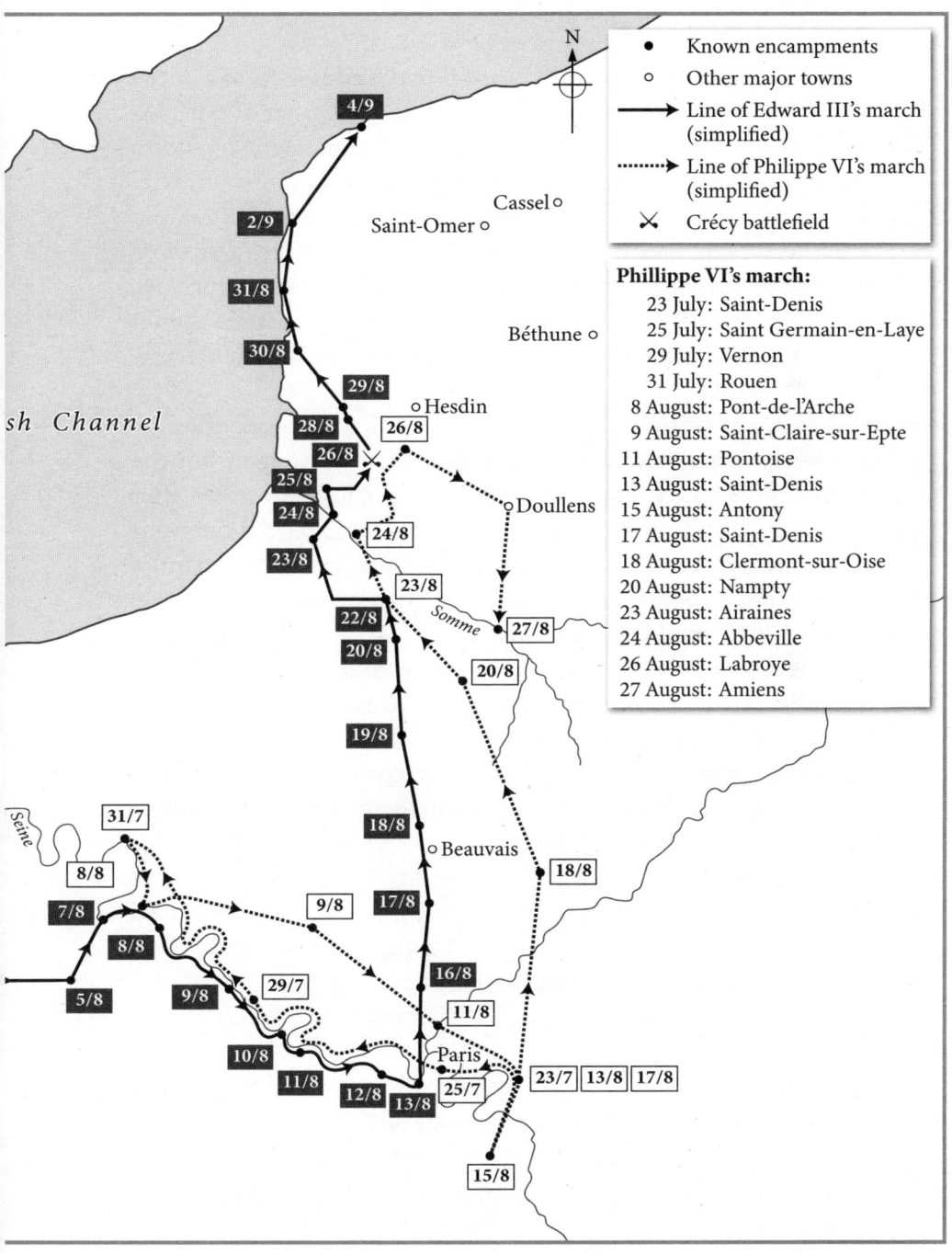

Known encampments
Other major towns
→ Line of Edward III's march (simplified)
····► Line of Philippe VI's march (simplified)
✕ Crécy battlefield

Phillippe VI's march:
23 July: Saint-Denis
25 July: Saint Germain-en-Laye
29 July: Vernon
31 July: Rouen
8 August: Pont-de-l'Arche
9 August: Saint-Claire-sur-Epte
11 August: Pontoise
13 August: Saint-Denis
15 August: Antony
17 August: Saint-Denis
18 August: Clermont-sur-Oise
20 August: Nampty
23 August: Airaines
24 August: Abbeville
26 August: Labroye
27 August: Amiens

Cassel
Saint-Omer
Béthune
Hesdin
Doullens
Somme
Beauvais
Paris
Seine
sh Channel

weather conditions – he was able to disembark almost entirely unopposed.

We can see how quickly Edward progressed thanks to a document found in England's National Archives: a register of expenses incurred by the king's kitchen during the campaign. It's not a glamorous manuscript. There are no grand illustrations or exciting stories. It's more or less a list of receipts that detail not just what was eaten and how much it cost but also *where* and *when* it was eaten. Thanks to this long-ignored document – which my colleague and I named the Kitchen Journal when we published it – we can track much of the English army's progress with remarkable precision.[25]

What we can see is that the English made quick work of securing not just their beachhead at Saint-Vaast-la-Hougue, but the whole of the Cotentin peninsula. On 26 July, just two weeks after their initial landing on the shoreline, they had reached the walls of the great city of Caen, the heart of Normandy, roughly 70 miles away as the crow flies and at least 90 by the route of the medieval roads that Edward had followed.

To contemporary ears this may not seem like much of an accomplishment, but the army that Edward brought to France in 1346 consisted of roughly 14,000 fighters: 2,800 men-at-arms, 2,800 mounted archers, a further 5,000 archers on foot, and the rest common infantry.[26] And beyond these thousands were so many more. The Kitchen Journal attests to not just the existence of the king's cooks but also his accountants. That Edward and his commanders got them all ashore, got them all organized and got them moving across so many miles of foreign territory is a triumph of both leadership and logistics.

As his army approached Caen, Edward must have been shocked by what he saw.

Medieval cities were built around a historical core that had been walled for defence. We might call this a 'downtown' or 'city centre' today, but in the Latin that dominated the Middle Ages it was called the *urbs*. It often happened that more people were drawn to the security-driven prosperity of a medieval city than would fit within its walls and gates, so cities spread out beyond them. These additional buildings, springing up 'under' the shadows of the city's walls, were in Latin quite literally *sub-urbs*, from which the English word derives.

Most of the time, faced with the threat of a major assault, a medieval city would choose to abandon its suburbs. Residents were unlikely to be people of power and influence, and without defensive walls their homes were deeply difficult to defend.

So Edward, approaching Caen, surely expected to see suburbs emptied of people and supplies ahead of his coming as everyone took what they could and huddled behind the walls of the Norman capital. Instead, he found the city's militia outside the suburbs, behind no wall or fortification whatsoever. Facing the loss and destruction of their homes, the common people had decided that they'd rather stand and fight, and they'd convinced many within the city itself to stand with them.

It would have been a triumphant moment if it had worked.

Edward arrayed his lines for battle. The townspeople had heard how many men he had, but the human mind is ill-suited to imagine such large numbers. It would have been a staggering sight. Then the English archers loosed. There were some 7,800 of them, but Edward surely didn't have them all shoot at first. Each archer had been provided with two sheaves of arrows, roughly twenty-four arrows in total. They wouldn't want to waste them.

Even if only a thousand arrows took flight at that first command, it would have been enough. The people of Caen, so boldly ready to fight for their homes, turned and ran for the safety of the city walls.

The English ran after them. Edward and his commanders tried to call for a halt, but the English soldiers – our sources highlight the archers in particular – were not listening. With a roar they rushed after the fleeing French like wild dogs after injured prey. The gates of the city, opened for its retreating people, couldn't close fast enough. A screaming wave of terror and blood rushed into Caen.

For five days that wave washed over the city as it was sacked. By the time it receded, half the population was dead.

So much was looted from Caen that the English couldn't carry it onward. Edward, ever the logistician, decided to send the wealth – and the ransomable French he'd captured – back to England in the ships that had brought his army over the Channel. It was a much-needed win for his war effort, both in terms of finances and morale-boosting propaganda. He also sent home orders to have more men and supplies meet him at Le Crotoy, on the mouth of the River Somme. This was over 150 miles away across enemy territory, but Edward's confidence was high. He'd had little difficulty so far, and he seems to have thought that he would make a raiding march that entire distance and then be able to once again offload his plunder and resupply. At that point, he could either pull out of France or connect with a smaller allied army that had invaded French holdings from the Low Countries.

It would not be that easy.

As Edward was leaving Caen, Philippe was already in his way. The French king's army was gathering at Rouen, on the north bank of the Seine. The English army turned upriver, seeking a way across, but found the bridges all broken or too heavily defended to use. Philippe patiently paralleled on the opposite bank, no doubt pleased at his enemy's growing frustration.

By 13 August, the English were in Poissy, just west of Paris. They were tired and far deeper into France than any of them wanted to be. Philippe was in Saint-Denis, gaining in strength. In a flurry of messages back and forth, the French king came to believe that Edward had agreed to fight in a pitched battle that would be arranged on a field south of Paris. He marched there to meet him. Meanwhile, the English had rebuilt a broken bridge over the river and, under cover of night, bolted north, heading for Le Crotoy and the ships that were supposed to be waiting for them.

Flinging accusations of treachery and dishonour at the English king's heels, an enraged Philippe pursued with his massive army while his fastest riders tore north along the fastest roads in order to get ahead of their quarry.

They succeeded, and by the time Edward reached the next major river in France, the Somme, it was already held against him. Once more, he was stymied by water. Only this time he also had a massive army – roughly twice the size of his own – bearing down on him from behind. The English probed in vain at the few bridges still standing, then rolled west towards Saint-Valery to buy time.

Edward's campaign would have come to a horrible end if it hadn't been for the unexpected news – perhaps from a prisoner of war – that there was a hidden ford called Blanchetaque between the sea and walled bridge town of Abbeville. Here, for a short time on either side of low tide, the Somme could be crossed by a few men at a time.

To try it was the utmost desperation. But it was the only chance the English had.

In the pre-dawn hours of 24 August, the English made their way to the river to wait for low tide. When the sun came up, they were spotted by the French on the opposite bank, who quickly spread the alarm. When the first of the English splashed into the river, their enemy was waiting for them. Crossbows hummed in the morning air, thudding into the men trying to fight their way through water and fire both.

It came to be known as the Battle of Blanchetaque. If not for the glorious victory at Crécy, just days away now, it would be far better known.

The English fought like the desperate men they were. When one fell, his corpse flipping over in the current, another pushed past him. Many English died, but some made it through the river, pushing, fighting step by step onto the north shore.

The French finally broke and ran for the safety of Abbeville. Philippe arrived on the shore the English had left behind, just in time to see the last of the English wagons drawn up across the river, the tide now in too far to make the crossing himself. Enraged even further, he, too, went to Abbeville. His army gathered there, four kings strong: himself, King John of Bohemia, John's son Charles, the king of the Romans, and King James III of Majorca.

Edward and the English were safe for the night, but not for long. The ships he'd ordered to come to Le Crotoy were not waiting for him, and Abbeville was only a few miles away. He decided to try to march for an allied army from the Low Countries that he believed was besieging Béthune, but Philippe got ahead of him again. Trapped up against the dense forest of Crécy, the English took the best position they could and readied for yet another fight for their lives.[27]

Battle of Crécy, 1346

The Battle of Crécy began late on 26 August. The English took position on a slight high ground, using what terrain advantages they could as they arrayed their army in the manner that had served them so well in Scotland at Dupplin Moor and Halidon Hill: a centre made up of dismounted men-at-arms, with thousands of longbowmen stretched out in wings to either side. These wings were under the cover of trees and hedges, preventing them from being seen and protecting them from any enemy charges. The French, streaming to the battlefield, had little idea how effective this formation could be – and Edward had still more advantages. One was his decision to surround his position with his wagons, tipped over onto their sides to create a field fortification that we call a *wagenburg*. According to one story, the English formation was described to King John of Bohemia, a now-blind veteran of many campaigns who had come to help Philippe. He replied that if they rushed in upon the English, the French forces would be destroyed.

That is exactly what they did, though. The French forces were arriving on the field by multiple roads, relatively late in the day, but few were interested in delaying the battle. They had chased the English across northern France, twice watching their enemies barely escape across rivers meant to trap them. They'd at last run their quarry to the ground. They wanted to finish the hunt.

The first line sent into the attack was made up of mercenary Genoese crossbowmen. Such was their rush, their confidence and their ignorance of what they were facing that these men went forward without their helms or their pavises – large shields that they could plant on the ground and crouch behind to do the slow work of reloading their crossbows.

The English let them march forward unimpeded until they dropped down into a natural bowl at the foot of the English wagenburg. Behind that protection – and hidden in the trees

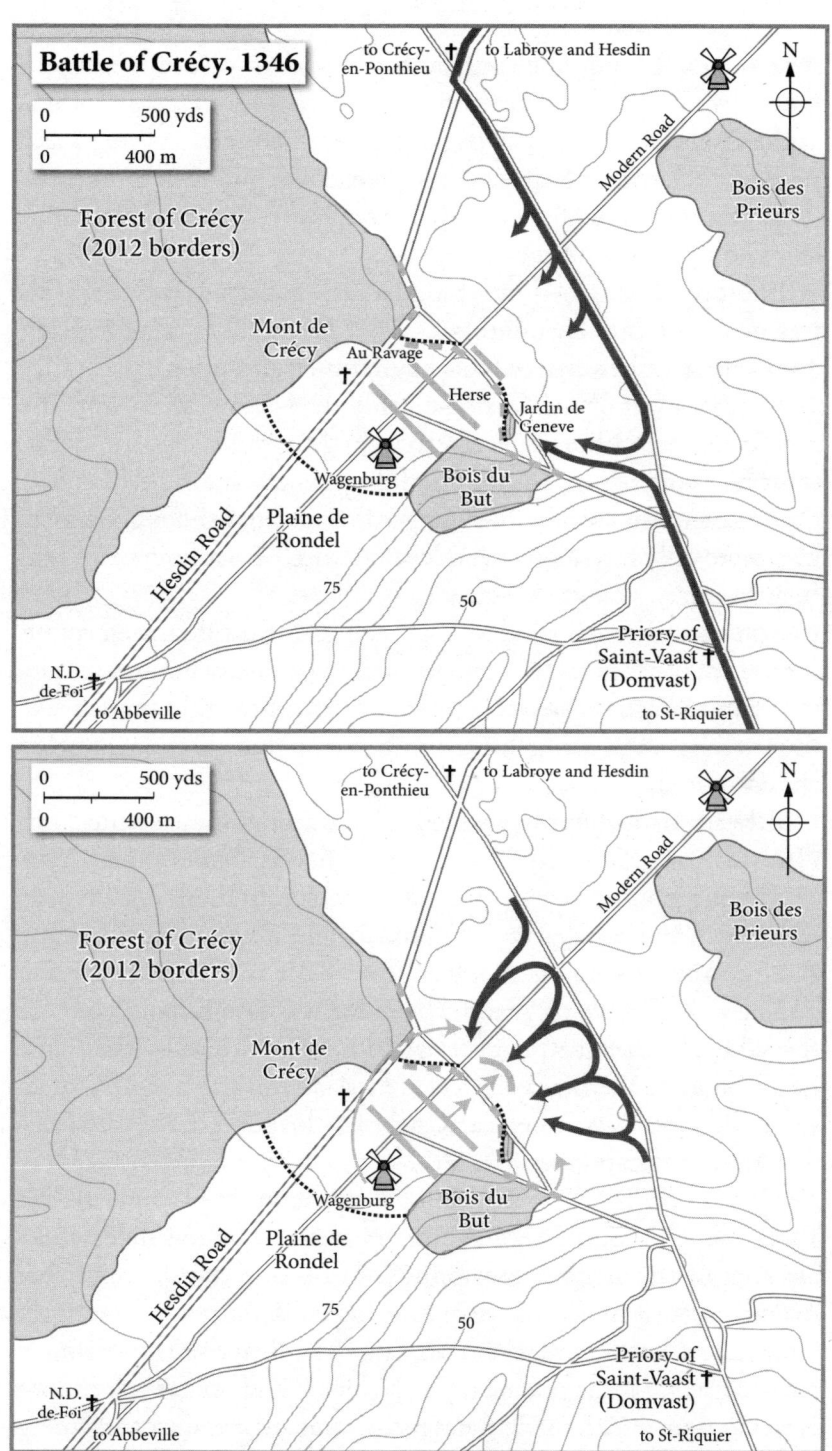

Battle of Crécy, 1346

to Crécy-en-Ponthieu
to Labroye and Hesdin

N

Modern Road

Bois des Prieurs

Forest of Crécy
(2012 borders)

Mont de Crécy
Au Ravage
Herse
Jardin de Geneve

Wagenburg
Bois du But

Plaine de Rondel

75
50

Hesdin Road

Priory of Saint-Vaast
(Domvast)

N.D. de Foi
to Abbeville
to St-Riquier

to Crécy-en-Ponthieu
to Labroye and Hesdin

N

Modern Road

Bois des Prieurs

Forest of Crécy
(2012 borders)

Mont de Crécy

Wagenburg
Bois du But

Plaine de Rondel

75
50

Hesdin Road

Priory of Saint-Vaast
(Domvast)

N.D. de Foi
to Abbeville
to St-Riquier

stretching out along one long flank of the bowl – the longbowmen took cover. They let the crossbowmen loose their first shots. Then, as the Genoese laboriously began to reload, the archers stood and stepped forward. They drew back their bows, and they loosed.

When the French lines behind them heard screams, they probably thought they were English.

Philippe already had his second attack galloping forward. This was a line of French knights on horseback, all vying for glory. They charged forward, only to be met by the sudden appearance of what was left of the Genoese, who were fleeing in horror. The lines of men and horses, each struggling to go in opposite directions, got tangled up. This blunted the French charge. Worse still, the jumbled mass was an ideal target for the English longbowmen, who were only too happy to send thousands of arrows hurtling off their humming bows.

Still more French tried to approach, and Edward's men set off several small cannons they had brought with them. Few men there had ever seen these devices, which belched fire and boomed like thunderclaps, spooking horses into terror that further mangled charging French lines.

Edward had superbly wedded his position and his tactics. His plan was going perfectly. His son, though, was about to mess it up.

The wagenburg was not completely solid. There was a wide opening in the carts facing the French, and it was in this opening that the king placed his vanguard, under the command of his son and heir, the Prince of Wales. His name was also Edward, but for the sake of keeping things straight I'll refer to him by the name he'd later earn: the Black Prince. He was on this day a mere sixteen years old, and it was here at Crécy, so the legend goes, that he would 'earn his spurs' as a knight.

No one on the French side could mistake the banner of the Black Prince, proudly held aloft in what appeared to be the weakest part of the English position. And no one could doubt that capturing the young man would bring a literal princely ransom and quite possibly end the Two Hundred Years War in a single stroke. French lords practically fell over each other for the chance to get at him, which made them ready targets for the archers lining out to either side. Volley by volley, the longbows steadily ripped the attacking lines apart.

The din must have been extraordinary. Metal scraping and clashing. Hooves pounding. Cannons thundering. Arrows buzzing. Banners snapping in the dust-choked air. Above it all, the screaming of tens of thousands of men and beasts.

Suddenly, the English vanguard advanced. We don't know for sure why this was. Certainly, it was in their best interests to hold position and let the enemy keep trying to reach them through the terrible onslaught of arrows. Perhaps the Black Prince was every bit as eager for glory as the French lords trying to reach him through that deadly storm.

As soon as the vanguard made contact with the French lines, the English longbows had fewer and fewer targets. No one wanted to shoot the Black Prince in the back. What had been a one-sided slaughter now became the chaotic butchery of a melee.

In this pivotal moment, the myth of Crécy differs greatly from the likely reality of the fight. According to English chroniclers – and the generations of historians who dutifully repeated their accounts – a group of concerned English warriors came to King Edward, who was watching the battle from a windmill. They asked him for help to extract and protect his engaged son. Edward denied them. 'Let the boy earn his spurs,' he said. When some of these men went to find the Prince of Wales anyway, they discovered he needed no help at all. The young man was resting amid piles of dead French, calmly awaiting the next wave to kill.

Our sources that aren't tied to the English crown tell a very different story, however. According to them, the concerned Englishmen were right to worry. The Black Prince had advanced into the chaos of the melee and been bested. He had fallen to his knees, surrendering.

We will never know exactly how long he was a prisoner in the tumult. But for those minutes – agonizing and terrorizing for the English, quite the opposite for the French – the Two Hundred Years War was very likely over. That the war continued, and that the English writers would be free to concoct a very different spin on the event, is due to a few brave Englishmen, including the bishop of Durham, charging through the fray to grab the boy and drag him back to safety.

King Edward, meanwhile, rather than disdainfully leaving his son to sink or swim on his own, had left the windmill and ridden out from the wagenburg in a panic in order to help secure his safety. It makes sense that he would. Edward was no fool.

Late in the day, Philippe withdrew from the field. Such was his loss of command and control that he did not signal a retreat. Much of his army tried to fight on without him. The blind King John of Bohemia, knowing that the fight was lost, asked two of his knights to lead him into the thick of the fight, preferring to die in battle rather than home abed. He got his wish.

The killing continued until there was no light left to continue. And while the English had done well, they had no idea of the scope of their victory. They passed a restless night anticipating more fighting with the dawn. Their guess was right: another French army, unaware of what had happened the previous day, stumbled upon the English position and attacked. It met the same fate as the first.

Crécy was a victory with few parallels. Almost all the losses were on the French side. Edward had broken Philippe's army in the field. Among the dead were the king of Bohemia, the duke of Lorraine, the counts of Alençon, Blamont, Blois, Chaumont, Chemillé, Flanders, Harcourt, Salm and Sancerre, along with a huge number of lesser lords and many thousands of ordinary men. For a moment, all paths were open to him.

He chose to march north, to the great port city of Calais. On 4 September, he placed it under siege.

Battle of Neville's Cross, 1346

The story of Neville's Cross begins in June, when Philippe, aware that the English would be invading his border somewhere, wrote to David II of Scotland – who had managed to re-take control of his kingdom in 1341 – and asked him to fulfil his part in the Auld Alliance and attack the English: any distraction that the Scots could provide would siphon off men and materiel that would otherwise be brought to bear against France.

An attack from Scotland wasn't immediately forthcoming, but the landing of Edward's army in Normandy in July made an assault on England not only a pressing desire for the French but a tempting target for the Scots. The northern frontier, as Philippe explained in a second letter encouraging David in July, was 'a defenseless void'.[28]

But although it was true that Edward had taken a substantial portion of his kingdom's military assets to France, he hadn't taken all of them. He knew better than that. When the Scots probed the border they found it suitably defended. They agreed to abide by the terms of a truce then in place: there would be no major attack until after it expired on 29 September.

In the end, the invasion didn't come until 7 October: perhaps as many as 10,000 well-armed Scots poured over the border. They plunged towards Carlisle, whose citizens bought them off, and then they advanced east along the Roman wall to Corbridge before heading south towards Durham. Their passage was marked by the smoke of destruction.

The English had anticipated an attack and had a response plan already in place. Though gathered almost entirely on the march to the enemy, the English defence that confronted the invasion might have numbered up to 6,000 by 17 October, the day the two forces met in what would be called the Battle of Neville's Cross.

The English took a strong position on high ground, probably just north of where the famous stone cross associated with the battle is located today. The Scots took their own position north of this, but their ground was more uneven and broken. Both sides wanted to fight on the defensive, but as the invaders the Scots had a more pressing need to come to blows. They likely knew they also had more men. The stalemate was broken in mid-afternoon, when English longbowmen moved forward and began loosing arrows into the assembled Scots, who responded by launching an attack.

For some time the Scots tried and failed to break the English position. Failing to do so, part of the Scots army withdrew. This not only evened the odds in numbers but also allowed more bows to be brought to bear. At some point, King David took two arrows to the face.

Whether due to their own exhaustion and fear or to whispers about their king's horrific wounds, the Scots finally broke. The battle became a rout, and several thousand Scots never returned home.

Astonishingly, David survived his injuries. English soldiers found him hiding beneath a nearby bridge and took him into custody. Two surgeons from York managed to extract the arrows, but one of the arrowheads could not be removed. He spent the next eleven years an English prisoner. Until his death in 1371, he was periodically crippled by blinding headaches.

Siege of Calais, 1346–47

Back in France, holding court in the siege lines surrounding Calais, Edward was no doubt thrilled at the course of events. In the span of weeks the English had beaten the king of France and captured the king of Scotland.

After his defeat at Crécy, Philippe had clearly thought that Edward would continue marching towards his Flemish allies. Assuming the immediate English threat was leaving, he'd disbanded his army to save money. By besieging Calais, Edward had surprised everyone, hunkering down to receive much-needed supplies from England in relative safety. He'd also made quick work of running lines of supply and even trade to his allies in nearby Flanders.

Meanwhile, the French army that had been trying to take Aiguillon had withdrawn and marched north to help against Edward's invasion, but it, too, had been disbanded after the disaster of Crécy. So Grosmont now had an extraordinary degree of freedom to manoeuvre in Gascony. In sending him there in 1345, Edward had commanded him to do what he thought best 'if there is war', and now Grosmont very much did. He seized towns and castles that England had lost in the War of Saint-Sardos. Soon enough he'd struck the rich city of Poitiers, and there was a great fear in France that he might come against Paris itself. When Philippe started gathering a new army, there was genuine confusion over which threat it was meant to face: Edward in the northeast or Grosmont in the southwest.

The only really bad news for Edward was that Calais was proving to be a stubborn target. The city was very well fortified and provisioned, with a strong garrison. It also proved difficult to fully invest: Edward could control most of the land approaches, but the sea was a far harder thing to barricade. Ships were reaching the city, keeping it supplied.

The siege of Calais proceeded through the spring of 1347. By then the English were at last managing to cut off French resupply efforts, and conditions in the city were worsening dramatically. The English siege encampment, meanwhile, was becoming a kind of parallel town to its French companion. Neuville, it was called.

In early summer, Philippe was at last getting close to having an army that he thought might relieve the suffering city. In June he sent an initial force to sever the line of contact between Calais and Flanders. If the French could secure that flank, they'd have a shot at weakening the English siege and then breaking it.

This attack met a Flemish army near Cassel, the very place where Philippe had won his great victory in 1328. This time, the French were defeated.

Hot on the heels of this loss came news of another. On 20 June, Charles of Blois had attempted a knockout blow of English forces in Brittany by laying siege to La Roche-Derrien with the largest army he'd ever assembled. The opposite happened. Charles of Blois had himself been captured and now joined the Scottish king in English hands.

Five days after that, the beleaguered French garrison in Calais reported that they were at the edge of starvation. Philippe took what strength he had and marched within sight of the town, but it was too little, too late. He didn't have the numbers to break Edward's grip on the city. On 1 August, he retreated without a fight. Philippe's authority, already weakened by the events the previous year, took still another blow.

Two days later, the once proud city surrendered. One month shy of a year after it started, the siege of Calais was over. The map of Europe was being rewritten. And this was just the start.

5

The Years of Jean, 1347–64

Black Death | Winchelsea | Execution of Raoul | Company of the
Star | Charles the Bad | Great Chevauchée | More Chevauchées |
Poitiers | Noble Prisoners | Three Estates | Jacquerie Revolt |
Treaty of Brétigny | Free Companies | Honourable King

After eleven months of siege, the high stone walls of Calais were stained and scarred by fighting. And the marshy, diseased land over which they loomed was cut through by ditch works half-filled with debris and stinking of refuse. The tents of the English encampment – by now large enough and in place long enough that people had taken to calling it New Town – smelled little better. The only things outnumbering the pits and piles of rotting filth were the flies.

So the stage that had been built in front of the city's gates after the surrender seemed something out of a dream. Bright colours rippled upon its clean flags and banners, its opulent canopies and its two high thrones. And the king and queen who sat upon those seats, wrapped in resplendent clothing, were, unlike so many of the thousands who'd gathered to watch, well fed and healthy.

In front of them, between the seats and the city, a second stage had been constructed. It held a platform – elevated so that as many people could see it as possible – topped with the thick timbers of a fresh-built gallows. It was long enough for six men to hang at once, and surrounded by a sprawling, restless, hungry mass of men held back by sergeants. This was the army of Edward III.

Thousands had gathered within the city, too. Survivors stood upon the walls, crowded balconies and even perched on roofs for a chance to see what was going to happen.

At last the gates of the city opened, creaking on their great hinges like a mournful sigh. Under the gaze of so many thousands, six men walked out beneath the August sun. Long shirts of sackcloth hung loosely about their bodies. The eyes with which they took in the crowds were dark and sunken from fatigue and starvation.

One of them carried the keys to the city. Another held the keys to its castle. These were the traditional signs of their surrender. But each of the men also had a hempen noose tied around his neck. This was as Edward had ordered it: if six leading citizens would hand themselves over for death – tying the knots that would kill them – he would spare the lives of the rest. These six had volunteered.

As the men walked to their appointed end, sounds washed over them like competing waves. From inside the city came mournful wailing. It was the sound of loss: the lives of these men and then the homes and possessions and places of all those they left behind. From outside the city came jeers and mockery, along with the buzz of men anxious to loose their pent-up rages.

Over five centuries later, the French sculptor Auguste Rodin would attempt to capture the mixture of determination and pained anguish in the faces and the forms of the six men that day. His 'Burghers of Calais' is a testament to heroic self-sacrifice.

That sacrifice would not be realized, however. As the men were preparing to be hanged, Edward's queen, heavily pregnant, begged him to have mercy. Whether the moment was staged or not, he granted it.

The burghers rejoined their families and the citizens of Calais emptied out, like a wave pulling back from the shoreline. After that, a corresponding surge of the English roared in.

A few weeks later, the pope orchestrated the Truce of Calais. There would be peace at least until the following July, with the English retaining Calais along with everything else they'd gained.

Edward III's turn of good fortune in 1346 and 1347 had been remarkable. Three times he'd been on the edge of ruin in France – on the Seine, then at Blanchetaque and finally with the capture of his son at Crécy – and each time he'd somehow triumphed. He'd defeated the king of France in battle. On other fronts, his men had captured the king of Scotland and the rival claimant to Brittany. And now, as the summer of 1347 came to a close, he'd gained one of the foremost cities of France. Not only did Calais offer an enormous amount of much-needed booty, but it also gave him a vital base of operations on mainland France – one that, unlike Gascony, was within easy reach of London and the Low Countries both. It was a strategic, geo-political and economic boon, though he would not have long to enjoy it. The Black Death would soon descend.

Black Death, 1347

When the Black Death arrived in the fourteenth century, it was not the first time it had been seen in Europe. Strains of the plague, which is caused by the bacterium *Yersinia pestis*, had been infecting Europeans all the way back to the Neolithic Age, and at least one variant of it was responsible for the Plague of Justinian in the year 541. Recent research reveals that the plague had almost certainly struck in pockets of devastation in Europe many years before it began to make the news with an outbreak in Crimea in 1346.[1]

Though the plague may not have been entirely novel, its present devastation was. Large numbers of people began taking fevers and then – suddenly, quickly, terrifyingly – dying. At the start of his book *The Decameron*, the writer Giovanni Boccaccio describes what was happening to victims in Florence in 1348:

> In men and women alike it first came to view in the form of tumors emerging in the groin or the armpit – sometimes growing to the size of a common apple, other times the size of an egg. Sometimes there were many of them, sometimes there were few, and the people called them *gavoccioli*. From these parts of the body the deadly lumps quickly began to propagate and spread – randomly, in all directions – and then the form of the sickness changed, with spots that were black or livid appearing on the arms or the thighs or elsewhere on the body, first large and in few numbers but afterwards small and numerous. Just as the lumps were an infallible token of approaching death, so, too, were these spots when they appeared on anyone.[2]

We will never know how many died. It has been estimated that the vast majority of those who were infected – probably upwards of 80 per cent – did not survive. Most died within a few days to a week. The plague didn't care for a person's station in life, their riches, their church attendance, whether they were kind or cruel, a parent or a child. Attempting to say goodbye to a loved one or to care for them in their illness was often a death sentence. Bodies were left to rot in their beds or upon the streets where they fell. Most scholars argue that half the population was lost one way or another during the Black Death's initial run through Europe. Even the most conservative of estimates suggest that a third of Europe died within just a few years.

Some towns were almost entirely spared. Others were completely wiped out. Even in the best of circumstances, the Black Death ripped holes in the fabric of life, from farming to transportation, from trading to taxation, causing further indirect harms to an already shaken system. The total losses swelled further as weakened community and social structures faltered or outright collapsed.

In these circumstances, it was difficult to make war. There were fewer people to fight, fewer funds to pay them with and fewer supplies to manage it. Though the Truce of Calais had only been planned for a year, it was soon enough being extended annually.

Battle of Winchelsea, 1350

Philippe VI died on 22 August 1350, though he managed to escape the plague. He was succeeded by his son Jean II, who inherited a nation barely holding on to stability. The population of France had been devastated by the Black Death, with the new king's own first wife among the dead. One of the realm's key ports was now firmly in English hands. Much of the French nobility was understandably wavering in their support for the Valois kings.

Even before he could be crowned, just a week after his father's death, Jean got the news that the English were once again on his doorstep. Edward had personally led a fleet of fifty ships into the English Channel, aiming to break the stranglehold that a French-allied Castilian pirate fleet had on English shipping.

The combatants met on the waters south of Winchelsea, close enough to shore that people gathered on the cliffs to watch.

The large Castilian ships towered over their English opponents, as the chronicler Geoffrey le Baker put it, like 'castles over little houses'. But the English had a few more ships than their adversaries, and gathered their forces more tightly than the scattered Castilian fleet to further their advantage.

The Battle of Winchelsea was brutal and bloody. The ships crashed in upon one another, splintering timbers as the men on the decks and perched above hurled arrows, bullets and stones into their enemies. Grappling lines were thrown, binding ship to ship, and the men fought in vicious melee for possession of the shared, shifting 'ground' beneath their feet. In the end, the English had the better of the fight. Le Baker describes the awful aftermath:

> There you could have seen ships painted with blood and brains, arrows fixed in masts, sails, beams, and castles, archers collecting arrows from the wounds of the dead and those fruitlessly praying, for the battle would be renewed on the following day... They care for the helpless wounded, throw the dead and dying Spanish down into the sea, restore themselves with food and slumber, and nevertheless commit a vigilant watch with armed forces... The king but reluctantly returned to England with triumph, yet with great peril prepared for him and his men. They brought back namely wounded heads wrapped in linen to hold them together, arms and legs perforated by bolts and spears, and teeth torn out, also noses cut off, lips cleaved, eyes plucked.[3]

The English won at Winchelsea, but in immediate terms the action did little more than make the English Channel safer for English shipping. Not entirely safe – not by a long shot – but safer. This made it easier to move men and goods between Gascony and England. And that, in time, would help lead to a renewed outbreak of fighting there.

But with populations on both sides still trying to re-establish order and stability in the wake of the Black Death, there was no immediate means for the English to press their advantage.

Execution of Raoul, 1350

Winchelsea had important *indirect* ramifications, however – both immediate and long-term. When Edward had seized Caen in 1346, he'd taken as prisoner Raoul II of Brienne, the count of Eu and Guînes, who'd been tasked with Caen's defence as the Constable of France – the chief military lieutenant to the king. Just a few months after Winchelsea, in November 1350, Raoul was released by the English to return home and raise the money necessary to pay his own ransom.

But instead of welcoming Raoul home or helping him raise the funds necessary to buy his life, King Jean had him immediately taken into custody and executed.

Jean le Bel says that there was a rumour 'that the king had been informed of some liaison that had either occurred or been planned' between his wife and Raoul.[4] The truth instead seems to be that Raoul had promised to forfeit some of his lands to the English in lieu of his ransom and that Jean had found out about it.

Right or wrong, as one historian has put it, 'the sudden fall of such a great nobleman created a sensation in France'.[5] For many, shock turned to rage when the king, recognizing that the position of Constable of France was now vacant, filled it with the leader of the defeated Castilian fleet at Winchelsea, Charles de la Cerda. A cousin and friend to Jean during their shared youth, de la Cerda had fled the battle with the remainder of his ships to the safety of French ports and then rejoined the king at court.

This rapid rise in status from defeated Castilian admiral to Constable of France was enough to ruffle feathers in general, but Jean went even further: he named his cousin count of Angoulême. And *this* ruffled some very specific feathers: Queen Jeanne II of Navarre had held title to Angoulême until she succumbed to the Black Death the previous year, and her son Charles felt that he should have inherited Angoulême from her as well as Navarre. The fact that its county seat was located halfway between the rich and important cities of Poitiers and Bordeaux meant that Angoulême was both a lucrative revenue source and a strategic military position. During Grosmont's run through Aquitaine, Jeanne had actually made a deal with him to spare her holdings in exchange for his free passage through them, which had infuriated the French crown. It's little wonder that Jean wanted tighter royal control of these lands.

The king tried to smooth things over by marrying Charles of Navarre – traditionally remembered as 'Charles the Bad' – to his daughter on 12 February 1352 – but history would prove that this wasn't enough to bring peace between the two rulers.

Company of the Star, 1351

To contend with the surge of anger over the sudden execution of Raoul, King Jean sought to bolster his support, and restore the connection between the crown and the fighting class, by founding a grand order of knighthood, the Company of the Star, on 6 November 1351. Jean's model for the foundation came from England. In 1348, Edward had returned to his earlier promise to establish a chivalric band – the abandoned Order of the Round Table – and founded the Order of the Garter. The Garter was, at its inception, meant to support those who were dedicated to Edward's claim on the throne of France. Even its motto – 'Shame on him who thinks evil of it!' – is a direct reference to the claim.[6]

Whereas the Order of the Garter comprised the king, the Prince of Wales and twenty-four others, Jean's Company of the Star consisted of 300 knights. Not only was it much larger, the Company of the Star dedicated itself to magnificent opulence: during its lavish inaugural ceremony in January 1352 the men feasted off gold plates.

For all its pomp and circumstance, the Company of the Star did not have an auspicious start. One of the knights who attended that inaugural ceremony was the man in charge of the strategic castle of Guînes, which Raoul had supposedly tried to give to the English. While he was away, an obscure Englishman named John Doncaster, by all accounts acting on his own, recruited a group of men in Calais and crept into Guînes under cover of darkness. Murdering the guard, they seized the castle.

Among the knights in the Company of the Star was Geoffroi de Charny, whom we last saw captured by the English at the Battle of Morlaix in 1341. Once ransomed, he continued to go wherever the fighting was, and he continued to be held in high esteem. While the rest of the French army failed on the field at Crécy, Charny was successfully defending the city of Béthune from the attack of Edward III's Flemish allies. Looking for someone to serve as a role model for his demoralized knights, Philippe VI gave him the honour of being the bearer of the Oriflamme in battle. Charged with the recapture of Calais after it fell to the English, Charny made a deal with Aimery of Pavia, a Lombard mercenary in charge of one of the city gates. Aimery swore an oath that he'd let the French in, but on the night of the planned assault it turned out that he'd double-crossed them. English troops were waiting in ambush, with King Edward himself among them. Charny was captured again, and this time King Jean II paid for his ransom – a very high one for a man of no great title – and by 1351 he was once more earning victories.

Now, in 1352, Charny was given pride of place within the Company of the Star, for whom he wrote a set of questions about chivalry that they were meant to discuss. He was also the author of a poem describing his life and career as a knight dedicated to preserving his honour and proving his prowess. It is full of remarkably frank observations about the realities and inherent dangers of this dedication. 'If you're not killed you'll be captured,' he writes. 'And if you're captured you'll be held imprisoned, and a price will be set for your ransom that you'll think absurd!' What is *not* an option, Charny says, is surrender: 'One thing I forbid: you must never take up arms unless you're prepared to die rather than suffer shame.'[7]

Perhaps not surprisingly, given Charny's central role in the Company of the Star, its members all had to take an oath that they would never retreat from battle. Once an engagement began they could withdraw roughly 900 feet from the front-line fighting to allow for tactical manoeuvring, but they could go no further. Though intended to encourage bravery, this would lead to utter slaughter in years ahead.

As populations recovered from the Black Death, so did the armies. For Jean, this meant a strike intended to dislodge the weakened English forces in Brittany and put an end to the Breton War of Succession in favour of the House of Blois. In the summer of 1352, a Franco-Breton army rolled out, and it quickly retook Rennes before pressing onward, aiming for the Anglo-Breton forces defending the castle of Ploërmel. Within this Franco-Breton army were some eighty-nine members of the Company of the Star.

Knowing that the Franco-Breton army marching against Ploërmel significantly outnumbered them – more than two to one – the Anglo-Gascons opted to advance out to meet them in the best defensive position they could manage. They found the ideal ground near Mauron.

The formation the Anglo-Gascons adopted on 14 August was, in many respects, much like the one that the English had taken at Crécy: a dismounted line of men-at-arms flanked by wings of archers.

The Battle of Mauron was yet another victory for the English – one made all the greater with the loss of all the members of the Company of the Star who had fought there. They had kept their word. Facing defeat, they'd stood their ground and refused to withdraw. So they died there.

Charles the Bad, 1354–55

On 8 January 1354, Charles de la Cerda – the constable turned count of Angoulême – took lodgings at an inn in the Norman village of L'Aigle. While he was sleeping, a group of assassins broke into his room, torches and swords in hand. Among the assassins was Charles the Bad's brother, Philippe, and a number of titled men, including the lord of Harcourt.[8] They found the constable in his bed, naked. 'Then the constable knelt before Philippe of Navarre with his hands clasped together,' the *Chronicle of the First Four Valois Kings* tells us:

He begged him to have mercy on him. He swore that he would pay for his freedom with his weight in gold, and that he would even relinquish his claim on his lands [in France] and flee overseas, never to return. To this, the count of Harcourt said, 'Lord, if you want to be a protector of good hostages, have pity on him.' But Philippe was inflamed with such anger that he would hear none of it.

The assassins set upon him with their blades, in an 'abhorrent' attack: his body, found in a pool of blood, had eighty wounds.[9]

The king of Navarre, Charles the Bad, made no attempt to hide his involvement in the murder. In an open letter to the pope and various secular rulers, he made clear that from his standpoint the murder was not only justified but was for the 'common good of the realm' of France: 'Know then that... it was I who ordered the death of Charles of Spain... If the King is angered by what I have done, then I am sorry. But I say that when he has reflected on it a while he should rejoice at being rid of such evil counsel.'[10]

At almost the same time, Charles the Bad opened talks with the king of England. Edward would have been happy to work with any potential ally to further his aims in France, but Charles the Bad held particular potential. His mother, Jeanne II of Navarre, had been the only surviving child of Louis X of France, cut out of the line of succession even though her father declared her legitimacy on his deathbed. Her lands in Normandy were part of her compensation for that loss. So in 1354 Charles the Bad had something far more important to the English than a claim on the strategic position of Angoulême. He also held Évreux, Mortain, parts of Vexin and – most important of all – a sizable chunk of the Cotentin. That peninsula had been the one Edward had used in 1346 to make his landing for the Crécy campaign. An alliance with Navarre would give England that landing point free and clear.

Jean was furious. He wanted to attack Charles, but he recognized that doing so would surely cement connections between Charles and Edward, which was the very disaster he needed to avoid. The French king did what he could with a weak hand. He cut a deal in February 1354 – the Treaty of Mantes – that expanded Charles's holdings as a means of ensuring peace between them.

Edward thought he'd been double-crossed, but it was only a matter of months before Charles had flipped to double-crossing Jean. Once more he was flirting with the English and threatening to open the doors of Normandy to France's enemies.

Back in England, Edward was chomping at the bit to re-engage his claims in France. By now, the Black Death was clearly in recession, and Jean's weakness was evident. As the summer of 1355 approached, the king of England believed he'd struck a deal with Charles that would allow him to land in Normandy and press upon his rival's lands from the north. Meanwhile, he planned to send to Gascony an army led by his son, the Black Prince. In the years since he'd so nearly cost his father the whole war at Crécy, the Prince of Wales had proven himself a commander capable not just of throwing himself headlong into the fight – exactly what had got him into trouble in 1346 – but of knowing when it was tactically sound to do so. His men were loyal, experienced and exceedingly capable.

The Black Prince set sail for Gascony on 8 September 1355. The invasion could not be kept secret. Jean well knew that the new English threat in the southwest would be bad enough without a second force in Normandy, so on 10 September the French king once more grudgingly cut a deal with the duplicitous king of Navarre – the Treaty of Valognes – to keep him from switching sides.

Great Chevauchée, 1355

Without a secure landing point in Normandy, Edward's planned invasion there had to be called off, but the Black Prince went ahead with his own plans. In October 1355, he rode out from Bordeaux at the head of a small army to conduct what came to be called the Great Chevauchée.

The *chevauchée* was a terrorist campaign meant to cripple the French tax base and demoralize its people. The prince was undertaking a fast-moving, mounted raid that was designed to devastate

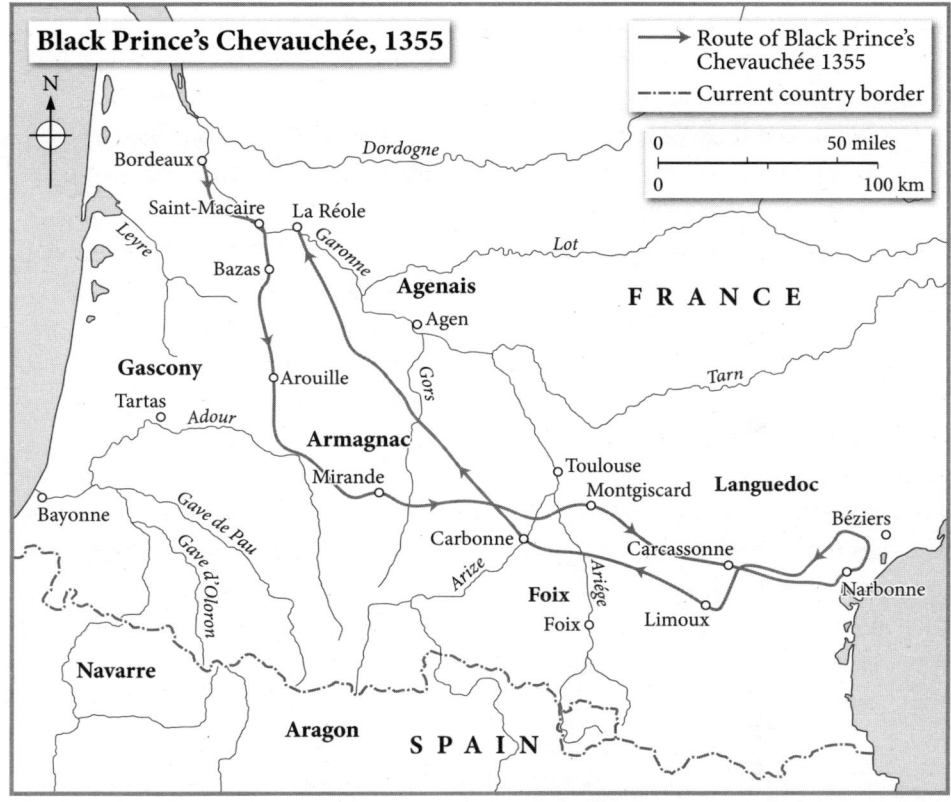

- through whatever harms it could manage – what population it did not imprison for ransom, to plunder whatever wealth could be carried off and to burn whatever was left behind.

The Black Prince was savage, ruthless and successful in this work. For two months his *chevauchée* scorched a path from the Atlantic Ocean to the Mediterranean Sea and back again. As one historian sums it up, 'the Anglo-Gascons had destroyed about 500 villages lying in a band about 200 miles long by forty miles wide across southern France. They had ruined at least a dozen walled towns and the trading and residential quarters of three major cities.'[11] Those who survived were now left in a desolate landscape that had been stripped not only of its wealth, but also the recently gathered harvest on which their lives depended. And that wealth was massive. As Jean le Bel informs us:

They turned back with all their prisoners and loot; and truly, those captives paid such huge sums in ransom that all the knights and squires were rich with the rings and the treasures they received: those still alive are still living off the proceeds, as will their heirs after their deaths. And every foot soldier, even the lowliest fellow, spurned silver coin and cups and goblets and cloths and furs and gowns: they were only interested in good gold florins and rich brooches and jewels.[12]

Winter brought an end to much of the Black Prince's raiding, but Jean's problems endured. Double-crossing the French king yet again, in December 1355, Charles the Bad took part in a struggle against Jean that appears to have been an attempted *coup d'état* with the aim of replacing the king with his son, who was *also* named Charles. By virtue of being the heir of France, this Charles was known as the Dauphin. Just as calling Edward's son 'the Black Prince' saves us from talking about an Edward son of Edward, calling the French king's son 'the Dauphin' will save us from a confusing multiplicity of Charleses.

Though he could hardly have been surprised, Jean had apparently had enough of Charles the Bad's treachery. That spring, on 5 April 1356, Jean surprised Navarre and his supporters at the Dauphin's castle in Rouen. Charles of Navarre himself was arrested and imprisoned, but four of his fellow nobles – two of them among the party that had murdered Charles de la Cerda – were summarily beheaded, their headless corpses hung on gruesome display as a lesson to others who might oppose royal authority.

It is striking just how far the prestige of the crown had fallen and how quickly it had done so. At Crécy in 1346, the king of France had fought with the kings of Bohemia, Majorca and Rome at his side, and the unquestioned support of his kingdom behind him. But since that momentous loss, it seemed as if a cascading series of disasters had chipped away at the vaunted unity and esteem. Calais had been taken. The French army had lost far more battles than it had won, including horrific disasters such as Mauron. It's hard to imagine someone like Charles the Bad thumbing his nose

1 (*above*) Pope Leo III crowns Charlemagne as Emperor of the Romans on Christmas Day, 800 – still viewed with wonder centuries later.

2 (*below*) The tomb effigies of Eleanor of Aquitaine and her second husband, King Henry II of England, in Fontevraud Abbey.

3 (*above*) King Philippe II of France charges at Holy Roman Emperor Otto IV during the Battle of Bouvines in 1214 – an important but little-remembered battle.

4 (*below*) A murder on Quémènès, a mile-long island in the Molène Archipelago, was the first of the countless deaths in the Two Hundred Years War.

5 (*above*) Edward I of England kneels to perform homage to Philippe IV of France in 1286, the very thing English kings would soon refuse to do.

6 (*above*) The root of so much death, the Treaty of Paris ratified by
Henry III in 1259 still exists in France's National Archives today.

7 (*above*) The Battle of the Golden Spurs in 1302 looked like a mismatch on paper, so the victory of the Flemish militia over the French knights was shocking.

8 (*below*) Edward III of England pays homage to Philippe IV of France in 1329, re-establishing a peace that would not last long.

9 (*above*) The Battle of Sluys in 1340 was an astonishingly bloody engagement at sea. Today, the site is peaceful green fields.

10 (*left*) Edward III's coat of arms, from his tomb in Westminster Abbey, combining the English and French arms and thereby staking his claim to the French crown.

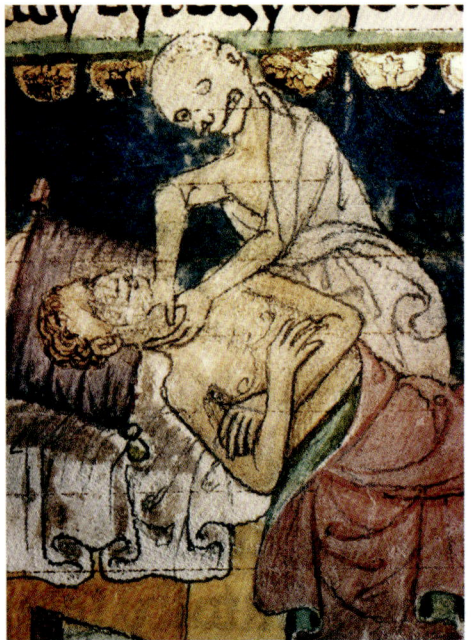

11 (*above*) Three other kings joined France's King Philippe VI at the Battle of Crécy in 1346, but it was England's Edward III who came out the winner.

12 (*left*) Death strangles a victim of the Plague in this fourteenth-century image. Metaphor was one way people grappled with the unfolding horror.

13 (*above*) One of several castings of Auguste Rodin's famed Burghers of Calais stands in Victoria Tower Gardens, London.

14 (*right*) Though Jean II of France would come to be known as 'the Good', his reign was hardly good for his realm.

Cy pule de la bataille a meaulx
en brye ou les Jacques furet
desconfitz par le cote de foix

chalons que la duchesse de
normandie et la duchesse
dorleans et bien .iij.c. dames

so openly at the Capetians, but under the Valois kings it was a different story altogether.

More Chevauchées, 1356

Philippe of Navarre, who'd led the assassins who slaughtered Charles de la Cerda, was not about to accept Jean's imprisonment of his brother. He declared his defiance to the king, took control of his brother's possessions and then used these bases to begin attacking the king's lands. Jean retaliated, ultimately laying siege to the city of Breteuil in April 1356. Philippe of Navarre called on the support of the English, who were only too happy to make this civil war worse. Henry of Grosmont, by now the duke of Lancaster, landed in the Cotentin and on 24 June set out with several thousand men on a *chevauchée* towards Breteuil, which they relieved and resupplied on 5 July. From here, the English rode on, slashing their way in a southern loop back towards Normandy. The French army got close and tried to take position for a fight, thinking that Lancaster would meet them in a pitched battle, but the English avoided them, and an infuriated Jean marched back to Breteuil to take personal charge of a re-established siege that began on 12 July.

The French king was desperate for a win – *any* win – that he could proclaim against his enemies. Unfortunately for Jean, things were about to get much, much worse.

The Black Prince had spent the winter and spring in Gascony, but as the calendar turned to July he was again on the move. Once more, he engaged in a *chevauchée* through the French countryside. This time, rather than riding eastward out of Gascony, he headed north, planning to rendezvous with Lancaster, who by now had refreshed his army in Brittany and was burning his way towards the valley of the Loire.

To cut through the length of France was a bold plan, and it went well at the start. Through the months of July and August this army tore through the regions of Limousin and Berry. According to the Italian chronicler Matteo Villani, the Prince of Wales was 'burning and devouring with iron and fire anything that stood against him. He had already seized an immeasurable amount of

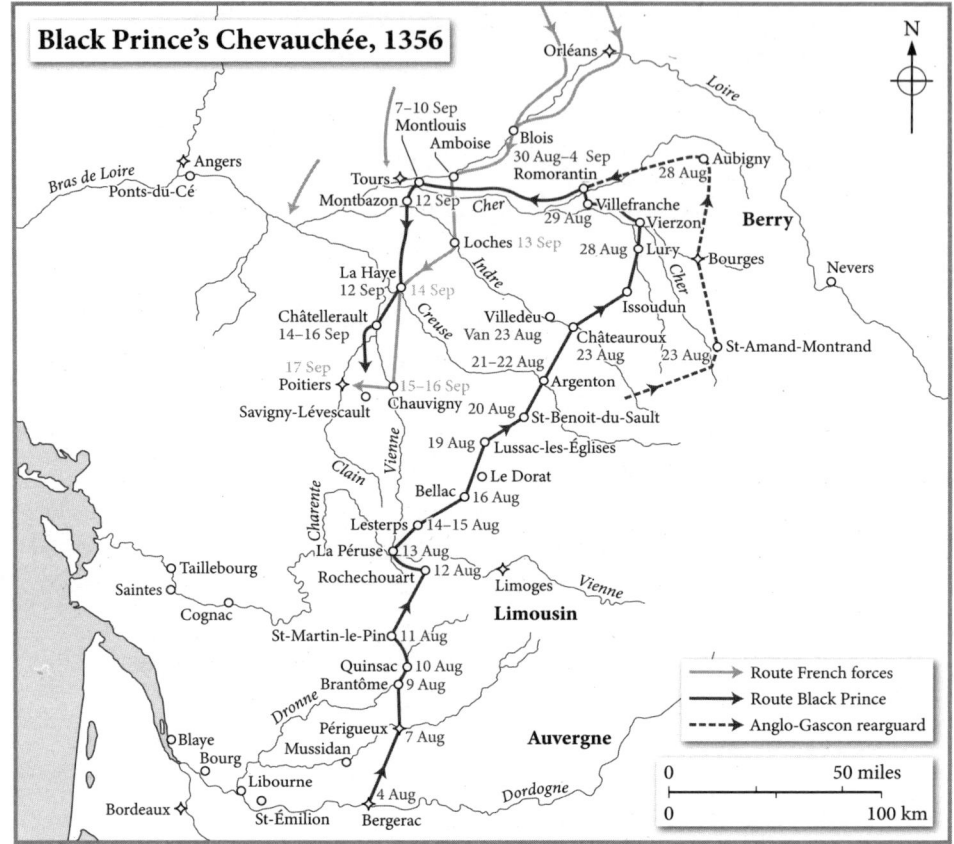

Black Prince's Chevauchée, 1356

booty, since he had plundered 1,500 dwellings, more or less, having stolen and burned without opposition.'[13] The swathe of destruction was dozens of miles wide.

The Black Prince's freedom to raid with such impunity was only possible because the French king refused to budge from Breteuil. But as the situation in the southwest grew more dire, Jean at last disengaged: he offered the besieged garrison the most generous terms possible – and a bribe, to boot – if they'd open the gates. As soon as this 'victory' was achieved, he marched his army south to intercept the English threat. His forces gathered in Chartres, then moved towards Orléans.

The Black Prince was meanwhile looking for a way across the Loire, which was running higher than usual. Lancaster had been stymied trying to do the same from the opposite bank. With the water levels so high, they needed a bridge, but the French had wisely destroyed or fortified them all. In early September, Lancaster pulled back towards Brittany. The Black Prince, near Tours, decided to do the same towards Gascony, though Jean was closing in on him fast.

On 14 September, the Black Prince took position on the River Vienne near Châtellerault. He knew that the French, able to move faster through their own territory, were about to fall upon him. He'd seen this dance before during the Crécy campaign, when his father's march to Flanders had been overtaken by the pursuing French. Unable to escape, Edward had taken the best position for battle he could and wrested a magnificent victory from that challenge; his son now hoped to do the same. He took the best position he could, ready to meet Jean when he rolled into Châtellerault.

But two days later, on 16 September, the Black Prince received the surprising news that Jean was instead crossing the Vienne at Chauvigny, roughly 20 miles away south of him. Astoundingly, the French had marched right past the English position and now stood between them and the safety of Gascony.

Jean knew full well what he was doing. A conservative guess is that the English army at this point was no more than 6,000 men, whereas Jean had perhaps 11,000 – a far cry from the chronicler Jean Froissart's claim of 48,000, but a significant advantage nonetheless. After the frustration of thinking he'd have a fight with Lancaster near Paris only to have him slip away, the king wasn't leaving anything to chance. He was determined not to let his enemy escape.

The chronicler Villani says that at this point the Black Prince, weighed down by 'all the booty that he'd collected, seeing the force of France arrayed against him, realized that he could not save himself by fleeing unless by losing his honor'. His problems were many, but chief among them, according to a letter he wrote to London several weeks later, was the fact that his army was 'short on supplies'.[14] During the running raiding of the *chevauchée*, they had largely resupplied through plunder as they advanced, but keeping ahead of Jean left little chance to do this.

What was approaching, though no one could know it, was the Battle of Poitiers, one of the most important in the history of the Two Hundred Years War.

Battle of Poitiers, 1356

The two armies marched south from the Loire, engaged in a cat-and-mouse game. The Black Prince was prepared to fight if necessary, but he knew well the dangers of being caught in a disadvantageous position. Yet his men and his horses were tired, hungry and thirsty. The longer this game lasted, the weaker he got.

He rolled the dice on an attempt to ambush the king. As soon as the English knew Jean was south of them, the Black Prince says that they

> decided to hasten towards him on the road which he would have to take in order to fight him. But his battalions had already passed when we got to the place where we expected to meet him, and only part of his army, some seven hundred men-at-arms, fought us. We captured the counts of Auxerre and Joigny and the lord of Castillon and many others were taken or killed on both sides; and our men pursued them for twelve miles, as far as Chauvigny.

The road that the Black Prince hoped to catch the king on was that running through forests east to west from Chauvigny to Poitiers, so it would appear that it was on this road that this attack on the rearguard occurred. Villani, who seems to be a strong source of information about the days leading up to the battle, provides more detail from the French side. He writes that the English, knowing that the French would need to follow that road if they went directly through the wood, tried to set up an ambush there – just as the Black Prince says – but that Jean recognized the danger. He had the road scouted, and his reconnaissance sussed out the close proximity of the English forces. Jean therefore took his army around the forest and into the safety of Poitiers. Unfortunately, part of the king's rearguard – the chronicler Geoffrey le Baker calls it 'the rear of the enemy'[15] – didn't get the message. They were caught by the English as they marched through the forest.

For the Black Prince, this was truly a desperate gamble. Lacking a main road heading south through the forests from Châtellerault, there was no place for the easy passage of an army. Yet he made it through anyway. Had things been timed just a little differently, he might even have burst from the treeline and destroyed the French army while it was still marching in a column.

The English now plunged back into the forest and continued south. It may be that they'd learned that Jean had taken the road around the forest in that direction and still had hope of catching him there. More likely, the Black Prince knew how badly he needed to get ahead of the French on his march to safety in Gascony.

The English emerged at the south end of the forest. Once more, it is a testament to both the determination and desperation of the English that they had managed the dreadfully difficult movement through the woods in just a few hours. In a letter written after the battle, the English commander Bartholomew de Burghersh says that they fought an engagement with another group of French near a castle he calls *Chabutorie*, which was after they had crossed the road and left the forest behind:[16] this would put the fight somewhere in the vicinity of Savigny-Lévescault, with *Chabutorie* being the fortified manor now called La Chaboissière.[17]

Daylight fading, the English settled down to camp for the night. They'd had two successful actions and grabbed a few prisoners, but the Black Prince could not have been confident. The forest had helped to shield their movements, but those who'd escaped from the day's skirmishes would have reported what they knew. Any advantage of surprise was gone. Whatever small chance the Black Prince might have had at slipping away was diminishing by the minute.

Villani tells us that at this point 'less than two Parisian leagues' – about five miles – separated the English and French camps. Roughly eight miles separate Poitiers from La Chaboissière, so Jean's encampment was close to four miles from the city, a distance

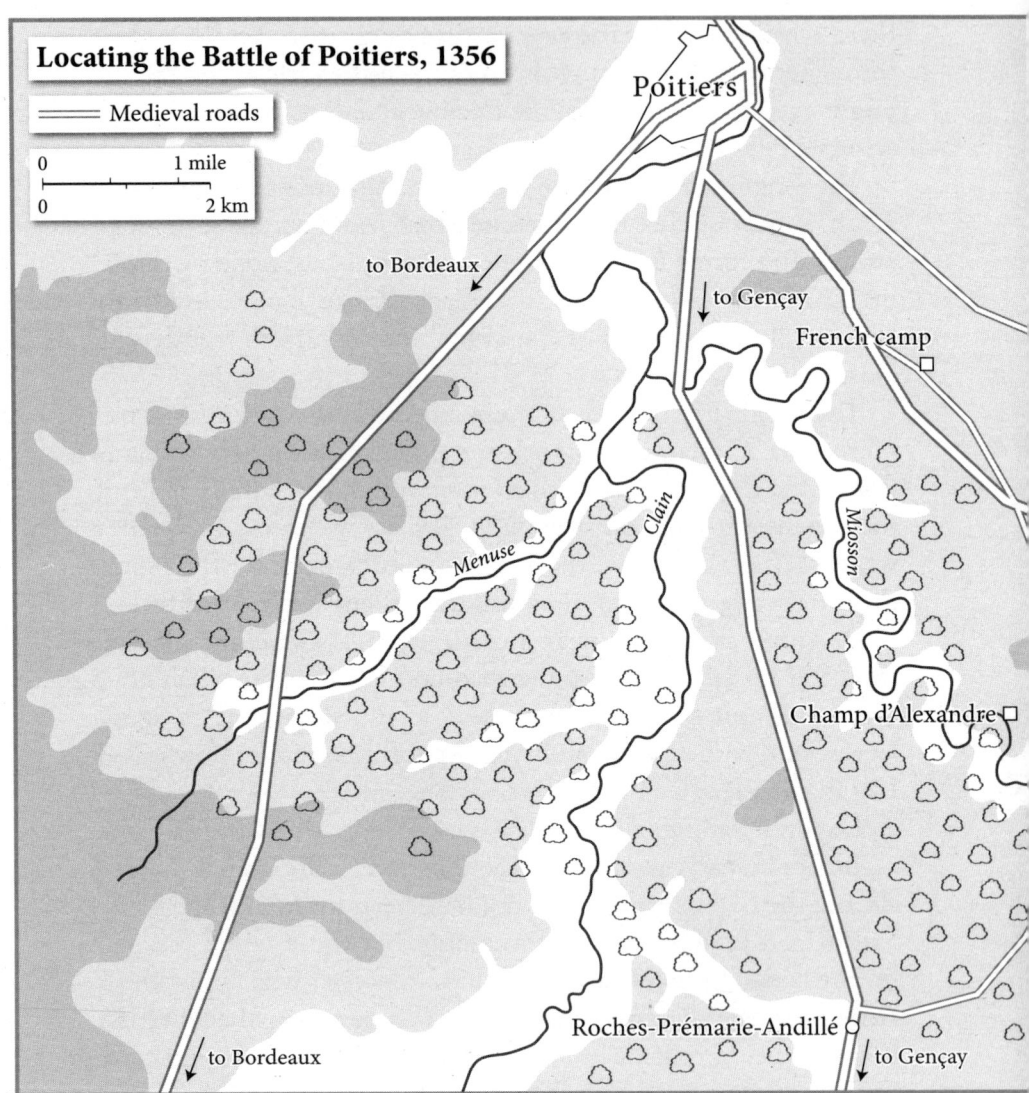

Locating the Battle of Poitiers, 1356

Medieval roads

0   1 mile
0   2 km

Poitiers

to Bordeaux

to Gençay

French camp

Clain

Miosson

Menuse

Champ d'Alexandre

Roches-Prémarie-Andillé

to Bordeaux

to Gençay

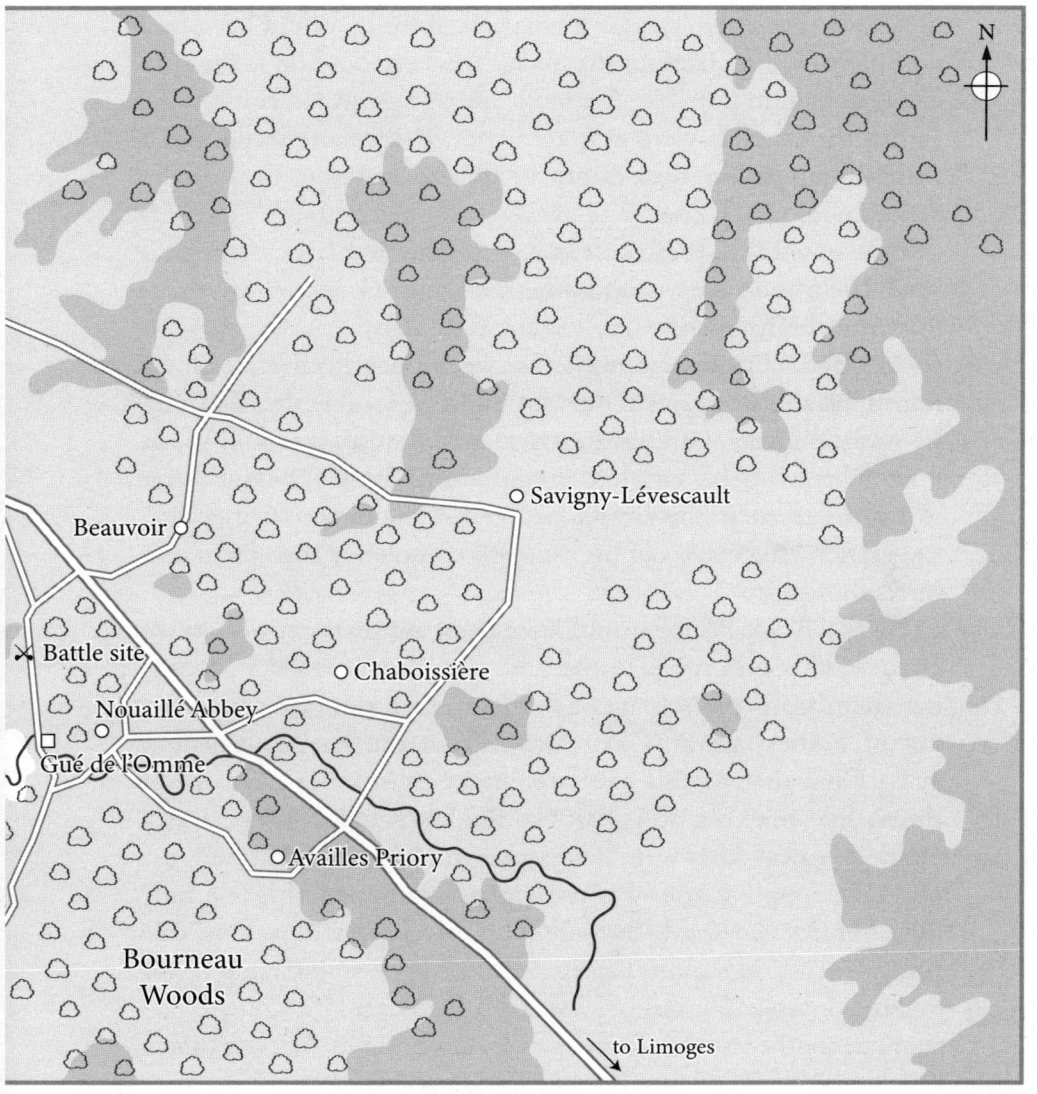

N

Savigny-Lévescault

Beauvoir

Battle site

Nouaillé Abbey

Gué de l'Omme

Chaboissière

Availles Priory

Bourneau
Woods

to Limoges

also confirmed by the Black Prince's letter. That would put the French somewhere near the Centre Hospitalier Universitaire de Poitiers today.

Whether in his heart of hearts the Black Prince wanted to fight or simply retreat, we cannot know. Certainly, he would have said nothing of falling back to his men, especially once he knew that it was next to impossible. A good leader, he projected confidence.

But the English were in a hard spot. With food, water and a defensible position, they might be able to hold out against the greater numbers of French – but they had none of these. There was still the possibility, they must have thought, that Lancaster could reach them and even the odds or – the hope of hopes – turn them to favour the English.

The Black Prince also needed to keep open his avenues for a retreat back to Bordeaux. Outright flight was surely the last thing he wanted to do – unlike a tactical withdrawal, it would mean leaving his booty, his men and potentially his honour behind – but if it came to such dire straits, he needed the option. Otherwise, the French king could cut his route off completely and starve him into submission.

As the Black Prince would have been aware, there were three main southbound roads in the area. The first, if we start counting them from the sea, was the main route running southwest out of Poitiers towards Bordeaux. From the English position at La Chaboissière, this road was about eight miles due west of them. That may not seem far, but the landscape between was a tangle of forests that were likely even thicker than what he'd just pushed through. Closer was the second main road, this one running almost due south from Poitiers to Gençay. Reaching this route, too, would require a struggle across open country, but it was half the distance. Closest of all was the third option: a Roman road that ran southeast from Poitiers to Limoges – this was less than a mile east of La Chaboissière and readily accessible.

It would surely have been tempting to take this Roman road towards Limoges. It was wide and well travelled, and the English could have made good speed. Trouble was, the French could do the same, and at the moment they were encamped a few miles away on that very same road. If the English tried to take it, they'd be hounded all the way. And while the road was headed generally south, it was not the fastest way to safety in Gascony.

To the Black Prince's relief, his scouts would have been able to inform him that there was a local road that could get him to the town of Roches-Prémarie-Andillé, which was on that second road – the one headed south to Gençay. If the English could get *there*, they could follow that faster road for a couple of miles before taking another local road across to the town of Vivonne on the main Roman road directly to Bordeaux. This was the way to go.

From La Chaboissière, the English marched across the Roman road to the Benedictine abbey of Nouaillé (today Nouaillé-Maupertuis), where presumably they took fresh water and such supplies as they could. From here, the local road that they needed – its path close to the D142/Route des Roches today – crossed a bridge over a small river called the Miosson, whose winding valley it then tracked west. A half-mile west of the bridge as the crow flies there was another crossing of this river, a ford called the Gué de l'Omme. Today the ford has been replaced by another bridge beside a lovely park. This was the end of an adjoining road that ran from the Route des Roches almost due north up the slope out of the valley and across hilly farmland to meet up with the Roman road a couple of miles closer to Poitiers. It has various names along its route, but we'll call it the Rue de la Garenne: that's the name it holds on the slope down to the ford, where a modern memorial to the Battle of Poitiers stands today.

If we were to zoom out, we might roughly describe this immediate network of roads as a very pointed triangle: its left side would be the Rue de la Garenne; its right side, the Roman road; its base, the winding squiggle of the Route des Roches. In 1356, much of the space within this triangle was filled with thick woods, part of which still stands on a height above the abbey: the Nouaillé wood.

The Black Prince marched west along the Route des Roches, the Miosson to his right with the great woods beyond it. Where the road joined with the Rue de la Garenne, it turned southwest and continued into different woods on this side of the valley: the Bourneau wood. One of our only contemporary sources to give a fairly precise location for the battle to come is the *Petite French Chronicle*, which was likely written about a month after the fight. It claims that 'the two armies established themselves... between a manor of the bishop of Poitiers, called Savigny-Lévescault, and a large wood belonging to the abbey of Nouaillé, called Bourneau. Most of the enemy [i.e. the English] army had entered into this wood.'[18] The Route des Roches is the road between those very points.

The English plan would have been to follow this road all the way to Roches-Prémarie-Andillé and its larger, more arterial road south to Gençay. But instead – if we assume the traditional site of the battle is correct – the Black Prince turned north, crossing the Miosson at the Gué de l'Omme and marching up the Rue de la Garenne: every modern reconstruction of the battle has the English positioned on this road, with the Nouaillé wood either behind them or at their right flank. (I am of the latter opinion.) The banner of the Black Prince stood on the high ground where the Rue de la Garenne crosses the ridgeline above the Miosson.

Why the Black Prince turned north to recross the Miosson, rather than southwest out of its valley, may be explained by the account of Geoffrey le Baker, who provides us with a description of the landscape that might be one of the most quoted passages about the battle. The Black Prince, he says,

> observed that on one side nearby there was a hill, which was surrounded on the outside by hedges and ditches, but on the inside it was very open: you see, one part of it was pasture-land covered with dense briars, another part of it was planted with vineyards, and the rest was fallow land. He judged that the full strength of the French would take position on that fallow summit.

This would track with a decision in the river valley. The Black Prince had looked up the Rue de la Garenne and recognized that the ridge it crossed dominated the landscape. If the French, a few miles north up that road, decided to seize it, they would be able to take his force while it was marching in column – the very thing he had intended to do to Jean the previous day. Recognizing the danger, the Black Prince was determined to take the height first:

> Between us and the hill there was a wide and deep valley and marsh, fed by a rushing stream. At a fairly narrow ford, the Prince's division with his wagons crossed the stream and, coming out of the valley, beyond the hedges and ditches, he occupied the hilltop, where he was easily concealed in a strong position among the thick brushes, on high ground above the enemy. The field, in which our first and second divisions were safely positioned, was separated from the open ground occupied by the French army by a long hedge and ditch, the far end of which ran down into the aforesaid marsh. The earl of Warwick, general and leader of the first division, held the slope running down to the marsh. In the higher part of the hedge, far away from the slope, there was a large opening or gap, which cart-drivers made in the autumn. A stone's throw away from this stood our third division, led by the earl of Salisbury.

The English position would have stretched from the high ground just south of the little village of Les Bordes (the English left under Warwick) to the Nouaillé wood (the right, under Salisbury). In keeping with the standard English deployment we have seen since Dupplin Moor, it would have featured wings of archers to either side of a centre of dismounted men-at-arms. The English made their encampment along the slope of the Rue de la Garenne – quite possibly near where the monument to the battle stands today. This gave them shelter, protection and access to the water of the Miosson below. The French were roughly three miles north of this as the crow flies.

It was at the English encampment near Les Bordes that the cardinal of Périgord entered the picture, trying to broker a peace deal. Exactly what offers were on the table depends on who is reporting them. Geoffrey le Baker, an English chronicler, says that it was merely a truce that would 'last until Christmas'. Also biased to the English was the author we know as the Chandos Herald. In his *Life of the Black Prince* he doesn't explicitly state the English offer, though he does record that Jean told the cardinal that there would be no peace unless the Black Prince agreed that 'the castles and lands that he has wrongfully ravaged and laid waste since he left England are returned to us, and unless he abandons the quarrel for which he has started the war again' – that quarrel, surely, being his father's claim to the throne of France. The Black Prince, in response, says that although he is willing to fight, he desires peace, but that he cannot make certain concessions himself: 'if the damage and losses and deaths can be avoided, I will agree, if my father also agrees'.[19]

The chronicler Jean le Bel provides something of this bigger offer, pointing out that the English army 'hadn't tasted bread for the past three days' and that they 'feared being starved' even more than they feared fighting. The Prince of Wales therefore 'offered to relinquish all the towns and castles he'd captured and release the lord of Craon and many more of his fellow prisoners, if King John would let him leave the country; the prince would also swear not to take up arms against the kingdom of France for the next seven years.'[20]

This would have been a remarkable offer indeed, but it pales in comparison to what we have from Villani, whose information may have come from the papal court in Avignon.[21] According to him, in return for a safe withdrawal from the field the English offered truly staggering terms: the Black Prince would return every English gain from the previous three years, pay the French an enormous amount of money in reparations, and – in return for the duchy of Angoulême and taking Jean's daughter as his bride – swear himself a vassal to France. Villani says that Jean wanted to accept the prince's offer – not a surprise, since the terms were so generous that they might have ended the Two Hundred Years War then and there – but he was dissuaded when the bishop of Châlons objected. The churchman's argument was simple: 'Tell me, sire, what vengeance have you taken for yourself, what has been done for your honour, and for that of the whole kingdom, if this peace is made?' Insisting that the negotiations were, in fact, an English ruse to stall for time to get reinforcements or supplies from Lancaster, the bishop proclaimed: 'You should not forsake the vengeance for the offences you have received, and you should not let the full victory that God has prepared for you escape through the delays of negotiations and advice.'

It was enough to turn the king's council against a peace deal. They would take to the battlefield the next day.

On the morning of 19 September, the French army formed up in four divisions. Up front was the smallest of them: a line of mercenaries who would soften up the enemy. Behind this came a second division. Some sources treat these two lines as one, suggesting that they were coordinated: landing in rapid succession, they would be a one-two punch. After this would come the third division, under the command of the duke of Orléans and the Dauphin – the brother and son of the king of France. And last of all was the division of the king himself.

The Black Prince had meanwhile been busy making plans of his own. He knew his position was not a good one. It had some water, but whatever foodstuffs they'd procured from the abbey would not have lasted. If the English stayed where they were, they'd likely starve. So the prince's ideal move remained the Route des Roches through the Bourneau wood to Roches-Prémarie-Andillé. If he could withdraw back across the ford of the Miosson and get up into the tighter confines of the landscape to the south, he and his army might shake off the French pursuit and escape.

During the peace talks, the English had reckoned the distance to the French encampment while further reconnoitring the Route des Roches. The Black Prince was apparently reassured by what he was hearing. After the failure of negotiations, he thought he had the space and organization to make his move. He was wrong, but the error won him his greatest victory.

The Black Prince himself tells us of this key moment:

> Because we were short of supplies and for other reasons, it was agreed that we should retreat in a flanking movement, so that if they wanted to attack or to approach us in a position which was not in any way greatly to our disadvantage we would give battle. This was done and the battle took place.

The Chandos Herald, whose source was on the field that day, says that early in the morning on the day of the battle the Black Prince instructed Warwick and his vanguard 'to cross the ford and guard our wagons'. He and the rest of the men, the Black Prince assured them, would follow. A typical march would have the baggage trailing behind his army, but with the enemy potentially nipping at his heels he knew he would need to reverse this. At daylight, this action was already taking place. The Black Prince had 'moved off; he rode away, because he did not wish to fight that day but to avoid a battle'.

This movement appears across nearly every account of the battle, because the French had scouts of their own. They saw that the English position was shifting.

What happened next was so essential to the outcome of the battle that later English writers considered it a clever stratagem. This is certainly the story told by Thomas Bisset, writing around 1363. The English, he says, knew their long odds:

> Seeing that they had no hope of escape, and greatly fearing the multitude brought against them, they did not dare to openly attack the French, who stood in their array and did not move. But then, through careful thought and subtle ingenuity, in order to separate the French from each other, they pretended to return to their own country by another road near them. When the French and the others saw this, and believed that the English were fleeing from them, their unfortunate urges broke their ranks at once. They thought it would be as easy as swallowing a gnat.[22]

The sudden assault by the French first line was something that no one on either side had anticipated. The second line of the French was rushing to catch up with the first, but the two larger bodies of French behind them were not yet prepared to make an immediate assault. The English were meanwhile well into their tactical withdrawal: according to the Herald, the rest of the army had already crossed the ford when Salisbury, in command of the rearguard, did exactly what he was meant to do. He sounded the alarm and then turned to face the frenzied initial assault that threatened to run them all down from behind. Assuming a defensive position – no doubt using the hedges to strengthen his line – he hunkered down and took the hit. Archers sped out into positions they'd formerly occupied and began to loose.

After fierce and bloody fighting, most of it focused on the gap in the hedges through which the Rue de la Garenne ran, the English rearguard was victorious in holding position against the disorganized assault.

The Black Prince was meanwhile rushing back over the ford and up the hill with his men. The earl of Warwick was close behind. It was clear now that there would be no chance of a withdrawal. The Herald says that they marched 'up the hill' – presumably the slope leading up from the ford – in order to deploy for a pitched battle. As they streamed up onto the high ground, they spread out. They'd held this same position for more than 24 hours. They knew where to go. And more French were coming.

One group likely did not rush back up into the prior deployment, though. Geoffrey le Baker claims that in the middle of the battle a Gascon lord in the company of the Black Prince rode out to flank the remaining French in a manoeuvre that had to have been planned the prior day:

> Meanwhile, the Captal de Buch advanced by an oblique path, retreating down behind the slope of the hill that he had just left with the prince. Secretly going around the battlefield, he came to the place from which the first pickets of the king had emerged. From there he climbed up to the high field by the road just trodden by the French, suddenly bursting out of hiding and using the noble banner of Saint George to signal to us that he was a friend.

We can trace this path, beginning with the Captal de Buch over the river with most of the army when the alarm was raised. He and his men did not follow the road across the ford and up the hill. Instead, they rode for the bridge beside the abbey of Nouaillé. From there they shot north, following the Roman road towards Poitiers, the thick Nouaillé Wood keeping them hidden from view.

To sweep around to the northern end of the woods in this way was a ride of just under two miles – hardly a great distance for a mounted force. On level ground a horse could cover that in 15 minutes at a trot, but the local topography and desire to keep these mounts fresh for the fight ahead surely stretched it out to something close to half an hour. Thirty minutes, even more, and the timing lines up very well with having this force suddenly explode into the French flank.[23]

Even with the clever manoeuvre of the Captal de Buch, the Battle of Poitiers is a fight the French ought to have won. That they instead lost – and lost badly – stemmed from a failure of command and control. It was much like the cascade of poor decisions and poor communications at Crécy. Here, the first line was over-hasty in making its engagement. That impetuous action was exacerbated by the second line taking too long to come in support and being destroyed in turn. The battle had hardly started, the Captal de Buch was still riding, and already two out of the three divisions of the French had been demolished.

The third line was that of the Dauphin. The Herald says that he, too, tried to make his way 'through a gap in a little hedge', but the English poured in, plugged the gap, and the Dauphin withdrew from the field entirely. Other sources report that the Dauphin fled without striking any blow at all, and the question of just why he did so was a hot topic in France after the disaster became clear. One suggestion was that the king had ordered him away for safety – a story likely coming from Jean himself as part of an effort to restore the honour of his heir. Just as possible, the Dauphin had seen the scant survivors of the first two lines streaming into his own in panic and either lost his own will to fight or his ability to help his men find theirs. Either way, he pulled off the field, probably marching northwest in a beeline for Poitiers.

All that remained now was the fourth and final division, led by the king of France himself, 'with so many troops it was astonishing to see them', as the Herald says.

The Black Prince, flush with the flight of the Dauphin and no doubt hoping to neutralize his lack of numbers by instilling fear in his opponent, did not hesitate. Jean may have lost command

and control over his men, but he had not. He opted for a bold and ultimately victorious charge. At nearly the same time, the Captal de Buch plunged into the French flank and rear.

From the moment the alarm had been raised, the English had performed masterfully. Salisbury's quick work had bought time for his commander to return and take control of the field. The Black Prince had experienced men, and it showed. He re-established his position quickly. He pressed his advantages unerringly. When he saw the Dauphin's division retiring and only the king's division left, he charged.

The French who remained did their best. But in truth they were pressed on all sides, and the English were wreaking havoc. The carnage that took place in this final phase of the battle is horrible to imagine, though Geoffrey le Baker tries to give us a sense of what it was like as the French attempted to rally and defend their now ragged banners:

> Men trod in their own guts and spat out their teeth; many were cloven to the ground or lost their limbs while on their feet. Dying men fell in the blood of their companions and groaned under the weight of corpses until they gave out their last breath. The blood of serfs and princes flowed in one stream into the river.[24]

Some surrendered, but this, too, was chaos. The count of Dammartin later testified to the English court what happened when he was bested by a man on the field:

> He called on me to surrender, and I immediately did so and gave him my fealty in such wise that he should save me. He said I should be quite safe and need have no fear. Then he went to take off my bascinet [helm], and when I prayed him to leave it to me he answered that he could not properly save me unless he took it off. So he took it off, as well as my gauntlets; and as he did so another man came up and cut the strap and frog of my sword, so that it fell from me altogether. Then I told the [first man] to take the sword, for I preferred that he should have it rather than anyone else… Then he made me mount his horse and handed me

over to the keeping of a yeoman of his, and left me thus… Then a Gascon came up and demanded my fealty. I answered that I was already a prisoner; but all the same I gave him my fealty, simply so that he should save me. He took an escutcheon of my coat-armour and left me. As he went, I told him that since he was leaving me in this way I should give my fealty to any other person who might come up and be willing to save me. He answered, 'Save yourself, if you can.' Then another man, who belonged to Sir John de Blankmouster, came up and demanded my fealty. I answered that I had already been taken by two persons; but I gave him my fealty, simply so that he should save me.[25]

Many, though, no doubt preferring death to the perceived shame of surrender, fought until the bitter end. Among these was the king himself. His father, Philippe VI, may have fled the field at Crécy, but Jean would not do likewise at Poitiers. According to Villani, his youngest son, the fourteen-year-old Philippe, was still with him. The king ordered him taken away, but Philippe rushed back to stand with his father. 'Unable to use weapons, he watched for the dangers to his father and would cry out: "Father, look to the right, or to the left, or to the other side" – wherever he saw the attackers.'

Geoffroi de Charny was also there. Among the things he'd written in his *Book of Charny* was the importance of honour as a knight, and how hard it could be to achieve it:

you'll have plenty to cope with, including fear, as you see your enemies bearing down on you, lances lowered, ready to strike, and returning to attack with swords while bolts and arrows rain down on you – you don't know which to defend against first! You witness men slaughtering each other; some flee while others stay and die; your friends are struck dead: their bodies lie before you. But your horse is still alive and fit; thanks to him you could save your skin: he could get you out of there – but without honour. If you stay it'll earn you everlasting honour; if you flee you'll bring dishonour on yourself.

Is he not a martyr who commits himself to such work?[26]

In the end, Charny got his honour, amid just such a field of death. He was cut down at Poitiers, still holding the banner of the king in his hands.

Villani describes the circle growing tighter around Jean and his guard as the French knights, like Charny,

> were killed or were wounded and clinging to each other when they were finally struck down and died around the king. He, surrounded by the English and Gascons, was asked to surrender. Seeing all around him his dead barons and living enemies, without any hope in being able to sustain the fight any longer, he requested to surrender to the Gascons and put his weapons and banners in their custody. His son, small in body but great in spirit, did not want to surrender. But having been begged and commanded by his father to surrender, he did so.

For his bravery at such a young age, the boy would come to be known as Philippe the Bold.

And so, as the last of the men surrendered, the battle ended. It was a staggering victory, with thousands dead on the field and Jean a prisoner of the English – alongside his son Philippe and several thousand of his countrymen. 'By the time the English were all back round the Prince,' Froissart says, 'they found that their prisoners were twice as numerous as themselves, so they conferred together and decided to ransom most of them on the spot.'[27]

The English, many having fought that day on near-empty stomachs, were also able to enjoy a great feast after ransacking the French encampment, which had no shortage of food and wine. The Black Prince, perhaps remembering the display his father had made after Crécy, welcomed the captured French lords to his table in order to enjoy the choicest delicacies that had so recently been theirs.

Poitiers doesn't have the fame of the earlier Battle of Crécy or the later Battle of Agincourt, but it's arguably more important than either of those fights. Because in the end, the Black Prince, who'd been put to his knees at Crécy, at Poitiers brought the king of France to his knees.

The next day, the English army packed up and left, carrying everything they could. That night they stayed in Roches-Prémarie-Andillé, and from there they indeed cut across to the main road to Bordeaux. The Black Prince made haste to Gascony as fast as he could manage. He knew the great prizes he was hauling in both treasures and men. But he didn't need to hurry. With its king captured, France was in complete disarray.

On 2 October, the Black Prince and his army safely reached Libourne, 20 miles east of Bordeaux. For two weeks they stayed there, while preparations were made in the Gascon capital to celebrate their victorious return. When at last the Black Prince entered the city, he was met with all the rapturous, raucous joy of a Roman Triumph.

The long struggle was surely over, they must have thought. The enemy king was captured. Peace was at hand, or so it seemed.

Noble Prisoners, 1356–57

It was several days before the people of France knew what had become of their king. He'd been seen on the field at Poitiers, surrounded by the enemy. His standard had fallen. So many had been struck down, their torn bodies left exposed in a scavenger's feast. Had the king been among them?

In the absence of concrete information, rumours spread like wildfire. People at all levels of society were understandably gripped with confusion and panic. The news, when it came, that Jean was alive but in English hands did little to alleviate it all.

Word of what had happened at Poitiers reached England only a little later. Edward in London heard not long after the Black Prince was being lauded on the streets of Bordeaux.

Through little direct action of his own, Edward now had *two* rival kings in his grip: King David II of Scotland and King Jean II of France. If geopolitics was a game of poker, his might seem a very good hand indeed.

There are many reasons why the capture of the French king didn't end the Two Hundred Years War. We catch glimpses of them in Edward's announcement of Jean's capture, sent in a letter to the prelates of England so it could be declared in churches. 'Although we do not rejoice in the deaths of men,' the king wrote, 'we see in this how the merciful compassion of God extends all around us, our son, and his army; and we rejoice in the Lord, hoping that we will gain from this a better, swifter, and more de-sired peace.'[28] Edward was clearly pleased with the turn of events, but by no means did he view it as a final victory. His reaction was, in a word, tempered.

One reason why Edward wasn't wildly celebrating Jean's cap-ture is that he knew as well as anyone what it meant to be a king. France and Scotland may have lost their kings, but if someone else could take up the reins of power, their fights would go on.

This didn't make the captured kings useless to the English, though. The chaos that their imprisonment caused in their respec-tive kingdoms was not only a strategic advantage, but an economic one. Men of title promised money in ransom. Men claiming the highest of titles promised extraordinary wealth. So almost as soon as the English army had reached the safety of Bordeaux, Edward and his triumphant son were cutting deals with the men who had laid claim to choice prisoners on the battlefield. The clear aim was to transfer them into royal hands in order to extract the fullest advantage from them.[29]

The main prize, of course, was Jean. And on 5 May 1357, the Black Prince arrived in England with the prisoner king. The wel-come he had received in Bordeaux surely paled in comparison to what the pent-up months of waiting in England had wrought. The kingdom was overjoyed.

The king's status as a medieval prisoner may conjure up some rather frightening images in the mind, but imprisonment for Jean was hardly undignified. He was, at worst, under what we might call a 'house arrest' in England. He moved between royal estates, enjoying the trappings of a regal life that few English could conceive of: sumptuous food, delicate fineries and even his own astrologer.

He also had frequent visitors and access to a steady stream of letters and reports from France. So although he could do little to help, he was well informed of what faced the Dauphin – his eldest son, Charles – as he took up the reins of government and tried to stiffen the kingdom's spine. It was not an easy task. The Dauphin's situation was desperate, and it would only get worse.

Three Estates, 1357

The Dauphin was eighteen years old when he retreated with his 22-year-old uncle – the duke of Orléans – from Poitiers. It was later claimed that they'd been ordered by the king to make the withdrawal in order to keep safe the Valois line of kings. Some believed this. Many did not, pouring derision on those who had retreated and lauding those who, like the king and Charny, had faced the disaster with honour.

The enormity of what the Dauphin faced after Poitiers cannot be overstated. Few could point to anything good having happened since the Valois princes took the throne. The solution was easy to promise but difficult to deliver: he needed to do better.

Before he could get to doing better, though, he needed to get to doing something. The state was virtually paralysed. The king wasn't alone in his imprisonment. With him in English custody were the Dauphin's fourteen-year-old brother, Philippe the Bold, along with an enormous number of titled men. Some were quickly ransomed. But many others languished in captivity. All of them had been cogs in the machinery of France's industry, her economic and military power, and her most pivotal systems of governance.

The state was also close to broke. Jean had been forced to manipulate the realm's currency to keep the power of the crown afloat amid the storm of the war, and now the treasury was gravely depleted at a time when that same crown desperately needed funds to stabilize the kingdom. There was no question that the English would press the new advantage that Poitiers had given them.

With the future of France teetering on a knife's edge, the Dauphin and his advisors had little choice but to raise taxes.[30] Doing so nearly broke the kingdom.

Since medieval kings could not directly enforce taxation across all the citizens in their realms, they generally relied on the same kinds of relationship structures that gave their crowns the power and authority to get the money in the first place. This is simplifying things quite a bit, but in essence a king could lean on a count to raise taxes from a county. The count would then lean on lesser lords, who would lean on even lesser lords below them, all the way down to the lowest local level.

So when the Dauphin needed to raise money for the defence of the realm and the ransom of the king, he first had to acquire the consent of the kingdom's citizens. He did this by calling upon the Estates General to gather in October.

The Estates General was a kind of parliament that represented the three 'estates' or classes of medieval French society: the clergy, the nobility and the commons – the last of these being elected speakers from selected towns of the kingdom. It had been formed by Philippe IV in 1303 to provide representative support for his struggles against the pope and for his other efforts to centralize power within the court. In time, it became an advisory body: it was the Estates General that had affirmed – likely after some persuasion – that the so-called Salic Law meant that a woman could not succeed to the throne of France. The Estates General was also, due to it being loosely representative of the tax base of the kingdom, a mechanism through which the king would request and receive subsidies. If a king needed money, he could call on the Estates General both for consent to taxation as well as for the enforcement of the collection via the representatives who had agreed to it.

But this time, when the Dauphin called upon the Estates General to raise funds for a new army and his father's ransom, it loudly refused. The leading voice among the naysayers was the provost of the Parisian merchants – akin to the mayor of Paris – named Étienne Marcel. He and his fellows produced a litany of complaints against Jean and his court advisors – the very men who were presently advising the Dauphin – and a set of demands that needed to be met before they'd be willing to give the Dauphin the money he wanted. Among their requests was that Charles the Bad, who had many friends among them, be released from prison.

Although he'd previously been friendly with Charles the Bad, the Dauphin was well aware that Navarre's on-and-off dalliances with England might well be an existential threat. Navarre's brother had fallen in with the forces of the duke of Lancaster, helping the English destabilize French authority in Normandy, and there was genuine concern that the imprisoned king himself could do far worse if he was freed.

On 9 November 1357, that hypothetical problem became a reality. Charles the Bad, then held in the northern castle of Arleux, was sprung from prison by partisans, who took him to the city of Amiens. The people welcomed him with elation, a scene that was repeated when he entered Paris itself later that month and – with the support of Marcel and other disaffected members of the Estates General – presented the Dauphin with a list of demands.

It was quite a list: a blanket pardon for all acts committed by him or by his followers in his name; payment for all damage done to his property during his imprisonment; and, perhaps most astonishing of all, title to Normandy and Champagne, lands that had been his mother's.

The Dauphin did what he could to drag out negotiations, looking for a better solution. As he did so, news arrived from England: the imprisoned Jean was nearing a negotiated peace with Edward. No one knew for sure what the final terms would be, but the king of Navarre was certain that they'd be bad for him: with France and England at war, Charles had been able to play them off against each other to his advantage, but that would no longer be the case. Worse, their agreement might settle the borders in a way that would negate any of his own claims.

Desperate men in desperate moments do desperate things, but even by that standard what Charles the Bad did next was truly shocking. He opened the prisons in Paris, creating such chaos as to derail any hopes of achieving an immediate peace. Parts of France were plunged into anarchy as Charles the Bad fled to his Norman holdings, where he quickly allied with the English.

Not long afterwards, in February 1358, a mob led by Étienne Marcel killed two of the Dauphin's chief military officers right in front of him. The Dauphin was forced to flee Paris. The chaos was only growing.

Jacquerie Revolt, 1358

Like wars, revolts have no singular beginning. They are, most often, brief and violent moments when numerous storms all suddenly blow in the same direction, ripping holes in the social fabric. In the spring and summer of 1358, the storms were many, and their winds were fierce indeed.

One problem was obvious: the English – and now the Normans – had ravaged huge swathes of the kingdom, and the king who was meant to protect France was presently in prison and working to cut a deal with the English for his release. Since political and economic systems like the French administrative state were fundamentally rooted in a system of collective defence, the state's inability to produce a satisfactory defence inevitably undermined any faith that citizens had in the monarchy.

Adding to this, the relationship between the Estates General and the crown – whether that was the imprisoned king or his son, the Dauphin – was unquestionably broken. This fracture exacerbated the problem of protecting the realm from its enemies, as it prevented the necessary funds for its defence from being raised.

Meanwhile, bad harvests – thanks to both military predations and uncontrollable climate changes – meant that the prices for life's essentials were high. The economy was every bit the wreck that the government was. France's stability was mountains of dry tinder just waiting for a spark.

Ignition occurred in late May at the little hamlet of Saint-Leu-d'Esserent, less than 30 miles north of Paris, where fed-up peasants gathered together over shared grievances. Energized by their mass, the gathering became a protest. Turning violent, the protest lit the match of a political rebellion we call the Jacquerie, which spread from village to village with terrifying speed.

Separating fact from fiction in a revolt such as this is difficult. Jean le Bel, for instance, reports that peasants assaulted a knight 'and bound him tightly to a stake and raped his wife and daughter before his very eyes; then they killed them both – and the wife was with child – before slaughtering the knight and all his children' and setting fire to their home. In another instance, he says, 'they killed a knight and stuck him on a spit and roasted him in front of his wife and children; and after ten or twelve had raped the lady they tried to force her to eat his flesh before they killed her horrifically'.[31] Horrible as these stories are, it is unclear what truth lies behind them. Those who compiled these stories, like Le Bel, usually had a vested interest in exaggerating what happened to support their own political ends. Close study of the evidence shows that 'despite the Jacquerie's reputation for violence against women, all but one of the identifiable victims were male, and there is almost no evidence of rape'.[32]

Marcel, working to tighten his grip on Paris, was by now fiercely against the royals. He saw in the Jacquerie a ready ally in this fight. This only furthered his strength, as the Dauphin struggled to organize a counter to what was roaring over the landscape.

The opportunistic Charles the Bad, seeing the chance to prove his worth and his strength – and also no doubt keenly aware that a peasant revolt was no help to his own lordly interests – marched out from Normandy with a couple of thousand men, intent on restoring order.

The Jacquerie had built something of an army of their own. It had several thousand more men, but they were a ragtag bunch with relatively little experience. At their head was a farmer named Guillaume Cale from the village of Mello, not far from Saint-Leu-d'Esserent. He formed his force up on a hill near his hometown.

The king of Navarre recognized the difficulty of a direct attack on the larger peasant army, so he invited Cale to join him in talks that might prevent bloodshed. The peasant leader accepted and came down from the protection of his own lines.

Cale had been assured safe passage to and from the talks. This was fairly standard for a negotiation of this kind: safety in discussions was paramount. Yet as soon as he crossed into his camp, Charles the Bad had him seized. The king of Navarre then mounted up and ordered his men to charge the suddenly leader-less army of the Jacquerie.

The so-called Battle of Mello, fought on 10 June, was a massacre. The peasant lines were shattered by the charging knights, who ran down every man they could. Many were killed in the rout that followed. The campaign of vengeance and suppression in the subsequent days and weeks killed thousands more.

In a bald play for power, Charles the Bad now rode for Paris, but the move backfired: while many in the ruling class had been happy to support him against the peasants, supporting him against the Dauphin was something else entirely. His support dwindled, and he skulked away.

By the end of July, Marcel had been assassinated by Parisian guards, and the city haltingly returned to peace.

Treaty of Brétigny, 1360

In England, meanwhile, Edward and Jean had been busy in negotiations. By March 1359 they had an agreement: the Treaty of London. England would keep Gascony and Calais, plus the old Angevin lands of Anjou and Aquitaine would be restored to them, in addition to the counties of Maine and Normandy. The Breton Succession would be settled for the English side. Virtually the entire western half of France would be firmly in English hands. And, vitally, these lands would no longer be held as fiefs of the French king.

And that was just the territory. The French would also pay a ransom of 4 million crowns for Jean's release. The gold content of those coins would be worth 1.26 billion dollars today.

Little surprise, then, that the Estates General ultimately refused to accept the treaty. It was too much. They preferred to leave their king in hock.

Edward was furious. He held the king of France in one hand and an agreement with him in the other. For the kingdom itself to resist was unfathomable.

He summoned his army once again. He knew what France had lost at Poitiers. He knew how fractured she was now. He was

confident that an invasion now would enforce the deal he had...
or perhaps gain one *even more* in his favour.

Edward and the Black Prince marched out from Calais in
November. With them were the duke of Lancaster and the earls
of Warwick and Northampton. It was a veritable Who's Who of
England's most powerful, commanding a total of some 10,000
men. Their target was Reims, that coronation seat of French kings.
The French had denied him half of the kingdom, so Edward
planned to take the whole thing.

The English besieged the city through December and into
January, but it stubbornly refused to fall. With supplies dwin-
dling and the winter doing its brutal work on his army, Edward
broke off the siege and marched to Burgundy, where he holed up
through the remaining cold months.

When the temperature warmed up, the English returned. This
time they marched for Paris, where they arrived on 5 April.

The Dauphin was in command of the great city. He ordered her
gates shut and strongly barred, trusting that her thick walls would
hold out against whatever the English brought to bear against
them.

It was a good bet. Formidable though Edward's army was, it
had little hope of breaching Paris. This wasn't Calais on the coast.
This was a major city in the middle of France. It would be nearly
impossible to put it to a true siege even if he could afford the time
to do so. He simply didn't have the manpower to surround it,
much less the men needed to protect supply lines back to friendly
territory.

The king of England challenged the Dauphin to come out and
fight. When the young man wisely refused, Edward taunted him
and had his men ravage the precincts outside the walls. This continued for days, but the Dauphin held firm.

Frustrated, Edward marched to the smaller, less defensible, but
rather wealthy city of Chartres. He could not take Paris, but *this*
was within reason. The threat that he might seize it, Edward surely
hoped, might pull the Dauphin out of Paris.

The English army's spirits were high as they made their way to
Chartres on Easter Monday, 13 April. The date would come to be

remembered as Black Monday, as a freak storm lashed the English lines: 'So much rain and hail fell all that day', the French friar Jean de Venette wrote, 'that most of the carts and their crews were bogged down on the muddy paths and roads. The horses could no longer pull, and they and their drivers were out of breath from the pelting rain and hail... It is said that the greatest losses of men and supplies came from this bad weather.'[33]

Perhaps not surprisingly, the dark day grew more vicious with each retelling: lightning ripping open the skies, the hail shredding tents and battering the terrorized men and animals. Legend would eventually claim 1,000 men and 6,000 horses lay dead when it was finished – a rather different picture than one gets from reading Jean le Bel, for instance, who says of the same sequence only that Edward left Paris for Chartres before moving on, 'always seeking out the most plentiful country' to support his army.[34]

In any case, Edward withdrew from Chartres, and he re-entered negotiations with the French. Three weeks after Black Monday, a new accord was struck: the Treaty of Brétigny. This wasn't quite the deal that the Treaty of London had been, but it was still an unquestionable English win.

Under the treaty, Gascony would still be greatly expanded. The French had taken Brittany, Anjou, Maine and Normandy off the table, but it was still an extraordinary revision of the map. Poitou, Saintonge, Agenais, Périgord, Limousin, Ponthieu and Calais were among some of the great lordships that would become subject to the English king. No longer would there be a duke of Aquitaine performing homage to hold possession under the king of France. Henceforth there would be a lord of Aquitaine, ruling English lands for the king of England. For the ransom of their imprisoned king, France would pay 3 million crowns, with his release to occur after the first million was paid.

In return for all this, Edward agreed to renounce his claim to the throne of France once the terms of the treaty were fulfilled.

Though made under obvious duress on the French side, the Treaty of Brétigny was a surprisingly thoughtful peace. It had been sixty-eight years since the outbreak of fighting after the murder at

Quéménès. After all those murderous decades, here, at last, was a real chance for peace – if it lasted.

Free Companies, 1361–62

On 24 October 1360, King Jean rode out from Calais. The Treaty of Brétigny had been signed and sealed, and although his side hadn't managed to cough up the full amount necessary to secure his freedom, the English had let him loose regardless. Keeping a king prisoner wasn't cheap, and Edward was glad to get that expense off his ledger. More than that, Edward knew that he had a better shot at seeing the terms of the treaty fulfilled if Jean was in France. Jean's second son, Louis of Anjou, took his place in Calais as a hostage to guarantee that the king of France would deliver on the agreed terms. To his credit, Jean tried very hard to do just that, especially when it came to raising the money that he'd promised for his release.

It was no easy task, however. Not everyone was pleased with the notion of peace.

Among those who had come to enjoy the warrior's life in the fourteenth century was Arnaud de Cervole. Born around 1320, he had become an archpriest, but the outbreak of war had proven to be its own calling. He was among those captured at Poitiers, and after his ransom he found himself among a class of fighters who recognized that their skills could provide rewarding careers as brigands and mercenaries.

Bands of these men came to be called Free Companies: small, independent armies that could be hired out by one king or lord to fight another. Left unpaid, they'd be more than happy to plunder the lands of *any* ruler.

The Archpriest, as Arnaud came to be known, soon found himself leading a group of Free Companies called the Great Company. It was a formidable force of nearly 3,000 men at its height. In 1357 the Archpriest marched them towards the relatively untouched lands around Marseille. Their route would take them through Avignon, and the French army was in no condition to stand in their way. So Pope Innocent IV hoped to stave off a potential disaster by inviting the Archpriest to Avignon, granting him a personal audience, and ultimately paying him a large sum of money to go away.

Soon enough, the Dauphin was paying him, too, and then the king: the Archpriest had a competent military force, while the royal army was in shambles and more and more predatory bands of out-of-work fighters were forming up.

It's easy to gloss over these events – they don't have the glamour of the great battles – but the human costs should not be forgotten. In one instance, we have the report of a rural priest describing a band of English coming to the village of Chantecoq in pursuit of loot:

> [I] put together a hut in the woods of les Queues and stayed there with many of my neighbors, seeing and hearing every day about the vicious and wicked work of our enemies: namely, houses burned and many dead left lying like animals... Seeing and hearing such things, I decided on December 16 to go to the city and stay there. But it happened that very night that these accursed English found their way to my hut so quietly that, in spite of the watchfulness of our sentinels, they almost captured me while I was asleep. But... I was awakened by the noise they made and escaped naked, taking nothing with me because of my haste except a habit and hood. Crossing into the middle of the swamp I stayed there, trembling and shivering in the cold, which was then very great, while my hut was completely despoiled.[35]

Among these Free Companies was *another* Great Company more famous than the Archpriest's. By the end of 1360 this other Great Company had at least 12,000 men and, as the Archpriest had, it descended on Provence. It captured Pont-Saint-Esprit, a small town astride the Rhône just south of where it flowed into the River Ardèche. From here not only could this Great Company halt traffic on the Rhône, but they were also positioned to attack Avignon downriver. If the pope had been worried by the Archpriest's group of brigands, this new one terrified him.

The pope had paid off the Archpriest, but this was no longer an option. For all the pope knew, word of that payoff was the very reason this second group was upon him. So he tried a different tactic. He excommunicated the members of this new Great Company and in January 1361 called for assistance, promising indulgences to any who would launch a crusade against the trouble-makers. Jean sent the Constable of France. The king of Aragon sent a few hundred men, too.

The Great Company had meanwhile continued to grow in strength, but those numbers were more a problem than a benefit: the force was too large to sustain itself without significant gains in plunder, and defences were coalescing to prevent just that.

In March, the Great Company cut a deal to move on. It crossed the Alps to fight in Italy.

The departure of this threat was welcome news, but it was only one of the many threats France was facing. The kingdom was shattered. The Italian poet Petrarch was a witness to how far the kingdom's fortunes had fallen, writing in February 1361:

> The French, so long famed for their glorious military successes, have been beaten so frequently and so unexpectedly... by fire and sword that I could hardly believe it was the same kingdom I'd seen so recently while there on business. Everywhere was lonely misery, devastation, and desolation. Everywhere were fields neglected and untilled, homes ruined and abandoned except where they were protected by the walls of cities or fortifications. Everywhere, the bitter traces of the English, the fresh and horrifying scars left by their swords.[36]

The Treaty of Brétigny had taken huge swathes of the kingdom. English garrisons possessing castles now delineated as French were expected to remove themselves, while whole populations of French elsewhere now received the unexpected news that they were behind enemy lines. Many groups stubbornly refused to go along with it all, leaving French and English officials to argue over who ought to set things right. Amid the chaos were the remaining Free Companies, their ranks swelling with fighting men who simply didn't know what to do in peacetime. This, in turn, induced further resentments and devastation. Even those who wanted to return to a peaceful life might find themselves unable to do so: homes, farms, livelihoods… with nothing to go back to, the blade could be a man's only way to make a living.

In 1362, the French king ordered a show of force against some Free Companies that were then ravaging Burgundy. This group is often called the Latecomers (in French, *Tard-Venus*). The army would be led by Jacques de Bourbon, who was among those displaced by the recent treaty: he had been count of Ponthieu and La Marche, but the former had been handed over to the English. One of Bourbon's commanders was none other than the Archpriest.

An initial target was Brignais, a small town just south of Lyon that the Free Companies were using as a base from which to launch raids. Bourbon marched there and tried to take it back. In the battle that followed, the Free Companies came out on top. Bourbon and his heir were both mortally wounded. So, too, were the counts of Champagne and Forez. A massive number of their men were killed. At least a thousand were captured. The Archpriest was among these, but as soon as he reckoned that he wasn't likely to be paid by the crown, he switched sides to join the Free Companies in brigandage once more. Everything was falling apart.

An Honourable King, 1363

Jean's losses weren't confined to battles. The English had released him from imprisonment on the assurance that the king of France would raise the remainder of his ransom as agreed in the Treaty of Brétigny. Edward was fully confident that Jean would not cut and run. Whatever else the English king thought of his enemy, he correctly believed him to be a man of honour.

Jean did his best, but with each passing month it became more and more clear that the French king would be unable to fulfil his promises. His realm was painfully short of money: he couldn't give the English what he did not have, and he didn't have it because fifteen years of disasters had not only left the crown's treasury in disarray but also crippled the administration down to the local level that would be needed to restore it. And what money could be scrounged was being spent on paying off mercenaries one way or another: either to keep themselves from being attacked or to make an attack on someone else in a devolving landscape of local bickering and civil wars.

Far worse news reached Jean in the middle of 1363. His son Louis, who had been left in Calais as his replacement hostage, had escaped. Glad tidings, most of us would think, but for Jean it meant he was *doubly* dishonoured.

That November, the king of France made the sudden surprise announcement that he would – of his own free will – return to England. It is often said that he was doing so in order to hand himself over to his enemy: his son had been a hostage in his place, and now that Louis had escaped Jean was honour-bound to return to prison. Perhaps this is so, but we do not know for certain. Just as possibly, Jean believed that he could negotiate new terms face to face with Edward.

Jean II reached London in January 1364. Edward was in a position to be magnanimous. He welcomed the French king with feasts and a great show of how *his* kingdom was doing just fine. Meanwhile, negotiations were begun to resolve the outstanding issues that were preventing the fulfilment of the Treaty of Brétigny.

If they thought there was still time to forge a lasting peace, they were wrong.

6

The Years of Charles, 1364–77

Navarre and Burgundy | Cocherel | Auray | Du Guesclin and Spain | Nájera Campaign | Nájera | Tides Turn | Pontvallain | La Rochelle | Gaunt's Chevauchée | End of an Era

On 8 April 1364, in the chilly dark before dawn, a small company of men rode up the wide road along the Seine to the closed gates of Mantes-la-Jolie. The town was a crucial point on the frontier of Normandy, one of several fortified positions that controlled travel on the river between Paris and the sea. At the moment, it was also functioning as a centre for the Norman administration of Charles the Bad, who was, once again, at odds with the king of France.

The watchmen at the gates were wary. The riders had come up from the direction of Rolleboise, another Navarre-held castle downstream, which last they knew was being besieged by the king's forces. The guards called down to the horsemen, who by the light of the flickering torches looked haggard and exhausted.

One of the riders trotted forward. He was, he told them, the marshal of France. Robbers had ambushed him near Rolleboise, and he needed to find safety. After they were assured that he meant no harm to their town, the guards opened the gate. The grateful marshal rode in, and his men filed in behind him.

But behind *them*, streaming out of the dark, were more men. A far larger company, led by a man named Bertrand du Guesclin, slipped into the marshal's wake. They pushed forward, one after another, through the gates and into the town. Then, revealing their true intentions, they seized Mantes for the crown and began purging it of the Navarrese loyalists within.

That's one story of what happened, anyway.

Another story has it that the small party was led by du Guesclin, not the marshal, and that they were disguised as grape harvesters seeking work. This ruse, too, is said to have got the gates opened, though it assumes that the men on guard – or, more likely, the audience of the story – were willing 'to swallow the idea of an April vintage within the town walls', as one historian put it.

A different story altogether says that it was Olivier de Mauny, du Guesclin's cousin, who managed the surprise capture of the town. He and 160 men-at-arms were waiting in the dark when the gates were opened to let a wagon out onto the road. Seeing few guards in place, Mauny rushed the gate and took control.[1]

We will never know which story is true, if any. It is often the case that a simpler explanation is more likely than a more complicated one, which might incline us towards the last story. But if it *was* the more complicated ruse that opened the gate, I have little doubt about who thought it up. Bertrand du Guesclin was a minor Breton noble who years earlier had begun making a name for himself in the War of the Breton Succession, fighting for the French-backed Charles of Blois. Du Guesclin turned out to be an extraordinary commander. Among his most identifiable traits – beyond his reported ugliness – was his single-minded determination and his ability to maintain control over men of varied background and experience. In Brittany he had also acquired a reputation for focusing more on winning than on niceties like chivalry and fair play. A sneak attack on Mantes was very much his style.

The French and the Navarrese were back at each other's throats at a momentous time, because a new power vacuum was about to open up: back across the Channel in England, the king of France had only hours to live.

The illness that struck Jean II down isn't known. Plague had been in some resurgence. That winter had also been miserably chilly. And Jean had been under extraordinary stress. Though he was only forty-four, his health had been fragile for some time. Whatever it was, he died early on 9 April.

Peace may have died with him. The terms of the Treaty of Brétigny had not been fulfilled: only a fraction of Jean's ransom had been paid, and there were still outstanding difficulties in making the new borders on paper a reality on the ground. With so many issues unresolved, Edward III had never renounced his claim to the throne of France.

Meanwhile, both France and England were experiencing a generational shift of leadership. Edward was in his fifties now. Many of the men who had fought so successfully alongside him were dead. This diminished the realm's military capabilities, but it also diminished its political capabilities. History often reveals a keen difference between the diplomacy of veterans who have experienced war first-hand and those young and green enough to still be exuberant for the fight. England's economy was also in difficulty. Though the realm was at peace internally, Edward had begged and borrowed against his future income to pay for his many past fights. Those bills were coming due.

In France, the situation was even worse. Twice the Dauphin had served France as regent in his father's absence. He would serve her now as king. Few would have looked to the young man's coming rule with a great deal of hope. The Valois kings had done little for the kingdom. They had instead diminished it greatly, and the 26-year-old who would now travel to Reims to be crowned Charles V had done little to inspire confidence that a change in French fortunes was coming.

Yet change *was* coming. Under this new king's leadership, the kingdom would claw back into the fight. Within decades Charles would undo almost everything the English had accomplished to this point in the war. History would remember him as Charles the Wise. Among his new weapons was the clever du Guesclin – a man many called 'the Black Dog of Brocéliande' – who could do far more than overtake a town's gates. He would prove his worth on the field even before Charles could get to Reims and his coronation, in a battle that was all about Burgundy – one of several new and important players being sucked into the spiralling war between England and France.

Navarre and Burgundy

The old kingdom of the Burgundians had, by the end of the thirteenth century, splintered into a number of counties and other regions that more or less independently became vassals of France or the Holy Roman Empire. Quite confusingly, two of the most important of these regions continued to use the name of Burgundy. The duchy of Burgundy, with its seat at Dijon, was closely tied to France. The county of Burgundy, with its seat at Dole, was closer to the empire. In this book, we will most often be concerned with the duchy of Burgundy because of the central role it plays in the Two Hundred Years War from this point forward, beginning with the death of the duke of Burgundy back in 1361 – a death without an immediate heir.

After the duke's death there were two primary claimants to the duchy. One was King Jean II of France. The other was Charles the Bad. Each claim rested on a different but potentially valid progression of inheritance rights, so the choice of duke came down to who could win the support of the Burgundian ruling class.

In this, there was little competition. Navarre's previous acts – including his self-serving flirtations with England and his dalliances with the populist uprisings in Paris and elsewhere – had badly damaged his reputation with the nobility. Few in Burgundy had any interest in him becoming their duke. So the duchy went to Jean, who then named one of his sons – Philippe the Bold, who'd stayed with him at Poitiers – the duke of Burgundy. This would keep the proud duchy close, while assuaging Burgundian fears of being subsumed by France.

Predictably, Charles the Bad was upset. Once again, he'd been within a hair's breadth of major influence outside Navarre – a seat at the head table of power in France – only to have it slip away. When Jean left for England, Navarre tried to reopen the question of his claim to Burgundy. Thinking the king-to-be weak, he rattled spears from his bases in Normandy, threatening to march out and take Burgundy by force.

The Dauphin had responded by sending his army against Navarre's holdings in Normandy. It was this that had brought du Guesclin – or whomever it was – up to the gates of Mantes just hours before their king died.

Battle of Cocherel, 1364

In England, Edward was only too happy to see renewed conflict between Navarre and the Dauphin, which could only serve to weaken the French. Yet the English couldn't *openly* support Charles the Bad. The Treaty of Brétigny was still in place, and if the English hoped to get all that was promised to them, they needed to hold to it. The upshot was this: Edward didn't directly send men to aid the cause of Navarre, but he didn't stand in the way of those who wanted to help and could do so without violating oaths of their own. Chief among these men was the Captal de Buch. This Gascon nobleman was a highly respected military figure. Almost as soon as he agreed to support Navarre's cause, he was in charge of the military efforts entirely.

One of his first priorities was to gather strength to push back against du Guesclin, who'd followed up on the seizure of Mantes by chipping away even further at the Norman frontier. Towards the end of April, the Black Dog had taken Vernon, the last of Navarre's positions on the Seine. The situation was urgent, and the Captal de Buch, who had by now gathered a sizable army in Évreux, marched out to take it back.

Just over 16 miles separate Vernon from Évreux. The medieval road between them crossed a bridge over the River Eure at a small hamlet called Cocherel. When the Captal de Buch, marching east, came over the ridgeline to look down upon the river on 14 May, he found du Guesclin waiting for him, arrayed on flat land just west of the bridge. There would be no getting to Vernon without a fight. The Captal had numbers, but he was reluctant to leave the high ground. So he settled into a defensive position, hoping that du Guesclin would charge uphill into the teeth of his army just as the French had done at Crécy and Poitiers. The Black Dog wisely refused.

The struggle had all the hallmarks of civil war. A Gascon lord, the Captal de Buch was reportedly heartbroken to see that there were Gascons in du Guesclin's force, too. So mixed were the men, in fact, that they could not depend on appearance, language or even banners to differentiate friend from foe. Battle cries had been another means of recognition in earlier fights – the French were known to shout 'Montjoie!'; the English would shout 'Saint George!' – but this, too, was unreliable here. While they sat at a stalemate, the men on du Guesclin's side debated what they would shout to each other. According to Froissart, they decided upon the cry 'Our Lady and Guesclin!' He clearly had the hearts of his men, and the Battle of Cocherel, fought on 16 May 1364, would prove the honour well placed.[2]

The action began when parts of du Guesclin's force began to withdraw over the bridge to the other side of the river. Seeing this movement, one wing of the Navarrese army broke ranks and swept down towards the French. The Captal de Buch, knowing he could not leave such a large contingent of his army to fight alone, sent the rest of his men to support them.

That initial move from the Navarrese side is understandable. Most battles, as we have already seen, end in rout. One side breaks and tries to run. The other side then runs them down. With du Guesclin's men in apparent retreat, the Captal de Buch's men thought the moment of victory had come. But in their confidence, they relinquished the high ground.

Du Guesclin had made no mistake. Though some historians have doubted the commander's intentions here, he was too experienced to think he could conduct a wet-gap crossing under the ever-watchful eye of his adversary. He *wanted* the Navarrese to attack, which is exactly what Froissart – in the last version of his frequently revised chronicle – says he was doing.

For good reason, a feigned retreat is considered one of the most difficult tactical manoeuvres. No matter how well planned, it can easily become an *actual* retreat in the terror of the moment: the urge to sprint pell-mell is nearly undeniable once the enemy is bearing down on you. But du Guesclin masterfully maintained command and control amid the roar of the oncoming enemy. When the Navarrese descended onto the flatter plain, the French army turned and took them on. Whatever battle cries actually went up, most were quickly lost as the organized battle lines 'were scattered' into a horrific chaos of individual combats across the meadows, Froissart tells us: men striking at each other with spears, swords and all manner of weapons 'for as long as they had strength to hold them'.

The battle, now on even ground beside the river, might still have gone to the Navarrese given the disparity in numbers, but du Guesclin had a Breton force in reserve – one more reason to think this a planned action. Once the two lines were fully engaged, he sent this contingent barrelling around the flank of his enemy and into their rear. The Navarrese lines, who'd only minutes before thought they had the battle won, broke and scattered. The Captal de Buch was captured for ransom. Most of the men he commanded had poorer fates.

Battle of Auray, 1364

News of du Guesclin's victory reached Charles in Reims on 18 May, the day before he would be crowned as king. It must have seemed a sign of divine providence for the success of his coming reign.

For Charles V, the road ahead was already coming into focus: his father had agreed to a treaty with England, but Charles had no good reason to honour it. We have seen this before. Henry III signed the 1259 Treaty of Paris, but his son Edward I was only too happy to break it after taking the crown in 1272.

One of Charles's first acts as king was to reconfirm his younger brother's hold on the duchy of Burgundy. This severed any possible bridge to a peace with Navarre, but by this point that bridge had already gone up in flames. Investing Philippe the Bold with Burgundy was just kicking the last cold ashes into the water. An appropriate image, perhaps, since all rivers run to the sea, and once Bertrand du Guesclin had won at Cocherel he'd pushed all the way to the English Channel.

Du Guesclin's success in Normandy was unquestionable, but it came at a price for his homeland of Brittany. In the years since the Treaty of Brétigny, Brittany had swelled with out-of-work soldiers, including some Free Companies that French officials had managed to pay off to go there. The presence of these experienced soldiers had added new dimensions to the ongoing War of the Breton Succession between the English-backed claim of Jean de Montfort and the French-backed claim of Charles of Blois.

In the years leading up to Cocherel, Bertrand du Guesclin had masterfully navigated these additional elements to the benefit of Blois, but the Black Dog's sojourn into the war against Navarre – successful though it was – had taken him out of this fight and given new life to the Montfortist cause. This was exceedingly well timed from the English perspective. After the death of her husband, Jean de Montfort, in 1345, Joanna of Flanders had fought hard for the rights of their infant son, named after his father, but she'd been forced to flee with the child to the court of Edward III. The young man had now returned to Brittany to press his claim himself, so he was able to take advantage of du Guesclin's absence by laying siege to the town of Auray in the summer of 1364. Its inhabitants, low on supplies, agreed to hand the town over to the Montfortists if the siege was not relieved by 29 September.

With mere days to spare before the deadline, du Guesclin reappeared along with Charles of Blois himself, intent on lifting the siege and securing Auray. As this Franco-Breton army approached, Montfort and his Anglo-Breton army issued out to block it. In command was John Chandos, who like du Guesclin had risen far above his expected station thanks to his remarkable acumen in war: he had played important roles at both Crécy and Poitiers and become a close companion of the Black Prince.

On 29 September, the day of the deadline, the two armies arrayed for battle. Negotiators hustled back and forth between the two armies. Montfort reportedly made a substantial offer for peace. Many wanted to accept, but hotter heads prevailed. According to the French *Chronicle of the First Four Valois Kings*, du Guesclin himself was one of these, calling the Anglo-Bretons 'dirty cowards' and promising Blois that by force of arms he would deliver a Brittany free of them.[3]

The Battle of Auray did not go as the Black Dog hoped. Many of his fellow Bretons deserted rather than fought, even as the battle was getting underway. The Montfortists already had the advantage of higher and firmer ground, and now they had an increasing advantage of numbers, too. Sensing that a loss was only a matter of time, more and more men on the Franco-Breton side made that defeat a surety by slipping away. Seeing his chance, Chandos immediately launched his core strength at the standard of Charles of Blois. When it fell, the remaining Franco-Bretons broke and ran, pursued by an Anglo-Breton mounted reserve under the command of Hugh Calveley. He had wanted to be in one of the main lines of attack, but Chandos had insisted that he instead be ready to lead this last charge for just this purpose.

There might have been 3,000 men standing with Blois at the start. By the time Calveley had finished his work, at least 800 of the Franco-Bretons were dead, with Charles himself among them. Nearly twice as many were captured, including du Guesclin, who survived even as his own standard-bearer was slain beside him, only to be taken prisoner by Chandos himself.

As the story goes, Chandos knew of du Guesclin's pre-battle boasting. He took his prisoner to see where the corpse of Blois lay amid the carnage. The deaths, he said, lay at the feet of the Black Dog, who ought to wish he'd never been born. Then he pointed to Montfort, who was standing before his victorious men: 'Look upon these "cowards" of Montfort,' he told du Guesclin. 'Thanks to you, he is this day made the duke of Brittany.' Chandos was right. When Charles of Blois breathed his last on the bloody field of Auray, so too did the War of the Breton Succession. It took time, but on 12 April 1365, both sides agreed to what would be called the First Treaty of Guérande. This covenant declared that Jean de Montfort was the rightful duke of Brittany. In making the peace, the widowed Jeanne of Penthièvre, through whom Blois had made his claim in the first place, was allowed to hold the title of duchess of Brittany until the end of her days. After more than two dozen years, the War of the Breton Succession was over – but that didn't mean that the tug-of-war for its possession was over. England and France would again and again return here to fight. And du Guesclin would be in the middle of much of it.

Du Guesclin and Spain, 1366

As the fighting wound down in Brittany, the Free Companies once again reared their heads in France: the out-of-work fighters needed something to do.

There were many attempted solutions – sending them on a crusade, sending them to Italy as had been done the last time round – but the one that stuck probably came from the king's brother, Louis of Anjou: leading them over the Pyrenees into the middle of two related wars that would reshape the balance of power on the Iberian peninsula. Put in charge of this effort was none other than du Guesclin, whose ransom was guaranteed by the king in exchange for his release.

To understand why the Black Dog was about to head over the Pyrenees, we have to step back to the year 1350, when King Alfonso XI of Castile died. The crown of Castile passed to his wife's sixteen-year-old son, Pedro, but the succession was not straightforward. Though Pedro was the dead king's eldest son *by his wife*, Maria, the daughter of the king of Portugal, he had an older son, Enrique, with his long-time mistress and undoubted favourite, Leonor de Guzmán, the widowed daughter of a lesser nobleman. Such was Alfonso's affection for his lover that after Maria had given birth to Pedro – after the box marked 'legitimate heir' had been checked, in other words – the king had lived with Leonor instead, bestowing as many honours as he could upon their *ten* children together. Enrique himself was eventually made count of Trastámara.

The fact that Enrique was the elder son and had been given some political power made him a distinct threat to Pedro's authority. Atop this, after years of feeling slighted by the presence and prominence of Leonor and her children, the new king's mother was more than ready to make her own superiority known. No fools, Leonor and her children headed for the hills as soon as Pedro stepped forward for the crown, only returning when agreements to keep the peace were made. But after a sequence of uprisings against Pedro's rule, the king had Leonor imprisoned and then executed. It was the first of many instances in which Pedro would prove willing to go to extremes to accomplish his ends. History – depending on whether those writing it agree with those ends or not – has labelled him both Pedro the Just and Pedro the Cruel.

Now orphaned by his half-brother, Enrique of Trastámara fled from court to court, seeking allies. Early on, he found support in neighbouring Aragon in (modern-day) northeastern Spain. Its ruler, Pere (Pedro) III, was more than happy to expand his influence by taking advantage of internal divisions in Castile. Now, when the end of the War of the Breton Succession had raised the need to send out-of-work fighters somewhere outside France, Enrique knew just the place for them to go.

After much negotiation, in 1365 a deal was struck to raise a mighty army in France, blessed by the pope, that would march under du Guesclin's leadership into what is now southern Spain, passing through the Aragonese lands of Pere. The heart of it would be the Free Companies. Many of those leading the individual companies had fought against du Guesclin at Auray, including Calveley, the man who'd led the final cavalry charge there. That they'd so recently been at odds didn't seem to matter. They were joined by a different mission now.

On paper, their mission would be to attack the Moorish emirate of Granada in what is today southern Spain. That was the price of the pope's blessing. But the leaders themselves knew better. The Free Companies weren't coming to fight for God. They were coming to fight for money. And the one sure way to get it – a *lot* of it, Enrique of Trastámara assured them – was to invade Castile instead. Overthrow his half-brother Pedro and the rewards would be plentiful indeed. By the time du Guesclin's army was on the roads out of France, it was well over 10,000 strong.

In Aragon, Pere was initially thrilled. He'd paid handsomely to help fund this army and had agreed to give it free passage through his lands. In his mind, he'd bought a wolf, and he was keen to see it attack his enemies in Castile.

N

Santiago
de Compostela
Galicia

Asturias

Bisc

Camino de Santiago

León

León

Burgos

Valladolid *Douro*

Porto

Salamanca

Avila

Madrid

Coimbra

Toledo

Tagus

C R O W N   O F   C A S T I

Castilla la N

Extremadura

Lisbon

P O R T U G A L

Castilla la Vieja

Córdoba

Jaén

Seville *Guadalquivir*

Córdoba

Seville

Granada

G R A N A

*ATLANTIC
OCEAN*

Ceuta

Iberian Kingdoms, 1350–1450

But wolves are as likely to bite the hand feeding them as anything else. As du Guesclin's army passed through Aragon, it left devastation in its wake. Pere found himself paying even more money – plus lands and titles to its leaders – to keep its depredations to a minimum.

In early 1366, du Guesclin finally reached Zaragoza on the River Ebro. Pedro was in Burgos, about 150 miles away as the crow flies: the frontier between these two cities of Aragon and Castile was mountainous, difficult terrain, and Pedro positioned his forces in the passes, largely centred on the town of Soria. The only way around would be to march up the Ebro, through Navarre, and the king of Castile thought he had an alliance in place with Charles of Navarre that would prevent such a march.

He thought wrong. Charles the Bad was smart enough to know that he couldn't fend off the massive force that was marching on Castile. So rather than hinder them, he double-crossed his ally, inviting them to move through his lands with all possible speed in order to surprise the king in Burgos. Du Guesclin and Calveley marched out from Zaragoza at the end of February. In only a few short weeks it was all over. They'd shot through Navarre – extracting still further money from its duplicitous king – and steamrolled the meagre Castilian forces that stood between them and Burgos. Pedro fled at their approach, and on 29 March, Enrique entered the city to proclamations of his rightful place as king.

Pedro, on the run, tried to organize resistance, but many in the nobility had long disliked his authoritative demeanour. They were more than ready for the change Enrique promised. The deposed king fled to the court in Portugal, where his mother had been raised. He tried to have the royal treasury shipped there, too, but it was intercepted. Enrique used it to pay off the great army that had won him his crown. He'd seen first-hand the destruction that they could cause, and he wanted them gone with good wishes as soon as possible. The roads back to France filled with newly rich mercenary warriors.

Du Guesclin and Calveley stayed, enjoying the enormous riches and titles that they'd gained. For all that they'd done to try to kill each other in Brittany, they'd proved a winning team.

Within months, though, they would be enemies once more. The war between England and France ensured it.

Nájera Campaign, 1367

Though he'd lost his kingdom, Pedro wasn't completely bereft: he had a long-standing relationship with Edward III, the powerful enemy of the French king who'd supported Enrique's seizure of his throne. In 1345, when they were around eleven years old, Pedro had been betrothed to the English king's favourite daughter, Joan. The match was considered a good one, and both kings were greatly pleased. Under heavy guard, Joan had sailed from England to Gascony in 1348: she would tour some of her family's French holdings, and then she would proceed to Castile to wed the Castilian crown prince, called the Infante. Her ship landed in Bordeaux just as the Black Death broke over the city. Attempts were made to seclude her, but they were in vain. Brought the news of her passing, Edward wrote a sorrow-filled letter to the would-be groom's father, Alfonso:

> Racked with intense sorrows in my heart, I must tell you that grievous death – which spares no one, taking both old and young and reducing the rich and the poor to equals – has seized from us both our dearest daughter, whom we sincerely loved most of all, as befit her great virtues. If we are struck to the core with the sting of bitter sorrow, none can blame us. But we have placed our faith in God, whose hands have held us safe through the gravest dangers. So we give thanks to him that one of our family, free from every stain, whom we have loved so purely, has been sent ahead of us to reign among the choirs of virgins in heaven, where for our sins she can gladly intercede with the Lord.[4]

This connection between England and Castile had not been forgotten in the years since – least of all by Pedro. Now, knowing that he needed help if he was going to have any chance of getting back at Enrique, he sailed for Bordeaux to meet with the man who might have been his brother-in-law: the Black Prince.

In August 1366 the Black Prince, Charles of Navarre and Pedro forged an agreement to restore the crown of Castile. Signed the following month as the Treaty of Libourne, the agreement called for the Black Prince to raise an army to aid Pedro. Charles of Navarre would give this army free passage through the passes in the Pyrenees and into Castile. When it was done, a restored Pedro would pay back all that the Black Prince had spent on the expedition and give him the province surrounding Bilbao. For his troubles, Navarre would receive the Castilian provinces that stood between his lands and the Atlantic, opening up vital sea access for his kingdom.

Raising the army was quick work. The Black Prince called up his considerable personal retinue, along with a groundswell of Gascon soldiers. Joining them were men from far and wide seeking their fortune. Among them were the Free Companies that Enrique had paid off and sent home, who were by now crossing over the Pyrenees on their return to France. When they heard that the Black Prince was raising an army to remove Enrique, they eagerly answered his call in return for promises of yet more Castilian riches. The fact that they had been the ones to put him on that throne mattered to no one at all. Business was business, and their business was war.

All told, the Black Prince's army is said to have numbered some 10,000 men when it marched south for the Pyrenees in January 1367. Some say it was even larger. Enrique had nothing like it in Castile, nor could he possibly raise enough men to counter it.

There was little doubt about the Black Prince's invasion route. Centuries earlier, the Romans had built a road through the mountains to connect their provinces of Aquitaine and Hispania. The modern road between Roncesvalles and Gainekoleta, crossing over what is today called the Ibañeta Pass, is a close approximation of its route.[5] It was along this mountain road that Charlemagne's rearguard was attacked by Basques in 778 in what is called the Battle of Roncesvalles Pass, famously fictionalized in the French epic *The Song of Roland*. A couple of centuries later, the road over Ibañeta had become the preferred route through the mountains for the countless pilgrims making their way from France to the sacred shrine of the Apostle James in Santiago de Compostela. The Camino de Santiago ran from Roncesvalles down the valleys to Pamplona, then westward through Logroño to Burgos, the ancient seat of Castile, before continuing to its ultimate destination in the west. It was, in short, a highway leading straight to where the Black Prince wanted to go.

But the route through the Pyrenees was narrow. It was an ideal place, as Charlemagne had learned, either to ambush an army on the march or to halt it with a relatively small force. This was the reason that Charles the Bad was a necessary signatory to the Black Prince's invasion: Navarre controlled the pass.

Enrique knew the same thing, so as the Black Prince approached the great wall of mountains, Enrique cut his own deal with Charles the Bad: in return for a pile of cash and the transfer of the Castilian city of Logroño to Navarre's control, the passes would be closed. The ever-duplicitous Charles agreed. A furious Black Prince found himself stuck on the north side of the mountain range. Fortunately for him, Hugh Calveley was already on the south side with some 400 cavalry. And although they had just played a crucial role alongside du Guesclin in getting Enrique crowned, their first loyalty was to the Black Prince. Calveley left Enrique's court and led his company against Navarre with frightening speed.

Charles the Bad responded by flipping his position once again and opening the pass. In the end, he rode over it with his 'allies': the Black Prince and Pedro likely wanting him close at hand during the dangerous crossing to keep him from pulling any further stunts.

The Anglo-Castilian army was divided into three divisions.[6] The first started up the pass on 14 February. It was under the command of the Black Prince's younger brother, John of Gaunt, who five years earlier had been made the duke of Lancaster. His wife at the time was pregnant. The child, born in April, would be a son, Henry. As we will see soon enough, he would begin England's Lancastrian dynasty after deposing the son of the Black Prince, Richard, who was himself born just weeks before the army started their arduous climb.

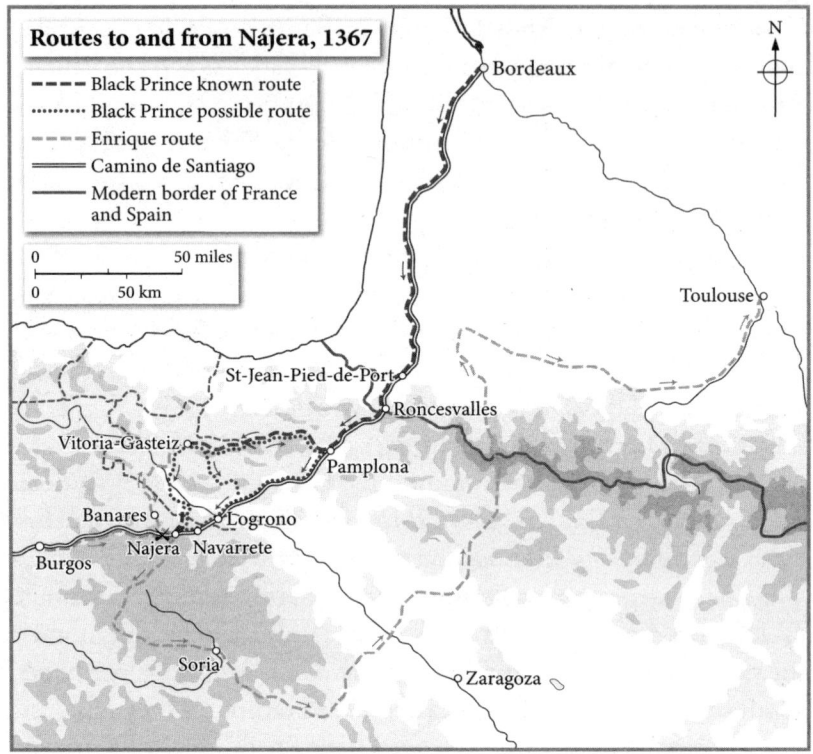

Routes to and from Nájera, 1367

- - - Black Prince known route
.... Black Prince possible route
- - - Enrique route
═══ Camino de Santiago
─── Modern border of France and Spain

0 ——————— 50 miles
0 ——————— 50 km

Bordeaux

Toulouse

St-Jean-Pied-de-Port
Roncesvalles
Vitoria-Gasteiz
Pamplona
Banares
Logrono
Najera Navarrete
Burgos
Soria
Zaragoza

At Gaunt's side as the army headed up into the snow-capped Pyrenees was John Chandos, a veteran of the Crécy campaign, whose herald would later write a poem that provides us with a key source to subsequent events. The Chandos Herald, as we call the unnamed poet, writes of the crossing: 'Since the just God suffered death for us on the cross, there was no such painful passage, for one saw men and horses, that suffered many ills, stumble on the mountain; there was no fellowship; the father made no tarrying for the son; there was cold so great, snow and frost also, that each one was dismayed.'

Among the first questions to be answered in this important campaign is why the Black Prince began it when he did. This was not only a bad time of year to be attempting the high mountain crossing, but also a bad time of year to be conducting any kind of campaign *at all*. Medieval life was largely seasonal, following a cycle of planting crops in spring to be harvested in autumn.

This harvest provided sufficient food to last through the winter. February was precisely the time of year that these supplies were most likely to give out, leaving nothing for the campaigning army to beg, borrow or steal on the march. We don't know who really coined the maxim 'an army marches on its stomach' – it's often attributed to Napoleon – but an army needs food, and February was about the worst time of year to find it.

Most likely, the timing was the result of the absolute necessity of using the Camino de Santiago. If the preceding years had proven anything about Charles the Bad, it was that the king of Navarre was as changeable as the wind that screamed over his mountains: a pass open today might not be open tomorrow, so the army had to get over while it had the chance.

Within days of the army's successful crossing and arrival in Pamplona, Charles would indeed show how unreliable he truly was. He had made a grand show of assuring the Black Prince that he had been on his side all along, offering to add a few hundred fighters to the cause and insisting that he would, in fact, ride all the way to Castile to fight Enrique himself. But on the side, he cut another deal with one of du Guesclin's Breton cousins, Olivier de Mauny, who agreed to fake the capture of Charles during a hunt and then 'imprison' him in Olivier's castle in Borja until the fighting was finished. Remarkably, Charles managed to screw *him* over, too: some weeks later, the king summoned his second son to take his place as a 'hostage' in Borja while he himself went to arrange for the promised transfer of money and lands to Olivier. When the Breton knight came to collect these, Charles seized him and held him prisoner – for real this time – until Olivier agreed to the son's release in return for Olivier's own freedom and no other reward.

Within days of the army's arrival in Pamplona, the Black Prince had decided on the next route of his march, which was head-scratching to say the least. Instead of taking the Camino west into the fertile valley of the River Ebro and following it straight into Castile, the invaders would instead take a slower and more dangerous path northwest towards Vitoria-Gasteiz in the relatively barren Basque Country. The coming weeks would prove this decision a grave and costly mistake, but it ought to have been obvious from the outset. Many English historians have tried to argue that the decision was part of some complex strategic plan – arguing that making the unexpected, clearly wrong move only proves the Black Prince's brilliance[7] – but the more likely truth is that it was masterminded by the ever-treacherous Charles the Bad. Medieval armies on the march relied heavily on local guides, who in this case would have been Navarrese, and beholden to Charles. Sending the invaders on the 'wrong' road up to Vitoria-Gasteiz would not only spare Navarre's fertile heartlands from being stripped of their few remaining supplies, it would also push the soldiers into lands that would become Charles's if Pedro won: the army was, in effect, conquering them for him.

Enrique had meanwhile been gathering his army at Bañares along the Camino de Santiago. Receiving news that his enemy had marched towards Vitoria-Gasteiz, he hastened there and fortified himself south and west of the town, where the route to Castile narrowed between the surrounding mountains. These weren't quite the treacherous passes of the Pyrenees, but they gave Enrique a major tactical advantage just the same. He had a nearly impregnable position on the heights, and without dislodging him the invaders could march no further.

The Black Prince seems to have thought a battle imminent now that the armies were close. He arrayed his forces on the plain and waited for Enrique to come down to fight. Then, he was left waiting. For weeks.

Storms blew through, and the bitter cold might well have been worse for the Anglo-Castilians down on the exposed plains than it was for the Franco-Castilians in the tree-covered mountains. The invaders were already suffering from a lack of food. What had been in short supply when they'd come over the Pyrenees was now all but gone as they held position through the interminable days. When foraging parties were sent out in desperation, many did not return: Enrique's forces seemed to be waiting in ambush in every direction. According to the account of Walter of Peterborough, who might have been present, 'there was scarcely a bean to eat'.

Towards the end of March, the Black Prince grew desperate. If he stayed where he was, his men would starve to death. So he broke camp and made all possible speed for the Camino. We do not know the route he took. A retreat back the way he'd come would have been easiest and safest, but there is some evidence that he might have taken one of several narrow tracks southward over the mountains.[8] One way or another, the Black Prince's army made it to the valley of the Ebro. On 1 April, it reached the southern bank of that river, following the Camino across a stone bridge in the city of Logroño. The next day he advanced to the village of Navarrete.

A clash now loomed. Enrique blocked his advance, as the Franco-Castilian army had taken up position in the small town of Nájera, ten miles ahead. The pilgrimage route between them – walked by so many seeking peace – would soon enough run red with blood.

Battle of Nájera, 1367

Enrique had managed a tremendously effective campaign to this point. Though he was outnumbered, he had used the landscape as a force multiplier. If the Black Prince had cried foul – insulting his honour for staying in the mountains at Vitoria-Gasteiz, for instance – Enrique had managed to ignore the baiting. His army was in good shape, and his enemies were tired, hungry and demoralized.

Enrique's new position should have allowed him to continue this strategy. Instead of mountain passes, the line of defence would now be the River Najerilla, which flows into the Ebro. Fed by the wet weather and the spring run-off from the mountains to the south, it was a torrent, running high and angry. The west bank of the Najerilla is a steep line of bluffs, giving any defender a superb high ground from which to control the approach on the road. With the ways around this obstacle blocked by rugged mountains to the south and the even wider Ebro to the north, an army perched here would be nearly impossible to dislodge. There was only one easy way across: a bridge at the little village of Nájera. All Enrique needed to do was to hold the small bridge – or collapse it – and his enemy would once more be trapped.

All of this makes what happened next genuinely puzzling. Despite holding such ideal ground, Enrique did not dig in. Instead, he marched his outnumbered army across the narrow bridge over the Najerilla and out onto the wide, flat plain east of the river, where he could meet his enemy on open ground.

In the early hours of 3 April, the Black Prince's army set out from Navarrete, marching west. Standard accounts of the battle rely on the Chandos Herald, who says that the English 'did not go the most direct road, but took the road to the right hand. They descended a mountain and a big valley, all on horseback, so nobly arrayed and in such fair close order that it was marvelous to behold.' Though no other sources mention this 'mountain', scholars have accepted its validity and presumed it to be the prominence rising just west of Navarrete. As one famous historian has concluded, the manoeuvre of going around the mountain even meant that 'the Prince achieved complete tactical surprise'.[9]

This is greatly overstating the case, I think. It is almost ten miles along the Camino from Navarrete to Nájera, with a 500-foot elevation gain halfway along the route. For the common, well-fed hiker following the paved road today, this would take roughly three and a half hours in good shoes. The Black Prince's men were already exhausted from a lack of food, shelter and rest on their long campaign, and now they were being asked to make this march in their full kit, potentially with the need to fight a battle immediately at the end of the journey. Taking the route around the mountain would add nearly three miles and another 100 feet of elevation gain to the task – the majority likely over broken terrain. This would not be wise.

Enrique knew full well that the Black Prince was marching from Navarrete. This was the reason Enrique had advanced onto the relatively flat landscape east of Nájera. He would have had scouts keeping watch – presumably some on the mountain between the two armies – in addition to spotters amid the camp-followers still on the bluffs he had left behind west of the Najerilla. And even if *none* of these were in place – which would have been a truly astounding failure of basic military tactics – the aforementioned flat plain stretches well away from Nájera before it meets the kind of foothills that could even conceivably begin to hide an army of 10,000 men and their many horses, not to mention the dust and noise of their coming. The Chandos Herald himself describes it as 'a fair and beauteous plain, whereon was neither bush nor tree for a full league around'.

Far more likely, the Black Prince followed the Camino for most of his march in order to keep his army as fresh as possible for the fight. The descent of the 'mountain' indicates a manoeuvre in the foothills near the village of Huércanos today, perhaps a mile from where Enrique's forces were likely arrayed in front of Nájera: Du Guesclin commanded a centre vanguard awaiting them, with the main body of the army, commanded by Enrique, gathered behind him. To either side were wings of mounted cavalry; the one on the left was led by one of Enrique's brothers, Don Tello.

Just as the Black Prince's earlier mistake was clear as soon as he decided to march to Vitoria-Gasteiz, Enrique's mistake was clear the moment he moved across the Najerilla to attempt this pitched battle. So why did he do it?

Pedro López de Ayala fought for Enrique at the Battle of Nájera, carrying the banner of the Order of the Sash – a Castilian counterpart to the Order of the Garter. He would later compose an extraordinary chronicle of his experience. Regarding Enrique's move out onto the open ground, 'this decision weighed heavily on many who were with him', Ayala reports, 'because the earlier position gave them a greater advantage than where they afterwards encamped. But Don Enrique was a man with a great heart and great strength and said he wanted to fight the battle on flat ground without any advantage.'

Most historians blame Enrique for the decision to advance, suggesting that if he didn't man up and fight, he was in danger of losing the respect of his men, the war and perhaps the crown.[10] In this explanation, Enrique might have wanted to maintain a defensive posture, but he felt that his only choice was to roll the dice on the bad odds of a bold attack. According to Ayala, when Enrique was still in Bañares at the start of the campaign, du Guesclin and another French knight, Marshal d'Audenham, told Enrique not to fight a pitched battle with the English. In response, the chronicler writes, the Iberian members of 'the council, who were diligent in his service, told him that if he showed any hesitation about giving battle he could be certain that the majority of the realm would desert him and go over to King Pedro... King Enrique accepted this counsel and told the French knights that it would be very dangerous to seem unwilling to fight.' Behind his high-minded chivalric pronouncements, in other words, were real-world political concerns.

But if this was the sense of things at Bañares, why had Enrique followed the French advice through the following weeks? And why, after those weeks had more than proved the advice both prudent and effective, was it such a sudden concern that the king needed to abandon the strategy in favour of a desperate gamble at Nájera? It doesn't add up.

A rather different picture emerges from a French work called the *Du Guesclin Memoirs*, which says that on the eve of battle du Guesclin was still advising delay, telling Enrique

> not to take risks since famine alone could reduce this great army which would soon be destroyed by it. He made [Enrique] understand that they had only to entrench themselves behind a ditch and place the wagons in front of them and with these two precautions they would be completely inaccessible to their enemies. Before three days were over, they would see them disband and separate from one another to go in search of the wherewithal [i.e. the food] to live in a distant country. And then, when they were dispersed and marching about without order or discipline and weakened by hunger, [the Spanish] could fall upon them and not leave any standing.

At this, however, an Iberian count objects, accusing du Guesclin of being a coward. This so affronts the Breton knight that he 'took an oath that he would fight and that on the following day, there would be a battle'. What's more, the *Memoirs* says that du Guesclin, not Enrique, made the actual plan the next day. The decision to array Enrique's men for battle 'with a river at their back' was made specifically because the Breton had no confidence in their willingness to fight the English. Forcing them to fight or die would 'make them give up any desire to flee and inspire them to fight well'.

When it comes to the fighting that day, we know that much of Enrique's army did indeed cut and run. The *Memoirs* is unquestionably biased in du Guesclin's favour and written with no small amount of hindsight, so it is unsurprising that it has du Guesclin 'predicting' this eventuality. But bias doesn't necessarily mean falsehood. It is hard to see why the *Memoirs* would depict du Guesclin directing battle arrangements for the losing effort, unless it were true and so well known that it could not be swept under the rug.

If it really was du Guesclin's decision to take the field, it must surely have been because he thought he could win. And the reason he would have thought that is that this is not the first time we have seen an outnumbered army take a forward position on the 'wrong' side of a narrow bridge with the river at their backs and then win. This is exactly what had happened at the Battle of Cocherel, just three years earlier, where du Guesclin had arguably won his greatest victory over the Captal de Buch – the very same man who now led the wing on the Black Prince's right at Nájera, the one facing Don Tello's on the far northern side of the battlefield.

But if du Guesclin hoped he could repeat at Nájera the feigned retreat that had won his fight at Cocherel, he was sorely disappointed. The command and control necessary for a feigned retreat is hard to manage under the best of circumstances. At Nájera, du Guesclin was in command of a multilingual force, which considerably complicated things.

Whatever the Breton commander intended, the battle's tempo got away from him. According to Ayala, a group of Castilians switched sides from Enrique to Pedro, prompting Enrique to start the battle before more of his strength could be lost. Likely seeing it as a great opportunity, Gaunt called out 'Forward! Forward, banner!' and the English vanguard under his command came straight at du Guesclin.[11] Overhead, volleys of English arrows slashed through the sky. Whether to get out from under this hellish rain of death or to recapture some advantage of his own, du Guesclin ordered his division to charge forward into melee combat.

As the Captal de Buch surged ahead on the far right of the English formation, Don Tello buckled under the onslaught. 'He and those with him', Ayala says, 'did not wait, but withdrew from the field in complete flight.' Some of the Captal's men no doubt gave chase, but most wheeled inward – driving straight into Enrique's left flank.

On the opposite side of the field, more English arrows were plunging into Enrique's right wing. It held longer than his left, but the killing points were too much. Enrique rode back and forth trying to keep his disintegrating lines together, but his men and their units were turning and running. All the while, the Black Prince was pressing his victorious wings against du Guesclin and the Franco-Castilian centre.

Order collapsed, and in the terrible chaos, the backbone of Enrique's army finally snapped. Most of the men fled for the bridge at Nájera, but it was only so wide. They clawed at each other to escape, trampling one another when they fell. Behind them came the army of the Black Prince, blades swinging like scythes cutting through ready wheat. Walter of Peterborough wrote that, in coming years, 'a thousand hacked-up body parts would be brought to light by the plough'. Of the advancing carnage he wrote:

> You would not believe the enormity of the slaughter,
> How many arms, legs, and feet are trampled upon.
> The Spanish give way, spitting their lives with blood,
> They change their position, trying to stop the damage.
> They close ranks, standing side by side,
> So densely packed that they cannot even fall in death…
> …
> From this hour, the English strike in front and behind,
> Like wolves upon cattle. Death comes without delay.
> Mouths, chins, eyes, our men dig out from it up to their knees,
> Butchering the people among the thorny plants on the field.[12]

When it was finished, thousands were dead. Those who weren't massacred in the rout were drowned in the raging waters under the bridge. 'The fear that gave them wings,' the *Memoirs* says, 'made many of them throw themselves into the river where the water suffocated them, preferring to let themselves drown rather than experience the pain caused by dying on the point of a lance or sword.'

All told, more than half of Enrique's army was lost. The Chandos Herald puts the death count at 7,700 men. The Black Prince's side suffered minimal losses in comparison.

The count of prisoners taken was nearly as large as the count of the dead. Among them was du Guesclin, once again in need of ransom.[13] Remarkably, the greatest prize of them all – Enrique himself – escaped both harm and capture. When all hope was lost, it appears that he fled up into the mountains rather than towards the river. He reached Aragon, and from there made his way back to France.

With Enrique's army annihilated and resistance to Pedro seemingly non-existent, all that remained was to settle the accounts of du Guesclin – who still owed money on his *prior* ransom – and stop vengeful Pedro from executing any Castilian prisoners he could find. Though retribution might seem politically expedient, the Black Prince knew that murdered men bought little in ransom. To head off escalating cycles of killing, the courts sorted out settlements for the complicated ransom cases, and on 7 April, Pedro entered Burgos to the public proclamation that he was king of Castile once more.

But things fell apart as soon as the Black Prince asked Pedro to hold up his end of the bargain. According to the terms of the Treaty of Libourne, the Black Prince expected lordship of lands and castles around Bilbao, as well as reimbursement for the great expenditures he had incurred to restore Pedro's crown.

This was beyond Pedro's means. Enrique had blown most of Castile's treasury paying off the mercenary army that he'd used to secure the throne almost exactly a year earlier – many of whose payees now stood ready to double-dip for payment getting it back. The Black Prince offered to take additional castles as a guarantee of future payment when the Castilian treasury filled up once more, but Pedro refused to let a sliver of Castilian real estate leave his hands, including what he had promised in the Treaty of Libourne. He agreed to produce at least partial payment on his debt, though, and he left for the southern parts of his kingdom ostensibly to begin collection.

For four months, the Black Prince and his army waited, spending still more money to sustain themselves. The summer heat brought to the English camps a wave of dysentery so punishing that chronicler Henry Knighton claimed that 'scarce one man in five returned to England'. Meanwhile, word had it that Pedro was carrying out a series of reprisals against anyone he thought disloyal.

When news arrived that Enrique had been welcomed back in France and was building a new army that could threaten a defenceless Gascony, the Black Prince had seen enough. The army packed up camp and began the long march back through the Pyrenees to home.

Tides Turn, 1367–70

King Charles was more than ready to support Enrique's efforts to gather a new army to re-reconquer Castile from the anti-French Pedro, whose cruelty and perfidy won him no new friends. Before the year was out, this force had crossed the Pyrenees, and Castile fell into a difficult civil war, with Enrique's position steadily improving. Among the many allies helping him was none other than Bertrand du Guesclin, who had secured his own ransom and release in January 1368.

By March 1369, Pedro had retreated to the hilltop castle of Montiel. Under false pretences, du Guesclin lured Pedro out of the castle and into a tent in the surrounding encampment. Enrique surprised him there. He stabbed his half-brother to death, earning himself not just the crown of Castile but the epithet 'the Fratricidal'.

The very thing that had brought Englishmen marching over the Pyrenees – fear of a French-allied king upon its throne – was now a certainty. Enrique would not forget his debts to France. In the coming years, Castilian fleets would be brought to bear against English ships and English trading routes – including the important one between Gascony and England – with devastating effects.

The consequences of the Black Prince's 'victory' in the Nájera campaign didn't end there. Pedro left behind a formidable array of unpaid expenses, leaving the Black Prince little choice but to levy taxes on the subjects of Gascony. Furious at the imposition, men like the count of Armagnac, who still regarded themselves as subjects of the French crown, took their frustrations to King Charles in Paris.

By the terms of the Treaty of Brétigny, the French king ought to have had no say in the matter. But Charles did not appreciate Edward III's refusal to formally renounce his claim to the French throne. He resented the English and Gascon-led Free Companies' campaigns of terror against the French people. And he simply did not like the Treaty of Brétigny, which not only took away lands that ought to have been his, but left him still paying the bill for his dead father's enormous ransom.

The French king recognized that the balance of power was shifting. Edward was no longer the active man he'd been, the Black Prince's star had fallen considerably, the once mighty Gascony was for all intents bankrupt and Castile was soon to be a staunch French ally. All the while, Charles was not only refilling his treasury but also populating his command with men like du Guesclin fresh from the battlefields of Iberia. All the king needed was an excuse to resume war with England, and Armagnac's complaint about the Black Prince's tax was a perfect opportunity.

On 25 January 1369, Charles summoned the Black Prince to appear in Paris to address the Gascon complaints. The Black Prince was livid. Kings of France had given these kinds of orders to the English rulers of Gascony before, but the Treaty of Brétigny should have put an end to such practices. The Black Prince fumed that, if Charles had the audacity to suggest that he only held Gascony under the sovereignty of France, he may as well arrive at the hearing wearing armour with an army in tow. In the end, he simply refused to show. Charles responded by declaring the Black Prince's lands forfeit to the French crown.

The Treaty of Brétigny was effectively shredded. The Two Hundred Years War was back on.

Charles is very often celebrated for learning from the mistakes of his predecessors. The experiences of men like du Guesclin helped him put into place a new approach to the war with England. Rather than insisting on large, pitched battles – fights like Crécy and Poitiers, which had gone rather poorly for the French – he was more than happy to conduct a war of attrition by seizing small opportunities. He understood that while a single sword stroke could kill a man, so could a thousand papercuts. It was slow, methodical, but devastatingly effective.

Even so, Charles's initial strategy was a bold one, intended to pummel the English from every conceivable angle. First, he encouraged former French holdings in Aquitaine to throw off the English yoke and refuse to pay taxes, siphoning strength from the Black Prince and furthering his financial problems. While these internal wounds festered, Charles would create new external ones: two of his brothers – Louis, the duke of Anjou, and Jean, the duke of Berry – would begin attacks along the Black Prince's border. All the while, every effort would be made to help his third brother, Philippe the Bold, the duke of Burgundy, to gather a fleet of ships at the mouth of the Seine. That fleet, in September, would invade England.

It went well at first. Parts of Aquitaine began to burn, and the Black Prince had a hard time extinguishing the flames. Despite his bravado, the Black Prince was in increasingly bad health. Contemporary evidence shows that he took ill in November 1368, and that his health took a dramatic turn the following February.[14] His frequent absences crippled the defence of his lands.

His brother, John of Gaunt, attempted to step into the vacuum. In July, as the army of the duke of Burgundy was gathering on the Seine between Rouen and Harfleur, Gaunt arrived in Calais with a small force. His plan was to relieve some of the pressure in the southwest by attacking French holdings from the northeast – an initiative made more urgent by the news that the French had overrun Ponthieu. Gaunt's ride out of Calais surprised the French, who had no real force in place to stop him. So Philippe

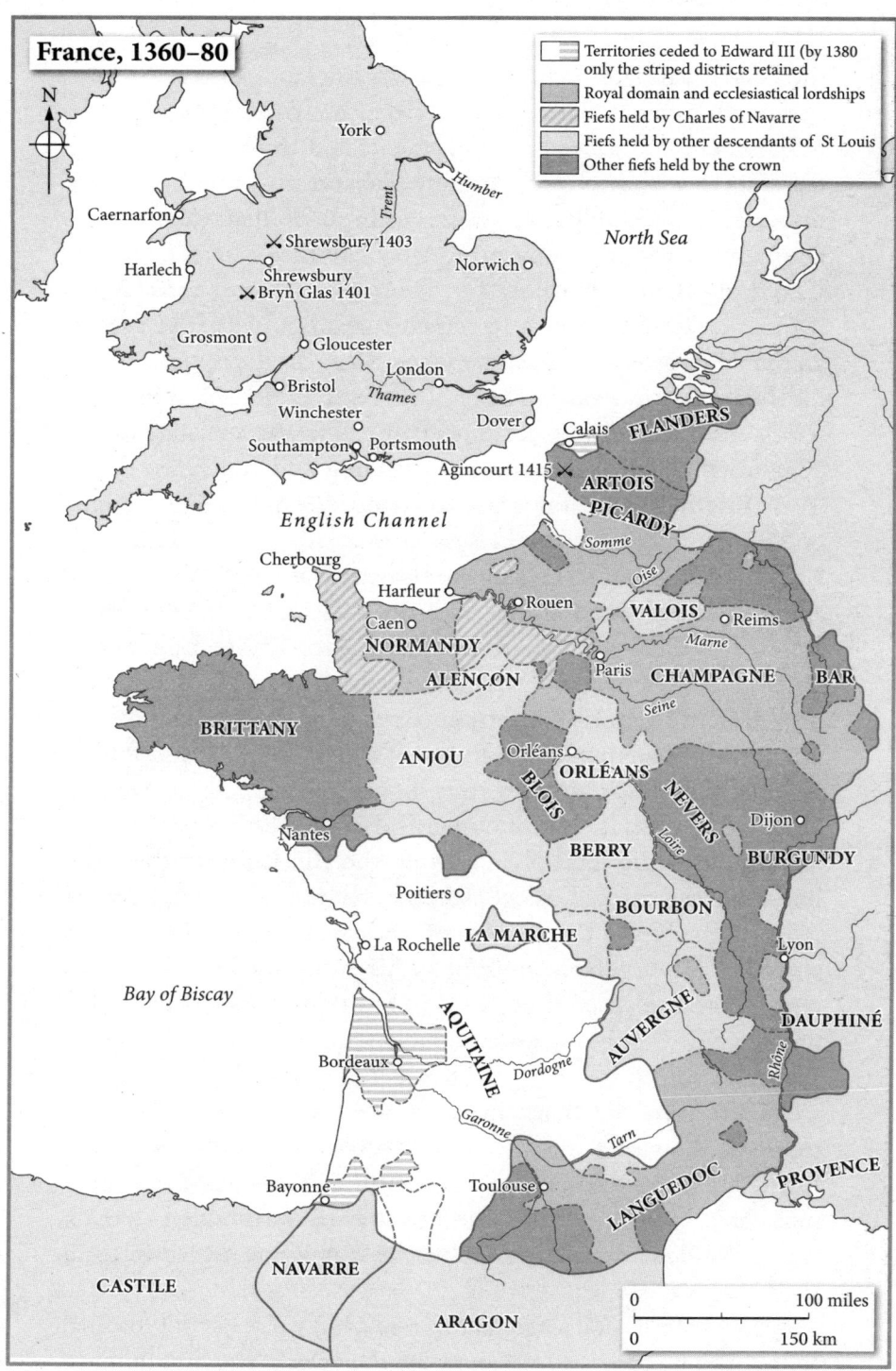

France, 1360–80

N

York

Caernarfon

Harlech

✕ Shrewsbury 1403

Shrewsbury
✕ Bryn Glas 1401

Norwich

Grosmont   Gloucester

London

Bristol   Thames
Winchester   Dover
Southampton Portsmouth   Calais
Agincourt 1415 ✕

English Channel

Cherbourg

Harfleur   Rouen

Caen

NORMANDY

ALENÇON

Paris

BRITTANY

Nantes

ANJOU

BLOIS ORLÉANS
Orléans

BERRY

Poitiers

La Rochelle   LA MARCHE

Bay of Biscay

AQUITAINE

Bordeaux   Dordogne

Garonne

Bayonne   Toulouse

CASTILE   NAVARRE

ARAGON

North Sea

FLANDERS

ARTOIS

PICARDY
Somme

Oise

VALOIS   Reims

Marne

CHAMPAGNE   BAR

Seine

NEVERS

Dijon

BOURBON   BURGUNDY

AUVERGNE   Lyon

DAUPHINÉ

Rhône

Tarn

LANGUEDOC   PROVENCE

Trent

Humber

Loire

Territories ceded to Edward III (by 1380 only the striped districts retained)
Royal domain and ecclesiastical lordships
Fiefs held by Charles of Navarre
Fiefs held by other descendants of St Louis
Other fiefs held by the crown

0   100 miles
0   150 km

the Bold's army didn't board ships for England. Instead, it hurried north to block the road from Calais to Thérouanne. After an impasse, Gaunt received reinforcements and Burgundy made the decision to withdraw and partially disband his army – whether due to England's military pressures or his own financial pressures is unknown. By now well informed of France's invasion plans, Gaunt marched to Harfleur and spent several weeks attacking it before disease forced him to retreat towards Calais. The French all the while struck at the army when they had the opportunity.

There was no rush for large-scale battles. No one wanted to repeat the disasters of Crécy and Poitiers. It was a change of approach with lasting ramifications. This renewed 'hot' phase of the Two Hundred Years War is characterized by a risk-averse patience on the part of the French. Progress was steady but not flashy.

For the English, this change in strategy was marked by a steady string of losses. Among the casualties was Chandos, who fell at Lussac-les-Châteaux, where the Roman road from Limoges to Poitiers crossed a bridge over the Vienne. The wily commander used this wet-gap crossing to entrap a French company on the last day of 1369, but over the course of the fighting, Chandos took a sword to the face, perhaps after slipping or tripping on his own long winter coat. It took him many hours to die.

Furious at the multiplying losses, the Black Prince drew the line when the city of Limoges surrendered to the duke of Berry in August. The loss of this important strategic position, as well as its revenues, was a personal affront to his authority. He resolved to retake it at once, even though his ill health had by now worsened to the point that he was occasionally required to be carried in a litter.

By the time the Black Prince arrived with more than 3,000 men, the duke of Berry had moved on. Even augmented by the town's militia, the remaining French garrison were probably outnumbered some ten to one. But the city was surrounded by thick walls. The defenders inside locked the gates and settled in for a siege.

We've seen several sieges in this book, but we've not yet stopped to talk about what they are and how they work. The first thing to understand is how active a siege is. Compared to the grand, cinematic sweeps of attacks and counterattacks in a battle, medieval sieges can *seem* passive, but they're actually highly dynamic.

Starvation is the most obvious weapon for besiegers, but cutting off food or water requires active and ongoing work. Disease is another obvious weapon, but disease can threaten both sides in such a struggle – to keep the siege active, after all, both attacker and defender need to remain in one place. Thanks to these dangers – and the fact that time is money – besiegers very often took active steps to end a siege as fast as possible by assaulting the target. This was *very* active indeed, because it meant going over, through or under the walls.

Each choice was costly and difficult. Over required ladders and siege towers to get atop the walls and fight the men defending them. Through required artillery or rams to breach the gates, or traitors to unlock them. Under required sappers to dig through the earth and rock below the walls, usually with the aim of helping the attackers go through the walls at the surface by weakening the foundations of the wall enough to cause a breach.

Because no one knew which tactic might work, besiegers often used all of them at once. This was certainly the case with Limoges in 1370. As soon as his men had invested the city, the Black Prince was working on ways to get inside, including sappers, who began their dark, dangerous work of attempting to mine under the walls. As soon as they began doing this, miners inside the city began the work of digging counter-mines, with the intention of intercepting the in-progress mines and killing the sappers. It was a cat-and-mouse game, played out in the cramped darkness under the earth.

The English sappers had succeeded in opening a significant void under one part of the wall by the evening of 18 September. It had been frightful work, as the men had used timbers to support the tunnel and chamber that they were digging out, and they were forced to hack away in the dark, praying that the groaning timbers wouldn't give way under the weight pressing down from above.

Now that the space was big enough, they *wanted* it to come

down. So they painted the wood with flammable oils and grease and filled the spaces between with kindling. Then they set it all on fire, trusting the flames to consume the wooden supports and bring it all crashing to the ground – hopefully with the walls above, too.

It worked. On the morning of 19 September, a significant section of the wall came thundering down. As soon as there was a breach, the Black Prince's men came screaming over the rubble, clambering through the dust and debris to get inside. Some worked to establish a kind of beachhead in the city as desperate defenders inside surged to the point of the collapse. Other attackers raced for the nearest gates to open them and let still more men inside. The full weight of the Black Prince's army soon poured into Limoges.

What came next is known most famously from Froissart's dramatic account:

> These were pitiful scenes. Men, women and children flung themselves on their knees before the prince crying: 'Have mercy on us, gentle sir!' But he was so inflamed with anger that he would not listen. Neither man nor woman was heeded, but all who could be found were put to the sword, including many who were in no way to blame. I do not understand how they could have failed to take pity on people who were too unimportant to have committed treason. Yet they paid for it, and paid more dearly than the leaders who had committed it. There is no man so hard-hearted that, if he had been in Limoges on that day, and had remembered God, he would not have wept bitterly at the fearful slaughter which took place. More than three thousand persons, men, women and children, were dragged out to have their throats cut. May God receive their souls, for they were true martyrs… The City of Limoges was pillaged and sacked without mercy, then burnt and utterly destroyed.[15]

Though these brutal images have haunted the reputation of the Black Prince, we should take care not to read them literally. There were not, for instance, 3,000 people *in* this part of Limoges to be slaughtered in the first place. Nor is it likely that the Black Prince would willingly damage the city beyond what was necessary to take control of it. Rampant destruction would harm the city's long-term ability to provide money and strategic advantage, both of which the prince badly needed. In fact, contemporary reports and some materials quite recently discovered reveal that there was no mass execution of civilians *at all*. Almost all the deaths came from the military task of taking the city, and the total dead was closer to 300 at most: 100 members of the garrison were killed, along with 200 members of the militia and some small number of civilians who fell in the chaos.[16] Whether Froissart or some copyist along the line added a zero to the body count – making 3,000 out of 300 – we may never know.

The Black Prince had won his victory, but he would not have time to enjoy it. Back in Bordeaux, his eldest and namesake son had taken ill with a reoccurrence of the plague. Before the month was out, the five-year-old was dead. Already weakened by his own illness, the Black Prince was broken by the loss. His doctors advised he travel to England with his wife and infant son, Richard. He would never return.

Battle of Pontvallain, 1370

More dark news for the English cause followed.

Du Guesclin had returned to the court of Charles, and the king of France had decided to name him as constable – a position that gave him military superiority over all but the king himself. The coming years would prove it a brilliant appointment. Long a brave warrior, able tactician and effective leader of men, du Guesclin had learned patience during his time south of the Pyrenees.

Du Guesclin also had his own eye for talent. Around the same time, he and Charles brought in a man who'd been an enemy to them both: Olivier V de Clisson. He was the son of the Breton lord Olivier IV de Clisson, who had been executed by King Philippe VI in 1343, and whose widow had become the fierce Lionesse of Brittany. The younger Clisson, from the age of seven, had been a sworn enemy of the French – and, when he grew old enough, a very effective one. He had commanded the right wing of the Montfortist lines at Auray in 1364, and it might well have been his battle plan that was followed to victory that day. Amid the melee he lost an eye, earning him one of his two epithets: the one-eyed man of Auray. His other epithet, given to him by his enemies, was simpler: the Butcher.

Though Clisson had served English interests well, he felt slighted by the returns he received for his service. When Charles offered him far more substantial rewards, he agreed to serve his cause. On 24 October, just a few weeks after du Guesclin had been named constable, he and Clisson made a written pact, sometimes called the Oath of Pontorson. In it, they swore to defend each other as brothers, to attack any who acted against one or both of them (with the exceptions of the king and other men to whom they owed allegiance), to keep each other informed of all rumours about one another, and to split equally any and all earnings from ransoms and rewards. Clisson thereby became a trusted right-hand man to du Guesclin in a brotherhood of arms, and the two men set about raising an army in Caen.[17]

The new constable's first target would be an English army that had been conducting a *chevauchée* between Calais and Paris. Nominally under the command of Sir Robert Knolles, a veteran leader in the War of the Breton Succession and Nájera, the army many thousands strong had been on the Continent since August. After marching out from Calais, they had raided up to Paris and then moved on towards Gascony. When news came that du Guesclin was headed to intercept them with the French forces at his command, Knolles advised a retreat up into the safety of Brittany. The other leaders refused, and the army fragmented into several smaller forces. On 4 December, du Guesclin pounced on one of these at Pontvallain. It was a significant victory, and it was closely followed by his destruction of a second part of Knolles's army at Vaas.

Knolles and the remaining English were hounded across the countryside, units picked off in opportunistic assaults, until they could reach the safety of firmly English holdings. The Battle of Pontvallain was a win not just in terms of enemy killed or captured, but also in terms of morale. It was the first major battlefield victory that the French had managed over the English in France.

Battle of La Rochelle, 1371–72

When Pedro of Castile had departed Bordeaux on the Nájera campaign in 1367, he'd left behind two daughters. Upon his death at the hands of Enrique, the eldest of these daughters became his undisputed heir. Her name was Constanza, and in September 1371 she was married to John of Gaunt, the duke of Lancaster and now, with the departure of the Black Prince, the man in control of Aquitaine. Her younger sister, Isabela, married his younger brother, Edmund of Langley, the duke of York. The third and fourth sons of Edward III had now married the two surviving heirs to Pedro's claim to the throne of Castile.

The union between the two houses had the possibility of being enormously beneficial. The sisters' only hope of dislodging the usurper Enrique from Castile was with the potential backing of England. Likewise, as the third son of Edward, Gaunt had no great prospect for his own ambition, but with Constanza he had the chance to be a king. More than that, he had a chance to be the man who brought the Iberian kingdom's power back into the service of England and not its enemies.

By the end of January 1372, Gaunt had already proclaimed himself king of Castile in his wife's name, and the next month he organized a dramatic royal entry for her into London. From this point forward, he was addressed as 'Monseigneur d'Espagne'. His determination to make good on this claim would consume much of the rest of his life, often to the detriment of more realistic goals.

This isn't to say that Gaunt was tilting at windmills. Enrique had made many enemies by seizing control in Castile – both within the kingdom's borders and around them. Many were willing to pledge their loyalty to Constanza's claim. Had England committed to a major assault on Castile – a refashioning of the Nájera campaign – Gaunt might have had his crown. Neither motive nor opportunity stood in the way. England just didn't have the means to undertake a successful war in Iberia, not with so many active fronts in France. As it stood, and as Gaunt knew first-hand, Aquitaine itself was on the ropes.

The problem was money. England's tax base fell far short of what either France or Castile could boast. And Gaunt's claim to Enrique's throne made certain that he would not face either power alone. Whatever else he thought he was doing in seeking a crown, Gaunt succeeded in bringing a significant fleet of Castilian ships into the service of the king of France. These ships would make an almost immediate impact.

For some time now, du Guesclin had been carefully tightening French control in Poitou, and it was clear to all that he had his eyes on La Rochelle. This seaport had been a significant concession in the Treaty of Brétigny. The English wanted it then for the same reason the French wanted it now: it directly threatened the sea route between England and Gascony. Aware of the threat, Edward ordered the earl of Pembroke to reinforce La Rochelle with men and supplies. The earl brought with him only a small army, but he was given enough cash to hire a few thousand more men when he got ashore. A small fleet was assembled to get it all across the sea. The journey went smoothly, right up to the point when Pembroke caught sight of La Rochelle on 21 June – and the Castilian fleet lying in wait for him.

The precise number of ships – and their exact types – is un-certain, but the Castilian fleet had more vessels on their side. For all Pembroke knew, still more might arrive. He gambled on run-ning the blockade to reach the harbour. The Castilian admiral was ready. His ships came forward, closing the gap on the English.

Fighting was hard. A couple of English ships were lost. As night fell, the two sides withdrew to anchor. The Castilians still blocked the harbour. Then, overnight, as wind and tide pressed the heavily laden English into shallow waters, the Castilian admiral pounced. The French *Chronicle of the First Four Valois Kings* de-scribes what happened next:

> The next day, at the rising of the sun and the tide, the sea was still so low that the English ships did not float. The Spanish came back at them, fast and fierce, and they tried hard to attack the

English ships with fire and oil. The battle there was hard and heavy. The English defended themselves very vigorously, but they had no way to guard themselves when they saw their ships all engulfed in fire. It was a horrible thing to hear, the tumult and the noise – both from the flames and from the terror of the horses burning in the holds of the ships… It was a great destruction and death of men and horses: so many burned, drowned, shot. Many leaped into the sea, driven mad by the fire upon their skin. Many of those who set out on small boats from La Rochelle to rescue the English were killed or drowned.[18]

It was a total Castilian victory. Those ships from the English fleet that could be salvaged and made useful were seized by the Castilians. The rest were burned to the waterline. Alongside a couple of hundred officers and lords, Pembroke was captured with his treasury. Without these much-needed reinforcements, there would be no resurgence of English strength in La Rochelle, no great force to stand against du Guesclin.

As news of what happened at La Rochelle spread, more and more people flocked to the French side. Poitiers fell. So did La Rochelle itself. By the end of the year, du Guesclin was conducting mop-up operations in Poitou, Saintonge and Angoumois. In Brittany, Jean de Montfort had at last thrown his lot in with the English just in time to find the French free to turn their growing strength against him. He tried to claim that he'd only been working with the English in order to counter the strength of Olivier de Clisson, with whom he shared a long-standing feud. The capture of a treaty he'd negotiated with Edward told a different tale, however, and the duke quickly found himself holding on to only a few pieces of his great duchy.

For the English, still more losses were to come.

Gaunt's Chevauchée, 1373–74

All winter, the English planned for a new year of campaigning in 1373: a great army, it was thought, could turn their fortunes around in Aquitaine. But how to get it there? The disaster at La Rochelle had made the idea of sailing there near impossible, so the fallback plan was to land in Brittany and march from there, aiding its beleaguered duke along the way. But even as plans were being made, Jean de Montfort showed up in England, cast out by the Bretons he was supposed to rule. Pockets of the duchy were still in his hands, including the vital port at Brest, but getting there might not be easy. The Castilian ships could be anywhere.

The latest English army instead landed at Calais, under Gaunt's command. With him were nearly 10,000 men and the exiled duke of Brittany, as well as multiple earls and veteran captains like Calveley. Montfort was no doubt hoping that they would march across Normandy to recover his duchy. The French certainly seem to have thought this was the plan, and they had prepared accordingly.

By every indication, though, Gaunt went where he'd planned to go all along: leaving Calais, his army would weaken France on a march intended to reinforce Aquitaine. From there, he probably still hoped to make a move for the throne of Castile, which would not just enrich him personally but also make safe the seas for England. Enrique was not blind to this desire. He knew Gaunt only had two remotely realistic invasion routes. One was over the Pyrenees, following in the tracks of the Black Prince during the Nájera campaign. This meant working with the notorious Charles of Navarre. The other was to go through the ports of Portugal, which meant working with its king, Fernando, who could make his own distant claim to the Castilian throne through his great-grandfather.

Yet while Gaunt's force was still preparing for its march, Enrique carried out a devastating pre-emptive strike on Portugal. This resulted in the Treaty of Santarém, in which Fernando agreed to stand with Castile and France against the English. Withdrawing from Portugal, Enrique marched to face down Navarre. Its king also capitulated. The news only seems to have hardened Gaunt's resolve to get to Bordeaux. From there, he still hoped to find some other means of making good on his claim.

Getting to Bordeaux would not be easy, though. The city was over 500 miles away by the straightest roads, but those ran

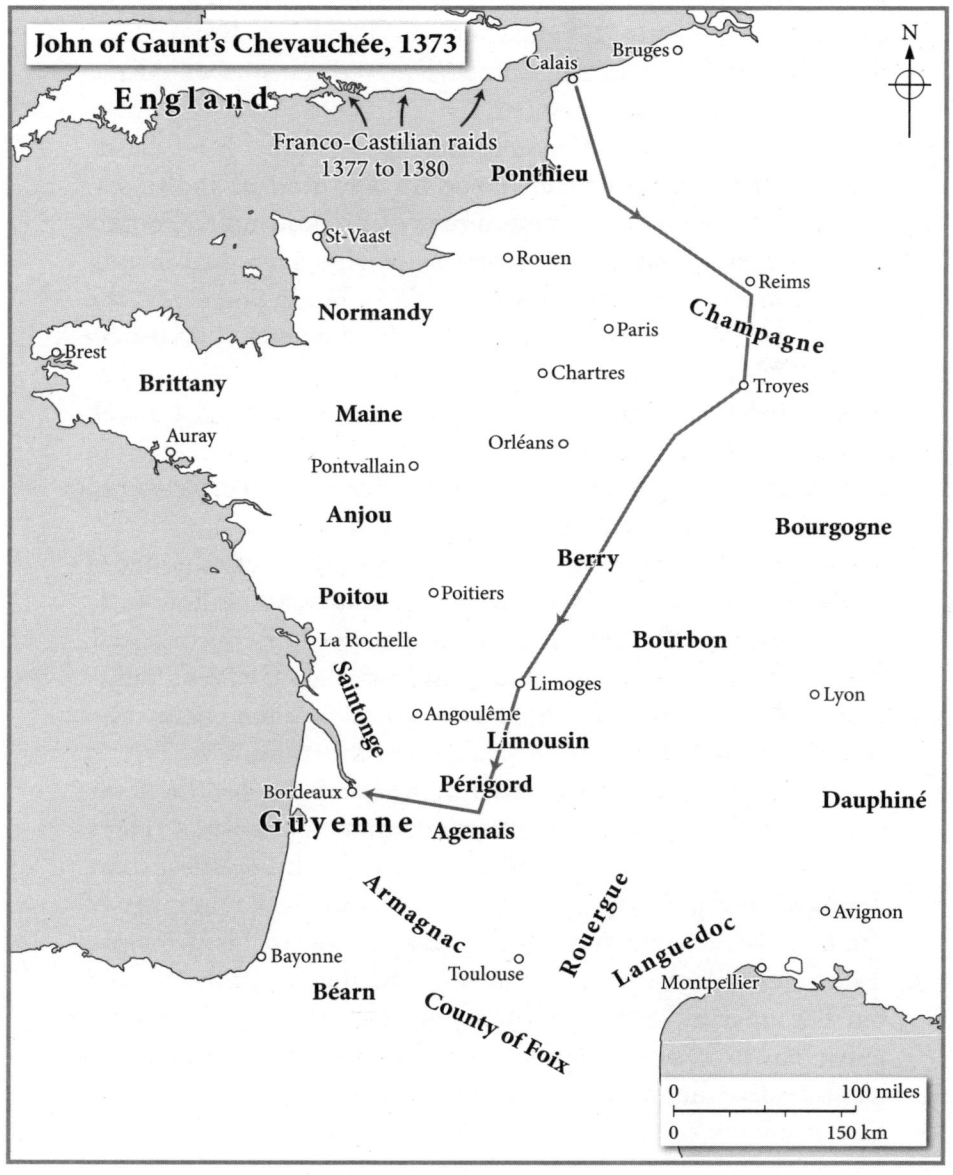

John of Gaunt's Chevauchée, 1373

England

N

Calais
Bruges

Franco-Castilian raids
1377 to 1380

Ponthieu

St-Vaast

Rouen

Reims

Normandy

Paris

Champagne

Brest

Chartres

Troyes

Brittany

Maine

Auray

Orléans

Pontvallain

Anjou

Bourgogne

Berry

Poitou

Poitiers

Bourbon

La Rochelle

Limoges

Lyon

Saintonge

Angoulême

Limousin

Bordeaux

Périgord

Dauphiné

Guyenne

Agenais

Armagnac

Rouergue

Avignon

Bayonne

Toulouse

Languedoc

Montpellier

Béarn

County of Foix

| 0 | | 100 miles |
| 0 | | 150 km |

through Paris or Rouen. The route Gaunt and his men would have to take would be double that. History would term it his Grande Chevauchée. It was an audacious undertaking. But though the army left Calais in August, its shattered remains would not reach Bordeaux until December.

Initially, the English march seemed to make good headway. But if the English had hoped for any kind of showdown with Charles – perhaps even a repeat of the lead-up to Poitiers – the French showed no interest in playing into their hands. While the English burned a wide path of destruction across the countryside, the people holed up in fortified cities and towns. So did the French armies. Du Guesclin kept them positioned between the English and Paris while maintaining a parallel march to the English advance. They stayed close enough to remain in contact and be able to harass the enemy when possible, but not so close as to provoke a battle.

Some French nobles were infuriated by du Guesclin's policy of non-confrontation. It was an unbearable stain on their honour to allow the English to march through their territory uncontested. Given that the very notion of kingship rested on Charles's ability to protect his land and people, refusing to face the enemy also posed a potential threat to the stability of the realm.

Charles summoned a council of war with his brothers, the constable and Clisson so that complaints about the strategy could be heard. The king called on du Guesclin to speak first. Though initially hesitant to speak out of turn in the presence of the high-born commanders, he eventually stated his principle: 'I do not say that they [i.e. the English] should not be fought, but I want it to be done from a position of advantage, as *they* know how to do so well and have done so often.'[19] Asked whether he seconded the opinion of the constable, Clisson showed no hesitation:

> As God hears me, my lords, the English are so filled with their own greatness and have won so many big victories that they have come to believe they cannot lose. In battle they are the most confident nation in the world. The more blood they see

flowing, whether it is their enemy's or their own, the fiercer and more determined they grow... So in my humble opinion it would be inadvisable to fight them unless they can be taken at a disadvantage, in the way one should take one's enemy.

Clisson pointed out that du Guesclin's strategy had given France a string of victories, whereas the rush into pitched battles had wrought little but defeat. It was a more than convincing argument.

Week after week it went on, with the French army using the towns to sleep and eat in relative comfort while the English slept in the field, reducing the increasingly meagre rations they'd been able to scrounge. Soon enough, fear grew alongside hunger in the English encampment. The army was forced to make its long journey through sparsely populated countryside while a cold and wet winter set in. Starving men, though forbidden to leave the safety of the main body, still did so in pursuit of food. The French were more than happy to pick them off.

In the end, an English path marked by starved corpses finally ended in Bordeaux. Less than half the mounts they'd started with remained. The carts that in men's dreams might have been heavy with booty – as they were on the Black Prince's returns from *chevauchée* – had long since been left behind, broken or stuck in frozen mud. Many men were lost. Still more would be begging for alms in the streets of Bordeaux, which was unprepared to host a half-starved force that doubled its population. Their entrance came with no parades. They had earned no great glory. As they dragged themselves into the city, they were, according to a French chronicle, 'in such a state that they had more than 300 knights on foot, who had abandoned their armor, some having cast it into the rivers, others broken it up, since they could not carry it, and so the French would not have the benefit of it'.[20]

Gaunt's would-be allies in Iberia were stunned when they heard of the news. The great strength that the Black Prince had shown when he'd marched over the Pyrenees seemed a distant memory. In 1374, with no real hope to reach Castile and only more losses in Aquitaine to show for his efforts, Gaunt returned to England. The whole affair had been a disaster. While the French were learning new ways to fight, the English were still trying to live in the past.

End of an Era, 1375–77

Though the French seemed to hold all the cards, there were growing voices for peace on both sides of the Channel. The expenditures of the struggle were enormous, and fractures were beginning to show in the uppermost reaches of power. In England, Gaunt wanted peace with France in order to press his claim to Castile unhindered. In France, the duke of Burgundy, the king's brother, wanted peace with England in order to maintain the economic prosperity of the holdings that he'd gained when he married Margaret of Flanders.

Despite continuing objections in some quarters, negotiations between England and France began in Bruges on 25 March 1375. The English position at the outset was that either Edward III ought to be made king of France or the full conditions of the Treaty of Brétigny ought to be restored. To the French, the first option was ludicrous, and the second only slightly less so: restoration of that treaty would mean the restoration of a very different map than the one they'd built over the past six years of fighting. Besides that, the English themselves had repudiated Brétigny. Step by step, more moderate compromises began to unfold, though the key issue of sovereignty remained a hurdle. When it was suggested to Charles V that he might give up some land in exchange for peace, he was aghast. Even in making deals with the Vikings, he said, recalling the distant example of Rollo and the formation of Normandy, the crown of France had never given away its sovereignty over the lands it handed out.[21] Positions were entrenched.

Even so, a temporary truce of two years was settled, with hope for a path forward when the heat of war was turned down. Diplomats on both sides tried to continue their delicate work, but England was experiencing internal crises that made it particularly difficult to move forward. Edward himself was declining. The Black Prince's health was worse. Meanwhile, broad resentment over a variety of domestic issues crystallized around the losses in

France, and when the English government's lack of coin forced the king to call a parliament it was in no mood to play nice. The Good Parliament, as it came to be called, tried to reform what it viewed as a corrupt government. After the death of the Black Prince in June 1376, Gaunt took effective control of the state and forced a new parliament – the Bad Parliament – to undo much of the reform. Amid all of this, a whole class of knights longed for a chance to claim new glories – or return to old ones – in a fight with France.

Across the Channel, Charles was preparing to give them just that. With his enemy in disarray, he planned to erase every English holding left on the Continent as soon as the truce expired. Anjou would strike at Bayonne and Bordeaux. Berry and Bourbon would attack the few positions left in the Auvergne. Burgundy would march on Calais. Clisson would take out Brest and Auray, the only footholds that Jean de Montfort had left in Brittany. A new Franco-Castilian naval force would conduct operations through the Channel – including land raids along the England coast – to keep reinforcements at bay. Meanwhile, it was hoped that the Scots would invade from the north in keeping with the Auld Alliance, while a descendant of Welsh royalty named Owain Lawgoch would raise rebellion in Wales. 'In truth,' the writer of the French *Grand Chronicles* observed, 'no one in the memory of man had ever seen such a great undertaking as what the king now planned to do'.[22] The whole enterprise was set to the timing of the truce: when it ended, the gathering waves would crash upon England from all sides.

And at this moment of peril, the one man most needed to keep the English safe was lost. On 21 June 1377, Edward III, the man who'd brought so many victories to England, died of a stroke. Because the Black Prince had predeceased his father, Edward III's ten-year-old grandson took the crown as Richard II.

Just three days later, the truce was over.

7

The Years of Civil Strife, 1377–1415

Everything Changes | Fighting in Flanders | Competing Invasions | Lords Appellant | Truce of Leulinghem | Madness | Negotiations | Crusade and Conflict | Usurpation | Owain Glyndŵr | France and Wales | Murder of Orléans | Hal to Henry V | Armagnac–Burgundian Civil War | War Renewed

Low tide came with the early dawn on 29 June 1377: the summer solstice had passed only nine days earlier. Jean de Vienne, the admiral of France, had likely been up since midnight, ensuring that his ships stayed together in the darkness of the English Channel, ready for their run into the estuary of the Rother. It was important, he knew, that they beach their ships at low tide. If they did so later in the day, then when the tide inevitably ran back out it would leave the ships high and dry – and that meant he'd have no escape if he needed it.

He had to be pleased with the French and Castilian captains of his fleet. They did their jobs well. When the sun broke over the horizon, it lit upon the masts of a steady line of ships sailing into the mouth of the river.

To port was the town of Winchelsea – a new town by that name, since the old one had been destroyed and abandoned almost a century earlier when the great storm of 1287 rewrote the map of this coast. New Winchelsea stood on the high ground at the end of a marshy peninsula. A prosperous enough place, though at the moment it was still recovering from the last time the French had come here in force. Some among Jean's crews might well have been there, seventeen years earlier, when another French expedition had sacked the town during a failed attempt to rescue King Jean II from English captivity.

This admiral's aim was far less lofty. Now that the English truce had expired, he'd come to raid.

His men disembarked on the beaches below Winchelsea rather than risk the shallow depths up the river closer to their target. Leaving a small detachment to guard the ships, the rest of his men marched up the paths edging the marshes and struck the town of Rye. The townspeople tried to make a defence, but it didn't take long for the admiral's men to overpower them. Jean was so confident in his position that he sent many of his men back to the ships to sail down the coastline in search of other targets. Meanwhile, he would pillage what he could.

It's unclear how long it took for word of the French raid to reach Battle Abbey, the remarkable monastery that William the Conqueror had founded as penance for the blood he shed in the Battle of Hastings in 1066. But it did. And its abbot, Hamo of Offington, swiftly reacted to the news by calling men to arms. Winchelsea was a dozen miles away. The abbot hurried there, following a track on the ridgeline, gathering men in his wake like fish drawn in a towing net. Winchelsea was soon swelling with men ready to fight.

Jean was stunned. Worried that the abbot would fall upon his remaining ships and leave him stranded, he pulled most of his men back from Rye to protect them. He tried to negotiate with Hamo, then tried to drive him away, but the abbot wouldn't budge. That night, the admiral ordered his men to board what they'd taken onto the ships – over three dozen casks of fine wine and a number of wealthy citizens who'd fetch a high ransom. When this was done, they set fire to Rye, pulled anchor and sailed out with the tide.

The histories of England laud Hamo for pushing the raiders away before they could do more damage. He had indeed done well. But he couldn't be everywhere at once. Behind him, the rest of Jean's ships struck Hastings and destroyed it. Then Lewes went up in flames.

England was a kingdom on the precipice. Even as Richard II's coronation was taking place on 16 July, men were readying defences along the nearby Thames in fear of an immediate attack on London. Though that particular strike failed to materialize, in August a raid from Scotland sacked Roxburgh. Just over a week after that, a Franco-Castilian fleet struck the Isle of Wight. The next month, Burgundy took two of the English fortresses protecting the approach to Calais. In the southwest, Anjou seized Bergerac and marched steadily towards Bordeaux. Clisson took Auray.

The new English king had little strength to respond. Only the onset of winter stopped further French advances, and at that point all the beleaguered English could do was to dig in and wait for spring. Less than a decade after holding nearly half of France, they now had little more than a scattering of castles and fortified towns clinging to the coasts.

England attempted to strike an agreement with Navarre to distract either or both of the kings of France and Castile, but French agents found evidence of the negotiations. In 1378, the king of France used this to move against Charles the Bad's remaining castles in Normandy, many of which willingly opened their gates to him. England tried to salvage what they could by taking direct control of Cherbourg on the tip of the Cotentin. That they were able to hold it was a small but vital victory given the staggering loss of everything else in the region. Charles the Bad, meanwhile, was further diminished when Castile stormed the Navarrese border and forced him, at long last, to submit to a binding treaty that not only neutralized an at times useful English ally, but also opened up Gascony to invasion from the south.

In this brief window, the French had built up enough momentum that they surely could have ended the Two Hundred Years War once and for all. That they did not was the result of financial pressures – ever a problem on both sides of the Channel – and a series of unexpected events that temporarily checked France's advance.

Everything Changes, 1378–80

Almost exactly one year before Navarre's submission, Pope Gregory XI died in Rome. The cardinals gathered and – supposedly under some local pressure – elected Pope Urban VI, who was neither French nor interested in going to Avignon. Shortly afterwards, a different gathering of cardinals disavowed this election and met anew, this time electing the preferred French candidate, Pope Clement VII, who journeyed to Avignon as quickly as he could.

With one pope in Rome, the other in Avignon, the Western Schism, as it came to be called, would last until 1417. The church – for there had been only one – was now split in two. The pope held the authority of the Vicar of Christ on Earth, with the power to excommunicate men and women from the church and cut their souls off from Heaven's grace. Now two such men claimed an authority that could only belong to one alone. Political differences became theological differences as countries put their stock in one pope or the other: France supported Clement, which meant that England supported Urban. And so it went, state by state, with Christians facing the threat of excommunication depending on which side they chose.

The Two Hundred Years War had taken on the vestiges of a holy war. The two countries had also lost the common ground of clergy who could help negotiate peace.

At the start, though, these spiritual fault lines were only cracks in the political landscape. The earthquake did not hit until Charles V made a disastrous error. At the end of 1378, he resolved not just to take Brittany from Jean de Montfort, but to annex the duchy into France. When the news reached the Breton nobles it managed to do the one thing all the fighting of the past years had not done: it unified them. In July 1379, the duke returned from his English exile, and to the apparent shock of the French was welcomed home in triumph. Within months, his position was so strong that he was able to call a truce with the French. Jean was once again duke over a unified Brittany. The following March, he had an agreement in place for mutual assistance with England, which sent an expedition under the command of the earl of Buckingham to conduct a *chevauchée* in France. At the end of July, it set out from Calais, aiming to burn a path of destruction all the way to Brest.

French reaction was stymied first by du Guesclin taking ill and dying only a few days before Buckingham reached Calais. It was a heavy loss, but an even more shocking death was still to come. On 16 September 1380, just after Buckingham marched through Vendôme, Charles V unexpectedly died of disease at the age of forty-two. 'When great men die, everything changes,' the French poet Christine de Pisan would write in 1405, looking back on this moment as 'the gateway to all our later misfortunes'.[1]

The king's eldest son was crowned as Charles VI. He was just shy of twelve years old – thirteen months younger than his distant cousin, the latest king of England – and his powerful uncles were to hold the reins of government until he came of age. The arrangement was a disaster for French unity. The individual desires of the uncles – like the duke of Burgundy's dedication to strengthening and hopefully growing his eventual inheritance in Flanders – had been kept in check under the older Charles V, but his young son was no match for them. Long-simmering resentments threatened to explode into outright hostility, and the new king was almost immediately reduced to a pawn. Even in appointing a new constable to replace du Guesclin they nearly came to blows before deciding to follow the late king's wishes in raising up Olivier de Clisson.

If there was any good news in all this, it was the fact that although Buckingham was free to march his way to Brittany, Jean de Montfort thought the change in kings might be a reason to reconsider his alliance with England. By January 1381, he had an agreement to do homage to Charles VI in return for a rollback of the royal decree confiscating the duchy. Buckingham, who'd marched across France to help him, now had little choice but to leave for England, his expedition a costly failure.

Fighting in Flanders, 1382–84

Remarkably, the young kings of England and France had to grapple with revolts at nearly the same time. Richard had to face down the Peasants' Revolt in England in 1381, and Charles VI had similar issues due to the combustible mix of war, famine, disease and high taxes in his own country: southern France was shaken by the Tuchin Revolt from 1378 to 1384, with smaller uprisings elsewhere.

The most important of these revolts began in Ghent in 1379. It centred, as so much did at that time, on the enormously profitable textile industry that was so intricately – and intractably – bound up with the English wool trade.

Ghent was hardly alone in its dependence on this business. Among its competitors in the region was nearby Bruges, but by the middle of the fourteenth century the Brugeois were already recognizing that the Zwin channel that connected them to the sea was silting up. Their solution was to dig a canal to the River Lys, and they acquired from Count Louis II of Flanders permission to do just that.

The canal, though, ran afoul of Ghent's interests. Squabbles broke out, then gave way to killings, and almost the next thing anyone knew a castle built by the count was torched by rioters. The revolt spread, and soon people were rising up in arms across Flanders, even in Bruges. By March 1380, the count was in Paris, hoping for help, but aside from his son-in-law, the duke of Burgundy, few in the court were interested: the return of Jean de Montfort in Brittany was their main focus.

Louis decided to take on the rebels anyway, and he managed to put the fires out throughout most of Flanders. Alone among the big towns, Ghent still held out against him, and in 1382 the city elected as its leader Philip van Artevelde, the son of Jacob van Artevelde, who had led the city's rebellion against the count's father some decades earlier. As the elder van Artevelde had done, Philip turned to England for help, emphasizing the economic ties between them. English leaders recognized that Ghent could once again be a base for attacks on France – as it had been for Edward III – but there were real questions about what the kingdom could financially afford to do.

While he awaited a final decision on whether the English would help, Philip carried out a bold attack on Bruges while the count was in town. The Battle of Beverhoutsveld, fought on 3 May, saw the Brugeois march out against van Artevelde, some of them drunk from a local festival. But the Gentenaars were well organized, well armed and utterly sober. They had brought artillery to pound the walls, and they were more than happy to now fire against the oncoming lines instead, scattering them. The army of Ghent then stormed the city, and the count only barely managed to escape with his life. The success brought more towns – and with them more and more men – to van Artevelde's side.

It also managed to get the attention of the French royal council. Uprisings in Rouen and Paris – the Harelle and Maillotin Revolts, respectively – had been put down in February and March, but Ghent's determination was bound to create more problems of this kind. Flanders had to be made to kneel. It had to be swift. It had to be hard.

Now fourteen, Charles VI led the army in name, though there was no question that the king's brother, Philippe the Bold of Burgundy – the count's heir – was in command. A French army some 10,000 strong gathered in Arras and marched north. Van Artevelde marched out from Ghent and took position on a hillside overlooking the road near what is today the Belgian town of Westrozebeke. But when the two armies fought on 27 November 1382, it was called Roosebeke.

On the eve of the battle, a sixteen-year-old was dubbed a knight. His name was Jean II Le Maingre, though like his father before him he would come to be known to history as Boucicaut, meaning 'the brave'. He was in the retinue of the duke of Bourbon. According to an anonymous and extremely flattering biography of Boucicaut, written in 1409, this freshly knighted young man made a great name for himself in the fight by killing an older, much larger Fleming with a dagger after the man had disarmed him: 'he thrust the dagger below his enemy's breastplate and between his ribs, and the Fleming fell to the ground overcome by pain – nor could he do Boucicaut any further damage. And Boucicaut said, mockingly, 'Is this a game for Flemish children?"[2]

Boucicaut was, as this likely fantastical story suggests, a man raised to be a fighter. Given his place in society, he would have known that he would eventually be made to fight on the battlefield, and his biography tells us that he trained hard to be ready when the time came:

He would train himself to leap fully armed onto his horse's back, or on other occasions he would go for long runs on foot, to increase his strength and resistance, or he would train for hours with a battle-axe or a hammer to harden himself to armour and to exercise his arms and hands, so that he could easily raise his arms when fully armed... He could do a somersault fully armed but for his bascinet, and could dance equipped in a coat of mail.

He was also reputed to be capable of powerful feats of jumping, an ability to climb between two walls built closely together and this: 'fully armed in a coat of mail, he could climb right to the top of the underside of a scaling ladder leaning against a wall, simply swinging from rung to rung by his two hands – or without the coat of mail, by one hand only'.[3] These stories are likely true. Fighting with heavy weapons under the encumbrance of armour was an enormous physical challenge that required strength, stamina and skill. Men in combat would either be up to the task or they would die.

At Roosebeke, the struggle lasted less than two hours from beginning to end, according to an Italian eyewitness named Buonaccorso Pitti, and it was absolutely one-sided: when the Flemings charged the French lines from the front, the French cavalry swept around to attack their rear. Those Flemings who didn't run were encircled, and those who didn't suffocate in the press were slaughtered. Froissart tried to give a sense of what it was like, beginning with the image of French men-at-arms attacking the largely untrained enemy:

Some had sharp axes with which they split helmets and knocked out brains, others lead maces with which they dealt such blows that they felled them to the ground. Hardly were they down then the pillagers came slipping in between the men-at-arms, carrying long knives with which they finished them off. They had no more mercy on them than if they had been dogs. So loud was the banging of swords, axes, maces, and iron hammers on those Flemish helmets that nothing else could be heard above the din. I was told that if all the armourers of Paris and Brussels had been brought together, plying their trade, they would not have made a greater noise than those warriors hammering on the helms before them.[4]

The biography of Boucicaut claims 60,000 Flemings died, though that's probably more than twice as many as were there. Froissart says 26,000 died. Pitti gives the number as 27,500.[5]

After the battle, the young king asked to see the Flemish leader, dead or alive. It took time to find van Artevelde, as the dead were already being stripped of their armour and anything else that might have value. But his body was eventually found. According to Froissart, 'He had been crushed in the press and had fallen into a ditch, with a great mass of Ghent men on top of him.' His corpse was dragged to the opulent tent in which Charles and his lords waited: 'When they had looked at him for a time they took him away and hanged him from a tree.'[6] With the rebel army crushed, the revolt in Flanders collapsed. The French took satisfaction in the destruction that followed over the next weeks, rooting out every vestige of rebellion that they could. Only in Ghent did the spirit of the struggle survive, and even there only barely. On 18 December, as the French began to withdraw, they took the time to stop in Kortrijk, where eighty years earlier their army had suffered its humiliating defeat at Flemish hands in the Battle of the Golden Spurs. Those gilded spurs of the dead French knights had hung in the church of Notre-Dame ever since. The French now took them down. They then set fire to every building they could on their way out of town.

England was too late to help the Flemish at Roosebeke, but the will to make a move into Flanders remained. It even had an added theological dimension now: the French, it was feared, would force the Flemings into obedience to the French-backed Pope Clement VII in Avignon rather than the English-backed Pope Urban VI in Rome.

In the summer of 1383, an English army arrived in the Low Countries under the trappings of a 'crusade' against the supporters of Clement.[7] It was led by the bishop of Norwich, Henry le Despenser, and it would eventually take his name. The effort was an unmitigated disaster. It besieged Ypres – an Urbanist city – for a month without success. Facing the fracture of his force and an approaching French army, Despenser called off the crusade and returned to England. Enormous funds had been spent on the endeavour, which had received the public support of Richard II, and all it had to show for it was a sack of the village of Gravelines on its way back to Calais. Accusations of corruption and mismanagement severely damaged the reputation of the young king and his government as a result.

Both sides were drawn back into peace negotiations in the wake of the disaster. On the English side, Richard could ill afford more war – neither financially nor politically. On the French side, the duke of Burgundy effectively ruled, and the last thing he wanted was more destruction in Flanders. The two sides met at Leulinghem, south of Calais. Among the proposals on the table was one that the French had unsuccessfully floated in 1375: a reduced version of Aquitaine could be reconstituted, but it would be under the control of John of Gaunt, not the English crown. Moreover, it would be held under the sovereignty of the French crown. Though the long-term trajectory of this plan seemed destined to create a Lancastrian dynasty local to France, English prospects were so bleak that they were apparently willing to consider it.[8] While matters were negotiated, a truce was agreed until October 1384.

Competing Invasions, 1385–87

In 1383, Fernando of Portugal died without a clear heir. Juan I of Castile – the son of Enrique, who had died in 1379 – claimed the throne on behalf of his wife, who was Fernando's only surviving child. The Portuguese, suspecting that Juan intended to subsume Portugal to Castile, threw their support behind João, Fernando's half-brother. It came to war, as these things tended to do, and Castile invaded. But at the Battle of Aljubarrota on 14 August 1385, João's forces obliterated Juan's army.

With Castile reeling from the loss, the duke of Lancaster had a perfect window of opportunity if he wanted to make a play for its crown, and João sent him a letter telling him just that. Portuguese sources inform us that Gaunt was unenthusiastic. He'd been bitterly disappointed when Richard had chosen to expend England's limited resources on Despenser's half-baked crusade rather than on his own aspirations, and this had resigned him to the fact that Castile would remain out of reach. It took the intervention of his Castilian wife and their daughter to convince him to try again, and he started making plans for a campaign the following spring.[9]

Meanwhile, the French were making plans of their own: they would conduct a massive invasion of England in the autumn of 1386, complete with modular, prefabricated defences made from 'the tallest trees in Normandy' that would be hauled ashore to protect the landing site. According to a French chronicler, Charles VI 'thought it appropriate that the English, so long accustomed to invading France, should tremble, trapped in their own homes when they saw that the French dared to cross the sea. He wanted to teach them a lesson: that instead of always being the aggressors, they should expect to be attacked themselves.'[10]

Preparations for this attack could not be kept hidden from the English, just as the build-up for Gaunt's expedition could not be kept hidden from the French. Neither side was especially clear on what the other intended, though, leaving the French particularly concerned about moving so many of their forces into one place for the planned invasion. It was only when Gaunt sailed for Castile in July that the French felt confident that he wasn't landing his force against France directly. This allowed them to mobilize everything, but it had also meant a significant delay.

Gaunt landed at what is now called A Coruña, in the northwestern corner of Spain, and he moved quickly to Santiago de Compostela. Here he paid his respects at the tomb of the apostle and eyed an entry into Castile via the Camino that his brother had once followed in the other direction on the way to Nájera. Juan of Castile had neither the men nor the money to respond immediately, but he got both when Gaunt's alliance with the Portuguese against Castile became well known throughout his kingdom. Winter was on its way, though, so the decision was made to wait for spring before trying to dislodge the English.

That same winter prevented the French from making their attack, too. By the time their great invasion force was gathered in port, the winds and weather had turned. The invasion was meant to have struck somewhere between Norfolk and Essex off the North Sea. These waters were now too perilous. It was a disappointing loss of money and morale. Plans were made to try again in 1387, but they would have to be much reduced. The delay that Gaunt had caused, by no direct intention, may have saved England.

Some of the many ships that the French had requisitioned for their invasion re-entered the Atlantic trade routes. One sizable group of them, on its way to Flanders in March 1387, was attacked by an English fleet under the earl of Arundel. The Battle of Margate, as it came to be known, saw the English seize seventy ships and some 8,000 barrels of wine.

In Iberia, João married Gaunt's daughter, Philippa, in February, and then the two kings rode into Castile in March. After the winter's encampment the English force had lost perhaps half its numbers and accomplished little. Weakened by a lack of supplies, they were forced to turn back towards the Portuguese border. Emissaries from Juan took advantage of the situation to broker a deal in June 1387. This laid the groundwork for the Treaty of Bayonne, which was officially sealed in July 1388. The son of Juan of Castile would marry the daughter of John of Gaunt, thus uniting the old line of Pedro with the new Trastámaran dynasty. In return for this arrangement – which included renouncing his own claim to the throne – Gaunt was paid a substantial sum to add to his already sizable riches. The agreement effectively pulled Iberia out of the Two Hundred Years War, strengthening the kingdoms there considerably and giving them the freedom – and arguably the cause – to look to the Atlantic for their futures.

Meanwhile, the reduced French invasion of England that was meant to sail in the summer of 1387 did nothing of the sort. On 25 June, the duke of Brittany arrested the man who was meant to lead it: Olivier de Clisson, the Constable of France. The two men had never liked each other. Clisson had been a supporter of the House of Blois in the war that Jean de Montfort had won, a rivalry that over the years had grown into outright hatred. Clisson's growing stature had worsened the situation, especially as he leveraged his wealth and political connections into major landownership traditionally reserved for the nobility. For Montfort this became a direct threat: he was still childless after the death of his second wife, and the complexities of the treaty that had ended the War of the Breton Succession meant that the duchy would pass to Charles of Blois' son, John, who was then imprisoned in England. Clisson entered into an arrangement to pay for the boy's ransom; in return, John would marry Clisson's daughter. Montfort was furious. On capturing Clisson, he apparently intended to have him killed. Only cooler heads around him prevented this.

Montfort knew that the king's uncles, the dukes of Berry and Burgundy, would support him against Clisson – both had their own reasons for hating him – but he gravely underestimated how close the nineteen-year-old Charles was to his constable. The king rebuked Montfort and helped arrange for the heir's ransom from England and his marriage into Clisson's family. Montfort submitted. But his hatred grew.

Lords Appellant, 1386–88

Civil fractures were even worse in England.

The days of Edward III's greatest glory were distant but still remembered fondly. What was holding the realm back, many thought, was Richard's court. Through no fault of his own, Richard had been thrust onto the throne young, and those formative years had solidified an unshakable belief in his own authority – what we might more generally call 'royal prerogative'. This ran afoul of a Parliament that was increasingly keen on flexing its own muscles. Worse still, in the minds of many, Richard's youth had allowed a series of individuals close to the king – councillors, courtiers and favourites – to influence policy towards their own favour rather than towards what was best for the realm.

When Gaunt left for Castile, this opposition grew. Chief among them were the duke of Gloucester, the earl of Arundel and the earl of Warwick, eventually joined by the earl of Mowbray and the earl of Derby. The last of these was Henry

Bolingbroke, the eldest son and heir of Gaunt and, through him, the king's first cousin.[11] They became known as the Lords Appellant, because they laid the charge (an 'appeal' in legal terms) against several of the king's favourites that their supposed misdeeds had damaged the standing of the kingdom.

The question of what to do with France lurked behind it all. It was clear that Richard wanted peace. Twice now the realm had dodged French invasions that might have been crippling. And what the crown was spending to maintain garrisons in its meagre Continental possessions cost more than could be extracted from them. War was a losing proposition.

The Lords Appellant said otherwise. Whether they believed it or saw it as one more charge to lay against their political enemies, they insisted that better leadership could turn the tide. Such was the toxic atmosphere that rumours swirled that Richard only wanted peace with Charles in order to enlist the French king's help in crushing the English king's adversaries at home.

At first, in what would become known as the Wonderful Parliament, the Lords Appellant were successful in their efforts to oust the realm's chancellor and put some checks on the king's power. But as soon as he was able, Richard undid every reform he could. It was both a political crisis and a battle of wills akin to that around Edward II and his favourites – and it was no less harmful to the government. Richard raised troops to move against the Lords Appellant, who likewise mustered men to resist. On 19 December 1387, they collided in the Battle of Radcot Bridge, with Bolingbroke leading the Appellant side in victory. The king became a virtual prisoner in his own kingdom, and the so-called Merciless Parliament of 1388 conducted a bloody purge of his household.

In foreign policy, the Lords Appellant repudiated all agreements that Richard had made with his counterpart across the Channel. They wanted war – though they quickly discovered that the financial problems of conducting one were real. The king hadn't been sitting on a secret pile of coin, and efforts to raise taxes for the needed funds were met with outright hostility across the kingdom. In the face of this reality, the fervour of the Appellant cause died down. Richard deftly regained control, presenting himself as uninterested in vengeance. He had been misled by others, he claimed. Henceforth, he would rule wisely as his own man. Among other things, he insisted that this would mean an end to the dreaded taxation of the past – a move that put peace with France back on the table.

In France, meanwhile, Charles VI – Charles the Beloved, many were calling him – was also proclaiming his emancipation with a similar message. His powerful uncles were pushed away, and a new group of advisors and administrators called the marmousets swept into the court. They were keen to stabilize the crown's treasury, and there was no better way to do that than to end the war.

Truce of Leulinghem, 1389

Representatives of both kings met outside Calais at the end of 1388. On 18 June 1389, the Truce of Leulinghem was sealed: a three-year pause in the fighting, during which a permanent peace could be determined.

There was an array of responses to the news of a peace. As happened after Brétigny, out-of-work fighters needed something to do, but the scale of the problem was nothing like the earlier days of the Free Companies. Most, it seemed, were simply tired of war. Many in the professional fighting class diverted their attentions into chivalric competitions, like the peace-time jousts at Saint-Inglevert, at which Boucicaut and a couple of other French knights announced that they would welcome any and all challengers to contest their arms in 1390.[12] The peace also ushered in developments in writing and the arts. Many of the survivors, sensing their place in a changing history, sought to preserve and share their stories. So many of the sources used in this book owe their existence to the agreement reached at Leulinghem.

One of those coming to terms with all of this was a man named Geoffrey Chaucer. After finding a place in the household of the duke of Clarence as a teenager, he had risen to become Clerk of the King's Works at the time of the truce. Less than forty years earlier, in the shadow of the Black Death, Boccaccio had written *The Decameron*, a story in which a number of the plague's survivors, having escaped to the countryside, tell each other stories to pass the time. Chaucer now followed this model in writing his monumental *Canterbury Tales* in the shadow of centuries of war: a number of pilgrims tell each other stories to pass the time while riding the roads from Southwark to the shrine of St Thomas Becket in Canterbury.

The poet penned himself into his work as one of the pilgrims. The other characters, recognizing him as a writer, ask him to tell a tale of mirth, and Chaucer gives them The Tale of Sir Thopas, an absurd parody of stories about hero knights and the glories of warfare. Presented in sing-song rhyme, it grates on his listeners' ears to the point that the leader of the pilgrims shouts him down: 'your rhyming isn't worth a shit!' The chastened poet then provides a radically different work for his fictional audience: The Tale of Melibee is hardly a tale at all, but instead a fairly close translation of a debate about violence and vendetta that had been written in 1246. In the story, a man's home is attacked, his family is assaulted and many urge him to go to war against his enemies. 'Gentlemen,' a wise old man interrupts,

> many who cry 'War! War!' know too little of what it is. At the start, war has such a great and bountiful beginning that men can rush in as they like and find it an easy thing. But what will come of it in the end, none of them knows. For truly, once a war is begun, many children still in the womb will starve to death because of the fighting, or else come of age in sorrow and die in wretchedness.[13]

Few students read these twin stories that Chaucer puts in the mouth of his fictional self. The earlier – and truthfully hilarious – Miller's Tale is much preferred these days. But the poet, who was himself captured by the French and imprisoned in Reims during Edward III's siege of the city in 1359, had seen much of the war's horrors first-hand. He knew what he was talking about.

Madness, 1392

As diplomats continued working to find a permanent peace, France was shaken by a seismic event. On 13 June 1392, just after midnight, Olivier de Clisson was on his way home from meeting with the king in Paris when six men burst out of the dark, swords in hand, intent on murder. The constable was on horseback, but the men came at him from all sides. There was nowhere to run as they laid into him, the points of their blades turned by his mail shirt. He fought back with a dagger. In the struggle, his horse bucked, and he was thrown from the saddle, head first into the door of a bakery. His assailants, thinking him dead, fled the city.

The fight had raised the guard, and soon Charles himself was running out to see what had happened. Remarkably, his constable was alive. Even more remarkably, he'd recognized one of his assailants: Pierre de Craon, who'd recently been banished from the city and had gone to the court of the duke of Brittany. Even as the manhunt for Pierre began, the constable was pushing the king to go after his old rival Montfort, the man who'd imprisoned and nearly killed him in 1387. The duke, Clisson assured him, was behind the whole thing. Likely he was not. Jean de Montfort's third wife – Joan of Navarre, the daughter of Charles the Bad – had given birth to a son in 1389, at last establishing for him an heir and eliminating the threat that control of Brittany might pass to Clisson's heirs. He had, in effect, won that fight. Assassinating Clisson in the aftermath would have been tremendously ill advised. On the other hand, Clisson now had every reason to try to implicate the duke in the affair: it was the only way he could possibly salvage his own plans for the duchy.

Whatever the truth of it, the king believed Clisson. Within weeks, he had made the decision to go into Brittany with a royal army that his constable lent him funds to help pay for. Philippe the Bold was beside himself. He never liked the upstart Clisson. More than that, after the death of his own father-in-law in 1384, he'd expanded his already substantial duchy of Burgundy with his wife's counties of Artois, Burgundy, Flanders, Nevers and Rethel. His power was enormous. His riches even more so. Changing the status quo was not something he wanted to see happen.

Supporting the king's decision, though, was his twenty-year-old younger brother, Louis, who just days earlier had been made the duke of Orléans. Seeing a chance to make his name, he announced that he would ride at the king's side.

The king's reality shattered on 5 August, as his army was riding through a forest near Le Mans. Jean Juvénal des Ursins, a French chronicler writing in the 1430s or 1440s, tells us that a man dressed in rags – himself likely not of sound mind – abruptly ran out of the woods in front of the king. He grabbed the bridle of Charles's horse and began screaming of treason in the king's ranks, warning him not to go further lest he fall into a trap laid by his enemies. The man was driven off, but not long afterwards a page accompanying the king grew drowsy in the summer heat and let drop a lance. The clanging of it startled Charles, who 'entered into a great and extraordinary frenzy, and he ran to and fro. He attacked anyone who came near and killed four men. Others immediately grabbed him and constrained him, and he was taken to his lodgings.'[14] Other writers give more detail – whether from rumour or their own imaginations – about how he killed the page first, and that Louis of Orléans had tried to stop his older brother and barely escaped the king's manic sword-swinging. The king could only be approached after his sword had been broken, some said, at which point he was wrestled to the ground. He fell into a coma and was rushed back to Le Mans.

Charles the Beloved had become Charles the Mad.

While the king lay catatonic, Louis of Orléans tried to take control of the situation, but he was quickly bulled aside by Philippe the Bold with the support of the duke of Berry. The king's uncles saw to it that the Brittany campaign was immediately cancelled. Before long, whether planted or rising organically, rumours began to swirl that Charles was the victim of a supernatural malevolence. The devil had targeted the crown of France, and it didn't take long for it to be suggested that the Constable of France and other 'evil' counsellors were to blame. Remembrances of how Clisson had once been aligned with the English didn't help his defence. Soon enough, even after the king was awake and semi-lucid, Clisson found himself on the run, condemned by the French Parliament.

The dukes of Burgundy and Berry took over control of the realm in the absence of clear governance from the king.

Whatever the exact nature of the king's illness – we just don't know – it had a grave impact. The death of a king had precedent. A king's madness had none. Charles VI was very much alive, a young man with many years to live. When he was lucid – or believed to be lucid – he was the king in all his power. When he was not, those around him had no choice but to maintain the fiction that he was still in charge, because there was no telling when he might be once more in control of his faculties.

For the decades that followed the attempted assassination of Clisson on the darkened streets of Paris, the crown of France wavered. Those close to the levers of power attacked each other more often than they did France's enemies. The king was the man to unify the kingdom, but his condition now all but ensured he would divide it instead. The effect this had on the war was, from the point of view of the French, nothing short of disastrous.

Negotiations, 1393–96

This new uncertainty shook the ongoing peace negotiations with England. The French tried to hide their king's condition, but word would inevitably get out – and it would leave them looking weaker. Worry over how this would impact the talks added to Philippe the Bold's anxiety and his determination to conclude a lasting peace as soon as possible. Everyone returned to Leulinghem, and the result was a provisional plan that represented a truly remarkable offer: the expanded English Aquitaine established by Brétigny would be returned to them, minus Poitou and northern Saintonge. The English could keep Calais, and a pile of coin for such diminishment from Brétigny as there was.

For the French, there would be a permanent peace, and the English would agree that the duchy of Aquitaine would be held in liege homage to the French king. There were a few wrinkles still to be ironed out – most of them questions that were known to have been flashpoints over the years, like whether the French king could hear appeals for cases in Aquitaine – but the overall sense was that it was going to work this time.

That it didn't was due in part to the French king's madness – he took a six-month leave of his faculties at the very point that he was supposed to be considering the proposal – and Richard's inability to steer opinion in England, where many still wanted to relive past glories.

France kept the pressure on. After Richard's wife, Anne of Bohemia, died in 1394, the hand of Charles's daughter Isabella was offered up. Diplomacy was as total as they could manage. In 1395, a French cleric wrote a letter to the earl of Somerset, asking him to help produce a final end to the war. The two countries, fighting openly for 'almost sixty years', he wrote, had seen horrors that 'no one would believe unless he had seen them':

> For who shall describe the slaughter, especially of so many nobles of the highest rank and even of kings? Who shall tell of the robbery and the burning even of sacred places? Who shall set forth the sacrilege, the raping, the violence, the oppression, the extortion, the plundering, the pillaging, the banditry, and the rioting? Finally, to embrace many crimes in a few words, who will portray the inhuman savageries… committed in this horrible and most cruel war?… But who, most sweet Jesus, will tell with dry eyes how children are snatched from the embraces of their parents, some slain on the very bosoms of their mothers, and others cruelly slaughtered at their parents' feet, how mothers and daughters are subjected to enemy lust, how many people of the highest rank are carried off into servitude, and how many are put up for sale like animals? O savage spirits, O cruel deeds, O men forsaken by humanity!

Even the fallen are not spared the devastation, he says, as many of the 'half dead or dying' are left to 'the mangling of vultures, and were slain and destroyed by the fangs of wild beasts, and many others – alas, how dreadful! – were greedily devoured by savage wolves'.[15]

War-hawks in England still tried to get a better deal, pushing for a re-establishment of English holdings akin to the Angevin empire at its height. Everyone knew this would go nowhere.

Facing the prospect that it would all fall apart, Richard agreed to an extension of the truce until 1426 with no other exchanges except a marriage to Isabella – and that without any claim to territories in France now or in the future.

Once again, there was peace, but nothing had truly been resolved.

Richard and Isabella were married in Calais on 4 November 1396. The widowed groom was twenty-nine. The bride was five days shy of seven. Her favourite dolls had been gathered to accompany her to England. Richard agreed not to consummate the marriage until she was twelve.

Crusade and Conflict, 1396–97

Now that a peace between the two kingdoms was seemingly secured, France and England went in very different directions.

For France, the peace left many of its knights free to participate in a long-desired crusade against the Ottomans, who were threatening to overrun the kingdom of Hungary and overwhelm Central Europe. After a successful march down the Danube, the crusader army on 12 September 1396 laid siege to the fortified town of Nicopolis, hoping to starve it out. In less than two weeks, though, Sultan Bayezid I had reacted to their presence with a swift, forced march that caught the crusaders completely by surprise.

The climax of this action came with the Battle of Nicopolis. The exact numbers involved elude us. Johann Schiltberger, who was sixteen when he was captured on the field, claimed that the crusaders numbered a mere 16,000 men, which historians have generally accepted as plausible. His assertion that the Ottomans fielded 200,000, though, is just as preposterous as the claim from Şükrullah, a fifteenth-century Ottoman historian, that the crusaders had 130,000 men. In reality, the forces were probably close to an even match. But numbers aren't everything in battle. On 25 September, the knights charged, winning neither glory nor victory. After they blasted through the first Ottoman lines and sent them running up and over a hill, the French thought they had the battle won, despite the insistence of the Hungarian king, Sigismund of Luxembourg, that Bayezid's main battle strength still threatened.

Cresting the hill, the knights came face to face with the rest of the Ottoman army, organized and stoutly defended from a mounted charge by stakes driven into the ground. The Christians were cut down. The counts of Eu, Nevers and La Marche were all captured and held for ransom, along with most of the French military leaders.

News of the disaster reached the courts in the west in December. While many in France went into mourning, Richard saw an opportunity to reassert his authority. In July 1397 he arrested three of his opponents among the Lords Appellant, the earls of Gloucester, Arundel and Warwick. Gloucester was smothered in prison. Arundel was found guilty by trial and decapitated. Warwick was also found guilty and exiled to the Isle of Man. Richard was settling old scores. One prominent exception was his cousin Henry Bolingbroke, the man who'd beaten the royal forces at Radcot Bridge. His place as John of Gaunt's son clearly gave him some protection: for all that Richard had done, taking on the powerful Lancastrian house was on another level entirely.

Usurpation, 1399

In 1398, another of the few Lords Appellant to survive the purge, the duke of Mowbray, told Bolingbroke that the king was coming for him and his father both. When Bolingbroke and Gaunt confronted Richard, the king denied it. Mowbray, cornered, turned on the Lancastrians, who in turn made new accusations against him. In the end, it was declared that Mowbray and Bolingbroke would settle the matter in a personal duel. On 16 September, just as they were about to fight before a crowd gathered at the walls of Coventry, the king put a halt to the proceedings. He had instead decided to exile both men: Mowbray for life and Bolingbroke for ten years.

Bolingbroke departed for exile in Paris. By a strange coincidence, he was given lodging in the mansion left vacant when Olivier de Clisson had been chased out of town. He was there, in February 1399, when word came that his father, John of Gaunt, was dead. The next month brought news from England that Richard had extended Bolingbroke's exile to life, and the great estates of Lancaster – the duke had been the richest man in the realm – were forfeited to the crown.

While Richard consolidated power in England, French power was divided among many hands. To address the uncertainties of Charles's madness, Queen Isabeau had worked hard to create a council of regents to govern the realm during her husband's 'absences'. The most dominating voice in the government, as he had been for quite some time, was the rich and powerful Philippe the Bold. With so much of his wealth centred in Flanders, the duke of Burgundy preferred a peaceful resolution to the long war with England. His rivals included the younger brother of the king, Louis of Orléans, who advocated for a more aggressive foreign policy towards Gascony in particular: likely because *his* wealth would be much improved if his lands extended further in that direction.

Orléans saw an ally in the exiled Bolingbroke and worked hard to befriend him. In the summer of 1399 they made a pact to support one another against their enemies. At nearly the same time, when word arrived that Richard had taken his army to Ireland to press English interests there, Bolingbroke saw his chance. Pausing only to receive a blessing from the abbot of Saint-Denis, he rode for Boulogne. From there he and a few hundred armed men took ship and sailed for England.

Henry landed near the Lancastrian holdings in Yorkshire, and by mid-July he had sealed an alliance with Henry Percy, the powerful earl of Northumberland, and his son of the same name, more commonly known by the nickname 'Hotspur', which he'd earned during many years of fighting on the borders of Scotland.

At first, Bolingbroke claimed to seek only his inheritance, but as his support grew so did the calls for regime change. In mid-August, Richard returned from Ireland and found no respite on English soil. Bolingbroke's forces cornered him at Flint Castle, and soon enough the king was imprisoned in the Tower of London. One month later, on 1 October, Richard was formally deposed by Parliament. And less than two weeks after *that*, Bolingbroke took the crown as Henry IV – the first Lancastrian king.

Almost as quickly as Henry took the throne, a number of lords set about trying to restore Richard. Their Epiphany Rising failed, but it convinced the new king that the old king had to go. One month later, Richard died in Pontefract Castle. Likely he was starved to death.

Across the Channel, many in France were shocked. The deposition of a king was a frightening prospect given the status of their own monarch. More than that, it was strongly suspected that the peace negotiated with Richard might not last under Henry. The duke of Berry wrote to his brother, the duke of Burgundy: 'Truth to tell, my dear brother, it is a great tragedy and a signal misfortune for our country. For as you well know, Lancaster governs by the will of the English people and the English people like nothing better than war.'[16]

Owain Glyndŵr, 1400–03

War is exactly what Henry had in mind – but against Scotland, not France. Henry understood that not everyone who accepted Richard's removal accepted his own claim to the crown: many were looking instead to the existing heir presumptive, an eight-year-old great-great-grandson of Edward III named Edmund Mortimer. A military victory, Henry was certain, would unify England behind him. So in the summer of 1400, the English army, perhaps the largest gathered since Crécy, rode north. The campaign would fail completely. Worse, it would cause *another*, far more impactful war to break out, reigniting the same tensions with France once again.

In a quiet, beautiful corner of Wales, two great landholders had been engaged in an ongoing property dispute. One, Lord Grey of Ruthin, was strongly connected to the English court. The other, Owain of Glyndyfrdwy – today called Owain Glyndŵr, though the English sources often name him Owen Glendower – was a Welshman who could claim descent from several lines of kings in Wales. According to some stories, when Henry put out a call to arms for his campaign into Scotland, Grey prevented it from reaching Owain, which prevented the Welshman from supporting the king. Henry threatened to come after Owain in response – this was surely

Grey's intention – but the Welsh lord didn't submit as expected. Instead, he was proclaimed the Prince of Wales by his supporters on 16 September 1400.[17] Because there already *was* a Prince of Wales – Henry's son and heir, the future Henry V, who had turned fourteen that very day – this was a declaration of open rebellion. Owain won an early and important fight at the Battle of Hyddgen in 1401, encouraging even more Welsh to join in the fight.[18] Soon enough Owain was flying the golden dragon of Arthur, drawing even more to his cause. He sent letters to leaders in Ireland and Scotland, attempting to draw them into an alliance.[19]

The king made several attempts to deal with the rebellion. None of them worked. And then, in June 1402, Owain struck the town of Knighton. The local English forces mustered out, led by Sir Edmund Mortimer, a man of wealth and powerful connections who was also uncle – and guardian after the lad's father had died – to the young Edmund Mortimer who some thought should be king. Despite this, he'd never shown the slightest hint of disloyalty to his cousin, Henry IV. On 22 June, he brought Owain to battle near a hill called Bryn Glas, which rises beside the small hamlet of Pilleth today.[20] The result was a complete and total victory for the Welsh. The English forces were destroyed. Mortimer was captured.

The defeat sent shockwaves through England.

Henry tried to blame the loss on Mortimer. Rumours swirled that the English leader might have even had a secret arrangement with the Welsh – that, like a boxer taking a dive, he'd thrown the fight. The king refused to ransom him, which drove a wedge into the crown's relationship with the powerful Percys in the north: Hotspur was married to the sister of Mortimer. In September, Henry added insult to injury after Hotspur and his father decisively defeated a Scots army in the Battle of Homildon Hill. A range of rich ransoms were taken from the Scots leaders, but Henry – needing money – insisted they be given to him. Northumberland was enraged.

Only weeks later, Henry seized Mortimer's rich estates, accusing him of being a traitor to the crown. There's zero evidence that this was true, but it became a self-fulfilling prophecy. Almost as soon as Mortimer was accused of being Owain's ally, he actually *was*: in November 1402 he married Owain's daughter, and on 13 December he openly announced his defection to Owain's cause.

On 8 March 1403, Henry put his son, Prince Hal, in charge of the royal response in Wales. It was against Owain that the future Henry V learned to make war. He was, by all indications, a quick student. We have a letter he wrote to his father, on 15 May, reporting that he had gone straight to Owain's home in Glyndyfrdwy:

> And there we torched a beautiful home in its park, and all the land around it. We camped there all that night, and some of our men issued out into the countryside and seized a significant gentleman of that place who was one of the chief supporters of Owain. He offered five hundred pounds for his ransom, and he promised to pay the full sum within two weeks if we would spare his life. We did not accept, and he was put to death. Many of his companions – taken on that same raid – suffered the same fate.[21]

The prince was sixteen.

Less than two months later, Hotspur and his father rebelled against Henry IV. On 21 July, their army and that of the king and prince met in the Battle of Shrewsbury. The carnage was astounding. Hotspur was killed. And although the future Henry V was in charge of the action that likely saved his father's crown that day – commanding the left wing of the king's line, he ordered a perfectly timed sweep into Hotspur's flank at the key moment – the young man was struck in the face with an arrow. It penetrated six inches into his skull and was only removed after a remarkable operation. His survival bordered on the miraculous and no doubt left its mark on his mind as much as on his body.[22]

France and Wales, 1403–05

In France, meanwhile, the rift between Louis of Orléans and Philippe of Burgundy had only grown during the king's frequent absences from sanity. This struggle was already preventing France from taking advantage of England's internal problems in Wales, and it was about to get even worse thanks to the return of conflict in Brittany.

At the end of 1399, around the same time that Henry IV was being crowned, Jean de Montfort had died. His widow, Joan of Navarre, took on the duties of administration on behalf of their ten-year-old son, who became John V of Brittany. Whatever else she'd learned as a daughter of Charles the Bad, Joan knew the costs of conflict and the political manoeuvrings needed to avoid it – especially with such a young man as the duke. She made a point of seeking to heal old wounds, including a successful effort to mend fences between the Montfortists and Olivier de Clisson, who after being removed as constable had returned to his sizable estates in Brittany. This edifice trembled, though, when in 1402 she made the surprise announcement that she would marry Henry IV, himself a widower since 1394. What's more, she would move to England. The marriage, for all that we can tell, had far more to do with affection than any great aspirations.

John V was not yet old enough to rule Brittany on his own, and Joan appears to have planned a short regency by none other than Clisson, who was sure to leverage his good relationship with Louis to strengthen Brittany's connections to Orléans. Philippe of Burgundy was aghast. Even setting aside his old antagonisms with Clisson, he knew Brittany's importance in the sea trade that enriched the Low Countries – we can think all the way back to what happened at Quéménès in 1292 – so he wanted to move the duchy closer to his own sphere of interests rather than those of his political rival in the French court. He got his way and was made regent. Orléans, though, was winning the fight in the heart of Paris. By 1403 he had successfully outmanoeuvred his uncles in order to take control of the oft-mad king and his crippled court. Among his immediate aims was to take advantage of England's turmoil by reopening hostilities. Brittany had long been a proxy battleground in the Two Hundred Years War. Wales could be that, too.

Orléans's shift from an ally of the exiled Bolingbroke to an enemy of the enthroned Henry IV is striking, if perhaps not surprising. For one thing, the peace between the kingdoms had been the work of Burgundy, and, petty though it might seem, Orléans was ready to oppose just about anything his uncle wanted. More

than that, though, he had his own reasons. England was perceived to be weak and vulnerable. If it came to war, the French
were confident that they'd have the upper hand. And if Gascony
contracted, Orléans stood to benefit. What's more, the ambitious
duke knew that the younger nobility chafed under the peace. They
were anxious to gain honour, esteem and profit in a war of vengeance
against the hated English. Orléans accordingly stoked anti-
English sentiment every chance he could, winning him many
allies who could be useful in his struggle for control of the court
and the country. To help push the realm to war, Louis had even
gone so far as repeatedly challenging the English king to a duel. In
response to one of these, Henry had replied by publicly remind-
ing him of his earlier promises of support – an effort intended to
make him look duplicitous in the eyes of the French – before
pointing out that a duel was beneath him: 'What a king does',
he said, 'he does for the honour of God and the common good
of his realm and of all Christendom, not for mere bombast
and greed.'[23]

In the summer of 1403 – as Henry IV was still conducting
mop-up operations in the aftermath of Shrewsbury – a couple
of hundred French and Breton soldiers landed in South Wales
under the command of a somewhat mysterious figure named Jean
d'Espagne. He was likely a Castilian, his force was something
akin to a Free Company, but about all we know for sure is that
they were welcomed by the Welsh, and they helped Owain seize
Harlech Castle the following spring. Other raids were hitting
elsewhere along the coasts, including one that was defeated in
Devon at the Battle of Blackpool Sands. War was in the air.

In April 1404, the man who had perhaps worked hardest to keep
the peace – Philippe the Bold – died. The enormous expanded
holdings of Burgundy that he left behind went to his eldest son,
who had fought so bravely before being captured at Nicopolis
that he was called Jean the Fearless. This new duke of Burgundy
would come to be a dominant figure in the Two Hundred Years
War, but at first his primary concern was to ensure his domination over his inherited lands.[24] This pushed the court even further
into the hands of Orléans and the men who, like him, wanted war

with England. It was to this court that Jean d'Espagne sailed in May 1404.

Though all but forgotten today, this ship would change the course of the Two Hundred Years War. Aboard it were two Welshmen – Owain's brother-in-law and chancellor –and they were seeking nothing less than an alliance between Wales and France.

That same spring, the truce between England and France was not renewed. And, as Owain held an independent Welsh Parliament in Machynlleth, his men were negotiating with Charles VI and his advisors. By mid-summer, agreements of support were signed between them, with the French also directing the king of Castile to support the Welsh. This was followed by an even more important confederation, signed between France and Wales, in the first days of 1405.[25]

Unlike the earlier fights between France and England in Brittany, what was happening didn't just threaten English holdings abroad. It aimed for the kingdom itself. On 28 February 1405, Owain, his new son-in-law Mortimer and Hotspur's father, the earl of Northumberland, signed a document that historians call the Tripartite Indenture. It was a remarkable agreement. Clearly drafted by the Welsh, it was a pact that would have broken England in three after Henry's overthrow: Owain would rule a greatly expanded Wales in the west, while the other two men would have split the remainder, Mortimer to the south and Northumberland to the north. It was a plan to end England, and there is every reason to suspect that Orléans had given it his approval.[26]

In the immediate months after that agreement was struck, the Welsh suffered a series of battlefield losses. In March, a Welsh force reported to be some 8,000 strong set the town of Grosmont ablaze. The English prince, now healthy and back in command in Wales, sent a rapid response force and won a major victory for the English. As the young man wrote to his father, the king, his men

were only a very small force in all, but it is very true that victory is not in the numbers of men, and this was well shown there:

in the power of God and by the aid of the blessed Trinity your men won the field and vanquished all the said rebels and killed by reliable account on the battlefield at their return from pursuit, some say 800 and some 1000, on pain of their life.[27]

The numbers – both in terms of the total Welsh force and its casualties – seem high, and the prince was undoubtedly anxious to inflate them. Both he and his father knew the fragile nature of Henry IV's hold on power. There'd been Shrewsbury, of course. But just the previous month Constance of York, the countess of Gloucester, had abducted Edmund Mortimer – the young man who had been Richard's designated heir before Henry's usurpation – and tried to spirit him away in an effort to use him as a figurehead for a new rebellion. She didn't get far before she was caught. The best guess is she was trying to take the boy to Wales.

At the start of May another uprising connected to the earl of Northumberland's machinations began in Yorkshire. Towards the end of the month, Richard Scrope, the archbishop of York, lent support to the revolt. It ended disastrously when he was arrested by loyalist forces. After a trial in June, he was beheaded. Northumberland fled for Scotland. Meanwhile, another Welsh force was defeated at Usk, with Owain's eldest son captured.[28]

Such was the situation when a French expeditionary force of at least 2,800 men finally showed up in July. It was led by Jean de Rieux, marshal of France, and several other lords. One chronicler tells us that they arrived in Milford Haven aboard thirty-two ships, though another source tells us it was 140 vessels.[29]

After some initial success in Wales, the combined Franco-Welsh army marched for England. On 7 August, a worried Henry IV ordered his forces to gather in Hereford to repel the invasion.[30] He made all haste to get there himself.

What happened next is something of a mystery. Apparently, Henry's forces deployed upon high ground at Great Witley about ten miles from Worcester. The Franco-Welsh took up position on opposing high ground. Threats were exchanged. A few knights engaged in duels or jousts between the armies. And then, for reasons we don't know, the Franco-Welsh force retreated back to Wales.

If a deal was struck, we have no record of it. Our sources are remarkably silent on what transpired – far more silent than we would expect given the depth of the incursion into English lands. Indeed, there are those who question whether the French invaded beyond the Welsh borders at all. Such an endeavour ought to have left a major mark upon the landscape of texts, and the landscape of towns and countryside, too. Whatever happened, the French wintered in Wales. Their presence now was a negative: they were more mouths to feed and more bodies to house in a land already stripped of resources.

The next spring, Owain tried to pick up the pieces. In March 1406, seeking support for his cause, he wrote to France, promising to change the allegiance of the churches in Wales from the pope in Rome to the pope in Avignon. The Pennal Letters, as they are called, went unanswered, because the duke of Burgundy had found a new way to destabilize the de facto rule of Owain's key ally in the court, the duke of Orléans.

Murder of Louis of Orléans, 1407

Jean the Fearless, the duke of Burgundy, was a cunning man.[31] During one of the king's periods of madness, Jean managed to secure for himself the position of guardian to the Dauphin – also named Louis, but we'll call him by his title to help keep things straight – and the other children of Charles. It was a brilliant, if Machiavellian, move. Louis of Orléans was furious. The rivalry between Burgundy and Orléans escalated. The two men began raising private armies and civil war loomed.

In 1407, the elderly duke of Berry stepped in and forced his two nephews to meet and agree to peace, solemnly promising that they'd do nothing rash. Three days later, Louis of Orléans was murdered in Paris. The assassination had been planned long before Jean the Fearless made his show of peace-making.[32]

The assassins rented a house near the Hôtel Barbette, the royal residence of the queen, where Louis often dined. On the evening of 23 November 1407, just after eight, Louis was falsely summoned to meet the king at the Hôtel Saint-Pol. Taking a mule, he started out with three companions and four attendants bearing torches. The duke was, eyewitnesses would later report, in fine spirits.

As he passed the rented house, a dozen men rushed out of the dark. Louis was dragged off his mount. One torch-bearer was killed immediately, another left desperately wounded. The duke's page played dead as the rest of his companions bolted. Louis, on the ground, asked what was happening. Then the killers set upon him.

The attempted assassination of the constable Olivier de Clisson on the streets of Paris in 1392 had led to the crippling mental illness of the king. That illness had now led to a successful assassination on those same streets.

It was fitting that the current constable, Charles d'Albret, was one of the first men on the scene after the duke's assassination. An axe had taken Louis's left hand. His right arm, raised to defend himself, had been shattered. His face was beaten in, his skull burst open. His brains were strewn across the mud.

The rented house of the assassins was in flames – an attempt to cover their tracks.

Jean the Fearless pretended to be shocked when he was told what had happened. He wept, and helped escort the duke's coffin to burial.

All the while, the Provost of Paris investigated the murder. In a tour de force of medieval detective work, he put the pieces together in just two days, announcing to the gathered lords of the realm that he needed to question them. Jean balked and, taking the dukes of Berry and Anjou aside, admitted to them that he'd orchestrated the assassination. A day later, Berry told the council. Jean fled Paris.

The murder set off what we now call the Armagnac–Burgundian civil war. On one side were the supporters of Jean the Fearless, the duke of Burgundy. On the other side were the supporters of Louis of Orléans's son, Charles, who received the early support of the count of Armagnac. What we think of as modern France was split between them, but the nature of medieval lordships and titles meant that there was no contiguous border between the belligerent parties. The country was a jumbled mix of allegiances, all loosely bound by their ties to a mad king. The kingdom's internal problems had already hampered France's ability to take the fight to England: the effort to help the Welsh had been significant, but by no means had it been a full-on invasion force that could decisively end the war. The further fracturing caused by Louis's murder meant even such small offensive efforts were impossible.

Hal to Henry V, 1407–13

Though France was riven by conflict, Henry IV was in no position to capitalize on the unrest. He didn't have the money, the men or the stamina to do much more than raid its coast. Everything changed, however, once Prince Hal stepped into the breach. His war tutelage in Wales had been largely successful. The Welsh leader was still on the loose, but at this point he was unable to do more than harass the entrenched English. This freed Hal to move into other positions of government. Political conflicts with his father spiked, then resolved with the king's passing. Prince Hal became King Henry V on 20 March 1413, just twenty-six years old with a legendary career ahead of him.

Separating the man from the myth of Henry V is difficult. The scale of the victory that lay ahead transformed mistakes into mysterious strategies, quirks into marks of excellence. Reports that he would 'rebuke even notable captains for looking him in the face when talking to him', for instance, are related in a positive light – the king had 'a forbidding public presence' – rather than in a negative light because he was the successful Henry V and not, say, the floundering Henry IV.[33] We see this kind of spin again and again not just among English contemporaries praising their glorious monarch, but among the French, who used Henry as a contrast to their rivals. If they wanted to blame the French loss to him at Agincourt on disorganization, they would paint Henry as the most organized king possible. If they blamed the French king for not being present in battle, they made sure to emphasize Henry's warrior status. If the loss was God's will, they strove to paint Henry as something akin to a priest-king.

Of all the characterizations of Henry, this last is likely the most accurate. His life to this point had certainly angled him towards

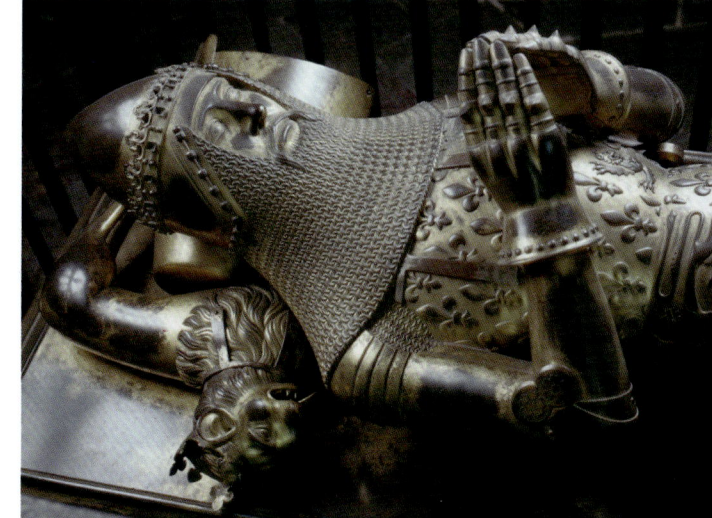

15 (*left*) The brutal and bloody defeat of the Jacquerie in 1358 included a massacre in Meaux, depicted here.

17 (*above*) The small town of Nájera in Spain, beside the river in which so many would drown in 1367. The high ground that Enrique abandoned can be seen behind.

18 (*below*) The bronze effigy of Edward the Black Prince at Canterbury Cathedral. Though he never sat on England's throne, he dominated decades of English life.

16 (*left*) A drone shot looking north from the Gue de l'Omme towards Poitiers. In 1356, the English likely took position on the high ground between the marshes at lower left and the thick woods on the right.

19 (*above*) Charles V of France hands the sword of the constable to Bertrand du Guesclin in 1370. The appointment was a brilliant one.

20 (*left*) Unlike his surviving funeral effigy, this bronze effigy of Edward III in Westminster Abbey shows no indication of the stroke that killed him.

21 (*above*) When madness overtook Charles VI in a forest near Le Mans, he wildly swung his sword at the loyal men around him.

22 (*right*) The chaos of the Battle of Shrewsbury in 1403 is made clear in this colorization of a sketch in the remarkable Beauchamp Pageants.

Here shewes howe att the batell of Shrewesbury betwen kyng henr the iiij & h henr percy / there was slayne the said h heur percy and many other wt hym And on the kyng psrty there was slayne the Erle of Stafford n many other in grett nombre

25 (*right*) A drone shot looking northwest from the initial point of contact between the French and English in 1415. Marching towards Azincourt in the far distance, Henry likely took position in the gap between the villages of Maisoncelle, in the trees to the left, and Tramecourt, in the trees to the right.

26 (*below right*) The difficulties of attacking over muddy ground are clear in this illumination of the Battle of Agincourt in 1415.

23 (*above*) A modern depiction of the assassination of Louis of Orléans on the streets of Paris in 1407, complete with the duke's severed hand.

24 (*right*) Henry V would be remembered as one of England's greatest kings. His depiction from the side may be due to the wound he suffered at Shrewsbury in 1403.

27 (*left*) The firepower that Henry V set against Rouen in 1418 is clear in this illustration based on an image in The Beauchamp Pageants.

28 (*below*) The assassination of Jean the Fearless upon Montereau Bridge in 1419 further split an already divided France.

Our ramener en   se de fane et acomplir la

29 (*above*) The English hoped that burning Joan of Arc at the stake would end her story. Instead, it transformed her into legend.

30 (*right*) In the absence of contemporary portraiture, Joan of Arc has long been depicted according to the needs and desires of artists.

31 In 1453, the Battle of Castillon was fought on these fields between the Dordogne (bottom right) and the Lidoire rivers (the line of trees leading to the left).

32 The meeting of France's Francis I and England's Henry VIII on the Field of the Cloth of Gold was an occasion of stunning splendor.

devotion. A Frenchman who spent a week at court in the run-up to the Agincourt campaign thought the king 'better suited to be a churchman than a soldier'.[34]

Enigmatic as Henry is, he was clearly aware of his family's tenuous hold on power. His father's usurpation of the throne from Richard II had frayed the fabric that held the country together. Revolt after revolt had nearly torn it apart. As prince he'd taken that arrow to the face at Shrewsbury facing Hotspur. He'd ordered men's deaths in Wales. He'd watched the kingdom's coffers empty and its prestige evaporate. It's little surprise that, as king, he set out to stabilize the realm.

One of his first acts was to issue a general amnesty to those who'd rebelled against his father. Soon after, he had the remains of the deposed king disinterred from the smaller church where Henry IV had ordered him buried. With ceremony, Richard II's body was moved to his tomb in Westminster Abbey. Both were respectful gestures towards healing old wounds, but we can't ignore their practical political value: behind every rebellion had been rumours that Richard might still be alive. Henry was, in the name of honouring the king, making it quite clear that he was not.

Still, Henry knew all too well that nothing created unity quite so efficiently as a war. It was the primary reason his father had gone to Scotland in 1400 at the outset of his own reign. That campaign hadn't gone to plan, but his son had bigger dreams. Where his father had looked north, Henry V now cast his gaze to the south.

Armagnac–Burgundian Civil War

As the king of England turned his eyes to France, the eyes of the competing factions there were likewise turning their eyes to him. The duke of Burgundy had, by 1409, rationalized the assassination of Louis of Orléans as an act of tyrannicide: the king's brother had been justifiably killed for his efforts to acquire power. With the Treaty of Chartres that year, Jean the Fearless was formally absolved of wrongdoing, welcomed back into court and made to reconcile with Louis's son, Charles, who'd taken up his father's title as duke of Orléans. It was a public resolution, but by no means was it an end to private scheming.

With a new king on the throne of England, the duke of Burgundy saw a chance to flex his muscles in the French court and lead negotiations for a new peace that would keep his own interests safe while countering the interests of the rival Armagnacs. That same spring and summer, though, the duke misplayed his hand in Paris by supporting the Cabochien Revolt. He'd hoped to use this popular uprising to pass new ordinances that would shift more control of the kingdom into his hands, but the revolt – after a few riotous and bloody months – had to be put down by force. Once again, the duke was forced to flee to his holdings in Burgundy. From there, he still tried to conduct negotiations with Henry V, but he had few cards left to play. He offered the English king the hand of his daughter, but the Armagnacs, now back in control of the French court, were offering marriage to Charles VI's teenaged daughter, Catherine.

Henry eventually agreed that he would not undertake any attack against France until February 1415. This truce gave him time to build up his strength and play the sides in France against each other. He was angling for a broad settlement in England's favour, something like the reinstatement of the old Treaty of Brétigny. No one on the French side had much interest in that. From what they could tell, Henry might not be long for the throne anyway: recent English history was a series of rebellions. As if to drive the point home, in October 1413 Sir John Oldcastle, a veteran soldier who had faithfully served Henry in Wales only to be declared a heretic for supporting a Christian reformation movement popularly termed Lollardy, escaped from the Tower of London and worked to foment an uprising that would take down both church and crown. It didn't come to much, as those who gathered for the planned uprising in January were decisively beaten by royal forces, but Oldcastle himself escaped and would remain at large – with fresh calls to rebellion only a rumour away – until his capture and execution in 1417.

At the end of 1413, Jean the Fearless declared that he'd received letters, supposedly written by the Dauphin himself, claiming that he and his mother the queen were being held prisoner in Paris at the Louvre. For the sake of France, the Dauphin was begging for rescue. Only the army of the good duke of Burgundy could save them.

No originals of these letters exist.[35] They were, almost assuredly, forged on the orders of the duke of Burgundy, who was anxious for a pretence to march on Paris and seize power. He'd failed to take the regency by assassination. He'd failed to take it by popular rebellion. Now he'd take it at the head of an army.

In January 1414, the Dauphin made public pronouncements that the letters were a lie. He and his mother were doing just fine. But there were many who still believed – or wanted to believe – that Jean the Fearless was coming to the rescue of the crown. North of Paris, the army of Burgundy began to gather. The Armagnac forces did the same.

By early February, Jean the Fearless and his army had taken position at Saint-Denis, just outside Paris. Inside the city, Armagnac supporters attacked anyone they suspected of supporting the Burgundian side.

Jean the Fearless didn't have a chance in hell of breaching the walls of Paris if they stood against him. His only hope was that the citizens would open the gates to him. But the public declarations of the Dauphin – the young man he was ostensibly there to save – were not helping his case. Worse, the king, who had been 'absent' up to this point, apparently recovered his wits long enough to make public appearances and declarations in favour of the Armagnacs. The gates of Paris remained locked, and it was clear they were going to stay that way. On 16 February, Burgundy retreated.

The next day, he was declared a traitor. By the start of April, the Armagnacs had turned from defence to offence and were marching north out of the city, a momentarily sane Charles VI at their head, the sacred Oriflamme held aloft. They were marching on Burgundy. All that month they forged ahead. The destruction was enormous. In the sacking of Soissons, the Armagnac forces reportedly killed some 1,200 of their countrymen.

The fighting dragged on through the summer, as Jean the Fearless tried to slow down the Armagnac advance, losing city after city. All the while messengers were on the move between the Armagnacs, the Burgundians and the English. Everyone knew that their opponents were talking to each other. Everyone wanted to end up with the winning hand.

But wars, as we've already seen so often, cost real money, and Burgundy was running out. The Armagnacs were scraping the barrel, too. In the Armagnac camp besieging Burgundian Arras, dysentery was rampant.

At the start of September, the Dauphin managed to negotiate an agreement to end the siege of Arras and, with it, the Armagnac attack on the duke of Burgundy. Peace was coming just in time – the ink was hardly dry when Henry V decided he would target France – but no one was certain if the peace would hold. The Dauphin had negotiated the peace without consulting the Armagnac leaders. Charles of Orléans, who'd come to get vengeance on the man who'd assassinated his father, only swore to uphold the agreement when forced to do so by the Dauphin. Distrust was rampant. And across the Channel the English were preparing for war.

War Renewed, 1414–15

Shakespeare famously attributes Henry's determination to an insult: in the summer of 1414 the Dauphin had sent him a gift of tennis balls, implying that the new English king was immature and unready for real games of war. Offended and enraged, Henry retorted that he'd send back English cannonballs. The story goes back to within a decade or two of the supposed event, so it may have some truth.[36] But his timing was surely motivated by more pragmatic considerations: Henry clearly didn't think that the newly forged peace in France would last. And as far as England was concerned, that made the moment ideal.

Henry clearly felt secure in his own lands. By 1 December 1413, Owain's imprisoned daughter, the wife of Mortimer, was dead, along with their daughters.[37] It had been a long time since anyone had heard from the Welsh rebel himself, and up north the Percys were pushing up the daisies. The following May, Parliament officially declared the Welsh rebellion over. The threat from the west had passed.

For years, France had been crippled by the madness of its king. All that time, England hadn't taken advantage of the French weakness. Now France stood even further divided by the fighting between the Armagnacs and Burgundians. Henry, at last, was ready.

In June 1415, French ambassadors arrived in England, still hoping to stave off war. The military build-up across the Channel was not a secret. The French knew what Henry planned to do, even if they didn't know where or when.

When Henry received the ambassadors at Wolvesey Castle in Winchester on 30 June, one of the first things he did was to ask after their king's health.[38] It was a subtle comment on the madness of their sovereign. He then told them that they'd get to business soon.

The ambassadors had safe conduct until 7 July, so their anxiety surely increased as they were left cooling their heels day after day, watching the comings and goings of military men. Henry made it clear that he was too busy preparing to invade their country to talk to them.

On 2 July, talks began, but they made little headway. The English made it clear that Henry was coming for his rightful lands unless the French gave them to him. On 4 July, the French put an offer on the table that would let the English king hold the lands that had been given over in the old Treaty of Brétigny and taken back by the French in the years since – and even more in the region of the Limousin. It was a wildly generous offer. No one in France would welcome it. But no one in the weakened and divided country wanted a war, either. Henry told the ambassadors that he'd think about it.

He was lying. Holding lands in homage wasn't the way forward. This was the problem that had caused the Two Hundred Years War in the first place. He would *have* the lands, or he'd have war.

While the ambassadors resumed their wait, on 5 July Henry offered to pardon his old adversary, Owain Glyndŵr.[39] The rebel

– if he was still alive, he would have been about fifty-seven – never responded to the offer. He was never caught. Many in Wales say that he never died. He's just waiting, like Arthur, to return and once more raise the banner of the golden dragon to the sun.

The next morning, Henry delivered his counter-proposal to the French. Henry would give them a truce to be counted in decades in return for the lands he demanded and the hand of the French king's daughter – with a matching dowry. The ambassadors did not have the authority to accept. Discussions continued through the day, but it was all a prelude to one last grand act of theatre.

That evening, the ambassadors were brought to the great hall. Henry was enthroned in triumph, surrounded by his lords. It was a sight to inspire both awe and dread. Reading from a prepared statement – of which copies had been made to hand out to the stunned Frenchmen – the archbishop ran through the laundry list of England's many attempts to keep the peace and Henry's magnanimous offers to try to prevent war. Denied justice, the king of England had no choice but to go to war. Henry took horse towards Southampton, where his army, and the fleet that would take them to France, awaited.

As the French ambassadors were being escorted back to Dover, one was overheard telling a colleague that Henry ought to have been more receptive to negotiating, 'if he wanted to be secure' on his throne. It was widely understood, after all, that 'the king had many rivals in his own kingdom', including many who thought another man ought to have the crown, like the duke of Clarence or the earl of March. If instead the king continued raising an army for war with France, the Frenchman mused, 'he would expose himself to dangers both within and without. Internally, what happened to King Richard could happen to him.' When it came to France, Henry was courting trouble no matter what he did, the man said:

> If the king made only a brief incursion into France and then quickly came back, he would have accomplished nothing and spent a lot of money doing it, which would anger his people when he returned. If instead he stayed a long time – two or

three months, perhaps – then the armed forces of France would have assembled, and they were far better trained in arms than the English were used to, and the lords of France would by then be at peace and united, putting the king himself in grave danger.

In other words, Henry would be better off staying at home and leaving the matter alone.[40]

The ambassador was correct that the king lacked complete control of his kingdom. That much became clear on 31 July, when the earl of March came to Henry and informed him of a plot to unite Oldcastle's disaffected followers with the resuscitated dream of the Tripartite Indenture to split the monarchy between the Welsh, the Mortimers and the Percys. Within days, all those in reach of the king were arrested, and the ringleaders were quickly tried and executed.

Would more men try to steal away his throne while he was away in France? Henry couldn't know, but he couldn't back down now. On 11 August, he sailed for France.

8

The Years of Henry, 1415–22

*March to Agincourt | Agincourt | Different Directions |
Reconquest of Normandy | Paris Massacres | Siege of Rouen |
Assassination of Burgundy | Treaty of Troyes | New Nationalism |
Baugé | Siege of Meaux*

Just before dawn on 14 August 1415, a small ship laid up into
the low-tide rocks and mud along the estuary of the Seine. A
ramp crashed down its side, and a nineteen-year-old named John
Holland carefully led his mount out into the shallow water before
splashing towards shore. More men followed, their horses eager to
be on land after days spent in the cramped stalls of the transports.

The king's fleet had arrived offshore the day before: too late
to land many men safely, but too early for their many sails to be
hidden by the dark. The word that the English had come would
have spread fast and far in the hours since. All Normandy knew
they were here.

Holland's company formed an immediate defensive perimeter
around the landing site. A parade of ships dropped anchor behind
them. Henry V was committed to getting his many thousands of
men and horses ashore with all speed, counting on his great numbers to establish a viable beachhead. The small advance party had
to give them that chance.

The high cliffs of the Cap de la Hève, looming above the beach,
caught the first light of the rising sun to the east. Holland and the
others watched that high ground for any sign of movement.

As more English arrived behind them, and no French appeared
ahead, Holland advanced his company along the beach and then
up the slopes into the light of the warming sun, following the local

tracks up onto the heights themselves. At every turn they expected attack, but none was coming.

Henry had brought roughly 12,000 fighting men to France – 9,000 of them archers – along with some 20,000 horses. With them were thousands more: priests, surgeons, cooks, transport specialists, administrators and everything else that was needed to keep an army fighting in foreign territory.[1] It took three days to land it all, and the French made no move to repulse him. Their own forces, uncertain of the English landing point, had been thinly stretched across the lower Normandy coasts. So on the local level, they simply didn't have enough numbers to repel him upon the shore as he arrived. Instead, they'd quickly begun coalescing on the nearby town of Harfleur, just five miles east of the English landing. There was no question in anyone's mind that this would be Henry's first target, so they expended their efforts on preparing the fortification and supply of the town.

Harfleur sat in the valley of the River Lézarde, where the tidal waters of the Seine estuary filled a bustling harbour. Many of the town's 6,000 people fled in advance of what was expected to be a siege. Reinforcements to the garrison filed in and took up residence in the vacated homes while they frantically worked to repair and strengthen the walls and gates. Terrain defences were established, too, as the Lézarde was forced to overflow its channels and flood the areas around the walls. Timber spikes were driven into the river bottom from the harbour to the Seine in order to stave in the hulls of any English ships that tried to approach from that direction, and a chain was put across the water between the town's walls in case anyone nevertheless got through.

Henry's initial position was on the heights west of the town, but by 19 August the duke of Clarence had managed to get a substantial force onto the heights east of the town, too. The English, meanwhile, were busy hauling up the dozen or so artillery pieces they'd brought with them.

Gunpowder had first made its appearance in the Two Hundred Years War at Crécy in 1346. There, Edward III had used the few rudimentary guns he had to send charging French horses into a panic at the sight and sound of their fire. Now, nearly seventy years on, gunpowder weapons had become more common and more capable. The cannon Henry had were not large by any modern sense, but they still packed a frightening punch. And the English gunners settled into an efficient sequence of firing that ensured shots were raining down on the town almost continuously. Under this onslaught, Harfleur ought to have fallen in days. Certainly, Henry thought that it would.

But it wasn't until over a month after Henry's landing that the garrison inside finally agreed to give up. With the town's fortifications severely compromised and much of its interior ruined, on 22 September they learned that no help was coming from the French king and made terms for their surrender.

Henry had his first victory, but the cost had been dire. The weeks spent on the siege were weeks during which the great numbers of his army worked against him. Only so many men were needed for the attacks on the town. Any number beyond that was worse than useless: they cost money, they used up supplies and they profoundly multiplied the vectors of disease transmission within the filthy encampment. Among the great fears of an army holding position is one we have seen before: dysentery. This gastrointestinal disease – in medieval chronicles it's often descriptively called 'bloody flux' or 'bloody diarrhoea' – is an almost inevitable result of thousands of men, horses, and livestock pissing and shitting in one place: water supplies are fouled, creating a surge of the disease that, by its nature, spreads still further within the close quarters of camp.

By the time Henry had taken Harfleur, he'd lost thousands of his men to dysentery: they were either dead or so weakened as to be of no use. Henry decided to send them home.

It appears that there was discussion of Henry going with them, but he sensed that seizing Harfleur – especially at the high cost in men and money that it had taken – was an insufficient prize to quiet those at home who had been itching to take down the Lancastrians. He needed more.

He would get it at Agincourt. That battle would be such a glorious English victory that many historians have assumed that fighting the French was the intention all along.

Trouble is, that doesn't square with any of the facts on the ground. For one thing, if Henry wanted to fight the French, he knew *exactly* where they were. With the king once more incapacitated, the Dauphin was in charge of the realm's defence, and he was gathering his army to the east in Rouen, just up the Seine from Harfleur. Henry could have stayed where he was or taken up position almost anywhere on the 46 miles of ground between Harfleur and Rouen.

Yet on 8 October, he marched directly north, hugging the Channel coast as close as the roads would allow. His destination was Calais, which a day earlier had received word that he was en route. The French had heard that this was his plan as early as 6 October.

Henry had decided to win his glory by following in the footsteps of Edward III's Crécy campaign. Nearly seven decades on, his great-grandfather's march from Normandy to Calais was the stuff of legend. Henry intended to repeat it, even down to the detail of crossing the Somme at Blanchetaque. He would show his strength – and the corresponding weakness of his enemies – by marching unimpeded across northern France. It was the march he was after, not a battle.

But a battle was exactly what he was going to get. Henry could not have known it, but he was marching towards Agincourt, one of the most celebrated triumphs not just in the war, but in all of English history.

March to Agincourt, 1415

According to one of his own chaplains, who soon afterwards wrote a priceless eyewitness account of the events called the *Gesta Henrici Quinti*, the king ordered his men to carry enough rations for a mere eight days on the road.[2] With Calais over 150 miles away, the days getting shorter, and no small amount of time needed to take down and put up a military encampment every 24 hours, he and his men would need to keep up a very fast pace. They had no time for deviation. They took no siege engines or anything else that would slow them down.

The make-up of this army was also ill-suited to a pitched battle. The chaplain informs us that Henry left Harfleur with 5,000 archers and 900 men-at-arms. Modern researchers are certain he had more men in total, but the real point is the ratio of archers to front-line fighters. Most English armies up to this point had a relatively equal ratio between them, which was fitting for the standard English layout for battle that was so successful at Crécy and elsewhere. Henry's time in Wales had certainly given him an appreciation for the power of the longbow, but he couldn't possibly have thought a five-to-one ratio was right for facing the French army.

By 11 October, he had reached what is now called Arques-la-Bataille, and he was already moving too slowly. He lost more time when that town and castle stood against his passage, forcing him to negotiate. The king promised to leave their lands and homes alone if they'd just let him through. This they did, and Henry appears to have been as good as his word. So this wasn't a *chevauchée*, either. The English were not pillaging and terrorizing. They were simply trying to get from Harfleur to Calais as quickly as possible.

On 12 October, he reached Eu. The English army was now less than 20 miles from Blanchetaque. He could get there the next day, though the ford was only passable at low tide, which would happen a couple of hours after sunset. So his crossing would have been anticipated to start at dawn on 14 October. Once safely across the Somme, he'd still be some 60 miles from Calais as the crow flies – much longer by roads, of course – with his supplies scheduled to run out on 16 October. Things were not going well.

Worse news came that night. A minor but fierce engagement on the road had captured some French prisoners. These men reported, with no small satisfaction, that the French army was not behind Henry. It was ahead. Under the command of Boucicaut – who had risen from that young man at the Battle of Roosebeke to become the Constable of France – they had taken up a position on the north bank of the Somme at Blanchetaque.

In 1346, Edward had fought his way across that river in the Battle of Blanchetaque. Henry had surely heard the stories well enough to know that it had been a hard fight indeed. A wet-gap crossing against a committed enemy was a commander's nightmare. His great-grandfather had done it against a hastily assembled local force. Trying the same feat against an entrenched French army would be tantamount to suicide.

Rather than turn back towards the battered walls of Harfleur, Henry headed east, looking for another way across the Somme. The French stalked him on the opposite side of the river, lodging and replenishing stocks in the towns as Henry's men ate their increasingly slim rations in the cold open air.

On 17 October, the French used a defended bridge to make a small sortie against the English army as it was marching near Corbie. Henry managed to fight them off, but it was a near thing. It convinced him that if his archers were to be of any use, they would need protection. Edward had managed this at Crécy with trees, terrain and a wagenburg, but Henry was unlikely to be free to fight on ground of his choosing. So he borrowed the tactic of driving stakes in the ground that had cost so many French knights their lives at the Battle of Nicopolis. His archers set about making them as they shifted the march towards the southeast, seeking distance from the French and a way across the Somme to Calais.

They found it between the towns of Nesle and Voyennes. This was no Blanchetaque, with the men hurtling themselves across the water and into the enemy. Instead, the English stealthily crept single-file through the marshes on a local track. As they skulked across, the men threw wood, rocks and anything else they could find onto the sides of the meagre causeway they'd discovered, hoping to widen it and speed their passage. The effort was a success. On the evening of 19 October, they camped on the other side of the Somme.

Though the English had managed to cross the river, they were about to learn that their situation was, if anything, worse. The French army, which they'd thought was far away, was actually at Péronne, just 11 miles due north and *directly* in the line of any march to the safety of Calais. The night after their crossing of the Somme, the English camp was no doubt stunned by the arrival of three French heralds, who'd come to negotiate a time and place of battle. According to the *Gesta*, the French said they would fight

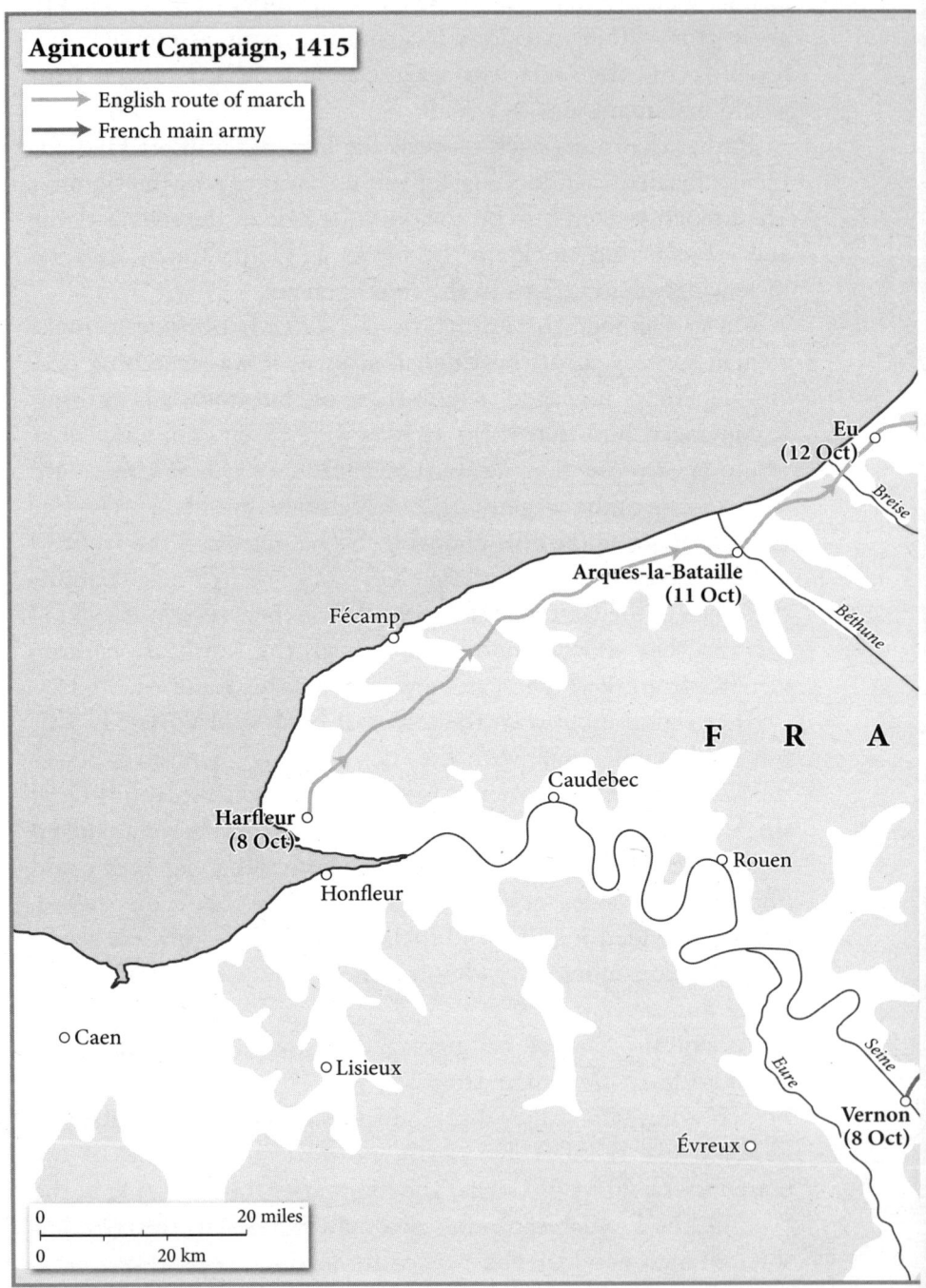

Agincourt Campaign, 1415

→ English route of march
→ French main army

Eu
(12 Oct)

Breise

Arques-la-Bataille
(11 Oct)

Béthune

Fécamp

F R A

Caudebec

Harfleur
(8 Oct)

Rouen

Honfleur

Caen

Lisieux

Eure

Seine

Vernon
(8 Oct)

Évreux

0   20 miles

0   20 km

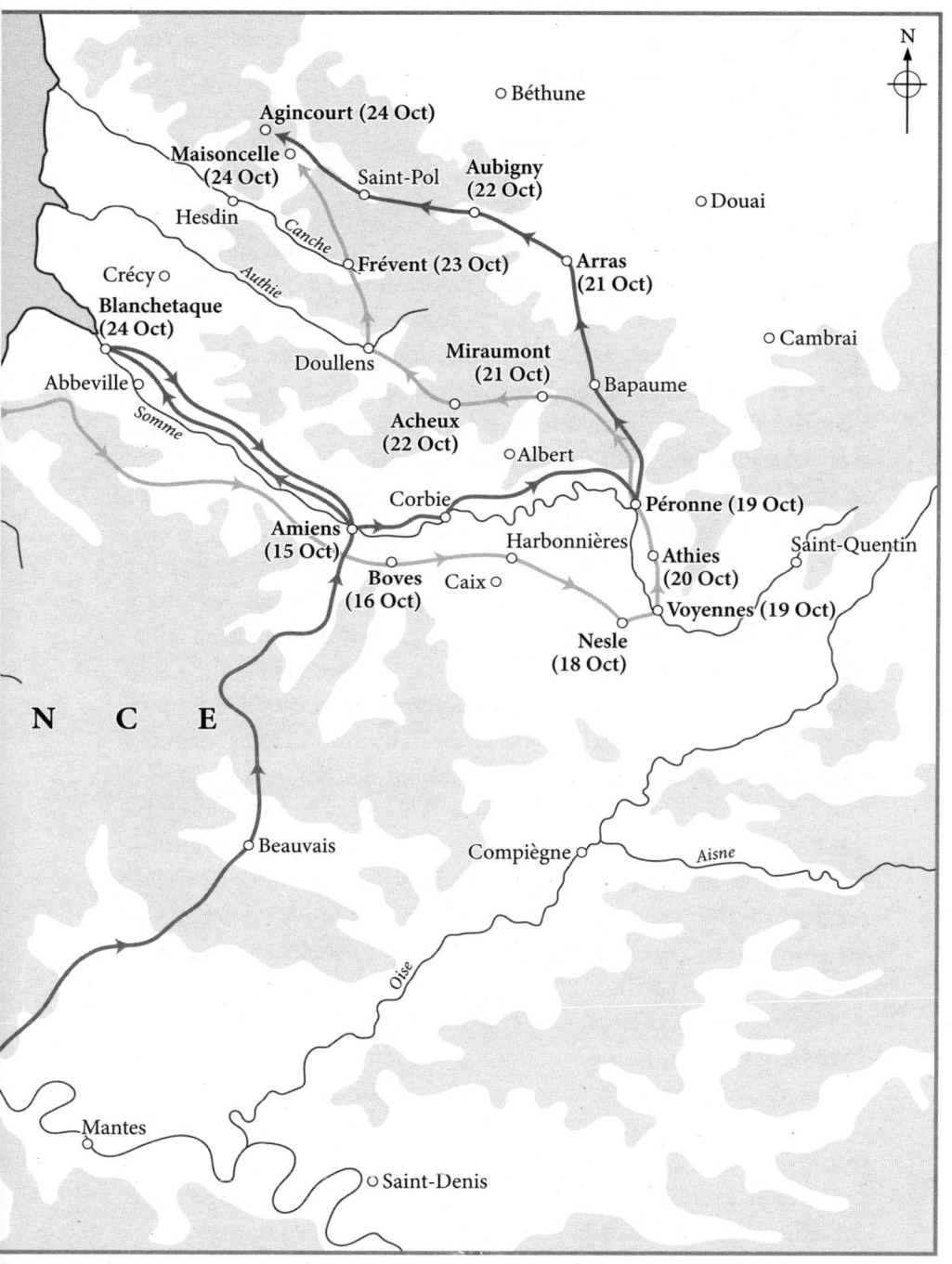

N

Béthune

Agincourt (24 Oct)

Maisoncelle
(24 Oct)

Saint-Pol

Aubigny
(22 Oct)

Douai

Hesdin

Canche

Frévent (23 Oct)

Arras
(21 Oct)

Crécy

Authie

Doullens

Miraumont
(21 Oct)

Cambrai

Blanchetaque
(24 Oct)

Abbeville

Somme

Acheux
(22 Oct)

Bapaume

Albert

Corbie

Péronne (19 Oct)

Amiens
(15 Oct)

Harbonnières

Athies
(20 Oct)

Saint-Quentin

Boves
(16 Oct)

Caix

Voyennes (19 Oct)

Nesle
(18 Oct)

N   C   E

Beauvais

Compiègne

Aisne

Oise

Mantes

Saint-Denis

Henry before he could get to Calais. But French sources claim that Henry agreed to meet the French on the battlefield at a very specific time and place: 24 October at Aubigny-en-Artois, which was about 40 miles north.

Counterfactuals are, by definition, unknowable. But it seems a safe bet to think that, had the French brought their forces to bear against Henry on 21 October, the English would have been destroyed. The French willingness to delay the battle and instead withdraw to another, agreed-upon position was a consequence of the distrust that pervaded France during the reign of the mad king. Many northern lords who had sided with the Armagnacs were wary of being engaged in the field against England only to have Burgundy swoop in and wreck their homes while they were away. A delay bought time not just for the king to head up his army, if he was able to do so, but also for the dukes of Brittany and Burgundy to arrive and create a unified French front.

It all depended on Henry keeping his word and showing up for the fight, but this he did not do. Instead, after the French withdrew from Péronne and headed north, the English walked in their footsteps – the roads were 'churned up by the French army', the *Gesta* tells us – but just before reaching Bapaume on 21 October, Henry suddenly tacked west and camped near Miraumont. He continued west, then northwest for two days, taking a strange, roundabout route if he truly intended to head for Aubigny. On 23 October he reached the main road from Doullens to Aubigny... and almost immediately left the road and headed away from Aubigny to the northwest. The writer of the *Chronicle of Normandy* is succinct in his summation: 'the English did not keep to their covenant that day'.

Henry and his exhausted men were still trying to get to Calais. The French, once their scouts brought them the news, were desperate to catch up with him and make him pay for what they considered treachery. It was a race, and it was one the English would lose.

After a gruelling cross-country march, the English crossed the River Ternoise at Blangy-sur-Ternoise on 24 October. They marched up a local track onto the plateau to the north. There, they caught sight of the French army to their right, 'filling a very broad field like a countless swarm of locusts', the *Gesta* says, 'and there was only a valley, and not so wide as that, between us and them'. The English were at this point on the fields east of Maisoncelle. The French were to their northwest, on the fields south of Ambricourt. There was indeed a small valley between them.

The English would later claim that the disparity in their numbers was enormous. The chaplain first says that the French outnumbered his side thirty to one – that would be close to 175,000 men – then later says they had 60,000. They most certainly did not. But the English *were* outnumbered. We are uncertain of the numbers on both sides, but it was closer to between two and four to one at the time the battle began.

Now in contact with one another, the two armies arrayed for battle in case the other decided to charge. This was smart. No commander wanted to be caught unprepared. Also smart was the fact that neither side gave up their high ground to cross the valley and charge up at the enemy. It had to be particularly tempting on the French side if Henry had indeed broken his word in avoiding Aubigny, but instead of giving Henry an advantage they took steps to ensure that he could not slip away. As the chaplain describes it, the French 'withdrew to a field, at the far side of a certain wood which was close at hand to our left between us and them, where lay our road to Calais'. It was this last bit that was especially important to the French. Manoeuvring northwest, around the trees that surround Tramecourt, they had taken position around the castle and village today called Azincourt, completely cutting off the road to Calais. Henry had nowhere left to run.

When darkness fell, the English army crept up to Maisoncelle and there passed a fitful night under a heavy and cold late-October rain. The French were encamped in the fields ahead of them, so close the men could hear each other talking.

Battle of Agincourt, 1415

As the sun rose over the muddied fields, the two armies arrayed for battle. The English lined up just north of Maisoncelle: their far left was pinned against a small wood there; their far right ran up against the woods closer to Tramecourt. The French were lined up a couple of bowshots in front of them, the castle and village of Azincourt behind them.[3]

We have a good idea what formation Henry wanted to take, because it would be the standard formation that the English had used time and time again. Wings of archers, their positions fixed by terrain and woods to prevent flanking attacks, would funnel the enemy into a stout centre of dismounted men-at-arms. But what had worked so well at Crécy and elsewhere was ill-suited for Agincourt. For one thing, the open ground was not of Henry's choosing. The distance between the protective woods of Maisoncelle and Tramecourt meant that the English position would have to be stretched thin: the men were only four rows deep, according to our sources, and there was no second line ready to come in behind them. The archers planted their stakes to give themselves a little more protection from cavalry charges, but this was a tactic that none of them had used before. There was no telling if it would work. And Henry's ratio of archers to men-at-arms was thoroughly out of whack. If he followed standard practice, his centre would be a small piece amid the great lines of bowmen, making it more likely that the French could break through those wings somewhere. Henry's solution was to modify the standard formation. Instead of a single line of men-at-arms, he created three of them by putting two 'wedges' of archers into that part of the formation, as the chaplain describes them. This widened his centre while compounding the killing zones in front of the wings. He placed himself in the middle of this centre, his banner proudly pronouncing his presence. In command of the right was the duke of York. In command of the left was the baron of Camoys.

It was a good plan, but no matter the 'game face' he wore, Henry had to have been worried. He had done what he could to make up for the deficiencies in his position and his army, but the hard truth was that the field did not favour him. He did not want this fight. His lines were perilously thin, and if the French broke through them – pretty much anywhere – it was game over.

The French must have seemed a massive, pent-up tidal wave

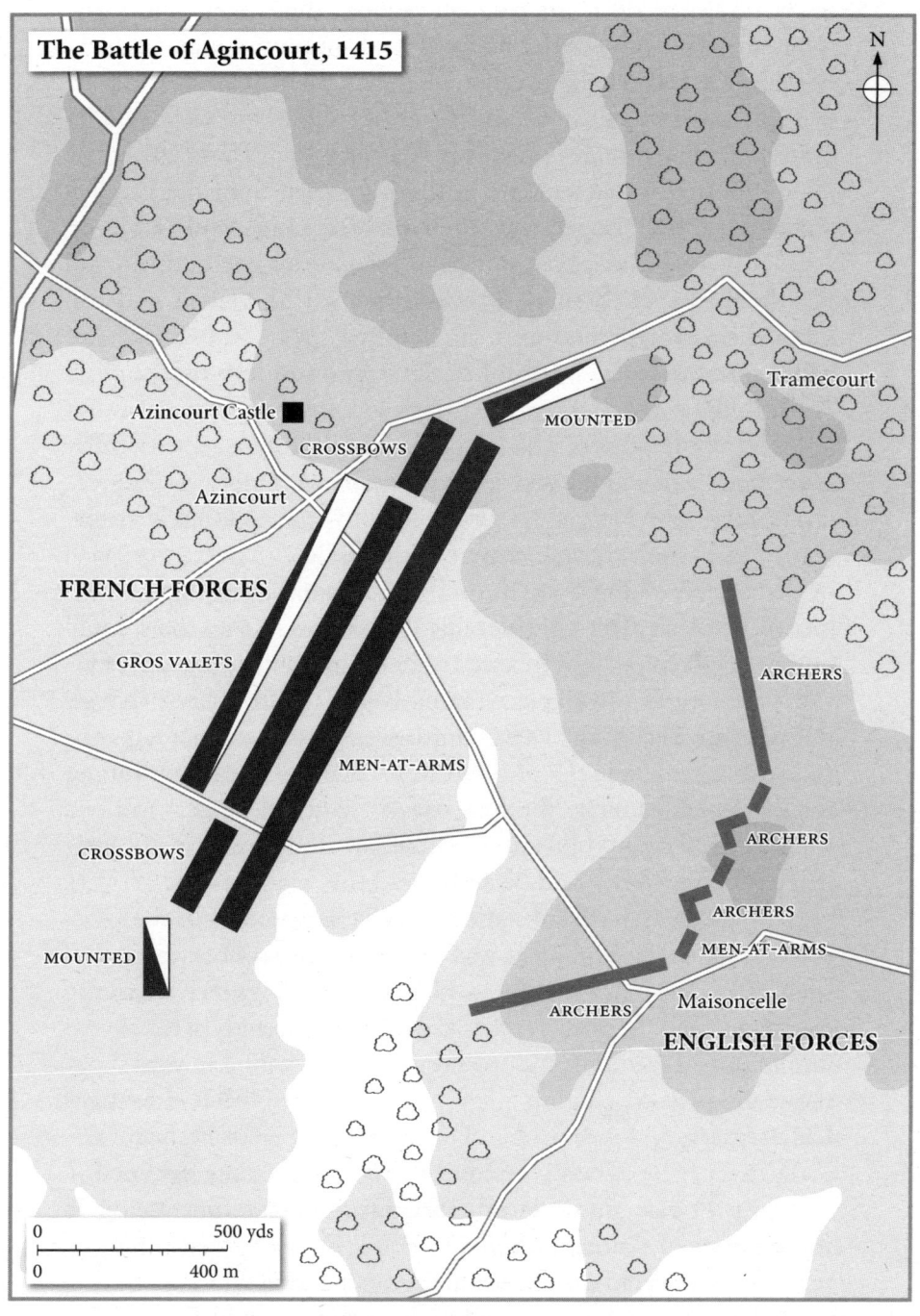

The Battle of Agincourt, 1415

N

Tramecourt

Azincourt Castle

CROSSBOWS

MOUNTED

Azincourt

FRENCH FORCES

ARCHERS

GROS VALETS

MEN-AT-ARMS

ARCHERS

CROSSBOWS

ARCHERS

MEN-AT-ARMS

MOUNTED

Maisoncelle

ARCHERS

ENGLISH FORCES

0   500 yds
0   400 m

ready to sweep over the English troops. Their front line – the vanguard – was an enormous mass of dismounted men-at-arms. Experience had taught the French much about the stinging attacks of arrows against horses. To either side there were smaller units of cavalry, though, which would charge first. Those taking the reins expected to encounter a withering storm from the English archers, but they hoped that their plate armour would hold up against it long enough to punch a hole in the enemy lines and put them to rout. Behind, a second line of the French had still more dismounted men-at-arms, flanked by crossbowmen who could shoot over the heads of the first line and into the English. A third line – the rearguard – was made up of squires and other lower-ranking fighters who, it was hoped, would need to do little more than watch and learn as their betters won glory for France.

As for those betters, the French army was absolutely front-loaded. A French chronicler we call the Religieux states that 'each of the leaders claimed for himself the honor of leading the vanguard', and that after 'considerable debate and so that there could be some agreement, they came to the rather unfortunate conclusion that they should all place themselves in the front line'. Though it is not true that *all* the French lords were in the vanguard, it's fair to say that far too many of them were. It was a matter of honour for these men to make the first attack. Standard-bearers strained their arms, trying to raise the banners of their lords just a little higher so that they could be seen amid the sea of others.

The leaders of both sides met. The chaplain author of the *Gesta* is once again silent on what was said, but other sources – most of them French – make plain that Henry made a significant offer in exchange for safe passage to Calais, though exactly what it was differs in the accounts. He would return Harfleur. He would pay money. He would offer up every fortress the English had south of Calais. He would give up his claim to the throne of France.

Whatever he actually offered, the French leaders declined it. Many in France would later condemn them for this, seeing in it memories of Poitiers, where the Black Prince's grand offers for peace were rejected only to see the French mauled.

By mid-morning, it was clear that there would be a battle.

Around this time, Henry ordered that his baggage train be moved up. These wagons had likely been stationed far to his left behind the woods west of Maisoncelle, and the king felt they were better positioned to his immediate rear, either to act as a possible counter to any attack from the rear or in order to better protect them. If it was the latter, he was right to be worried: the tail end of the baggage train was hit by locals while it was moving. According to the chaplain, they made off with 'royal treasure of great value, a sword, and a crown among other precious objects, as well as all the bedding'.

Henry likely didn't learn of this attack until after the fighting. He was busy starting the battle that would define his legacy.

And he *did* have to start it. For all their insistence on being the first into the fray, the French lords knew better than to do it on Henry's terms. They knew the English wanted to fight from a defensive position, and they could afford to be patient and instead force him to come to them. Henry's men were tired and hungry, many of them suffering from dysentery that they had picked up at Harfleur or in the miserable days since. Every hour, the English grew weaker and the French grew stronger. The king and Dauphin had not shown up. Neither had Burgundy. But Brittany had reached Amiens and was on his way. Other French lords from across the north were speeding to the field, too. Whatever Henry's chances were now, they would not improve with time.

Henry ordered an advance. Trumpets blared. Banners shook, and Henry's line moved forward. There, in the centre, was the monumental prize of the king himself. It was provocation. It was bait. And it worked. The French vanguard, eager to earn a literal king's ransom, advanced to meet him.

Once the French were moving, Henry's line likely stopped. He might even have pulled back a little towards his previous position. The point of his defensive stance, after all, was to give the enemy time to be pummelled by his wings of arrows before they ran into him.

On both sides of the advancing French vanguard, the cavalry was hurtling forward ahead of them. When they were about 300 yards out, the first English arrows were loosed into the air. Few hit. The damage would have been minimal. But the devastating power of the longbow is not contained in a single volley. It's the multiplication of thousands of archers shooting at speed.

In the movies, longbowmen loose arrows with such speed that they can look something like machine guns. But while it's true that a trained archer is capable of very rapid shots, in reality the men were more careful in choosing their targets and loosing their bows. They didn't have enough arrows to fire at will. Movies will also show their shots puncturing plate armour, which is something they did not do. Plate armour was built to withstand these impacts. To get to the man inside, an arrow needed to break the more vulnerable protections at a seam – like those that enabled movement at the neck, shoulders and groin – or by chance get the angle right to pass through an eye slit. Most of the arrows would have missed a target altogether and been buried in the mud. Those that did hit likely shattered on protective plate. Surprisingly, though, those splintering arrows may have been the most dangerous of all. Slivers of wood, careening arrowheads and broken shafts became chaotic projectiles of their own, glancing out at unexpected angles. With 5,000 or more archers able to let loose, the breaking arrows exploded among the French riders, spraying fragments like wooden grenades.

Only a few of the charging French made it through this awful storm to reach the stakes that protected the archers. Some horses were impaled. Riders who fell were killed by archers who used small daggers to dig for arteries. Animals and men screamed. The chaplain blandly reports that the French cavalry was 'forced to fall back under showers of arrows', but the brutal reality behind those words had to be truly horrific. And it was only the start of the carnage.

Many of the horses that had been turned back were wounded, driven mad by the stinging strikes of the arrows. Careening towards safety, they crashed into the advancing vanguard, smashing holes in the lines and crushing men.

The lordly banners in the vanguard shook, but they kept coming. Whatever else history would say about what happened at Agincourt, it cannot be denied that the French were brave, struggling through the thick mud that had been further churned by the hooves of the cavalry. But then came the hammering of the longbows:

> the terrifying thrum of 5,000 bowstrings singing in unison, the rushing sound of feathered shafts flying up then flying down, a sudden darkening of the light as the arrow-cloud obscured the sun, a deafening clatter of steel on steel, like the heaviest imaginable hail against a tin roof, mingling with a chorus of curses and screams as some of the arrow-tips sank into flesh.[4]

Naturally shying away from the swarming arrows, the men packed together as they advanced, and the chaplain tells us that the 'wedges' of archers that Henry had used to widen his centre thereby caused the French vanguard to break into thirds as it approached. When men tripped and fell in the mud, there was no time and no space to help them up. In the press, most were trampled further down, suffocating in wet, dark earth.

How many fell in that hellish march, we cannot know. But many, undoubtedly more than enough to punch through Henry's thin lines, got through. Shouting the glory of France, they stormed into the waiting English men-at-arms.

Henry's lines bent under the onslaught. The chaplain says they staggered backwards 'almost a spear's length'. But heels dug into the ground. No one turned away. When a man fell in front, the man behind him stepped forward into the gap. The melee was fierce, with the king himself in the thick of it, a crown atop his helmet. Someone struck him so forcefully in the head that one of its jewels was flung into the gore-thickened mud. The duke of Gloucester, fighting at his side, was cut through the groin.

But the English held. Step by step they began to push back.

If any in the exhausted French vanguard wanted to run, they could not. The second line, as planned, had advanced in their wake. It shoved them forward into the butchery. As the men fell, the piles of bodies became points of solid, high ground amid the hellish mud, with fighters scrambling atop them for firmer footing. The weight of it all smothered those who'd fallen but still lived. The archers, by now well out of arrows, launched themselves at the flanks of the French with any weapon they could get their hands on.

French lords removed their helmets and began to surrender, and as their banners fell the onslaught sputtered and died. Men were taking prisoners left and right. This, too, was chaos, as we saw at Poitiers. The chaplain remarks of the French that, 'even of their nobly born', some 'that day surrendered themselves more than ten times'. In ransoms, it meant riches beyond the dreams of most of the men on the field.

But then shouts rang out that the third line of the French, the rearguard, was now getting ready to advance. It probably wasn't true. But Henry didn't know that. All he knew was that his exhausted army had only barely survived. His archers, without arrows, could do little to stop them. Worst of all, many if not most of his men-at-arms were distracted with herding up their prisoners, who at this point probably outnumbered them. If the rearguard indeed charged, what seemed like an extraordinary English victory could quickly become an extraordinary English defeat. To survive, the king needed every man possible at the front line. Damn the ransoms.

In desperation, he ordered the prisoners executed. His men-at-arms balked at first. So a furious Henry immediately tasked an esquire in command of a company of archers to do the deed. They set upon the helpless men, slitting throats and bashing skulls.

At last, the French rearguard withdrew. It might have been because they were terrified by the barbaric murder of their comrades and lords. It might have been because those lords, having all been in the front lines, were simply leaderless. We are unlikely to know.

With their withdrawal, Henry ordered the ghastly executions halted, and the Battle of Agincourt was over. With his victory, Henry had secured his exalted position in England's history.

Different Directions, 1415–16

Agincourt towers in the English imagination for good reason: Henry should not have won. It was an extraordinary victory by a most extraordinary leader. And like Edward's similarly surprising victory at Crécy or the Black Prince's win at Poitiers, it would alter the trajectory of the Two Hundred Years War by sending the two kingdoms in very different directions.

In the aftermath of the victory Henry was glowing. He welcomed a number of French heralds to his tent, pointing out the totality of the French defeat and impressing upon them the fact that their sick king was incapable of such action. They didn't need to be told. It would soon enough be said all over Europe.

Yet the king of England was no fool. He was still in the middle of enemy territory, and his army was in worse shape than ever. Later English writers would claim there'd only been a few dozen losses on his side, but we know this wasn't true. French reports of roughly 600 English dead are far more likely, and as many as 10 per cent of his fighting force may have fallen. The survivors at least got to eat. The French encampment was well supplied, and the English took to it with all the abandon of an alcoholic at a brewery. Then they packed up and headed for the safety of Calais as quickly as they could. Henry had no interest in facing another army in the field. We have the names of nearly 300 prisoners that they took with them, including the dukes of Bourbon and Orléans, four counts and the marshal Boucicaut. Among the French dead left behind were the dukes of Alençon, Bar and Brabant, as well as nine counts, a viscount, an archbishop, France's constable and admiral, and over a thousand knights. Of the untitled men, there were likely thousands more.

The English reached the walls of Calais on 28 October, and returned to England just a few weeks later to a hero's welcome. When he had left for Harfleur, his throne had been anything but secure. There was no whisper of that now. What's more, the English dream of winning in France, after a generation in abeyance, seemed suddenly and vibrantly real.

When Henry had attacked, France had only just begun to pull itself out of the civil war between the Armagnacs and the Burgundians. The court of the mad king was so fractured that Jean the Fearless – whose forces might well have reversed the outcome – had not even shown up to the Battle of Agincourt. Instead, the

French army that *did* show up was very largely Armagnac. Henry's victory had thereby tipped the scales of power between the two French parties wildly out of balance. By mid-November, the duke of Burgundy was gathering men to march on Paris in the name of protecting the king.

It was a play for power, and one that the Dauphin quickly diagnosed. He mustered forces in the capital and tried to out-manoeuvre Burgundy by sending word that not only was the king perfectly protected, but also that the English army was already sailing back to England. When Jean the Fearless continued his march towards Paris, the Dauphin appointed as constable one of the only major Armagnac leaders left: the count of Armagnac himself, who'd been overseeing the French forces in Gascony during the Agincourt campaign.

Just days before Armagnac's arrival in Paris, the young Dauphin died, likely of dysentery. His position was taken by his young-er brother, who was being raised in Hainaut, in the court of his father-in-law. For the time being, the new Dauphin refused to take a side in the dispute, which freed Armagnac to crack down against his adversaries. Burgundy backed off for the moment, but it was clear that the kingdom was once more on the verge of civil war.

Looking for a win that would both bolster his party's status and set back the English threat, Armagnac turned his attention to the recapture of Harfleur. He had good reason to be hopeful of its recovery. Henry V's long siege had left it in near ruin, and his expulsion of the town's French inhabitants had left few hands to rebuild the fortifications, restore the buildings and begin recreat-ing the kind of military bastion that could serve English interests. The English garrison that Henry had left behind had done its best over the winter, as had the first waves of English colonizers. But it was still vulnerable.

In March 1416, a significant part of the English garrison was on a foraging raid along the coast north of Harfleur when Armagnac's forces caught them unawares. In a pair of actions sometimes called the Battle of Valmont, the English barely escaped ruin. The con-stable, furious, put fifty of his own men to the noose for what he considered their failures in the field. He then put the English in a metaphorical noose: he blockaded Harfleur with a fleet of French and Genoese ships, then established a land-side siege of the town to starve them out.

Jean the Fearless, though, still continued to be a vexing thorn in Armagnac's side: at multiple points the constable had to rush back to Paris to block one Burgundian plot or another, and each occasion was a chance for the beleaguered English garrison to survive a couple more weeks. They managed to hold on until 15 August, when an English resupply fleet under the command of the duke of Bedford fought its way through the blockade in the Battle of the Seine. A costly, largely forgotten battle, it relieved the siege. And it wasn't the only harsh blow to hit Armagnac that summer.

We met Sigismund of Luxembourg, the king of Hungary and Germany, at the Battle of Nicopolis in 1396, where his sage advice to the French nobles was rejected as cowardice, resulting in ruin for the crusaders. The experience had made him both wary of the French and resolute in his conviction that Christendom had to unite against the Ottoman empire. The Western Schism had to end. To make it happen, he had managed to get representatives of the popes – by now there were *three* of them – to come to the Council of Constance beginning in 1414. The aim was to get them all to resign so that a new, universal pope might be chosen. By 1416, though, Sigismund felt that the French were against the effort. After a sequence of what he felt were personal French slights, he decided to turn against the French: he signed the Treaty of Canterbury with Henry V on the same day the English ships reached Harfleur. The two men agreed to help each other against their common enemy in France.

That same summer, the frustrated duke of Burgundy came to an agreement with Henry: the English would not attack Burgundian lands, and the Burgundians would not fight against the English. The last thing that Jean the Fearless wanted was a peace between England and France that would see the full weight of the French kingdom turned against him. So this was, in essence, a doctrine of neutrality. For the Armagnacs, it was treason.

Once more, the two sides in France were at each other's throats, and tensions only grew when the latest Dauphin – less than two years after his brother – died unexpectedly in April 1417. This made the mad king's eleventh child the *fifth* Dauphin during his reign. The boy, like two elder brothers who died before his birth, was named after his father. We will hear much about him in the later chapters of this book, as he would eventually come to the throne of France as Charles VII. At the moment, though, he was fourteen years old and a prize in the tug-of-war between the Armagnac and Burgundian factions fighting to take control of the realm.

Crisis led to crisis. Jean the Fearless promulgated stories that he alone was a loyal retainer of the king and no one should pay taxes to the crooked Armagnacs. Men flocked to his banner. Cities did, too. Armagnac and the constable tried to staunch the bleeding, but the flow was too great. Hearing that Rouen was threatening to throw in with Burgundy, the latest Dauphin rushed out from Paris and managed to hold it at the end of July. But the same day, up the Seine on the opposite side of the capital, the city of Troyes gave itself over to Jean the Fearless. In Paris, the count of Armagnac brutally repressed any voices in support of Burgundy.

All hell was breaking loose, and Henry hadn't even arrived.

Reconquest of Normandy, 1417

After his success at Agincourt, the king of England was convinced that he could not only get the French to reinstate the Treaty of Brétigny, but that he could add to it his gain at Harfleur. The dream for England was to make this port into a second Calais, but Henry and his advisors recognized how dramatically different the two situations were. In 1346, Edward had managed to take control of not just Calais but also a significant ring of land beyond it: the Pale of Calais. This had provided both a military zone of control to protect the city and a landscape for agricultural production to help sustain it. Regular support ships still needed to make the 25-mile crossing of the Channel from Dover to Calais, but on those instances when the sea was too dangerous – whether due to weather or attack – the Pale was a vital backstop. In 1415, though, Henry had seized Harfleur alone. And it sat more than 100 miles across the Channel, in the very heart of French waters at the mouth of the

Seine. Harfleur, even more than Calais, needed more land.

To acquire what Harfleur needed – and to bring the French to a final, lasting peace – the king of England decided to invade France again in the summer of 1417. Though his army was not quite as large as that which sailed in 1415, it was nonetheless formidable.

Exactly what he planned to do with it is less clear. Henry's strategy in 1417 is frustratingly hard to follow, probably because it changed repeatedly.

His initial intention, it seems, was to begin his campaign from Harfleur. This would have made sense. It would enable him to secure that port and use it as a base to expand English control of the ground precisely where he needed it. Yet when his army made its landing on 1 August, it did so not in friendly Harfleur on the north bank of the Seine but instead on the French beaches near Deauville on the south bank of the Seine.

Judging from his initial actions here, Henry's new plan was bold: after landing, his scouts rode east with all speed in advance of his army, seeking the surrender of the port of Honfleur, which sat almost directly opposite Harfleur. If he could take it, he'd control the mouth of the Seine from both shores.

The Dauphin was up the river at Rouen, less than 50 miles away. It's easy to imagine his despair. Henry would never be more vulnerable than he was in landing. But the strength he was bringing ashore was greater than the force that the Dauphin was using to keep the great city of Rouen under control. The Dauphin stood a good chance of losing the fight in the field. And even if he *did* win, he might well find that Rouen and perhaps even Paris had fallen to the duke of Burgundy in his absence.

Still, the Dauphin decided to withdraw to the capital. He had to hope that the English invasion would unify the kingdom of France behind his authority, negating Burgundy's threats and giving him the power to take the fight to Henry in the field more evenly matched. Normandy, at least for now, would have to fend for itself.

Remarkably, the first reports out of the region may have been positive. According to the Religieux, the Armagnac authorities had sussed out Henry's plan to assault Honfleur, and they'd prepared accordingly: 'they had taken care to supply the town, already surrounded by thick walls and a deep ditch, with supplies of food and all manner of defensive weapons, as well as a strong garrison'. When this garrison refused to budge after both threats and bribes, Henry put Honfleur to siege: 'the king ordered his archers and siege-machines to be stationed around the town, and they built machines that hurled massive stones, which made noise like a horrible thunder, as if they had been launched from the very gates of Hell'.[5]

Day after day, the garrison of Honfleur held out. The Religieux suggests they even managed a few surprise sorties against the besiegers.

Most histories omit or gloss over this siege of Honfleur. Henry himself likely wanted it forgotten. It certainly wasn't what he would have hoped for in 1417. Memories of what he'd suffered in taking Harfleur were surely surfacing. He'd salvaged that campaign with Agincourt, but he knew how easily that could have gone another way. He couldn't afford to be bogged down again.

After several days, he abruptly lifted the siege. His scouts were telling him that Honfleur's defiance was the exception in lower Normandy. To the east, the roads were clogged with refugees, and the emptied towns they left behind were ripe for the picking.

A couple of weeks later, Henry followed those roads to the walls of Caen, the great capital that Edward III had sacked and briefly held in 1346. Two great church complexes, both founded by William the Conqueror, overlooked the proud city just as they had in Edward's day. Henry's army used both as bases for attack, hauling artillery up onto their heights in order to rain fire upon the city below.

It didn't take long for Caen to break. When the English got through on 4 September, the sack was as ruthless and bloody as it had been in 1346. Henry gave orders that women, children and priests ought to be spared, but there's little evidence he was obeyed. Amid the looting, nearly 2,000 people were massacred in the streets and squares.

All the while, Jean the Fearless continued to press forward. He insisted that he was not in league with the English – this was technically true – and that he only intended to purge France of the Armagnac sickness that had kept her from adequately fighting against the invaders. Among Burgundy's strengths was a formidable artillery train, whose use – or the threat of it – led many to surrender quickly.[6] In August he took Doullens, Reims and Beauvais, among other great prizes. He'd swept north and west around Paris, crossing the Seine at Meulan-en-Yvelines. Vernon and Mantes-la-Jolie – the latter of which we saw taken by some sort of sneak attack in 1364 – gave themselves over unasked along with many other towns. By 21 September, the Burgundian army was in Montrouge, roughly three miles from the Île de la Cité in the heart of Paris. The Parisian Metro connects them today. Jean the Fearless was so confident that the Armagnac garrison would come and face him that he drew up a battle plan for the occasion.[7]

In truth, the constable was paralysed with indecision. The fall of Caen had been followed by a sequence of towns giving themselves over to Henry, who was so confident in his conquests that he was setting himself to the necessary work of establishing regulations for the administration of his new gains. Odd as it may seem, the tedious normalcy of this bureaucracy was welcomed by many who had grown weary of the back and forth between the Armagnacs and the Burgundians. The English foothold grew. On 1 October, Henry marched on Alençon, whose duke had died at Agincourt. He had its submission by the end of the month. Amid it all, the queen fell into league with Jean the Fearless and set up a kind of breakaway government outside the Armagnac-held capital. When she made pronouncements against the Armagnacs, the Dauphin and constable trotted out the mad king to make pronouncements against her. Hardly anyone knew who was truly in charge.

Paris Massacres, 1418

In the darkness just after midnight on 29 May 1418, a gate of Paris was opened, only a few blocks south of the Pont Neuf today. Waiting outside was a host of armed men. A few weeks later, roughly 2,000 citizens had been killed.[8] The Paris Massacres were massively important in their own right, but they also allow us to see how violence worked during these times – why it happened, what it looked like and what we can learn from it.

First, the facts.

Under the leadership of Jean de Villiers de l'Isle-Adam a few hundred Burgundians had, with the help of spies inside the walls, plotted their action for days. On 29 May, after making their entrance, Villiers and his company quickly made their way across the Seine to the Grand Châtelet, at that time the judicial and penitentiary centre of the city. A growing crowd of Parisians had already gathered there, armed with whatever they could find. They fanned out through the city, shouting for more support. The people answered.

The Burgundian attack on 29 May 1418 was a literal surprise, but in retrospect the bigger surprise might have been that so little blood was shed in the immediate hours after the people of Paris broke free. For close to five years now the Armagnacs had ruled a city that despised them. And the more that the populist Burgundian elements within the Parisian citizenry had resisted Armagnac rule, the more the Armagnacs had tightened their fist.

The Burgundian leaders had three high-priority targets. First was the king. Mad though Charles VI might have been, he was nevertheless the theoretically unifying figurehead of the state. From the Grand Châtelet, Villiers made a beeline for the Hôtel Saint-Pol to secure him. This they did.

The second target was the count of Armagnac, who as constable had been king in all but name. He managed to escape his mansion in disguise and hid in the cellar of a neighbouring mason on promises he'd be kept safe. He was betrayed, and the mason turned him over to the Burgundians.

The third target was the Dauphin. By the time the Burgundians reached his lodgings, the fifteen-year-old had already been roused by an Armagnac knight named Tanneguy III du Châtel, who hurried him to the security of the Bastille, where he gathered some of the remaining supporters with the standing garrison there. From there, Tanneguy got the heir out of Paris and out of Burgundian reach in Melun. Failing to secure the Dauphin was a costly error for the Burgundians, though no one could have known it yet. There were instead peals of bells ringing in the city he left behind, a city that thought itself free. The Burgundians had seized the capital, and they had done it with little cost of life – though the toll would swiftly increase.

A few days later, Tanneguy mounted an attempt to retake the city for the Armagnacs. His force was also let into the city by partisan conspirators, but they did not meet with the same success. Hundreds of Armagnac fighters were killed or captured. Many more ordinary citizens died in the following hours as Parisians hunted down suspected Armagnac sympathizers in retribution. Even more died on 12 June, when rumours reached a fever pitch that a far larger assault was being planned by the iron-fisted Armagnac party, and angry citizens descended on the prisons to butcher the Armagnacs held within. Many, including the count of Armagnac himself, were ripped to pieces in the frenzied onslaught of people shouting 'Peace! Peace! Long live the king and the duke of Burgundy!'

England had seen something similar in 1381 during the Peasants' Revolt. Flanders had seen multiple insurrections, as far back as the revolt that was crushed at the Battle of Cassel in 1328. France, too, had already had its share of revolts. The Jacquerie in 1358. The Capochien in 1413. What is striking, however, was how many of those hacking people to death on the streets of Paris could do so while calling for peace.[9]

What happened in the Paris Massacres – and how it changed France, the war and ultimately the monarchy itself – depended upon the Armagnac and Burgundian parties, which to this point we have more or less treated as political labels. But ordinary people were willing to fight and die over these tribal loyalties. They didn't do so because the civil war was important to Jean the Fearless or any other rich noble but because it was important to *them*.

The duchy of Orléans and the county of Armagnac – the twin foundations of the Armagnac party's power – were situated in the western and southwestern parts of France. We can broadly categorize their party as being that of the coast: focused on the maritime trade routes of the Atlantic ports, they felt that a strong

Anglo-Gascon state – especially one on the expanded borders of the Treaty of Brétigny – correspondingly weakened their own powers and prosperity, making them necessarily anti-English.[10] A less obvious but more important corollary is that they tended to be in favour of a strong and centralized monarchy. A realm in which power was divvied up among the lords was a realm that could not enforce its claim to Gascony or maintain control over the trade routes. Given that Paris was the traditional capital of the realm, the Armagnacs were dedicated to its control, but they were not Parisians themselves. No one in the ruling classes was in favour of rule *by the people* – not in any sense that we would mean today – but it was nevertheless true that the Armagnacs appeared more opposed to such an idea than the Burgundian party might have been. The Armagnacs were perceived as foreign rulers in Paris, dedicated to propping up a mad king perpetuating a mad war against England that had cost the deaths at Agincourt and so much else, and all for their own power and profit.

The Burgundian party had come to stand against these things, as men of the Continent. Gascony was not their concern. War with England was not in their interest. Neither was centralization under the existing system: the murder of Louis of Orléans, so shocking to the establishment, had been justified as tyrannicide, a blow against centralization and perhaps even against monarchical power itself. And the Burgundians – with their power base in northern and eastern France – had an affinity with Paris, perhaps especially so with the tradesmen and the lower classes whose lives depended on stability and Continental trade. Jean the Fearless had made this pitch more or less directly to the common people while still claiming to uphold the best interests of the king and his kingdom.

But both the Armagnacs and Burgundians bought into the idea that the king was king because God wanted him to be. This was the reason that they could not simply be rid of him, mad though he might be. In the king, there was unity. Even so, because he *was* a mad king, he could not himself unify his people. This left the fighting factions to create structures of unification of their own, while never giving up on the firm and fundamental belief that the people *must* be unified. It was this potent mix that proved to be such a dreadful recipe for violence.

When the people dragged the count of Armagnac from his prison, stripped him, beat him to death and then carved the jagged red cross of Burgundy into his corpse before hanging it up for all to see, they believed the violence was not only justified, but *proper*. Rich prisoners could buy their freedom and renewed privileges in ways that the commons could not. Stripping him stripped away that class separation, and executing him publicly enacted punishment in the open rather than in secret. It was, they would have thought, how God willed it.

Something of this supernatural sense of justice can be seen in the journal of a bourgeois of Paris, who records that after one of the massacres had left over 500 battered corpses in the streets, 'it rained so hard that no one could smell any bad odor, and the wounds of the dead were washed clean: in the morning there was no butcher's blood or filth upon them'.[11] In such a view, the city was being cleansed, with God's blessing. And the result would be a unity that would bring peace.

Those on the other side, of course, saw the violence in a *very* different light. One observer of the killings wrote that 'the murders were perpetrated by a popular fury', and that they were 'unthinkable and unheard of up to now'.[12] In time, this view took a firmer hold. So while the Burgundians 'won' the Paris Massacres – they were the ones who, in the end, held Paris – it was, like the Black Prince's win at Nájera, a Pyrrhic victory. The sheer scale of the horror made the revolt... well, *revolting* to a great many people. There was a sense that something had fundamentally changed in the world. And although Jean the Fearless had himself made efforts to curtail the violence, he was nevertheless the one most identified with the bloodshed, and it tainted his reputation considerably.

For the Dauphin, his dangerous flight from a murder-minded city at the age of fifteen left a lasting impression. It also instilled in his party an even greater sense that absolutism was the answer to the kingdom's ills. The people had to be kept in check. For the ruling class, this was the natural order of things, which meant that any rebellion was an abomination. From this low point, the powerful, divine-right French monarchies of the future would grow.

In the moment, though, no one could suspect that the teenaged Dauphin would change the direction of the kingdom. He was outside Paris, trying to blockade the Burgundian-held city, trying to create a working government out of the shattered remnants of his Armagnac allies, and trying to insist that any orders purportedly given by his royal parents were actually those of the duke of Burgundy who had them in his control.

Siege of Rouen, 1418–19

All the while, Henry had resolved to take Rouen. Sitting on the north bank of the Seine, Rouen was one of the largest cities in France, and among its most heavily protected. Its thick walls were almost four miles around and crowned with sixty towers. Its gates were heavily fortified. And it had a garrison of over 2,000 men in addition to at least 10,000 citizens who were prepared to defend their homes with their lives.

The English army arrived on 29 July, and it was immediately clear that Henry had learned lessons from his siege of Harfleur. Although that fight had been successful, it had cost him dearly in men. What was more, his artillery had so thoroughly destroyed the town that the cost of rebuilding and refortifying it had been a significant drag on his war efforts. So although the English sited their cannon to threaten the town, he never ordered the devastating barrages that had beaten Harfleur into submission. Rouen, a true jewel in the crown of France, would not be left in rubble. He'd starve it to death.

Barricading a city was no easy task, but the English set themselves to it with resolute determination. Lines of supply extended out from their existing conquests in Normandy, bringing needed men and materiel, a lifeline that helped maintain their strength in the field and reduce the likelihood of disease in their camps. Patiently, they encircled the town and ran chains across the mighty river beside it, cutting off any chance of supply by water as well as land. By October, the city was on its own.

The siege of Rouen can be held up as a testament to Henry's superb planning, but it was just as equally a testament to France's civil war. A relief army might have crushed the English against the city's daunting walls, but no one was in a position to send one. The duke of Burgundy's strength was dedicated to holding his Parisian prize against his Armagnac enemies. The Dauphin's strength was dedicated to overcoming him. In their absence, Henry had only local forces to contend with.

Inside Rouen, conditions worsened daily. By Christmas, its starving citizens had already been reduced to fighting over scraps of dead vermin. Several thousand 'useless mouths' as they are often called – women, children, the poor and those otherwise unable to aid in the defence – were cast out from a city that could not afford to keep them alive. The English refused to let them through the siege lines, forcing them back with arrows until they were huddled in the cold amid the refuse at the base of Rouen's walls. Day by day, they starved there.

Rouen asked for a negotiated surrender on New Year's Eve. The people had little to bargain with besides the prized city: they knew Henry saw it as a capital, so they threatened to begin destroying it from within if they received no mercy.

On 19 January 1419, negotiations were completed and the city surrendered. Rouen was a great city in its own right. But its control over Normandy brought more towns into submission, each advance securing the gains behind it.

Assassination of Burgundy, 1419

The taking of Rouen was a wake-up call for both the Armagnacs and the Burgundians. For all the animosity between them, they ran a real risk of fighting over the last oar on a sinking ship. And now the English frontier was less than a couple of dozen miles from the walls of Paris.

That summer, the Dauphin and Jean the Fearless met at Pouilly-le-Fort. Neither man was in a strong position. The Burgundians had possession of Paris and the mad king, but the cost had left their coffers empty and their reputation in tatters.

The Armagnacs worried that the duke's history of friendly relations with the English – and his economic connections to them through the Low Countries – might lead him into an alliance with Henry V that would leave the Dauphin completely isolated. Ironically, Jean the Fearless had the same fear: if the Dauphin made peace with Henry, Burgundy would stand alone.

On 11 July the two French leaders forged the outline of a way forward. In the Treaty of Pouilly-le-Fort they swore their friendship and made peace, and they made common cause against the English. The bells of Paris rang in celebration.

Exactly how the Armagnacs and Burgundians would work together to oust Henry V was initially unclear. A further meeting was planned at Montereau, just outside Paris. There was a significant castle there, standing at the confluence where the Yonne entered the Seine, guarding bridges over both rivers. The fortress was in the possession of the Dauphin, but it was agreed that he would withdraw to the town itself, which was on the south side of the confluence. The duke could hold the castle, and the two men would meet on the bridge between, the waters of the Yonne slowly rolling beneath them.

In preparation, timber walls were built on either side of the bridge's midpoint, creating a private enclosure for the negotiations. The duke and the Dauphin were allowed an escort of only ten men each, and all would be sworn to oaths of peace before they were allowed through the doors into the meeting. No one was supposed to be armed.

On 10 September, the two groups arrived. Jean the Fearless, it was later said, had misgivings about the situation, but he decided to proceed anyway. In the enclosure, he made a show of kneeling to the Dauphin before giving a speech reaffirming their agreement and the peace. The Dauphin listened, appeared to give him thanks. Then he exchanged a glance with Tanneguy, the knight who'd smuggled him out of Paris the previous year. Tanneguy produced 'a large war axe' that he'd been hiding.[13] Another man tried to grab it, but the knight used the weapon to drive him back. Then, turning, he swung the axe into Jean the Fearless, driving the blade between his shoulders. In a flash, the Dauphin's men were rushing forward, shouting 'Kill! Kill!' Someone produced a blade and began slashing at the duke, who vainly tried to block the blows with his arm. His eyes were wide in horror. His right hand was nearly cut loose. Multiple blades opened hideous gashes across his face. Tanneguy struck again with the axe, splintering his jaw. More blades flashed out, plunging into the fallen duke. At some point – remembering how Louis of Orléans had been mutilated when he'd been assassinated on Jean's orders in 1407 – someone finished cutting off his right hand.

The Dauphin made no attempt to stop the violence. It was said that he only stood apart and watched. His indifference was one of several reasons that many suspected that the killing was premeditated, and that it had been done with the Dauphin's consent and encouragement. The murder was more than an act of long-delayed vengeance. The Armagnacs who conspired with the Dauphin that day thought that the removal of the powerful Jean the Fearless would end the civil war and unite France against England under the leadership of the Dauphin.

It achieved just the opposite.

Over a century after Jean's assassination, King François I of France was shown the skull of the duke in the monastery of Champmol. Among the gashes on the bone, one side of it had been caved in. 'Through this hole', the king was told, 'the English entered France.'

It was no exaggeration. For all his dalliances with the English, Jean the Fearless had ultimately decided his future was with the Dauphin and France. His murder changed all that. Rather than buckle under the authority of the Dauphin, the Burgundians buckled in to fight against him.

Treaty of Troyes, 1420

Henry V was a man who recognized opportunity, so when news of the killing was brought to him, he was thrilled. The Armagnac–Burgundian civil war had given him his victories at Agincourt,

Caen and Rouen. France's leadership devolving into a blood feud promised even more.

True enough, before the month was out, he received embassies from the city of Paris asking him to bring peace to the kingdom. He welcomed them while successfully besieging Gisors. His position was clear: he would take the hand of Catherine, the daughter of the mad king, and he would rule as regent until her father's death. After that, the crown of France would be his. The Dauphin would be disinherited.

Such a proposal would have gone nowhere before the assassination of Jean the Fearless. Now, many saw it as the only path forward.

While the queen and the new duke of Burgundy – Jean's son, Philippe the Good – considered the offer, Henry moved ever closer to Paris. In October, Meulan surrendered, giving his armies free rein to approach the city on both banks of the Seine. By November, Saint-Germain-en-Laye was in Henry's hands. There were real questions about what Paris might do if and when the English arrived at its gates. Henry might not need to fire a shot.

In December, the Burgundians settled on a peace with the English. It was the least ill choice available: they had no interest in making peace with the Armagnacs.

Over the winter and into the spring, the Dauphin tried in vain to strengthen his position. An attempt to use the chaos to flip leadership of Brittany into the Dauphin's control via *coup d'état* failed abysmally: it only succeeded in driving the Bretons more securely into Henry's arms. The Dauphin also tried to boost his military forces by importing an army of Scots. In March, a few hundred of them were lost in a military debacle outside Fresnay. The vultures seemed to be circling.

On 21 May 1420, Henry strode into the cathedral of Troyes in a carefully orchestrated formal procession. Charles VI was too ill to be present, so the duke of Burgundy and the queen of France acted in his name. Along with Princess Catherine, they met the English king and walked with him up the steps to the altar. There they concluded the formal treaty that cemented an

Anglo-Burgundian alliance between Henry and Philippe the Good, promised Catherine to the English king and further declared him the current regent of France, taking control of the mad king and all the authority of his crown. Furthermore, it made clear that at the death of Charles that crown would pass to Henry or his heir – whether this was with Catherine or not. By the terms of the Treaty of Troyes, the Valois dynasty was finished.

But *France* wasn't. It is often said that the treaty was meant to unify England and France, but this is not so. The two kingdoms would have a single ruler, but they would nevertheless remain separate kingdoms – though exactly how this political compromise would work in practice was wisely left unspecified. Unspecified, too, were the thorny issues of Gascony and Calais: would these continue as part of England or would they be subsumed back into France? How would all the enmities of more than a century of fighting be resolved?

No one could say. And to some degree it didn't matter. The bells in Paris once more rang in celebration. France was still split nearly in two, but at least one half of the kingdom could look forward to peace.

Edward III's original claim on the French throne had been, above all else, a political ploy: it was leverage to be used in the bargains and negotiations over the English hold on Gascony, the thing that mattered most of all. Though his successes against the French – Crécy, Calais and, perhaps most of all, Poitiers – might have made a claim on the throne feel closer to reality, it had still been a nearly impossible dream.

In only a few short years, Henry V had seemingly made it reality.

The New Nationalism

On 1 February 1421, Henry landed in Dover. It was the first time he'd set foot in England since leaving to make his attack on Normandy over three years earlier. He was greeted in grand fashion, and certainly it is easy to imagine that all was triumph for the man frequently lauded today as one of England's greatest kings.

But the reality in the moment was more complex than our modern myths. There were many English at the time, in fact, who had grave misgivings about the Treaty of Troyes.

No one doubted that it was an extraordinary accomplishment, but for whom? France stood to gain the most. This was the inevitable reality of the treaty's 'one king for two kingdoms' political concept: England was bearing an enormous cost in men and money to defeat the Dauphin and unify France. This would be good for Henry personally, but was it good for *England*? Would the French crown, rescued by the English crown, proceed to dominate it? Judging from history, a unified France would be larger, richer and more important on the world stage than England. At war, French gains were English losses. The same could be true in peace. Henry's long absence from England underscored the problem: the king of England seemed more interested in France.

Addressing these concerns was Henry's first order of business on his return. He and Catherine toured the kingdom, doing their best to be seen widely. He reassured Parliament that his French endeavours would be self-funded. There would be no need to raise taxes. England was and would be secure, he promised.

Back in France, meanwhile, Henry's men were continuing the hard work of making good on his French promises. Chief among these oaths was the isolation and destruction of the Dauphin.

Such is Henry's dominance in our histories that it is easy to think of the Dauphin as weak and ineffectual. But while his position at the start of 1421 was dire, he had done a remarkable job holding half of France together despite having few friends outside the kingdom and having been publicly disinherited by his parents within it.

Part of what was keeping him afloat was something no one could have expected or counted on: the defeat at Agincourt and the litany of disasters since had not broken the spirit of France. To the contrary, the tragedies were giving birth to a new sense of national identity.

Societies are bound together by relationships. Those links put a political system into motion, and the system will tend to stay in motion as long as they hold. Imagine society as a top, and its government as the hand that has balanced it upon its point and set it spinning. In perfect balance, in a vacuum, the top's momentum might let it spin for ever, but nothing exists in perfect balance, and the harsh reality of friction and other forces will slow the top down. Governments aren't inevitable, and they certainly aren't immortal.

France's government to this point was fundamentally personal. The rite of homage, as we've seen, is the foundation of that system laid bare: an exchange of oaths from one individual to another. When you swore to serve the king, you were swearing an oath to the particular king in front of you.

King Charles VI's madness was an obvious problem for this system, because he couldn't comprehend his part in the personal exchange. The solution was to emphasize the belief that God had given him the crown he wore. What Charles understood was secondary to God's will. It wasn't a perfect fix – we've already seen the enormous friction it caused – but although the top was wobbling, it still had momentum. It was still spinning.

The Treaty of Troyes threw it all out of balance. By its terms, Charles was relinquishing what God had given him. Whether he could actually do this was a rather thorny legal issue, but on a practical level it called into question the validity of all the oaths upon which the government was founded. Worse, it did so in the course of handing the crown over to the English. The treaty was, for many, nothing less than treachery against the crown, the country and even God.

The Armagnacs did all they could to benefit from this reading of events. They declared the treaty invalid and improper. They condemned all who agreed with it, insisting that the Dauphin was the true ruler of the kingdom. He was hardly an ideal figure: he had dishonoured himself by assassinating Jean the Fearless, and then he'd been disinherited by his own family. Rumours swirled – naturally fed by unofficial Anglo-Burgundian propaganda – that he wasn't even a legitimate son of the king.

The one unquestionable fact that the Dauphin and his allies could point to was that he was French – and that being French was an identity beyond oaths or actions. It was about the common bonds of birth, a connection not shared by the foreign power that had set its soiled hands upon the crown. It was a patriotic sense of Frenchness that existed outside of class structures, rooted in ideas of land and language, in myth and history and culture. The Dauphin did not invent this concept, but there is no question that he benefited from it. Despite his shortcomings, this sense of identity lifted him up as the leader standing against the Anglo-Burgundian alliance: he was the figurehead of French resistance, a unifying symbol for France itself.

Nationalism's power is undeniable, and it was about to change everything.

Battle of Baugé, 1421

With Henry's return to England, his brother, the duke of Clarence, was left in charge in France. Eager to press the next phase of English operations – and no doubt make his own mark – Clarence set off on a *chevauchée* into Armagnac-held Anjou, with roughly half of England's field army with him, perhaps 5,000 men.

Clarence was caught flat-footed by the French response. In the months since Troyes, the Dauphin had refined his strategy. The Scots who'd come to France had previously been dispersed under French command. Now, they were re-formed to fight as a single army of their own. And whereas the French were inclined after Agincourt to methodically oppose the English, the Scots had no such intentions. When word of Clarence's attack reached what had become known as the Army of Scotland, it rode out to intercept him in the field, the earl of Buchan at its head.

The numbers were nearly equal on paper, but this wasn't the case when the armies first came into contact with each other near Baugé on 22 March. Buchan's men were a cohesive force aiming to cut off the English. Clarence's men, on the other hand, were still widely dispersed, looting and scrounging for food. The duke was apparently unaware of the Scots army, a profound failure of reconnaissance that left him at a tremendous disadvantage. With no intelligence on the enemy numbers and disposition, and with less than 1,500 men ready to form up to fight, the English turned to meet their foe.

Many of Clarence's commanders told him to delay until he had more men and better intelligence, but he apparently ignored them. Counting on the army he was facing to be as unprepared as he was, he instead ordered his men forward in a fast strike.

In fairness, the Army of Scotland was not drawn up for battle. Clarence did catch their initial defence by surprise. But he was also outnumbered roughly three to one, and it did not take Buchan long to put his troops into order.

So many English victories had been the result of taking a defensive stand and allowing the longbow to corral and damage the advancing French. The Battle of Baugé neatly flipped the script. Clarence had few archers with him, and he was charging ahead of any he might have had. Buchan's Scots, on the other hand, did have archers, and they used them to thin and slow the English advance.

By the time it came to melee, Buchan's numerical advantage had already decided the outcome.

The duke of Clarence, at that point the heir presumptive of the still childless King Henry V, was among the first to die. Over a thousand Englishmen were slain with him in the charge or in the awful, bloody rout afterwards. Hundreds more were captured, including the earl of Huntingdon.

The disaster could have been far worse. What was left of Clarence's disorganized army, learning what had happened, fled north under the command of the earl of Salisbury. Though they were pursued by the Scots, they made it to safety in Normandy. And though Buchan urged the Dauphin to send everything he had at the English while they were on the ropes, the young French prince failed to do so. It was a costly error.

But the victory at Baugé was nevertheless enormous. It wasn't just Henry's brother who died there. So, too, did the myth of English superiority in the field. This considerably boosted morale on the Dauphin's side. It boosted his numbers, too. Many who'd been hesitant to join with an apparent lost cause changed their minds and rallied to his banner.

Siege of Meaux, 1421–22

Henry immediately tried to gather a new army and the shipping to transport it to France. But these things took money, raising money took time and he didn't reach Calais with fresh forces until June. After that, he moved on Paris and then into the field. His hope was to bring the Dauphin to battle, to avenge the loss at Baugé and reinforce his claim of superiority. Barring that, he would take on Buchan and the Scots.

The Dauphin withdrew rather than face him in battle, though, and the leader of the Scots was a far wiser man than Henry's brother had been. Buchan and Henry engaged in a careful dance between the Seine and the Loire as each tried to bring the other to fight on his terms. Both were canny commanders. Neither would give what the other wanted. It was a moving stand-off.

Meanwhile, conditions in Paris were deteriorating as the Dauphin's forces blockaded supplies. Knowing what a grave loss it would be to lose the support of the city, Henry had no choice but to try to knock out the nearest enemy strongholds to give Paris some breathing room. He took Villeneuve on 22 September, then moved on to Meaux, which controlled traffic running into Paris along the Marne. He placed it under siege in October. He thought it would be quick.

It wasn't.

The garrison of Meaux dug in, forcing the English to do the same. As at Harfleur, dysentery spread through the besieging encampment. But whereas Harfleur had held out for just over a month, Meaux held out for seven. So Henry was still there, hunkered down, when he learned that back in England, on 6 December, Catherine had given birth to a son who would take his father's name. By the terms of the Treaty of Troyes, he would in time wear two crowns.

No one thought that time was coming soon.

On 11 May, Meaux finally surrendered. Henry had his victory, but it was costly. He'd lost thousands of men. Strategically, though, it was worth the heavy toll: the fall of Meaux allowed desperately needed supplies to flow into Paris. It also gave Henry and his allies a boost that rocked the balance of the war back in their favour. The Dauphin was again on the back foot.

At the end of the month, Tanneguy led an army of several thousand French and Buchan's Scots into the county of Nevers, which was then controlled by the duke of Burgundy. The English and Burgundians made haste as best they could in that direction, but the French seized La Charité and its bridge over the Loire. They then moved to besiege nearby Cosne, which made an agreement that it would surrender unless relieved by 12 August. Though Henry and Philippe were caught off guard by Tanneguy's attack, Henry in particular was pleased with the turn of events. He now knew exactly where he could find a French army and bring them to battle. Heralds were sent ahead to arrange a location for the fight, while the king, the duke and their other allies cobbled together an army that was at least three times the size of what the Dauphin had waiting for them. Henry had reason to be confident.

He had, we now know, only a few weeks to live.

It is often said that Henry died of dysentery that had afflicted him since the siege of Meaux. Disease was certainly running rampant there, and one doubts that even in his privileged position within the encampment he could have passed the months untouched by it. When dysentery kills, though, it tends to do so quickly, and there is every indication that Henry was in good enough shape to campaign through May and well into June.

It was only at the end of that month that he developed debilitating symptoms, which grew worse as the Anglo-Burgundian army moved towards the Loire. By the time they reached Corbeil at the end of July, it was clear that there was no chance of the king leading his men once more unto the breach. He was by now so wracked with fever and pain that he could hardly move. The army pressed ahead under the command of his brother, the duke of Bedford, reaching Cosne on 10 August. The Dauphin's forces had withdrawn ahead of them. When the appointed day of the battle arrived, the allies waited in vain on the agreed-upon field for the opposing army to show up.

Tanneguy and Buchan had decided not to fight. Their enemies cried foul and accused them of dishonour, but the Dauphin's commanders knew that they were outmatched. A fair fight on even ground was no chance at all. It was, in truth, the same decision that Henry V had himself made when he'd broken his agreement to fight the French at Aubigny in 1415. Dishonourable it might be, but it meant survival.

Henry had no chance to acknowledge any of this. By mid-August he'd been carried to the Château de Vincennes, just east of Paris. Bedford and other English luminaries met him there, and on 30 August they heard his last will. The duke of Gloucester was appointed as the tutor of his son. Bedford was to be the keeper of Normandy and, if Philippe the Good declined the position, the regent of France. These instructions given, on 31 August, 'between the second and third hour after midnight', the king died.[14]

For all the tragedy of it for England – he was two weeks shy of just thirty-six – Henry V's early death froze the memory of the man at the height of his kingdom's accomplishments in France. The remaining decades of the Two Hundred Years War would be played out beneath the shadow of this singular warrior king, a man whose accomplishments had rightfully positioned him to 'be the king regarded by most generations after him as the greatest medieval ruler England ever had'.[15]

9

The Years of Joan, 1422–31

Bedford's France | Treaty of Amiens | Cravant | La Brossinière |
Verneuil | Vacillating Allies | Siege of Orléans | Rouvray | Joan of
Arc | Patay | Coronation | Reims to Compiègne | Joan's End

On 6 November 1422, two knights wearing Henry V's coat of arms rode through the doors of Westminster Abbey.[1] In their hands were the helm and the crest of the dead king. Another pair of knights followed close behind, bearing the arms of England and of France. Behind them rode an earl, carrying a battle-axe turned upside down.

The men rode in solemn silence up a path of sand and straw that had been laid down through the main aisle to mute the sound of the heavy mounts. Behind them came five more horses, pulling a chariot bearing Henry's lead coffin. Atop it, on a bed of red silk and tooled gold, lay the crowned effigy of the dead king, made of boiled leather and painted to mirror the body beneath it. The effigy wore the finest of garments and jewels. Its hands held two royal sceptres.

Behind the chariot wheels, a procession on foot made its slow way into the great space. The dukes of Gloucester and Exeter were the first to enter, followed by King James of Scotland, a prisoner of the crown who'd fought alongside Henry in France, and Queen Joan of Navarre, Henry's stepmother. Hundreds more mourners followed – nobles and knights, clergy and civic leaders, and more – all filing in by social rank.

The chariot halted at the choir. The effigy-topped coffin was carefully lifted down and carried forward into a 'blazing chapel' that had been constructed for the event: an extraordinary structure of wrought iron, covered with at least two hundred lit candles. Sixty paupers, each paid a shilling for the task, gathered around the structure holding candles of their own.

Under the dancing light of the fires great and small, a requiem mass toned into the stillness. The bells of the great abbey tolled. Through the long night, dirges were sung as the priests raised prayers for the soul of the departed.

The following day, the funeral rites were held. Hooves once more trod through the open doors of the sanctuary:

> Three war-horses, with their riders displaying in splendour the arms of the king of England and France, were led up to the high altar of Westminster, as is customary, and there the riders were stripped of their armour; and when the arms had been completely removed, as well as the banners, the arms of St George, of England and France, with images of the Holy Trinity and of St Mary, were continuously carried around the corpse.[2]

At the end of the requiem mass, one final horse made its solitary way up the main aisle. Upon its back sat a knight, crowned, wearing Henry's coat of arms, his sword and his shield. These were ceremonially stripped away and offered up at the high altar.

The dead king was laid to rest, as he had desired, close beside the tomb of the saintly King Edward the Confessor. In the coming years, an elaborate chapel was built above it, according to his will, where further prayers could be said for his soul.

If Henry VI was present for his father's funeral, he can hardly have remembered it. The new king was less than a year old. His father had never laid eyes upon him.

Someone who very certainly was *not* at Henry's funeral was his younger brother, the duke of Bedford. Just four days after his brother's burial, clad in the black cloth of mourning, Bedford walked behind the coffin of another dead king as it entered the abbey of Saint-Denis, where France's royalty had long been buried.

No one had expected that the mad Charles VI would outlive the vigorous and valiant Henry V, who was in his early thirties when the Treaty of Troyes was concluded. Indeed, many of the French who were wary of the treaty's promise of a Lancastrian king had nevertheless agreed to it on the assumption that Charles did not have long to live, and that Henry was the only route to long-term stability. The assumption had turned out to be half-right. Charles outlasted his new son-in-law, but by just over seven weeks.

As at Westminster, the royal mausoleum at Saint-Denis was awash in candlelight as the king's coffin made its way inside. A cloth of gold had been draped over the king's effigy, and it would have seemed alive under the dancing flames. The bishop of Paris began his prayers. The burial was, as Henry's had been, a rich affair, burning far more in coin than it did in wax.

It was, however, strikingly bare when it came to royal attendance. Neither the widowed queen nor the disinherited Dauphin were in attendance. The duke of Burgundy, who like his own father had long used the mad king as a pawn, decided he had better things to do. So it fell to Bedford, who'd taken on the regency, to bear witness as the coffin was entombed. Afterwards, the abbey's monks and the dead man's servants squabbled and came to blows over the effigy's cloth of gold, an apt metaphor for the state of France itself.

In less than a decade, the course of the war would reverse, because a young woman named Joan would, in 1429, ride across France at the very moment of its lowest fortunes.

Bedford's France, 1422

For a little more than eight months in 1421 – from the death of the duke of Lancaster at the Battle of Baugé in March to the birth of the future Henry VI in December – Bedford had been his brother's heir. In all likelihood, he would have been up to the task: on multiple occasions he'd served as Henry V's lieutenant in England, maintaining the kingdom while his brother was campaigning in France, and he'd performed his duties well. But with a son finally in place, the dying Henry had asked him to make his future on the Continent, working to secure the future that he'd won.

According to the Treaty of Troyes, the crown of France now belonged to the infant Henry VI of England. Even before his father's death, many had opposed Lancastrian rule. Those numbers seemed sure to grow now. Whatever his sins, the disinherited Dauphin was not only a Frenchman, but at nineteen seemed far more capable of rule than a foreign-born child in swaddling clothes. Even more problematic, the treaty was predicated on the belief that Henry V had the strength to unite France, to end the dance of death, disunity and destruction that had plagued it for so long.

Yet even when he was alive and at the height of his powers, the chances that Henry could have seized the half of France still held by the Dauphin were probably slim. In January 1422 he himself had declared that the fight to take the 'kingdom of Bourges' – the derisive name given to what the Dauphin controlled from that capital – would be 'a long business, dangerous, risky and very difficult, especially between well-matched parties': casualties, he'd known, would be high, and the financial costs even higher. At the time, Henry had considered peace through mediation – via the duke of Savoy or the pope – and even on his deathbed had indicated to Bedford that he knew this would likely mean compromise. It's possible that the king would have been willing to give up the title of France if Normandy and Gascony were both surrendered to him.[3] In the Two Hundred Years War, that would have been victory enough.

Henry's death destroyed that chance. Bedford and the other lords of England could provide a voice for the king – the infant Henry VI – but they were not kings. Their power was limited to that which was deemed necessary to hold the kingdoms together until the new king came of age and could decide what to do. Thanks to the Treaty of Troyes, this meant not only keeping what they had but undertaking the potentially insurmountable task of defeating the Dauphin and conquering France entirely.

Bedford had no illusions about the difficulty of unifying France behind his nephew. But before he could even begin to deal with the Dauphin's supporters, he needed to be sure of his own. The great lords who'd agreed to the Treaty of Troyes must now dutifully pass their personal allegiance from Henry V to Henry VI and remain steadfast allies.

His first stop was the duke of Burgundy. Whatever small chance England now had in France depended upon his friendship, which made it all the more frustrating for Bedford that his younger brother seemed intent on making an enemy of Philippe.

The duke of Gloucester was, as one historian neatly sums him up, 'a disruptive spirit, assertive, opinionated, impulsive and intensely ambitious'.[4] He'd tried to claim that his appointment as Henry VI's tutor meant that he ought to be regent of England, but almost everyone favoured Bedford. On the one hand, this was mere expedience. The Treaty of Troyes was meant to establish two separate kingdoms under one king, but the court understood that there was no way for the administrative state of France – that is, the war-torn pieces over which Bedford could claim authority – to maintain itself alone. For the foreseeable future, that kingdom needed England's financial and military backing. Having Bedford serving as regent of both kingdoms – essentially, being what Henry V had meant to be, at least until Henry VI was old enough to take over the duties himself – made sense. On the other hand, it was also a decision driven by distrust of Gloucester, who was not the right man to take charge in such a diplomatically precarious environment. This was proven when, mere days after Henry V's death, Gloucester decided to marry Jacqueline of Hainaut, a woman whose claims to titles in the Low Countries made her one of the duke of Burgundy's greatest rivals. Her union to Gloucester meant that he, too – and thereby England – was likewise a rival. Gloucester had lit an entirely unnecessary and highly dangerous fire, and the task of putting it out now fell to Bedford.

Treaty of Amiens, 1423

Fortunately, Bedford was a man with political sense, aware that the key to unlocking a successful negotiation was to recognize what the other side wanted and then find the common ground between them. Philippe the Good was, Bedford knew, a man for whom Burgundy was an identity. For him, it was a kingdom in all but name, with a proud past and bright future. Though he had been no great friend to the English, Philippe had thrown his lot in with them when his father was murdered by the Dauphin and his Armagnac allies. To do otherwise would have been an affront to the great dynasty that he'd been handed by the preceding generations. As a man with no children, were he to die suddenly, the realm of Burgundy would have been split between his two sisters – one unwedded and one widowed. It had to be something of a nightmare for the duke: all that the family had worked to build might well be undone.

Bedford proposed a way to alleviate much of the uncertainty. He himself would marry Philippe's sister, Anne. This would strengthen the ties between England and Burgundy, helping to put out the fire that Gloucester's marriage had lit, reassuring Philippe that his sister would have a powerful ally moving forward. Meanwhile, Philippe's other sister, Margaret, would be married to Arthur de Richemont. Richemont had fought on the French side and been captured at Agincourt, but after his release he'd been instrumental in pushing English interests in the court of his older brother, the duke of Brittany. Richemont was widely considered a great field commander – which was something that Philippe knew Burgundy might well need. For Bedford, such a marriage presented the possibility of bringing Brittany into a formal relationship with the Anglo-Burgundian alliance. Knowing full well the devastation that the War of the Breton Succession had wrought, its duke had carefully navigated a middle ground between Brittany's economic interest, which was with England, and its political history, which was with France.

It worked. On 17 April 1423, England, Burgundy and Brittany signed the Treaty of Amiens. The two proposed marriages would go forward. The dukes of Burgundy and Brittany publicly acknowledged the Treaty of Troyes and Henry VI's position as the king of France. And all three dukes on hand agreed to support each other to the end of their days: should one of them be under attack, the others would personally send him 500 soldiers to help in his defence. Just one day later, the dukes of Burgundy and Brittany signed a separate agreement underscoring that even if one of them should make political peace with the Dauphin, this personal oath to support a fight against him would remain in effect.[5]

The Treaty of Amiens re-established the promise of the Treaty of Troyes. It was a good start for Bedford. With Brittany throwing its lot in with the Anglo-Burgundian alliance, the entirety of France's western and northern seaboards from Gascony to the Low Countries – save the ports of La Rochelle on the Atlantic and Le Crotoy at the mouth of the Somme – were now in friendly hands.

The Dauphin, though, had plans of his own.

Battle of Cravant, 1423

He might already be considered Charles VII, but it wasn't just his enemies who continued to call the French claimant to the throne the Dauphin. Whatever traditions there were in immediate monarchical continuance – the king is dead, long live the king! – there was also a tradition in France that its kings *became* kings when they were crowned in Reims and there consecrated with that holy oil that had graced Clovis. Unfortunately for the would-be Charles VII, Reims was in the hands of the Burgundians at the time of his father's death. The disinherited Dauphin was in much the same position that the English king Edward III had been when in 1359 and 1360 he'd besieged that city at great cost, hoping to authorize his claim to the throne there.

So almost from the moment the mad king died, a primary goal of Armagnac France was to recapture Reims and get the Dauphin crowned.

The Armagnacs made their first big move in June by sending an army over the Loire – the de facto border between the Dauphin's holdings and those of the Anglo-Burgundian alliance. It was a strong force of some thousands under the leadership of Buchan, the commander of the Scots who had destroyed Bedford's elder brother at the Battle of Baugé two years earlier. His destination was the stout castle of Montaiguillon, near the village of Louan-Villegruis-Fontaine today, east of Paris. A Dauphinist force under the nephew of Tanneguy du Châtel had seized it, exerting pressure on the city, and it was now besieged by English forces under the command of the earls of Salisbury and Suffolk. Buchan was to relieve the siege, then use Montaiguillon as a launching point for an incursion into Champagne and the securing of possible routes to Reims.

Buchan's army made good progress initially, but when it reached the Yonne he was convinced by the leader of a local warband that he would be well served to seize the town of Cravant, on its east bank. At the time it would have made some strategic sense. Much of the east bank of the Yonne was steep plateau; Cravant sat where a valley broke this line, so there was a significant bridge over the river west of the town, with ready access to several main roads on both sides of the river.[6] If Buchan could take Cravant, he'd be able to advance to Montaiguillon with a more secure route to his rear. And although the town was now held by Burgundian troops and Buchan lacked siege equipment, Cravant's walls were nothing terribly impressive. He probably thought it would be over quickly.

It was not. The defenders hunkered down, and Buchan doubled down. As days turned into weeks, the impact of the miscalculation became clear. Buchan's siege had burned up his advantage of surprise. Bedford and Philippe the Good had not been idle. While Buchan had encamped around Cravant, they'd gathered forces from across the north into a combined army that would meet at Auxerre, roughly a dozen miles downriver from Cravant. Salisbury came down from Montaiguillon to lead the English forces. The Burgundians would be commanded by Jean de Toulongeon. News of these movements brought more Dauphinist troops streaming in.

At the end of July, the armies on both sides were within contact. Buchan had at this point over 6,000 fighting men. The combined Anglo-Burgundian forces were probably closer to 5,000 – outnumbered, but hardly by two or three to one, as is often claimed.[7] As the English and the Burgundians marched up from Auxerre, they found Buchan standing on the high ground of the plateau northwest of Cravant, blocking the road. Salisbury and Toulongeon responded by backtracking towards friendly Auxerre and moving their army across the Yonne. This was a shrewd move, though not without its own dangers. It put the wet gap of the river between their forces and that of Buchan – a terrain defence that aided him nearly as much as high ground – but the landscape was otherwise flat and broad, meaning they could bring more numbers into an engagement. Strategically, and perhaps more importantly, their new position cut off Buchan's line of retreat. He was now effectively immobilized at Cravant.

Buchan responded by arraying his forces onto the flat plain between the besieged town and the Yonne, facing the enemy across the river. The bridge was a thin line between them.

For several hours there was a tense stand-off, during which the Anglo-Burgundians moved the pieces of artillery that they had brought up from Auxerre into a position near their end of the bridge. When this was done, the cannon opened fire as lines of longbowmen loosed. Arrows and stone shot tore over the peaceful water, the combined archery and artillery barrage ripping into Buchan's men. Behind this storm, Salisbury and his men charged the bridge on foot, hacking and slashing their way forward. It was awful work in close quarters, but as soon as they had a foothold on the other side, more English and Burgundians were streaming over behind them.

Meanwhile, no doubt set in motion by the thunderous noise, companies of men under the command of Robert Willoughby pushed into the water upstream on the Anglo-Burgundian right under cover of their own waves of arrows. The water was waist-deep, and the struggle across was intense and bloody, but he, too, reached the opposite bank. As soon as he did so, he plunged into Buchan's flank.

Pieces of Buchan's army started to melt away. The Scots, one source says, were swearing 'in their atrocious French' at the men retreating.[8] Then all hell broke loose when the defenders of Cravant – despite enduring a month under siege – opened their gates and attacked Buchan's rear. Hit on every side, his army disintegrated in a panicked rout.

We don't know the exact casualties on the English side. As usual, we only know the losses among the men of status: just thirty. Probably the total losses ran into the hundreds. On the other side, total losses may have run as high as 3,000. Buchan and several hundred others were captured.

Though the Anglo-Burgundians had taken the offensive at Cravant, the battle was strategically a defensive one: Cravant was theirs when the day began, and it was theirs when night fell. The victory changed relatively little on their side. For the Dauphin, though, it meant the loss of the Army of Scotland – not French lives, perhaps, but one of France's strongest weapons in the fight. In Paris, the news was celebrated in the streets with 'great bonfires and dancing'.[9]

Battle of La Brossinière, 1423

Both sides were learning what Henry V had foreseen: there was no longer sufficient manpower, willpower and treasure for the two crowns to do much more than trade blows along a relatively stable front. It was, as one Parisian wrote during 'this war accursed by God', as if 'the English would sometimes take one place from the Armagnacs in the morning and lose two in the evening'.[10] No one had the strength to deliver a knockout punch.

It might be for this reason that Sir John de la Pole, the brother of the earl of Suffolk, did something unexpected. Near as we can tell, Bedford had directed him to take 2,000 men – a significant portion of the English strength – and lay siege to Dauphinist-held Mont St-Michel. Instead, in September, de la Pole decided to go in the opposite direction in every sense: he mounted a raid instead of a siege, and he led it south into Anjou.

The raid was initially successful, as many of the *chevauchées* of the previous century had been. De la Pole soon had wagons full of booty, ransoms aplenty and even a massive herd of cattle fat from a summer of grazing. It had gone well, but the fruits of its success were its greatest danger: none of these prizes moved at speed. By the time he turned around at Segré, French forces were already coalescing, like blood coagulating around a wound, intent on preventing his return to Normandy. Led by the count of Aumale, they gathered at Laval while scouts tracked the English advance and decided where and when to pin them down.

On 26 September, the English were crawling along an old Roman road north of La Gravelle near La Brossinière – today's hamlet of La Brécinière – when they came face to face with Aumale's much larger army, arrayed for battle. According to one chronicler, the English were less than two miles from the French when they recognized the danger.[11]

The English tried to recreate something of what they'd done at Agincourt. Caught in an unprepared position, the archers planted stakes to hold off a cavalry charge while men-at-arms massed together in the centre. The French did what they'd done at Agincourt, too – but this time successfully. There was no hesitation, no mud and no mistakes. Their cavalry charged. At such a close distance, the English would have had roughly 15 minutes before the horses were on top of them. The archers tried to respond with waves of arrows to hold them off, but the French were too many and too fast. The riders either flowed around the stakes or broke through them, the hooves of their horses pounding into the English backfield. The archers shattered, scattered and utterly failed to disrupt the vanguard of the French army that was already advancing on foot even as Aumale's cavalry now turned to plunge like a dagger into de la Pole's flank.

The English fought hard over the next few hours, just as the Scots had at Cravant, but the results were similar. Surrounded, those who weren't taken for ransom were slaughtered.

At Agincourt, the French corpses had piled up. At La Brossinière, the corpses were English. Well over 1,400 of them were cut down. De la Pole and most of the other leaders were captured. It was nothing short of a massacre.

Battle of Verneuil, 1424

The French were not blind to the blow that had been struck at La Brossinière. Normandy's frontier garrisons had been pared down to field de la Pole's army, and that had been destroyed. Normandy was weak and highly susceptible to an attack. But, as it was for the Anglo-Burgundians after Cravant, the French could not leverage the win immediately.

It was a problem of relative numbers. The weakness of one's enemy is of advantage only when one has the strength to exploit it. The Dauphin did not.

His wife's mother, Yolande of Aragon, was already putting together a plan for that, though. It was well known that the duke of Brittany had been hesitant to agree to the Treaty of Troyes, and Yolande knew that if this could be undone, it would be a double blow: the numbers gained for one side would be lost by the other. The key to Brittany, it was thought, was the duke's brother, Arthur de Richemont, who had married the sister of Philippe the Good as part of the negotiations meant to keep the Anglo-Burgundian alliance secure. He was known to be displeased with Bedford, and he'd previously been a loyal Armagnac. Throughout the winter of 1423–24, Yolande helped to lead talks in Nantes that ultimately conspired to bring not just Brittany to the Dauphin's side, but Burgundy, too. No official agreement was made, but all sides seemed positively inclined to it.

The Dauphin's position grew even stronger on 7 March 1424, when a new army from Scotland arrived at La Rochelle. Nearly 7,000 strong, it was led by a ransomed Buchan and the earl of Douglas, and it came just in time. That winter the English had at last cut a deal to release the long-imprisoned King James of Scotland in return for a massive ransom and the promise that Scotland's sons would no longer be sent to fight with England's enemy on the Continent. Crucially, the agreement conceded that James could not be held responsible for any Scots who were already in the field in France. By the time James was crowned at Scone on 21 May, the Dauphin's plans for a campaign against the English was well underway. Douglas had already been named duke of Touraine. France couldn't count on more reinforcements from Scotland, but the ones they had were there to stay.

In addition to the Scots, the Dauphin hired a couple of thousand heavy cavalry from the duke of Milan. These, along with other mercenaries and his own substantial numbers of French units, gave the Dauphin a fighting force of some 15,000 men. He put them under the command of the count of Aumale, who'd just beaten the English at La Brossinière. It was an army meant for a decisive strike: to defeat the English in the field, drive them from France and enable the Dauphin to at last be crowned.

Bedford, meanwhile, was trying to establish greater security for English-held Normandy by pushing back on the closest Armagnac holdings. One of these was the town and castle of today's Ivry-la-Bataille, on the River Eure. On 22 June, the earl of Suffolk reached it with a few hundred men, though his numbers were set to grow as the English garrisons were scraped to the bone for reinforcements.

Despite his numbers, Suffolk took the town quite quickly. The castle overlooking it to the west was a different story. Its commander held out, but he agreed that if he was not relieved by 15 August, he would hand over the position. The Dauphin sent word that relief would come.

It was, for both sides, a ticking clock. The Anglo-Burgundian numbers around Ivry grew, with Bedford himself arriving to take command on 14 August. At that point, he had just over 10,000 men, and they mustered south of the town in a strong position, arrayed for battle. On the appointed day, however, Aumale's great army – probably between 14,000 and 16,000 men now[12] – didn't show.

Aumale very likely knew he had strength in numbers over Bedford. He knew, too, that he would lose honour by not giving battle at Ivry as had been promised. At the same time, he was also a canny commander. Many of his forces were still stretched out along the roads southwest of Ivry. And his scouts had meanwhile reconnoitred Bedford's position and no doubt reported it a difficult one to assault. Losing face was bad, but losing the Dauphin's army would be far worse.

So on the day he was supposed to meet Bedford in battle, Aumale was at the English-held town of Verneuil-sur-Avre, about 30 miles west. He sent heralds to its closed gates, informing them that he'd defeated Bedford in battle. To help sell the lie, some of his Scots were splattered with blood and then paraded nearby, bemoaning their fate in passable English. The town opened its gates.

At sunset, Bedford accepted the surrender of the garrison at Ivry – only to learn that the French had now taken Verneuil.

Worse, a significant number of Normans now abandoned the English, either fading into the night or marching to join Aumale's force. This, plus the need to garrison Ivry meant that his army, when he readied to march towards battle in the morning, would be even more outnumbered.

And thus we come to the first puzzle of Verneuil, one of the most important battles in the Two Hundred Years War. Because at this moment, already outnumbered and now facing the prospect of fighting on ground not of his choosing, Bedford willingly weakened his force even further: he sent away his Burgundian allies. This may have been as many as 2,000 men. Some historians have chalked this up to Bedford wanting to project supreme confidence. As one says, 'it was certainly a magnificent gesture, and one is loath to condemn it'.[13] But in truth it *would* be condemnable. We may know the outcome, but Bedford most certainly did not. What he would have known instead is that any battle is perilous. So the only plausible reason to deprive himself of so many men before the fight must be that he believed his position would be paradoxically stronger without them. And the only reason to accept *that* is to assume that he did not trust them. He knew that the Burgundians had engaged in productive talks at Nantes with representatives from Brittany and the Dauphin just three months earlier. Seeing some of the Normans desert him, Bedford must have made the calculation that the Burgundians might follow suit. And if they turned against him during the fighting, it could prove disastrous. He was sacrificing strength in numbers, it was true, but the trade-off was certainty in his ranks. And he knew that command and control, as we have seen time and again, could win the day.

So it was with an army of around 8,000 that Bedford set out for Verneuil. He spent the night at Évreux, but his advanced units were already at Damville, around a dozen miles from the French, who at this point outnumbered him three to two, if not two to one. The road between the two armies roughly followed that of the D51 today, passing through a forest whose vestiges can still be seen southwest of the hamlet of Piseux. By midday on 17 August, Bedford's army – now largely an English army – had passed through this forest and was only a few miles from Verneuil.

Aumale was already arrayed for battle ahead of them, spread out across the open plain in front of the town's walls.[14] He and his fellow commanders had argued the previous day about whether to fight at all, but the prevailing view had been to make a stand and force the English to engage. Their front line was some 2,000 Lombard cavalry, at least 700 of them in full armour on armoured horses. This was a force far more formidable than the one that had charged so disastrously at Agincourt – the Lombards had already proven their worth against the Burgundians the previous year at La Bussière.[15] Their planned role at Verneuil, once it began, would be to smash into the English front. The main battles of the French and Scots men-at-arms would follow them on foot. Meanwhile, under the cover of an arrow storm from Scots archers on the French right, a large unit of French cavalry would swing around the English left to infiltrate the English backfield. Given Aumale's leadership, it is no surprise that this basic plan looks very much like what he'd done to destroy the English at La Brossinière.

As we have seen, it was common for leaders to conduct negotiations before a battle, if for no other reason than to say that they'd done it. As far as we can tell, Aumale actually hadn't done this at La Brossinière, opting instead to attack before the English could prepare. If so, this would have stained his honour every bit as much as his failure to fight at Ivry. So at Verneuil, the English forces were allowed to array for battle while Bedford met with Aumale and the other members of his multinational command.

The English plan was based on Agincourt: not only had that been a great victory, but it had been fought in a position chosen by the enemy, with no natural obstacles to protect the exposed archers from cavalry charges. As Henry V had done, Bedford had planned ahead and ordered his men to cut sharpened stakes that they could plant in the ground for protection. The archers, as was standard, would assemble in wings flanking a centre of dismounted men-at-arms. But again, per Agincourt, archers would be among the centre, too. We have no certain description of their formation, but it would make sense that they were in wedges, pointing towards the French. Again with Agincourt in mind, the wagons of Bedford's baggage train were circled to his rear, protected by roughly 500 archers in order to prevent the kind of raid that had happened to his brother. Thinking of La Brossinière, Bedford also took steps to be sure that the French cavalry could not wrap around his flank and get into his backfield: he gave the order that the army's horses – and there were more of them than there were men – would be tethered together into a line that would become a kind of living wall arcing around the backside of his position. Bedford had anticipated the French tactics. He was clearly no fool.

In the late afternoon, recognizing that the French were waiting to fight on the defensive, Bedford opened the battle. With a tremendous roar, his front lines marched forward enough for the archers to bring the French into range. The English loosed a volley. The archers from Scotland answered it, and soon the arrows from both sides filled the air, striking 'with such cruelty', said Jean de Waurin, a chronicler who was there fighting on Bedford's side, 'that it was a horror to look upon them'.[16]

At this, the Lombard cavalry surged forward. The archers tried to take them down as they'd done at Agincourt, but the better armour of the men and their mounts left them 'perfectly protected',[17] and they punched gaping holes in the English front as they stormed into the backfield. But unlike what had happened at La Brossinière, they didn't turn to trample down the lines of men into the flank of the English centre. Had they done so, Bedford's position might have been irrecoverable. Instead, they pressed onward, driving at the English baggage and falling upon the men trying to protect it. It was a perplexing move, and one historian suggests it was due to their visored helms restricting their senses to the point that they 'found it hard to follow the course of the battle'.[18] Stranger things have indeed happened in war, but these were men trained to maintain discipline amid the chaos. More likely, they thought their blow sufficient to set the battle into its final stages and wanted to be the first to get to the loot.

Meanwhile, the more lightly armoured French cavalry tried to dash around the English left. This they did, but their effort to stay far enough away from the enemy archers meant that they circled around too deeply. Quite unexpectedly, they came against the lines of the horses that had been tied together to stop just such a manoeuvre. As the French charge reined in short, many of the English archers that they'd tried to avoid had turned and brought them back into range. Arrows cut through the French, sending the horsemen into bloodied flight.

Our sources differ on exactly which unit of the infantrymen on the French side first decided to leave its defensive position and advance – some blamed the Scots, others the French – but its clear that *someone* saw the holes that the Lombards had blown in Bedford's lines and decided that the time had come to go for the kill. Once one unit hurtled forward, the others did, too.

The English lines were in disarray. Bedford's centre, with its waving banners and ransoms ready for the taking, must have seemed one strike from going into rout. This was how so many battles ended. But not this one.

Rallied by Bedford and the other commanders, the English centre stood its ground. 'I could not see or understand everything,' Waurin admits, 'since I was more than a little busy defending myself.' But he saw enough to know the horror of what happened as the lines

> came together with a great crash of noise and shouts and the tumultuous calls of trumpets and bugles. One side cried out 'Saint Denis!' The other, 'Saint George!' The hue and cry was so horrible that there was no man so brave or confident that he did not fear death. They struck with axes and thrust with spears, then put their hands to swords to deal great and mortal blows upon one another... The blood of the dead and wounded flooded over the earth and ran in great streams across the field.

For 45 minutes they grimly hacked at one other. By the end of that interval, the archers on the English right had reorganized themselves sufficiently to fall upon the flank of the attacking French on that side. Unit by unit, the French began to withdraw, seeking the safety of Verneuil's walls. Panic set in. A trickle of men became a cascading stream as they fell over each other in their attempt to flee. The Lombards, at last returning from the baggage, could do nothing to save the situation. They were themselves repulsed and put to flight.

The Scots alone fought on, but soon found themselves surrounded. Douglas and Bedford hated one another, so during the parlay they'd both insisted that quarter would neither be asked nor given. Accordingly, the Scots were slaughtered to cries of 'Clarence!' – a vengeance for the duke's death at Baugé.

The people of Verneuil, having seen the disaster unfold from their walls, now feared what the English might do to them once it was their turn. They closed their gates to the fleeing French, who were either cut down by the pursuing English or drowned in the water-filled ditches trying to get away.

Verneuil has often been likened to a second Agincourt. It's an apt comparison in political terms, and it works well in some tactical terms. In one regard, though, it does not: where Agincourt was a one-sided victory for the English, Verneuil saw remarkable carnage on both sides. 'The corpses [were] in high, tightly packed heaps, especially where the Scots had fought,' one source tells us. 'No prisoners were taken among them, and the heaps held the bodies of the dead English soldiers all mixed up with theirs.'[19] Bedford probably saw close to 1,600 of his men die in the desperate fight, a casualty rate of nearly 20 per cent. Many *losing* armies did not suffer such staggeringly high losses. Bedford's victory nevertheless lay in the fact that the Dauphin's great army had suffered far worse: 7,262 dead, according to heralds at the time, which was roughly half the army. Aumale, Douglas, Buchan and many of its other leaders were among the fallen.

The Dauphin's hope of ending the war in 1424 had nearly come true in the worst of ways. The loss at Verneuil didn't just prevent him from marching to Reims for his coronation, it also left his whole cause on life support. The Army of Scotland was again shattered – only this time with no hope of recovery given Scotland's new truce with England. In the coming weeks and months, many Armagnac-held positions along the frontier surrendered to Bedford, greatly solidifying the English hold on Normandy. Bedford himself was welcomed in Rouen and Paris like a conquering hero.

The Armagnacs did their best to pin the loss at Verneuil on the Scots and the Lombards. Cynical though it was, it fit with the Dauphin's positioning of himself as a 'true' Frenchman trying to save France from such forces. In truth, though, if the Dauphin was going to stave off an Anglo-Burgundian victory, he needed new allies, and he needed them fast.

He found one in Brittany.

Vacillating Allies, 1424–27

When the earl of Suffolk had gone to Ivry in June, Arthur de Richemont had objected, claiming that he should be the one to lead operations in the region. Bedford rejected this, very likely because he knew of Richemont's dealings with the enemy at Nantes – the same reason he would send the Burgundians away before Verneuil. Richemont had stormed off, determined to join the Dauphin's cause. Such was his temper that the loss at Verneuil did nothing to change his mind. He threw his lot in with the Armagnacs, and within a year had been made Constable of France.

There was renewed hope that Burgundy might abandon the English, too. Thanks for this were owed to the duke of Gloucester, who had decided on the heels of his brother's victory he needed one of his own. In October, he and his wife invaded Hainaut to press her claims in the Low Countries. The larger context of the Hook and Cod Wars – a series of civil wars in and around the county of Holland that dated back to the mid-fourteenth century – are of less importance than the immediate impact here: the adversary of Gloucester's wife was Philippe the Good. The fire that Bedford had thought he'd extinguished was raging once more, and in December he was forced to return to England to resolve the situation instead of leveraging his success at Verneuil to press towards a final victory. Worse for the English, Parliament looked upon his successes not as a reason to allow more money to flow to France, but *less*. What reason was there to think the Dauphin could do any harm to English interests now?

Through the winter Gloucester's campaign stalled, then was pushed back by Burgundy's response. The two dukes exchanged insults and threats, then agreed to a duel to the death, which Bedford only just managed to prevent. Through it all, representatives of Burgundy were continuing to talk with those on the

Armagnac side. There was much that they could agree upon, but the continued presence in the Dauphin's court of the men who'd murdered Philippe's father stymied any chance of coming to terms. The Anglo-Burgundian alliance was battered, but holding.

In the summer of 1425 Richemont helped orchestrate a major overhaul of the Dauphin's court. His influence – along with the continued efforts of Yolande of Aragon – led to new discussions regarding the possibility that Richemont's brother, the duke of Brittany, might join with the Dauphin: the negotiations were tense, but they bore fruit with the signing of the Treaty of Saumur on 7 October 1425. The duke brought more men to the fight, but perhaps more importantly he opened up a new front on land and at sea. Bedford had already been stretched thin, and this stretched him even further.

It may be that the duke of Brittany thought he could play both sides without incurring the wrath of either. If so, he was wrong. Some of the pressure on Bedford was relieved when Burgundian forces crushed those of Gloucester and his wife at the Battle of Brouwershaven on 13 January 1426. Just two days later, England declared war on Brittany. Almost at once, a small English army crossed into the duchy, raiding as far as the capital at Rennes. Richemont responded, hastily assembling a massive army to move against them. At the end of February, he had perhaps 16,000 men, and he marched on the small castle of Saint-James de Beuvron, just south of Avranches, where Sir Thomas Rempston had holed up with 500 or so English fighters. The odds were long, but the English held on in the face of significant bombardment. Meanwhile, Richemont was running into the same financial issues that had long plagued the Dauphinist side: he didn't have sufficient funds to pay his men. Fed up, many began to desert him. The siege ended on 6 March when an approaching force on horseback sent the Breton army into a panic. Whether this force was a group of fellow Bretons misidentified as English reinforcements or a complex sortie by Rempston is unclear. What is without doubt is that the Bretons began to flee, at which point the remaining English in the castle opened their gates and rushed out. Richemont's army dispersed in terror, with many hundreds of dead left behind, along with all their supplies and equipment, including their artillery.

The Battle of Saint-James changed the calculus for the duke of Brittany. When the English followed it up by bringing more men over the border, threatening a rapid conquest of the disorganized duchy, its duke promptly offered a truce. The next year, on 7 September 1427, the duke formally flipped his support back to the English and the Treaty of Troyes. Meanwhile, Richemont was fast falling out of favour with the Dauphin. He responded by declaring a rebellion, which threatened to tear Armagnac France in two. It eventually petered out as a practical threat, but it very much damaged the reputation of the Dauphin's court, which seemed incapable of holding itself together, much less taking the fight to the English.

Across these same months, Bedford's problem in the Low Countries was resolved. In January 1428, the pope declared that Gloucester's wife's previous marriage to the duke of Brabant had not been truly annulled in 1422. At the stroke of a pen, this invalidated the marriage that had brought Gloucester into conflict with the duke of Burgundy. Left without any military support, Jacqueline was forced to make peace with Philippe the Good in the Reconciliation of Delft, signed on 3 July. In the months between, Gloucester had moved on by marrying her former lady-in-waiting, Eleanor Cobham, with whom he'd had a long-running affair.

The years after the victory at Verneuil had hardly been smooth running for Bedford, but he had done more than just hold on to the lands that Henry V had won. Piece by piece, he had expanded them. The Dauphin was nearly out of money, nearly out of men and nearly out of support. Bedford was at last making plans to tear his way across the Loire and drive a stake into the heart of his enemy. Though it seemed that the end of the Dauphin was at hand, these months would instead be remembered as the beginning of the end not for the French, but for the English.

Siege of Orléans, 1428–29

In July 1428, the earl of Salisbury arrived on the Continent with a new army, nearly 3,000 strong. The long campaigns of the previous years had greatly diminished how many men could be raised in England, but even this small number was thought enough to break through the Dauphin's positions on the Loire. Bedford planned to have them attack first to the west at Angers, in order to connect English holdings in the north with those in Gascony, tightening the noose around Dauphinist France.

The new English army was very explicitly raised not under the banner of Bedford. Instead, it belonged to Salisbury, and his absolute command over it is generally believed to be the result of Gloucester getting payback against Bedford for their previous years of strife. And Salisbury – again, probably encouraged by Gloucester – had no intention of taking his army to Angers. His target was Orléans.

There was no questioning the strategic value of this extraordinary city. It stood on the Loire, about halfway between Paris and Bourges, where multiple major roads came together. Its proximity to lands friendly to the English – along with the transportation network connecting them – would greatly facilitate the logistics of military operations there. Orléans was also a far richer, far more glamorous prize than Angers could ever be.

Bedford was aware of all of this, but he was still in favour of Angers. As was often the case, he had an eye on the wider political landscape. For one thing, Charles, the duke of Orléans, had been a prisoner in England since his capture at Agincourt, and it was common practice not to attack a lord's lands when he was unable to defend them. Though far from a binding international law, men like Bedford liked to see the world through the lens of chivalric ideals, and viewed it as a matter of principle. Bedford had also been working hard to get Charles of Orléans to throw his support behind Henry VI and the Treaty of Troyes. The duke had held out to this point, but there were increasing signs that he might flip in the face of the Dauphin's apparent ineptitude. Invading his lands would harden his stance against the English at the very moment they wanted him to soften it.

Bedford had also been a man keen on taking small, cautious steps where he could be sure of his footing. An assault on Orléans was profoundly aggressive, a leap into the unknown. But because it was Salisbury's army, that's exactly where the new force headed. Augmented by the existing English retinues on the Continent and Burgundian allies, Salisbury descended on the Loire valley.

Instead of attacking Orléans immediately, he methodically cut the city off – as Henry V had done to Rouen – by seizing the towns upriver and downriver.

With the duke of Orléans imprisoned in England, oversight of the city's defence fell to Raoul de Gaucourt, the same man who had overseen Harfleur's heroic resistance to Henry V in 1415. As soon as Raoul had a sense of the English approach, he threw himself into the work of preparing the city for a siege, gathering supplies and strengthening its already formidable defences.

Orléans had grown up on the north bank of the Loire around a Roman town where five major roads converged. By the fifteenth century, the prosperous city was ringed by thirty towers atop massive walls. The gates where the roads passed through were protected by further fortifications called *boulevards*, which extended out from the ramparts. All traffic headed south funnelled onto a single bridge for the river crossing here, which was nearly a quarter-mile in length. By the fifteenth century the bridge at Orléans was a stunning nineteen spans of stone, with a small hospital and chapel roughly halfway across, along with a small fort called the Bastille Saint-Antoine. The bridge was further guarded by a fortified gatehouse at its southern end, called Les Tourelles in recognition of its two high towers. It was connected to the bridge and the shoreline by wooden drawbridges that provided additional points of protection. De Gaucourt strengthened this still further, ordering the construction of an additional earthwork on the adjacent shoreline. To deny the enemy any advantage, everything beyond this, including an Augustinian convent beside the Tourelles, was put to the torch.

On 12 October, Salisbury's army began the siege of Orléans.[20] With only around 4,000 men, he couldn't attain a complete investment of the city: the walls themselves were already an impressive length, but because the French were able to mount artillery pieces at strategic locations, the English lines would need to be some distance away, requiring siege lines of many miles. So the English began building multiple fortifications of their own from earth and wood – sometimes called 'fortlets' – that covered the approaching roads and the river. Determined individuals would be able to get

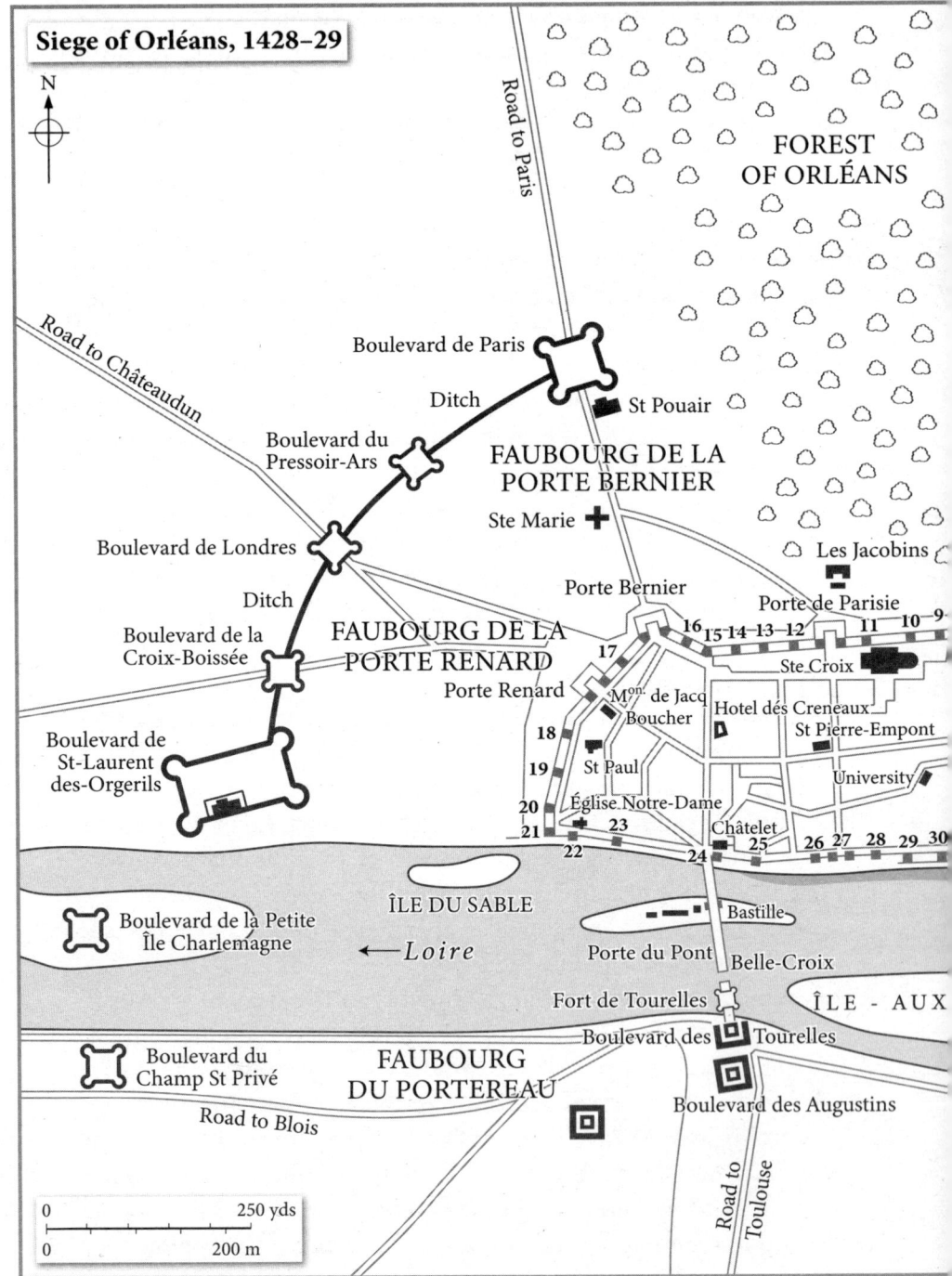

Siege of Orléans, 1428–29

N

FOREST
OF ORLÉANS

Road to Paris

Road to Châteaudun

Boulevard de Paris

Ditch

St Pouair

Boulevard du
Pressoir-Ars

FAUBOURG DE LA
PORTE BERNIER

Ste Marie

Boulevard de Londres

Les Jacobins

Porte Bernier

Porte de Parisie

Ditch

16 15 14 13 12   11 10 9

Boulevard de la
Croix-Boissée

FAUBOURG DE LA
PORTE RENARD

17

Ste Croix

Porte Renard

Mon. de Jacq
Boucher

Hotel dés Creneaux

Boulevard de
St-Laurent
des-Orgerils

18

St Pierre-Empont

19

St Paul

University

Église Notre-Dame

20

Châtelet

21

23

25   26 27 28 29 30

22

24

ÎLE DU SABLE

Bastille

Boulevard de la Petite
Île Charlemagne

←Loire

Porte du Pont

Belle-Croix

Fort de Tourelles

ÎLE - AUX

Boulevard des

Tourelles

Boulevard du
Champ St Privé

FAUBOURG
DU PORTEREAU

Boulevard des Augustins

Road to Blois

Road to
Toulouse

| 0 | | 250 yds |
| 0 | | 200 m |

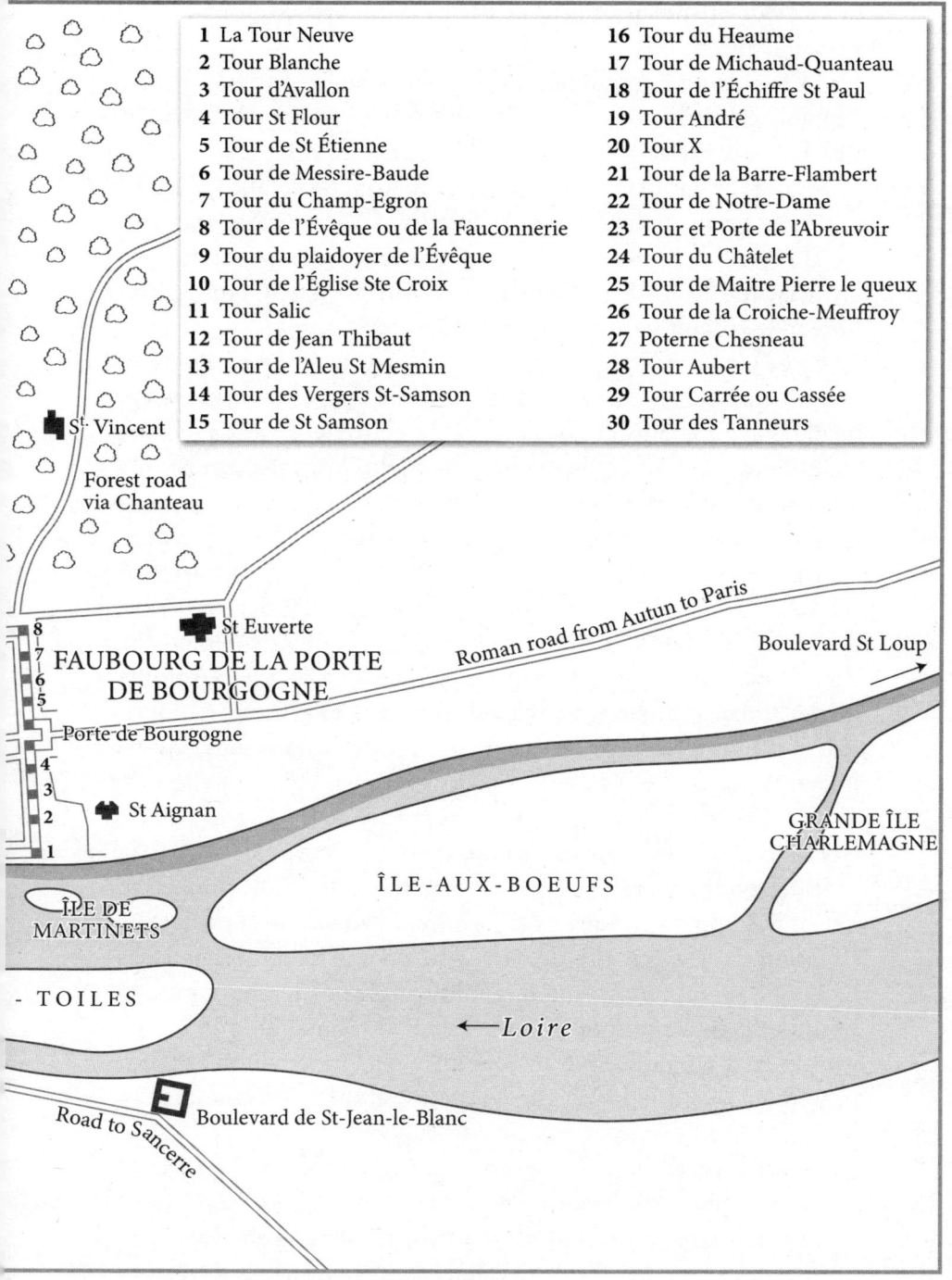

1 La Tour Neuve
2 Tour Blanche
3 Tour d'Avallon
4 Tour St Flour
5 Tour de St Étienne
6 Tour de Messire-Baude
7 Tour du Champ-Egron
8 Tour de l'Évêque ou de la Fauconnerie
9 Tour du plaidoyer de l'Évêque
10 Tour de l'Église Ste Croix
11 Tour Salic
12 Tour de Jean Thibaut
13 Tour de l'Aleu St Mesmin
14 Tour des Vergers St-Samson
15 Tour de St Samson

16 Tour du Heaume
17 Tour de Michaud-Quanteau
18 Tour de l'Échiffre St Paul
19 Tour André
20 Tour X
21 Tour de la Barre-Flambert
22 Tour de Notre-Dame
23 Tour et Porte de l'Abreuvoir
24 Tour du Châtelet
25 Tour de Maitre Pierre le queux
26 Tour de la Croiche-Meuffroy
27 Poterne Chesneau
28 Tour Aubert
29 Tour Carrée ou Cassée
30 Tour des Tanneurs

St Vincent

Forest road
via Chanteau

St Euverte

Roman road from Autun to Paris

Boulevard St Loup

FAUBOURG DE LA PORTE
DE BOURGOGNE

Porte de Bourgogne

St Aignan

GRANDE ÎLE
CHARLEMAGNE

ÎLE-AUX-BOEUFS

ÎLE DE
MARTINETS

- TOILES

←Loire

Road to Sancerre

Boulevard de St-Jean-le-Blanc

in and out of the city, but at least the main arteries for supplies were mostly cut off.

As for a major counterattack, Salisbury knew it would almost certainly come from the south. For this reason, taking the Tourelles was his primary target. If he could seize it, he'd have a fortified position that cut off any relief force. It would also allow him to seize the bridge, which could be used to mount a direct assault on the city. After several days of battering the position with artillery, the English attempted to storm it on 21 October. The Orléanais valiantly turned them back.

By 23 October, de Gaucourt and the Orléanais were beginning to think that the Tourelles could not hold. The English were known to be digging a mine from the ruins of the convent. It would only be a matter of time before these efforts brought down the gatehouse's stone walls, and the citizens knew the danger of letting the besiegers take the bridge. In order to maximize their chances of holding Orléans, they opted to hold the Tourelles only as long as it took to prepare a defence of the bridge itself. Within a day, this was done. The defenders brought down two spans of the bridge behind the Tourelles, then began an expansion of the Bastille Saint-Antoine on the bridge itself, along with forward barricades at the now broken end of the bridge. Unlike the Tourelles, these positions could not be undermined. On 24 October, Salisbury's men took the Tourelles, but the English were, if anything, even further from the capture of the city than they'd been the day before.

Then, on the evening of 27 October, the earl himself climbed to one of the upper windows of the Tourelles' towers to consider the situation. It was not the first time he or one of the other lords had done so, and, according to a soldier's chronicle, the habit had been noticed. A cannoneer in the city had trained his gun on the iron-barred window, and although he was away when the earl peered out over the Loire, the weapon was still loaded and ready.

Immediately the son of the master cannoneer noticed that there were people at the window. So he took the fuse and did just what his father, when going off for his dinner, had shown and instructed him. He fired the cannon and let fly a ball directly against the window, which broke the iron bars. The earl was hit on the head by one of the bars, or else by the shattering of the ball, to such an extent that it took out one of his eyes and smashed up a quarter of his head right through to the brain.[21]

Between the smallness of the target and the relative inaccuracy of gunpowder weapons at the time, it was a remarkably lucky shot.

The earl was taken to Meung-sur-Loire, but there was nothing anyone could do for him. His wounds were so horrific that it's unlikely the surgeons could even dull his agony. He died on 3 November.

Though Bedford had not wanted the siege to happen, there was now little choice but to see it through. He appointed the earl of Suffolk to take charge, and it took him little time to reckon that the city would not fall to assault. The bridge might have enabled that, as Salisbury had surely hoped, but the actions of the Orléanais had made it impossible with the current English strength. Both sides had to settle in for a winter's siege. For their part, still fearing the possibility that the Dauphin might send a French army, the English constructed extensive defences on the southern shore to protect the newly won Tourelles. The French earthworks were repaired and expanded into a larger, more formidable boulevard, itself surrounded by deep ditch works and a palisade.

The Dauphin, though, had no army to send. About all that could be managed was the smuggling in of more supplies and, in the following months, additional military commanders to preside over the struggle. Foremost among these was the 25-year-old half-brother of Charles of Orléans, Jean de Dunois. Due to the circumstances of his birth, he is commonly called the Bastard of Orléans. With him were some of France's finest remaining captains, including Étienne de Vignolles, more commonly known as La Hire, a veteran fighter who'd been a nuisance to Bedford for quite some time.

Battle of Rouvray, 1429

How poorly sealed off the city of Orléans was is clear from the arrival of these men. It was also clear from their departure, on 10

February, with perhaps 1,500 men of the garrison. The English needed supplies just as much as the city did, and the French had learned that a train of hundreds of wagons was en route from Paris, commanded by Sir John Fastolf. Among its supplies were many barrels of herrings, essential for the coming season of Lent. It was from these that the approaching Battle of Rouvray would take its alternative name: the Battle of the Herrings.

It was probably La Hire who cooked up the bold plan to intercept this convoy on the road.[22] Joining up with the men who sneaked out of Orléans were some 2,000 men who'd made their own approach from Blois, including a sizable mass of Scots who'd reformed after Verneuil. This combined force prepared to fall upon the English guarding the wagons, who would have less than half their number.

According to a contemporary chronicler – whose author might well have been there – Fastolf's convoy had followed the main road from Paris to Orléans to Janville, a walled town that had served as the English base in the region. They arrived there on 11 February and passed a 'freezing and very cold' night.[23] From here, rather than continue on the main road to Orléans, Fastolf swung westward to pick up the old Roman road from Paris to Blois, from which further roads ran down to his destination. This added some miles to his route, but it was a far safer path – the direct route ran through deep and perilous forest – that also led more directly to the English bases of operation for the siege, which were on the northwestern side of the city.

On the afternoon of 12 February, Fastolf's men spotted the French approach. Caught on the road somewhere near Rouvray-Sainte-Croix, the English didn't have time to withdraw to a safe location. So Fastolf circled his wagons with a single opening facing the enemy. It was something like the wagenburg Edward III had used at Crécy, only with the added element of Agincourt's stakes to help repel any cavalry charges.

After some hesitation and arguing over how to attack this field fortification, the French hauled up small pieces of artillery. They trained them on the wagenburg and began firing. For a couple of hours, the English could do nothing but sit and take it. A number of men died. Some wagons were blown to splinters. Had they 'persisted' in this punishing barrage, more than one historian has concluded, 'there could have been but one outcome – the ignominious surrender of the English army'. That they instead stopped firing to charge the enemy is attributed to their impulsivity and lack of patience.[24]

The French could well have grown impatient, but it's also unlikely that they could have kept up the artillery attacks. Theirs was a fast-moving strike force, not a besieging army, and it was operating in theoretically foreign territory. They would not have brought many guns, and those that they had were necessarily of a small calibre. Likely, they'd only been intended to frighten the horses of the guard while the convoy was in motion. For these same reasons, the ammunition to feed the guns would not have been plentiful. Having spent all or nearly all of this in the course of their bombardment, the commanders were probably certain that what damage they could do had been done.

When the charge did come, the English met it with arrows and bolts, then in a melee that sent the attackers running. Much blame for the loss followed the example of Verneuil. Some inevitably blamed the Scots, who'd been the first into the fray. Others blamed the French leadership, who'd hesitated before joining them. It didn't matter to the dead, 400 of whom were left behind. The English had lost very few.

Even as the defeated Bastard and La Hire slipped back into the city with the survivors, word of the loss at Rouvray was spreading. Orléans was still holding on, but morale across the Armagnac lands sank to perilously low depths.

But an unexpected new hope was coming. On that very day, some 200 miles away, a teenaged girl was about to change the course of everything.

Joan of Arc, 1429

In the Middle Ages, the boundary between Heaven and Earth was thin. Prophecies and the workings of the supernatural were commonly believed on all sides. For some, this might seem to diminish Joan of Arc's deeds. Devotion to the church was high in her time, as it often is in the face of peril and strife, and that intoxicating mix of religiosity and despair might well have prepared the French to believe in anything wrapped up in the trappings of Christ that might give them hope. France was crippled and fragmented. Desperate men can believe in most desperate things indeed.

Yet there was at the time a broad tradition of women, most of them young, who claimed to speak to angels or the power of divinity, and there were many other women who had fought in arms during the course of the conflict. Joan wasn't different in kind, but in *effect*. Her appearance on the scene didn't just save Orléans, it absolutely changed the course of the Two Hundred Years War. Before Joan, England might have been victorious. After Joan, France was destined to prevail. Seen through the lens of French nationalism, the story of Joan has earned her a statue or a named street in seemingly every town in France.

Exactly *how* Joan managed to be so important is a vexing question. One common answer is that of faith: she did what she did because she truly was an instrument of the divine. There can be no doubt that *she* believed that she was connected to God, but I think the truth or falsehood of that claim is beside the point. To do what she did depended not on her belief, but on the belief of others. The story of Joan is a story of inspiration and leadership.

At its core, leadership obviously depends upon belief. Above all else – above strength or charisma, above strategic manipulations or soaring oratory performances – to be a leader requires the belief of those who follow. Without their belief, no speech will ring true, no brilliant order will be carried out and no great victory will be achieved. No leader stands alone.

This fact, more than any other, points to the miracle of Joan of Arc: a teenaged girl rode, within a matter of weeks, from her quiet home to the court of kings, from the field of a farm to the field of battle. She rode there, she was followed there, and the men she inspired *won*. There are undoubtedly a great many reasons to marvel over Joan as a historical figure, but her ability to step into the leadership role that her life had not prepared her for is perhaps the most fascinating of all.

Born to Jacques d'Arc and Isabelle Romée around 1412, she grew up in the tiny village now called Domrémy-la-Pucelle – thanks to her self-identification as *la Pucelle*, meaning 'the Maid'. To call it a village may be too much: that word brings to mind picturesque settings and a quiet relaxation that Jacques and Isabelle surely did not know, even though they had a larger home than many other peasants. Theirs was generally a life of daily toil amid the fear of plague and unexpected weather. As Joan grew, fear of harm from raids or heavy taxation was added to the menu: set in the upper Meuse valley, Domrémy was a village of largely French loyalties in a part of France that was mainly controlled by the English and their Burgundian allies. In 1429, after she'd brought Charles VII to his crown and his throne in Reims, the new king asked Joan what she would have of him in return. A Domrémy free of taxes was her only request.

She learned to work the fields. She learned to sew. She was, by all accounts, an enthusiastic attendee at the local church. None of this was remarkable, and none of it would have been remembered if not for her visions, which began in 1425, the year after the horrific French loss at Verneuil. Saints Michael, Catherine and Margaret, she later testified, were telling her to take the Dauphin Charles to Burgundian-controlled Reims to be crowned king of France. Three years later, in May 1428, the voices had grown too persistent to ignore. Too young to travel alone, she convinced a relative to take her 12 miles north, to the town of Vaucouleurs. There she attempted to persuade the commander of the French garrison, Robert de Baudricourt, to give her an escort to Charles's court in Chinon, almost 300 miles to the west.

Baudricourt refused, but in the new year she was back and even more insistent. The voices were giving her more specific orders now. She would lift the English siege of Orléans that had begun only a couple of weeks earlier. That done, she would escort the king to his coronation.

This time, she convinced two lesser noblemen in the garrison that she had divine inspiration for her mission. They brought her back into Baudricourt's office again. While he still refused to help, he saw to it that she could go before the duke of Lorraine. This may have been an order from the duke himself, who by now might have heard of her and thought she might have the ability to heal him of an illness. Instead, she apparently scolded him for living with his mistress.

She was back in Vaucouleurs on 12 February, the same day that the French were defeated at the Battle of Rouvray. What transpired in Baudricourt's office that day, we do not know. But it's clear that *something* had changed his mind. She was given a horse and the clothing of a man – both to ensure a more comfortable ride and to make her less of a target on the road. He gave her the escort she requested, and on 22 February they departed for the difficult journey across France.

The legend of Joan of Arc truly begins with this furtive, dangerous passage to Chinon. But it's just as accurate to say that the leadership of Joan of Arc had begun, because the two men who'd brought her before Baudricourt, Jean de Metz and Bertrand de Poulengy, went with her. Though Joan's travelling party remained small, moving through hostile Burgundian territory under cover of night so as not to be detected by the enemy, word was already spreading ahead of her. Jean and Bertrand would come to be the first of many thousands of followers. Joan was, at her departure, perhaps seventeen years old.

After eleven days, the party reached Chinon. Soon enough, Joan was summoned to meet the Dauphin in the royal court, where legend says she saw through a ruse meant to trick her into speaking to a person disguised as Charles. From here she underwent a series of tests. In Tours, Yolande of Aragon joined other ladies of the court in testing the Maid's virginity. They found her pure. In Poitiers, a theological commission tested whether she was a good Catholic. They found her to be morally upright, and they further suggested that her claim to divine inspiration should be put to the test. Since she said that she would lift the siege of Orléans, no better test could be devised than to have her sent to do just that. She was outfitted with specially made armour, a banner and heralds. The duke of Alençon would accompany her, along with a newly raised force of hundreds of men, a great many of them drawn to the growing rumours of this remarkable young woman sent by God. They were to set out by the end of April.

When offered a new sword from the king to take to Orléans,

she instead asked that she be given the one that her voices told her was buried beneath the altar at the chapel of Saint-Catherine-de-Fierbois. Following a search, a sword was indeed found there, inscribed with five crosses. No one could explain how she'd known of its existence. It was just one of the many miracles that would come to be attributed to her.

As she prepared to depart, the teenaged Joan sent a letter to Bedford and the other English leaders, calling on them to surrender:

> I am a warlord, and in whatever place that I meet your people in France, I will make them leave, willing or unwilling. If they are unwilling to obey, I will have them all killed. If they are willing to obey, I will show them mercy. I am sent on behalf of God, the King of Heaven, to kick you all out of France, man by man, to fight against all those who wish to commit treason, so that the kingdom of France is not further damaged.[25]

So much of who Joan of Arc is – so much of what she became – hinges on the events after her arrival in Orléans on the evening of 29 April. The siege had been in place for 200 days at that point. It would end in nine.

There can be no overstating Joan's importance in what occurred during the days after she entered Orléans, but we would be wrong to attribute *everything* about that success to her, extraordinary though she was. Her legend could not have happened without the people of Orléans, who had held out far beyond anyone's expectations. For Joan to save Orléans, the city still needed to be there to be saved. That it had made it to this point was remarkable. But they needed hope. And when Joan entered Orléans in full armour, throngs of people jostled to see her, many of them clamouring for the chance to touch her, her clothes or the white horse upon which she rode. It was as if she was already a saint.

Joan wanted to mount an assault on the English right away, but the Bastard and the other French leaders were more cautious. She was an inspiration to the men, it was true, but in war numbers were still numbers, and Orléans did not have enough of them. The

Bastard rode for Blois, seeking reinforcements. He returned on 3 May with a couple of thousand men.

The next day, Joan got her first taste of fighting. The French made a sortie from Orléans against the boulevard of Saint-Loup, which guarded the eastern approach to the city. The Bastard apparently launched the attack without informing Joan. She learned what was happening when she heard shouts in the streets. Riding out, she found her countrymen starting to pull back. She rallied them, her banner waving, and the assault was renewed. The boulevard fell.

After a truce to celebrate the Feast of the Assumption on 5 May, the commanders in Orléans determined to assault the English defences around the end of the bridge on the south side of the river. On 6 May, after a hard fight – during which Joan appears to have stepped on a caltrop, thus suffering her first wound in battle – they took the Augustinian convent beside the Tourelles. The Bastard and the other leaders decided not to press further. The fortifications immediately around the Tourelles were too formidable to take on without significant reinforcements. Joan was livid. On the morning of 7 May she insisted that the attack be renewed immediately. More than that, she insisted on leading the assault personally. While climbing a siege ladder, she was shot by an arrow that entered between her throat and shoulder and probably exited near her shoulder blade. Joan tried to fight on, but she was dragged to safety.

As her banner moved off the field, French momentum stalled, then reversed. But Joan would have none of it. After a simple field dressing was applied to the wound, she brought her banner forward and rallied the men. At the same time, a fresh assault hit the Tourelles from the bridge side. The heavily outnumbered English panicked. In the confusion, the French gained entrance. The men defending the Tourelles were massacred or drowned in the river trying to escape. Joan reportedly wept for them. Then she entered Orléans in triumph as bells tolled in joy and the people shouted their thanks to God.

The next day was Sunday. The English formed up for a battle on the north side of the city, but Joan insisted that the French not take the offensive on the day that belonged to God. When it was clear that there'd be no French response, the English departed.

The siege had been lifted.

Battle of Patay, 1429

Joan never officially took command at Orléans. The French forces were under the command of the Bastard of Orléans. But it's equally true that the armies he commanded were not inspired to do what they did by him or any other leader. Their inspiration – indeed, France's inspiration – was Joan. Many men had died in the assaults that lifted the siege; many had English blood on their hands. But it was the Maid of Orléans, the girl who'd shed no blood but her own, who was credited with the victory.

The English, stunned by the events of Orléans, began putting together a new army to defend their remaining positions on the Loire. The French, flushed with success, began preparations to take them back.

In early June, the new French army was on the move. It was under the command of the duke of Alençon, but there was little question that many of those who swelled the Dauphin's ranks did so in eagerness to follow the banner of the young woman who rode beside him. Their confidence grew by the day, as English strongholds in the Loire valley folded. The town of Jargeau was taken on 12 June despite Joan being dazed when she was knocked off a scaling ladder by a rock thrown from the walls. The bridge at Meung-sur-Loire on 15 June. Beaugency fell on 18 June. For the French, inspiration and success became a feedback loop, all spiralling around the leadership of the Maid. Even Richemont had reappeared, leading a force of Bretons to support her.

The new English army was also in the field. Under the command of Sir John Fastolf, it had by now linked up with the remaining Loire forces, which were under the command of Lord Talbot. An aggressive and well-respected leader known for his willingness to get dirty, Talbot was something like an English Olivier de Clisson. The two men, both headstrong and ambitious, did not get along, and their bickering was at least partly to blame for the French ability to sweep up Beaugency, which occurred while they were preparing to retake the bridge at Meung.

The loss of Beaugency meant the loss of the Loire. The French had superior numbers and extraordinary momentum. Holding the bridge at Meung would be pointless even it was possible. The English withdrew, probably following the line of the road to the northwest for about five miles (roughly the line of the D104 today), before turning northeast up the old Roman road that ran between Blois and Paris. They were planning to regroup at Janville. The route would take Fastolf past the very spot where he'd won his victory at Rouvray just a few months earlier.

The French commanders might well have let the English retreat and been satisfied with securing their many gains of the past days. But this would not do for Joan. The duke of Alençon later recalled her words:

> Joan said: 'In the name of God, let us go fight them! If they were hung in the clouds, we would get them, for God sent them to us that we might punish them!' Asserting that she was certain of victory, she spoke these words in French: 'The gentle king shall have the greatest victory today that he has ever had. And my counsel says to me that they are ours!'[26]

The French set off in pursuit. The English instinctively tried to recreate their standard formation: a main body of men with the archers set behind stakes on either side. But time was running out, and Talbot sent 500 mounted archers rushing towards the French to delay them. There was a spot where the road passed between two hedges, and he planned to have them hide there in order to ambush the French vanguard. Once this was dispersed, they would rejoin the rest of the army. Fastolf, meanwhile, ordered their baggage and non-combatants to hide in nearby woods, along with the vanguard. On the road in front of this, he would assemble the rearguard and main body of the army for the fight to come. The vanguard's position in the woods likely points to a plan to use this, too, as an ambush: once the French engaged with the assembled army, the vanguard could sweep out into their flank and crush them.

Exactly where these locations were is difficult to see on today's landscape. The woods and hedges, so important to the participants, have long since disappeared in favour of open farmland. The same is true for much of the road the English were following: the only segment that remains in common use is southeast of Lignerolles – just beyond where the battle occurred, but roughly where Rouvray took place. With the help of old maps, however, we can reconstruct the road as it ran, and even recover hints to the areas most likely wooded in the fifteenth century. From this, it appears that the English rearguard was probably passing the little village of Saint-Sigismond when it caught sight of the first French riders. The army of Fastolf and Talbot was at that point spread out along nearly three miles of road up ahead.

The position Talbot chose for his planned ambush was close to Saint-Sigismond. There was a significant stretch of woods south of the road there, and hedges likely paralleled it along either side of the road in front of the small village. Fastolf's position, meanwhile, was on the road just north of Saint-Péravy-la-Colombe, near woods whose presence persists now only in old place names. He was only a few miles from Rouvray. The coincidence must have felt strange.

Though made in haste on unexpected ground, the English plan was a solid one. Given the French army's headlong rush, it might well have worked. But just as the French vanguard was about to ride into Talbot's trap, a stag bolted out of the nearby woods, running headlong into hidden archers. The men there cried out in surprise – just in time for the French to hear them.

The ambush betrayed, the French rushed it. The English archers fled, riding in a panic back towards the main army, which Fastolf was still trying to organize. The English vanguard, seeing the mounted archers in flight, turned tail and ran. Hardly a blow had been struck, and the English were already in a rout. Fastolf managed to rally part of the main army into a disciplined retreat, but a great many English were overrun in the chaos as the rest of the French army rushed onto the field. Well over 2,000 English died. Talbot was captured, along with several other major figures. Fastolf escaped, only to have Talbot later accuse him of being a coward whose dishonourable actions had caused the calamity. Though he was ultimately exonerated, he still wore the stain. Shakespeare immortalized him as Falstaff – with all the attack on his manhood that the name implied.

The Battle of Patay was a resounding defeat for the English – a reversal, it's often said, of their great victory at Agincourt – and Joan of Arc's stature grew despite the fact that she had been in the main body of the army and thus taken no direct part in the fight. Her life had already become legend, and the gravity of her story sucked in and warped the understanding of the events surrounding it.

Coronation, 1429

The English had never been able to physically possess all the towns that they claimed, and the years since Henry V's death had seen their resources steadily dwindle. Bedford had repeatedly scraped together armies out of his relatively few strong garrisons, weakening them for the chance to deliver the knockout blow against the Dauphin. The losses in the Loire valley, crowned by the crushing defeat at Patay, left him with a single pat of butter to spread over a whole loaf.

Many towns that had previously submitted to the Anglo-Burgundian alliance knew it. As word of Joan's victories spread, offers of loyalty came to the Dauphin. Roads long closed were suddenly opened, and the Maid of Orléans was eyeing Reims.

There was at this point some opposition to Joan from some of the members of the Dauphin's court. Part of it was jealousy over her success. But another part was diplomatic awareness. The route to Reims would pass through Burgundian lands, and there was still hope of driving a wedge between Philippe the Good and Bedford. But Joan was adamant. And the Dauphin, after all he had seen, was reassured that God was with them. On 29 June, the French army and its would-be king set out for his coronation.

They were now many thousands strong, and, two months since her arrival at Orléans, they were almost wholly committed to Joan.

The march was almost entirely without incident. Only two major towns held out against the Dauphin and the Maid – Auxerre and Troyes – and even these capitulated quickly and bloodlessly. On 16 July, the French army entered Reims. The English had stripped the cathedral of everything they could, but they'd been unable to lay their hands on the one thing that mattered: the Holy Ampulla, the miraculous glass vial with its sacred oil that had consecrated Clovis. All these years, monks loyal to the Dauphin had kept it hidden.

The next day, the Dauphin was at last crowned as King Charles VII. His crown had been hastily made overnight. Joan of Arc was standing by his side.

The moment was a profound turning point in the Two Hundred Years War. The Treaty of Troyes had disinherited the young man. Though the survival of the Dauphin's cause had shown that many were unwilling to accept that act, there was no question that many in France did. The crown upon his head threw all of them in disarray. The young Henry VI had not been crowned. Charles VII had – with the holiest of anointing in the sacred space of Reims. And all of it under the banner of the young woman sent by God to see it done.

The effect was immediate. More and more towns sent word of their submission to the new king. Whole regions that had been in the hands of the English or the Burgundians, like Champagne and Brie, switched sides. A few weeks later, Bedford at last received a couple of thousand men from England, but most had to be stationed in and around Paris to keep it from falling into the hands of the Dauphin.

Just days after Charles VII's coronation, the remarkable French writer Christine de Pizan, who'd retired to the Dominican convent at Poissy, was inspired to compose what would be her final work: sixty-one stanzas of lyrical verse entitled *The Song of Joan of Arc*. She lauds Joan as a new Moses, a greater leader than Joshua or Gideon. 'Esther, Judith, and Deborah were women of great worth and strength through whom God restored His people,' Christine writes, 'but more is done through this Maid!'[27]

Less than three months earlier, Joan had been a teenaged girl with no wealth, no connections, no learning and no indication of military prowess. Only a few had followed her from distant Vaucouleurs. But they'd believed in her, and so had the many thousands who had flocked to her since. It must have seemed, as she embraced her king at last upon his throne, that nothing could stop her.

Reims to Compiègne, 1429–30

In the summer of 1429, Charles VII's advantages were enormous. In a matter of weeks, the momentum of the Two Hundred Years War had swung wildly from his near defeat to his coronation. Many in his court, though undoubtedly grateful for what had happened, thought he should take the time to gather himself and consolidate his power before pressing onward.

Joan, once again, would have none of it. Her first two missions had been accomplished. Orléans was saved and the king was crowned. Now she had a new one: to push the English and the Burgundians from France entirely.

In other words, she aimed to take the major targets long in enemy hands and end the Two Hundred Years War once and for all.

Her first target was Paris, and after some debates and hesitations, Charles agreed to march on the city. Bedford led his newly augmented forces out to meet those of France, which resulted in a cautious dance as the two sides jockeyed for an advantageous position. On 15 August, they faced off on the fields northeast of Paris. Though it's sometimes called the Battle of Montépilloy, it was no battle. Both sides took defensive positions and tried to provoke the other to attack, but neither one took the bait. Both sides withdrew. More towns and fortresses submitted to the king, enabling him to threaten the roads to Paris. Among them was Lagny-sur-Marne, which not only gave the Dauphin a vital bridge over the Marne, it also allowed him to cut off much of the traffic on the river – traditionally an artery of food supplies for Paris.

Diplomats were busy rushing between the Armagnacs and the Burgundians, trying to work out an agreement for a final peace, but Joan was characteristically impatient. She seized Saint-Denis and pushed for the king to join his army in an attack on the highly defended prize of Paris. She was convinced that a show of force – a show of herself – would convince the city to hand itself over.

It did not. When Joan personally led an attempt to storm the Porte Saint-Honoré on the west side of the city on 8 September, defenders on the high walls met her with crossbow bolts. One blasted through her thigh. Another struck her standard-bearer in the foot. When he lifted his visor to look at the wound, another shot went through his eye. Her men tried to press on, but it was hopeless.

Hundreds died as Charles retreated to the Loire, disbanding the army that had taken him to Reims. Paris would remain out of his reach until 1436. Many of the towns that had submitted to him now found themselves in a political no man's land: the king had departed, but Bedford didn't have the strength to reoccupy everything. The contested territory became a nightmare of raiding and destruction.

So much of Joan's leadership was founded on her success – a fulfilment of the belief that she was sent by God and therefore *could not lose* – that her inability to take Paris was a hard blow.

Doubts crept in. The voices in the court that had suggested caution and diplomacy grew stronger.

Fully recovered from her wounds, Joan accompanied an army sent to Saint-Pierre-le-Moûtier, south of Nevers. Its orders were to root out Perrinet Gressart, who led what was one of the last of the Free Companies that had so plagued the kingdom. Gressart was a minor target. Sending Joan with the army appears to have been a means of giving her something to do that wouldn't destabilize negotiations with Burgundy. The campaign took Saint-Pierre after a siege, but by the end of the year it had failed to take La-Charité-sur-Loire after a multi-week siege and was forced to withdraw. This, too, did Joan's reputation no favours.

While the personal military position of Joan had weakened, there can be no question that the broader political position of

Charles had strengthened. Many, including Philippe the Good, were wondering if the Anglo-Burgundian alliance could survive. Bedford convinced the duke of Burgundy that they only needed to hold out a little longer. Henry VI was coming. Plans were already underway to crown the eight-year-old in England, after which he would come to France to be crowned there. They had just seen the political power of having a king in the field – even if they themselves did not view Charles as a legitimate king – and they had high hopes for the effect of having their own. More than that, it was expected that Henry would bring with him a new army. Burgundy agreed to hold on. They reached an agreement by which Bedford would take on the defence of Normandy and its surrounding territories. Philippe would defend the rest, including Paris.

That spring, as part of his efforts to secure the border, Philippe decided to march upon Compiègne, which sat at an important crossroads on the Oise river north of Paris. Joan had stayed there with Charles after his coronation. And whatever else she was, Joan of Arc was not one for waiting around and talking. With a handful of companions, she decided to ride for the town to help its citizens resist the coming siege. Her failure to acquire the king's permission to go was, by the letter of the law, treason.

What drew Joan to Compiègne may have been the fact that she had stayed there in the days after the coronation of Charles. She had seen and knew its people. But the same was true of many other communities now under threat. What Compiègne *did* have that many did not, though, was a remarkable similarity to Orléans. The town itself sat on the east side of the river, defended by towered walls and a broad moat fed by its waters. A single bridge ran across the river to connect to the roads on the opposite shore: a bottleneck, just as it was at Orléans. It is gone now, but the bridge extended from what is now called the Rue Jeanne d'Arc, a little over 150 yards downstream from the N31 bridge in the middle of town today. The town end of the bridge was protected by a fortified gatehouse. Its far end was defended by a moated boulevard that, although not as formidable as the fortification of the Tourelles beside the Loire, served the same role.

On 23 May, a week after her arrival in the area – and the morning after her secretive entry into the besieged city itself – Joan and a small group of Armagnacs decided to conduct a sortie against Burgundian forces on the other side of the river in the area where the town of Margny-lès-Compiègne sits today.

Sorties are risky. A successful attack against besiegers can greatly demoralize them or even cripple their ability to continue the siege. But in order to make such an attack, gates in the besieged city must be opened.

The man in charge of the defence of Compiègne was Guillaume de Flavy. He was a respected veteran of many engagements, a loyal supporter of Charles who had watched his coronation in Reims. He knew the dangers of what Joan was doing. He would have focused as much of his garrison as he could spare on the defences around the bridge. As soon as the gates were opened for the sortie, they had to be ready to hold back a potential Burgundian assault – to hold the line until Joan and the others got back in and Compiègne could be sealed once more.

Around nine in the morning, Guillaume was likely perched atop a gatehouse tower, where he could best lead the defence if it came to that. When he was sure of the preparations, he gave a signal for it to begin. The gates of the town crashed open and the company of some 400 men rolled out. Joan was on a grey horse among them, her banner whipping behind her as they thundered over the bridge. Ahead in the boulevard, the defenders lowered the drawbridge and opened their gates and barricades just ahead of the first rider. Swinging through these defences, pounding over that drawbridge, Joan and the others charged up the road and into the enemy.

The initial defence of the Burgundian camp scattered ahead of the sudden onslaught, and the French drove for the Burgundian encampment. But momentum would only carry them so far. After a back and forth – Joan would later recall making three attacks – the Burgundian defence had organized itself. The men around Joan begged her to turn back. She refused. Vital seconds were lost.

The Burgundian commanders knew the gates of the town were open. So even as Joan's sortie was stalling, many of them were already turning towards the boulevard at the end of the bridge – to take it or, at the very least, cut off Joan's line of retreat.

From his tower, Guillaume watched with mounting horror. Joan's sortie was now withdrawing towards the boulevard. The Burgundians were rushing it, too. The gates were perilously open. It was a race, and the survival of the town – the fates of so many thousands within – stood in the balance.

He would later be accused of treachery for what he did.[28] But he did nothing more or less than what any good commander would have done. As soon as he knew that the enemy would reach them first, he ordered the gates shut and barred.

Joan was cut off. She and the others darted into the fields, desperate to escape, but the Burgundians surged around them. Joan wheeled on her horse as men called for her surrender. She defiantly shouted back that she was pledged to a greater power. It was an archer who finally grabbed her robes and heaved her down out of the saddle onto the ground.

Scrambling to her feet, she saw two officers of John of Luxembourg within the tightening crowd. She surrendered to them.

Joan's End, 1430–31

Despite her recent defeats and the French court's growing doubt of her, Joan still held the hearts of many in France. And whatever Bedford and Philippe might say publicly, she frightened them. The allies were privately thrilled to have taken her off the board.

John of Luxembourg briefly held her at nearby Clairoix, but with the ongoing siege it was decided to move her to his castle at Beaulieu. When she nearly escaped her captors there, he moved her to the more secure castle at Beaurevoir.

There were a great many people who wanted to get their hands on the young woman, so for a time there was a frenzy of conversations and letters trying to sort out what should be done with Joan. Henry VI's council ultimately pushed for an ecclesiastical trial that would determine whether she was a sorceress. If she was found guilty of heresy, it would ruin not just her own reputation, but that of Charles, too: in effect, he could be branded as a king crowned by the devil.

The first step for the English was to get ahold of her. For this, John of Luxembourg demanded 10,000 *livres tournois*. It was a massive sum to pay for a prisoner of no personal wealth, but no one expected to ransom the Maid for hard currency. Her worth lay in the soft power of propaganda, which might be invaluable. A deal was struck.

Shortly after she heard of the exchange, a 'very angry' Joan leaped from the top of the tower of Beaurevoir and landed in a dry moat – perhaps 60 feet below. She was lucky to be only badly hurt, and at her trial she was asked what happened. She responded that she believed the people of Compiègne 'were to be put to the fire and the sword', and that 'she would rather die than live after the destruction of such good people'. Saint Catherine, who had 'told her almost every day that she should not jump', nevertheless comforted her after she'd done so.[29]

Asked to specify 'whether when she leaped she expected to kill herself', Joan said she did not, 'for as she leaped she commended herself to God. And she hoped that by the leap she would escape and not be delivered to the English.'[30] Did she think she would not die because God would somehow let her land safely and escape alive on foot? Or did she think, by surrendering her soul to God, that she would 'escape' to live in Heaven? Certainly, she would have known that to admit to a suicide attempt was its own sin, and that this was exactly the kind of theological error her questioners wanted to entrap her with. Like many of the answers she would give in her trial, it is an answer that defies certainty – which was almost assuredly the point.

Whatever had happened, her captors saw to it that she was kept under stricter guard – today we would probably call it a suicide watch – while she healed. As soon as she recovered enough, she was moved to Arras. She was probably there when word of the real fate of Compiègne reached her in November. Despite her despairing fears – and no doubt the high hopes of the Burgundians – her capture had not broken the spirit of the people. If anything, it had only encouraged them, and Guillaume had continued to prove himself a capable commander. After a series of humiliating setbacks, Philippe the Good had finally called off the campaign. The enraged duke blamed the English for failing to adequately support him. The people of the town had not just survived, but in doing so they'd helped to sever more of the threads holding the Anglo-Burgundian alliance together.

Joan was heartened by the news from Compiègne. It no doubt helped her endure the humiliations to which she was subjected as she was marched towards Rouen. The English wanted as many people as possible to see what had become of the Maid, and this long parade added still more miles to the astonishing journey she'd undertaken. A girl who'd probably never travelled far from her village had, from the time she left Vaucouleurs in February 1429 to the time she arrived in Rouen in December 1430, become a young woman who'd ridden an estimated 3,000 miles on horseback.[31]

In Rouen, the churchmen were waiting for her. Their ecclesiastical proceedings began on 8 January 1431, though the verdict was a foregone conclusion. For all the formal legality, the trial was about far more than the truth of the teenaged peasant girl who was brought before the court, day after day, week after week. Legal procedural rules were routinely broken. Trickery and threats were constantly at work. The whole affair was, by any reckoning, rigged – by both the English who brought her to the trial, helped pay for it and oversaw its work, and the mostly French churchmen who undertook it. The trial stood within a context of belief that, while it overlapped with political necessity, was not *merely* political. What Joan had done seemed inhuman. No one disagreed on this. Even if just a fraction of the stories about her were true, then she was quite literally supernatural, if only in her ability to convince men to act according to her wishes. For her enemies, though, the source of this could not be God, because it would mean that God stood against them. And if her powers didn't derive from God... well, in the cosmos of medieval Christianity there was really only one other option. It wasn't just the boundary between Heaven and Earth that was blurred in the Middle Ages. The devil, too, could do his work here.

To read the transcripts of her trial is to marvel at a young, largely uneducated woman compelled to tell the truth, yet able to confound some of the keenest theological minds of the age. 'Forced to be her own lawyer,' one historian concludes, 'she proved to be a good one.'[32]

The men in the tribunal actively tried to gather ammunition against her. They sprang rhetorical and theological traps. They even deployed stool pigeons in the jail. Joan repeatedly and frustratingly outmanoeuvred them. Her answer regarding her probable suicide attempt at Beaurevoir is emblematic of so many of her almost flawless answers. She not only failed to admit her heresy, but she also gave the judges precious little to hold against her.

Not surprisingly, though, the ecclesiastical tribunal found her guilty. On 23 May, she was handed over to a secular judge, who immediately sentenced her to be burned at the stake as a heretic. The next day, she was brought to an open space where stages had been prepared to help spectators witness the event. She was urged again to recant, while the charges against her were read out and the fire prepared.

Faced with her impending death, she suddenly interrupted and said she would indeed recant. After some confusion about what to do, she was asked to sign an admission to the truth of it – she made her mark with the sign of the cross – and was then sentenced to a life in prison. She was nineteen or twenty years old.

Before she was sent back to her cell, she agreed never again to bear arms or wear men's clothing. Among their many charges, the judges had argued that she'd committed a sin against God by wearing clothes of a different gender.

Joan had indeed 'cross-dressed'. Since women didn't usually fight in battles, armour was not typically made for them. By virtue of wearing armour in battle – a necessity given her mission – she *had* to wear the clothing of a man. Likewise, those thousands of miles she'd ridden and the company she'd kept along the way would have been made more comfortable in them. When initially asked about the issue during her trial, she had shrugged it off. The clothes were a small thing, she thought, that resulted from doing what her voices had commanded her to do.

Only days after recanting, though, Joan's jailers found that she was wearing men's clothing in her cell. Exactly how and why this happened is unclear. She may have been tricked into doing so: the jailers could easily have taken her women's clothes and left her only men's clothes to wear, in order to 'catch' her relapsing into sin. Another explanation is that she felt less vulnerable in male clothing. Unsaid, or at least unrecorded, is the implication that the guards who had been frightened of sexually assaulting a potential sorceress may have had no qualms about attacking her now that she'd said none of it was true.

Still another possibility is that it was a deliberate act of defiance. We do know that she felt remorse over recanting. When questioned after being found in the clothes, she told the judges that her voices had chastised her for betraying them, an act that 'had condemned her soul': 'Moreover, she said that whatever she had said and recanted on that Thursday had only been done for fear of the fire.' A scribe recording the proceedings knew exactly what she had just done. He wrote in the margin of his copy: 'Fatal response.'[33]

Whether or not she desired martyrdom, nothing could stop it now. On 29 May, the judges declared her a relapsed heretic, and she was again sentenced to die in flame. The next morning, she was taken to Rouen's Vieux-Marché. As before, her sins were read out for the gathered crowds to hear. Her only interruption this time was to ask to be given a cross. A soldier nearby quickly fashioned one with two sticks and gave it to her.

Joan was taken to the stake and bound to it, the little wooden cross tucked amid the ropes. A more formal processional cross was brought out from the church beside the square and held before her eyes. Beneath her bare feet, the fires were lit.

Her execution was meant to extinguish a powerful threat to English authority on the Continent, but we know now that her brief time at the centre of the war had truly changed the course of history. The slide towards England's defeat had already begun.

10

The Years of Negotiations, 1431–49

Frustrations Mount | Congress of Arras | Duke of York |
Three Sieges | Praguerie | Siege of Pontoise | Gascony in Peril |
Treaty of Tours

On 21 February 1432, Henry VI, the consecrated king of two kingdoms, at last returned from France to London. Accompanying the ten-year-old king, though riding well behind him, was a man named John Carpenter, dressed in his finest.

Carpenter had done well in his life. He'd been around forty-five years old when he was elected to serve as the town clerk of the City of London in 1417. Just two years later, he'd made one of several marks in history by compiling the *Liber Albus*, or *White Book*: the first book of English Common Law. Carpenter had served as London's town clerk throughout the years of Henry V and into those of his son. At one point along the way he'd even served in Parliament. But this chilly day in February might have been the pinnacle, reached at the respectable age of sixty. As the town clerk, it had fallen to him to organize this grand event – which meant this day, in a quiet way, belonged to him.

Carpenter wrote descriptions of what he'd organized in the city's letter book. His pride was clear. The occasion had been unprecedented, and all agreed the triumphal entry was its equal: the king was led past seven pageants that were presented in various parts of the city.

The poet John Lydgate was among those who witnessed it, and in the days that followed he used Carpenter's descriptions – with the clerk's help, we think – to compose a work to celebrate and remember it. The first pageant, we are told, was at London Bridge, where 'a pillar raised like a tower' had been built:

> And upon it stood a sturdy champion
> Who looked as stern as a lion,
> His sword held up proudly, to menace
> All foreign enemies and drive them from the king.

This 'giant' would defeat 'every assault of war' that might be made against the king's 'royal estate', because Henry VI was Christ's champion on Earth. Beside this stood two antelopes – a Lancastrian heraldic device – bearing the arms of England and France.[1]

Most of those celebrating their triumph on the streets of London had no sense of the real situation in France, but those who'd returned from there with the king knew it only too well.

Henry VI had arrived in Calais in April 1430. Celebratory bells rang in Paris and Rouen, but the king made no immediate move towards those great cities on the Seine. The resurgence of Charles VII's strength had made northern France a virtual war zone, and no one wanted to put the boy-king in danger. The English army that had come to France alongside him was sent out to make vulnerable roads secure. It took them until the last days of July to clear a path to Rouen.

A further advance up the Seine was impossible, in large part because a major Dauphinist garrison was holding out at Louviers. So the king was still holed up in the city's castle when Joan of Arc was burned at the stake at the end of May 1431. The king would not have seen her die. Nor would he have seen her ashes swept up and thrown into the Seine. But he would have known about it. He would have been told that it was a great victory: the English had fought the devil, and they'd won.

The effort to seize Louviers rivalled what had been thrown at Orléans. But after a seven-month siege and countless lives lost on both sides, its defenders capitulated at the end of October. At last, the English had a secure road to get their king to Paris. The expense incurred – in time, in coin and in lives – had been hard enough. No one had any expectation that they could get him to

Reims. Among so many other obstacles, Charles VII's growing garrison at Lagny-sur-Marne stood in the way.

So it was at the cathedral of Notre-Dame on the Île de la Cité, on 16 December 1431, exactly ten days after he'd turned ten, that the son of Henry V sat on a chair, the crown of England in his lap, and had the crown of France placed upon his head.

Henry VI's coronation in France was meant to be the first step towards resolving the crown's many struggles at that point. It would unite the various signatories of the Treaty of Troyes and reaffirm the authority of its dual monarchy across the Lancastrian and Burgundian domains in France.

In the end, it may have done more harm than good.

By crowning Henry VI, the English had effectively backed themselves into a corner. The one great thing they had to offer at any peace negotiation would have been his claim to the throne. While he was uncrowned, it might have been plausible to offer it up. Now that he had the throne, though, England was locked into its defence.

And if there's one thing that the king's nearly two years in France had revealed, it was that the Lancastrian cause was only barely hanging on.

As the king made his way through London, though, there was at least one glimmer of hope. In September 1431, the duke of Alençon, who'd fought beside Joan of Arc, had decided to make good on a financial claim he had against Brittany. To do this, he'd kidnapped the rival duke's chancellor and held him hostage at Pouancé, just over the Breton border. The duke of Brittany was understandably furious. He was also certain that the real player behind the plot was Georges de La Trémoille, the grand chamberlain of Charles VII. La Trémoille was a jealous man who would not tolerate rivals in the court. He had been one of the ringleaders in the expulsion of Arthur de Richemont, and he'd fought a personal and destructive war against him ever since. There's also a decent chance that he'd been part of the reason that no real effort was made to rescue Joan of Arc. It's questionable whether he really was behind Alençon's actions, but in one sense it didn't matter. Thinking that the French court was against him, the duke of Brittany had turned to the English one. Bedford was *thrilled* to do what he could to foment trouble for Charles VII. He agreed to send almost 2,000 men to help Brittany besiege Pouancé. Once this was successfully taken, the combined army of English and Breton troops would roll through Nantes and take Poitou, which would be granted to the duke of Brittany. The siege began in January 1432. By the time that Henry VI sailed for England, it looked as if it would be successful. Pouancé would fall, and a new front against Charles would open up.

But cooler heads on the French side recognized the foolishness of the whole affair. Among them was the king's mother-in-law, Yolande of Aragon, whose previous relationships with Brittany allowed her to step in and negotiate a solution.

On 22 February, just one day after Henry VI's royal entry into London – with all its magnificence and hope – the siege of Pouancé was lifted. It was a bitter blow for the Lancastrian cause. Not only was Bedford denied his attack on Poitou, but Yolande's negotiations between Brittany and the court of Charles VII led to the signing of the Treaty of Rennes, which effectively put an end to all their differences. It weakened La Trémoille's hold on the French court, and it paved the way for Richemont to return to his role as Constable of France. Much of this was internal French politics. For the English, the outcome was simpler: Brittany was no longer a path to victory. There were fewer and fewer paths to victory left anywhere.

Frustrations Mount, 1432–34

While the French court was putting aside past grievances, the English court was doing the opposite. When Henry VI returned to England, Bedford was once again regent in France. This left the duke of Gloucester to try to seize what control he could back home, which caused political distractions that lasted through the summer. Combined with continuing financial crises, England's ability to respond to the situation in France was badly hampered at the time it most needed attention.

Throughout 1432, Bedford was reduced to putting fingers in the holes of an ever-cracking dyke. In March, the Bastard of Orléans seized Burgundian-controlled Chartres. It was not only another city gone to Charles VII, but an important symbolic one within the history of France. More than that, it gave the French the ability to strike at nearly every road leading to the south side of Paris. Unable to be everywhere at once, Bedford resolved to make a single punishing strike that might give him some breathing room. The target was Lagny-sur-Marne. If the English could take it, the river and the roads leading into Paris from the west might be reopened. More, they would sever a vital connection between the French positions north and south of Paris. They had already made several attempts to retake the town since Charles VI's forces had seized it in 1429 – none of them close to successful.

Given its strategic location, Lagny was a strongly fortified town even before it became a target for competing armies in the fifteenth century. Standing on the south bank of the Marne, it was connected to the north bank by a stout stone bridge that sat roughly where the bridge on the D221 sits today. As was the case with many other towns in such a position – we saw it at Compiègne and Orléans – a boulevard had been built at the far end of this bridge. If the English were to have any hope, they needed to cut the combined defences of town, bridge and boulevard.

The earl of Arundel was put in command of the English army, which arrived at the start of May, marching from Paris on the road north of the river. After pushing the French forces back to the boulevard, Arundel was able to bring his artillery pieces within range of the bridge. As the gunners sited in and the bombards set to work, one by one its arches crashed into the river. The men guarding the boulevard were isolated, but they resolved to make a stand. Heroic as it was, it was in vain. Arundel captured the boulevard and took control of the whole northern shore. Arundel now built a bridge of his own, using barges brought up from Paris, that enabled him to encircle the town. Things had been going well, but after several of his assaults failed, Arundel's men grew frustrated. They'd not been paid, and the hope that a sack of Lagny might fill their pockets was looking increasingly unlikely. Many deserted. Arundel could barely maintain the siege.

Bedford came in July, having managed to scrounge more men. It wasn't enough to storm Lagny – serious reinforcements were delayed in England due to the dispute between the duke of Gloucester and the powerful Henry Beaufort, a legitimized son of John of Gaunt who wielded both ecclesiastical power (he'd been made a cardinal in 1426) and political influence (three times he served as Lord Chancellor of England) – but it was enough for the English to tighten their grip. The besieged garrison inside sent word to Charles VII that he must relieve them or lose the town. In August he responded with a force of perhaps 1,000 men and a train of supplies.

Bedford, hearing of its approach from the south, moved his army to block the French relief force. There was an exchange of cavalry attacks, but the French were reluctant to have a pitched battle. The English soon discovered why: while the force in front of them stalled, a second French army – and all the supplies – had taken a wide berth around the English. With the bulk of Bedford's army drawn away from the walls, they were able to fight through the siege lines and enter the city.

Lagny was relieved. And Bedford, after one more desperate attempt to storm it, had no choice but to withdraw to Paris in defeat.

The English failure to take Lagny further strained the already weakened Anglo-Burgundian alliance. For several years Philippe the Good had been trying to find either a way out of the war or the support necessary to win it, but to his mind the English stymied everything. They refused to make peace with Charles, but they also refused to do what was needed to win. More and more he was convinced that the English were unfaithful allies: interested only in their own gains, ungrateful for his support and careless of his costs – many of which they'd promised but failed to repay. He'd been angry after being forced to withdraw from Compiègne, and his ire had only increased as Charles VII's supporters had chipped away at his gains. At this rate, he might lose more than he'd won in the years since his father's murder.

Bedford was fed up, too. Frustrated by the lack of support from England – and Gloucester's constant mucking about – he returned to Westminster in 1433 to try to set the government on a stronger course. He found that the kingdom's finances were in even worse shape than anyone might have thought. At the time, according to the Exchequer, the crown was outlaying 126 per cent of its annual permanent revenues just to meet its expenses in England, Ireland, Scotland, Gascony and Calais. Its standing debt was already almost three times the total funds England brought in each year – without accounting for the debts owed to Burgundy and others.[2] Bedford simply lacked the money he needed for Normandy, Paris and everything else to support the Lancastrian cause in France.

It was probably around this time, while Bedford was pressing for help in London, that Carpenter, alongside his descriptions of the stunning royal entry that he'd organized, copied a very different text into his books. Composed in fifteenth-century French, the 'Complaint of Paris', as it is entitled, was clearly floating around. Its tone was far darker than the pageantry of hope that Carpenter had worked so hard to present.[3]

'I am Paris,' the poem begins, 'which does nothing but languish':

> Far from help, in pain and martyrdom.
> Ravishing wolves come to attack me:
> Day and night they want to kill me.
> I lose my people, my sickness ever worsens,
> So do not cease giving me comfort!
> It was long ago that the duke of Bedford
> Went for my sake to England,
> To his king and mine, to ask for help.
> Each day it fails to arrive, I lose hope.
> English lords, return to your good ways,
> Or you will lose Paris and all of France![4]

The poet would be disappointed. Before he'd left for England, desperate both to relieve Paris and to hold the Anglo-Burgundian alliance together, Bedford had directed as many men as could be spared to help restore the borders of the duchy of Burgundy and then clear out the French garrisons that were preventing supplies from reaching the capital city. It was in vain.

Amid all the violence of the Two Hundred Years War, what

followed in 1433 and 1434 may have been some of the worst. Brutalized by despair, the armies on both sides were ruthlessly savage in their treatment of anyone suspected of supporting the enemy. Through it all, the English and the Burgundians managed to roll back many recent losses, yet none of it changed the fundamental strategic situation. The major French garrisons at Lagny, Chartres and elsewhere were still choking Paris.

In the chaos of the broken, shattered landscape, cruelties multiplied. In Normandy, first in pockets and then en masse, a succession of peasant revolts erupted. The English, clinging to power, crushed them. The belligerents accepted the peace of the sword while sharpening their blades in the shadows.

As if it wasn't enough for the English to fear the French looming over the border, they could no longer trust their Norman subjects at home either.

Congress of Arras, 1435

At the start of 1435, a frustrated Philippe the Good entered into peace negotiations with Charles VII. Whether in spite of all the blood spilled or because of it, the discussions were surprisingly easy. Some basic positions were laid out, and an agreement was made for a major peace congress to be held in Arras over the summer that would bring England to the table.

At this point, the only thing stopping the duke of Burgundy from forsaking the English altogether was his oath to uphold the Treaty of Troyes in 1420. Yes, it was at a different time and to a different king. But it was still his word. It still meant something. So when the plans for Arras were made, he pushed for the English to attend. They agreed to come, but their ambassadors were given strict instructions not to relinquish Henry VI's French crown.

Philippe had agreed to a truce with the French to last through the proposed negotiations at Arras, but no such agreement was made with the English. So throughout the spring, the French were only too happy to keep the pressure on Bedford. This included a surprise attack that took the small town of Rue, not far from the crossing of the Somme at Blanchetaque. Bedford knew better than to let the enemy dig in, so he sent Arundel to deal with it as quickly as possible. The earl gathered a force in Gournay-en-Bray and prepared to march north.

It's unclear exactly what happened next. It might be that Arundel decided to make an overnight march with an advance portion of his army to surprise the fortified French town at Gerberoy en route. Or he might have diverted from his march simply to scout it with a detachment. Either way, the earl had a small number of men with him on 9 May, when he decided to pull back from Gerberoy and head back towards Gournay. Unfortunately for Arundel, the French had spotted him. Among their number was La Hire and another of Joan's former compatriots who'd been there at Patay. They pounced.

According to tradition, the Battle of Gerberoy began with a French ambush at Les Épinettes – today one of many undulating green ridges halfway between the two towns. Arundel rallied his men to make a stand on high ground backed by a line of trees and hedges. The French fired small-bore guns into them, then set spurs to their horses and charged. The English routed. Hundreds were killed. Arundel was found wounded on the field, his foot shattered by one of the shots. After he refused an amputation, the wound became gangrenous, killing him.

Arundel's death has made Gerberoy the most famous of the English losses that summer, but it was hardly alone. Everywhere France seemed to be on the rise. In response, a new expeditionary army of a couple of thousand men was raised in England: paid for by private loans from the leading members of the realm and led by Cardinal Beaufort.

As England's latest attempt to stabilize its hold on Normandy began, so did the peace talks. In June, the population of Arras more than doubled as ambassadors, their staffs and their guards all descended upon the city. Almost every constituency whose interests had been or could be touched by the ongoing fighting was represented. It was the medieval equivalent of the great peace conferences of the twentieth century.

Everyone was in place by the end of July, though it took until

10 August to be done with the many preliminaries. After that, the various players all got down to the business at hand.

The discussions between the English and the French did not start well. The French insisted that every scrap of land the English possessed in France belonged to Charles VII and ought to be held in homage to him. The English insisted that every scrap of land the French possessed in France belonged to Henry VI and ought to be held in homage to him.

The chasm between these diametrically opposed positions was, on the face of it, insurmountable. Over the days and weeks to come, though, there were at least some attempts to find a solution. The English suggested that they might be willing to agree to a decades' long truce and a marriage alliance. The French rightly observed that this had been tried before. Instead, after several back and forths, the French offered this: Henry would renounce his claim to the crown of France, but in return for doing homage to Charles he would have a greatly expanded Gascony along the lines of what had been in the Treaty of Brétigny – albeit not one that included Poitou. This was a good offer, especially in the light of France's relative military strength, but it was hardly good enough for the English ambassadors. Their king doing homage to another had been the problem from the beginning. Besides, such a solution left them none of the hard-won conquests of Henry V.

And so it went.

By the end of August, it was clear that the horse-trading of lands was never going to be the solution. There was no getting over the fact that two men claimed one crown, and neither was willing to give it up. Within a week, the English left the congress.

Burgundy and France remained. On 10 September – sixteen years to the day since his father's murder – Philippe the Good prepared to make peace with the man who'd watched him die. From the start, it was clear that the duke of Burgundy had no interest in performing homage to Charles or otherwise being made to serve him. He had no doubts about his complicity in the killing. So the French agreed to exempt Philippe from such duties, to save his personal honour. More than that, to save his family's honour, Charles denounced the murder, swore to name and punish the perpetrators, and agreed to make general atonement for it.

Philippe and his advisors were well aware that any peace made with France at this point would surely mean war with England. In political terms, they needed the inevitable costs of peace to be worth it. The French, understanding that politics and money were both rooted in lands, offered a massive expansion to the territories under his control. Some expanded the direct border of the duchy. Others multiplied his holdings in the Low Countries. All of it would be granted to him in return for the county of Tonnerre going to Charles… and Philippe's acknowledgement that Charles VII, not Henry VI, was the rightful king of France. *That*, of course, would fly in the face of Philippe's oaths to the Treaty of Troyes. So the cardinals that the pope had appointed to mediate discussions gave the duke leave to step out of that agreement with grace and absolution.

The Treaty of Arras was signed on 21 September. It simultaneously shattered the Anglo-Burgundian alliance and ended the Armagnac–Burgundian civil war that had begun in 1407. England now stood alone.

Duke of York, 1435–36

Bedford didn't live to see the final treaty that came out of Arras. After all his labours on behalf of England, his health had finally given out. He died exactly one week before the duke of Burgundy made his peace. But he'd known of the breakdown of the congress and approved of it. His was among the strongest voices to make clear that Henry's French crown was not up for negotiation.

He'd sacrificed so much to see his nephew crowned that it's understandable he was loath to see that crown as a bargaining chip. But Bedford of all people should have been able to see that the road ahead could only bring more losses.

The fracture of the Anglo-Burgundian alliance didn't just pull valuable military support away from Lancastrian France, it also gave a green light to further local resistance. Armed peasants revolted in the Pays de Caux in Normandy, and the French leveraged this to go on the offensive. They captured Dieppe in November, then followed it up with the taking of Fécamp and then Montivilliers. At the end of the year, Harfleur fell. The capture of so many ports was a devastating sweep in military and economic terms – it left Rouen in very real danger – but it was also horrifically damaging in political terms. Harfleur had been a symbol of Henry V's Continental gains, a first step towards English control of the seas. At its high point, the House of Lancaster and its allies had controlled almost the entire coastline from the Pyrenees to the Low Countries. At this point, only a handful of friendly ports remained between Bordeaux and Calais.

In England, a last-ditch effort was mounted to turn back the French advance in Normandy. Command of it was given to Richard, the duke of York. By the turns of fortune, he had gained wealth that exceeded all but the king's. He had also inherited a claim to the throne of England that might well have been better than the king's: he was the heir of Edmund Mortimer, the man who'd been Richard II's heir presumptive before he was deposed by Henry IV.

In 1435, York was twenty-four years old and had little experience on the battlefield or in France. His term of service was to be for a year, during which time the crown would figure out a permanent replacement for Bedford. Initially, it was hoped that York might arrive with the fresh troops early in the new year, but there were the usual problems of raising money to hire the men and then the ships needed to move them. There was also a lot of hand-wringing about the limits on York's power: he was going to France to do the job of Bedford, but he was not given the late duke's all-encompassing authority. Meanwhile, there were many who believed that a substantial number of the new troops ought to be kept at home. The Scots were still bound by the Auld Alliance with France, and the truce with Scotland was scheduled to lapse in May.

Three Sieges, 1435–36

For months Charles VII had been slowly tightening his control over the roads around the French capital in what would come to be called the siege of Paris. Exactly when these actions became a 'siege' in any technical sense is hard to say. Many date it to 1 June 1435, when, following up on their success at Gerberoy, his men seized Saint-Denis. This put the French in position to attack any English movement around Paris, severely curtailing the city's supplies, but it was by no means the construction of static siege lines. The English tried to fight back at multiple points, including a major effort that succeeded in retaking Saint-Denis, but such successes were the exception. It seemed that every time the English managed to push the French back in one area, they had to take two steps back in another.

The Treaty of Arras made the situation far, far worse. The Burgundians had been a strong and stabilizing presence in Paris. Some of them decided to stick it out with their English allies, essentially switching sides. Most did not.

The same shift of power was happening all across the north, threatening areas previously thought secure. Most vitally, the territorial exchanges contained in the Treaty of Arras had left Calais an island in the middle of Burgundian territory. For Philippe, this made the English city both a threat to his security and a tempting opportunity. Calais could secure and vastly expand his reach in the Low Countries – military, political and economical. By the spring, it was clear he was preparing to attack it. The English committed more of its newly raised troops to defend the city. It was the right decision, but it further delayed York's departure for Normandy and weakened the hand he had to play when he got there.

On 6 April 1436, Saint-Denis fell to Arthur de Richemont, who'd regained his position as constable under Charles VII. Paris was once more blockaded. This time, there was little energy – and not nearly enough men – to organize an effective counter-strike. Just one week later, the French appeared at one of the gates into Paris, the Porte Saint-Jacques, not far from where Clovis was buried at the abbey of Saint Genevieve. The Panthéon sits there today. Richemont and those with him presented an offer from Charles himself: a royal pardon for all who submitted to his authority. Word spread quickly. Angry mobs began filling the streets, clamouring for the gates to be opened, seething with pent-up resentment against the sixteen-year English occupation. When the constable and his men were finally let inside, the English garrison made an attempt to hold them back, but there was no stopping the wave that broke over the occupiers. Many were lynched. Others managed to flee to the Bastille, but even that was a temporary asylum. Trapped in a hostile city, the surviving English surrendered on 17 April and were allowed to march to Rouen.

Paris now belonged to Charles.

In England, the duke of Gloucester was spoiling for a fight with Burgundy. He was a man of action rather than diplomacy. One of the few things he and Bedford had agreed upon was a stand against the Congress of Arras. With the passing of his older brother, Gloucester was the heir presumptive to their nephew the king and able to throw his weight around in the king's council. He'd already shown his willingness to fight Burgundy when he'd defended his first wife's claims in the Low Countries. He no longer had that wife to support – since 1428 he'd been married to her former lady-in-waiting, Eleanor Cobham – but the Treaty of Arras gave him new reasons to want to attack the Burgundians.

He was not alone. The English viewed Burgundy's peace with France as a betrayal, and the threat to Calais was seen as existential. When Gloucester asked to be sent to defend it, he found many who were ready to join him. These were gathered as quickly as could be managed, but the Burgundians outpaced them. Gloucester was still in England when Philippe, after making quick work of its outlying English garrisons, attacked the city on 9 July.[5]

Calais had been well defended before Edward III had taken it in 1347 – there was a reason his siege had lasted nearly a year – but the English had spent the near century since fortifying the city further. After a first-day probe of the walls, the Burgundians made no direct assaults. Trying to storm an impregnable fortress would require the fanaticism Joan of Arc displayed at Paris. Philippe was no Joan. Her faith was in God. His was in technology. His army had cut off the city by land. His fleet would prevent resupply by sea. These were the basics of a siege. But rather than hunker down for a year, as Edward had done, waiting for despair to take its toll inside the walls, Philippe would speed things along. He possessed the largest artillery train in Europe, and he would use it to bring the city to its knees.[6]

For the first couple of weeks, he unleashed the guns at hand. It was a frightful sight, but the city's stout walls were relatively unscathed by the barrage. As for the defenders, they had guns of their own. Though not as numerous as Philippe's, they had a height advantage that gave them greater range. Still, Philippe's biggest pieces, called bombards, were still on the way. If anything could cripple the walls of Calais, they could.

On 25 July, Burgundy's fleet arrived to cut Calais off from the sea. After failing to sink ships in the harbour mouth, and aware that an English fleet would soon be arriving with Gloucester and his army, its admiral withdrew.

Philippe was in a hard spot. He didn't have a complete siege of Calais, and he had no way to stop the landing of Gloucester. Some of his men were already beginning to desert, recognizing the futility of the situation and anxious to get out of the way. Though it was a mark against his honour to do so, Philippe had no choice but to withdraw on 29 July.[7]

Within days, the assault from Scotland that the English had feared finally hit. King James took advantage of England's distractions to besiege Roxburgh Castle, some 50 miles southeast of Edinburgh. Despite significant planning, his siege lasted only weeks before it had to be abandoned. James had thought this a chance to solidify his status in Scotland after his many years in English captivity. It ruined him instead. The following February, he was assassinated in a coup largely driven by his failure at Roxburgh. The castle would claim the life of his son, too: after receiving his father's crown at the age of six, it took several decades for James II to take sufficient control of his kingdom to be able to turn once more against the English.[8] He did so by besieging Roxburgh in 1460 using artillery that he'd acquired in part through his marriage to Mary of Guelders, the great-niece of Philippe the Good. One of these cannons blew apart when he was standing beside it, killing him.

After the loss of Paris, the twin failures of the Burgundians and the Scots were welcome news. Had those sieges gone the other way, England might well have lost more than the Two Hundred Years War. But while it was good that two of their three enemies had been taken down a peg or two, these were hardly successes to crow about.

When the duke of York landed in Honfleur in June 1436, he was too late to save Paris, and his pared-back army was incapable of making a great offensive strike against Charles. The most that could be managed was to hold what was left of the English possessions in Normandy. York's replacement, the earl of Warwick, could do no better. The English had neither the money nor the manpower to do anything but try to cling on to a rapidly shrinking realm.

The French, meanwhile, continued their very successful strategy. Raiding parties, working with disaffected locals, struck as deep as possible into England's lands. This kept the English off balance, preventing them from concentrating forces in any one position. Bit by bit, the French chipped away at the English frontier, steadily securing what they had taken behind it. There was nothing flashy about what they were doing, but a war of lifetimes was never going to end with a single stroke. What France was gaining would, in time, end the conflict for good.

Praguerie, 1439–40

In July 1439, England, France and Burgundy attended yet another peace conference, this time near Calais. It had been arranged by Philippe the Good, who was now losing revenue thanks to his fight with England: not only was the lucrative wool trade bogged down in the dispute, but he was also paying a high price for standing garrisons to keep the English contained in the Pale of Calais. Less international in its scope than Arras, this far smaller conference was still a splendid affair. It was just as doomed. As before, the French demanded the English relinquish the French crown and agree to do homage to Charles for any lands held in France. The English refused to do either.

In lieu of a final peace settlement, the mediators conceived a complex thirty-year truce after an exchange of holdings that would produce more stable borders. During this truce, those who'd been exiled from Normandy would be allowed to return to their properties. This proposal was carried away to the courts of Charles and Henry.

Meanwhile, just as they had at Arras, the Burgundian ambassadors managed to cut a deal of their own on the side. This time, it was with the English. Without undermining their commitments to the French in the Treaty of Arras, they agreed to a cessation of hostilities with England. It was a much-needed respite for both sides.

Henry's court was not eager to agree to the truce, though there was at least some movement towards compromise. Certainly, no good news was coming out of Normandy. During the peace conference, Richemont had begun a siege of Meaux. In mid-September, the French took it despite the efforts of the audacious Lord Talbot – who after his ransom post-Patay had become England's primary general in Normandy.

Charles turned the question of a truce over to the Estates General. They met in Orléans in October. Many were willing to accept the truce, or at the very least discuss one. The king put off a final decision until their next meeting, which was planned for the following February in Bourges, probably because he had no interest in any peace that would compromise a single monarchy over France.

One thing that the Estates *did* manage to do was agree to a royal ordinance that nearly – and no doubt unintentionally – threw the kingdom into a new civil war. The ordinance centred on private military companies. The recent years of chaos had resulted in the same Free Company problem, with an added twist. Many of these private companies were effectively employed by French lords, who were more than happy to use them for their own personal gain. The depredations of these companies – especially when they were directed against the lands of fellow French lords – threatened the stability of the realm. The king's plan was to remove the companies from private employment and put them into his own service. In future years these would become the *compagnies d'ordonnance* – customary companies – whose permanent pay was connected to an overhaul of taxation practices that gave all powers of taxation to the crown. It was, in essence, the creation of the first standing army in France.

As progressive as this notion was, it marked an enormous shift in the power dynamic of the realm. Centuries of practice were being overturned. Few would call fifteenth-century France a 'feudal' society, but vestiges of its underlying structures still remained in tradition if not always in practice. Lords defended their lands with their own men. They taxed their own lands. Charles was taking it all away.

Among the nobles furious with this change was the duke of Bourbon. He objected on principled grounds, but there was no doubt his anger was also personal. For several years he had been a prominent patron of mercenary companies. Among his many targets was the house of Anjou, which had grown in power in the French court under Yolande of Aragon and her son, Charles of Anjou. Bourbon gathered to him every disaffected noble he could find, including the duke of Alençon. The rebellion that they began planning came to be called the Praguerie, due to its similarity to an uprising that had happened not long before in Prague.

Crucially, the conspirators took a page from the playbook that Philippe Augustus had used against the Angevins more than two centuries earlier: they convinced the king's eldest son that he'd make a better king than his father. Like Richard the Lionheart long before him, the Dauphin Louis was an easy mark. The teenager was frustrated to be so close to power yet have none of his own. The plan, concocted in February 1440, was for Louis to declare his father mentally incapacitated and declare himself regent in his place. In other words, he'd do to Charles VII what Charles VII had done to Charles VI.

The difference was that his father was not insane. The principles of the nobility nevertheless drew many to the rebellion. Most of the mercenaries were among them; they were, in the parlance of our time, fighting for their freedom. For several months the rebellion crippled the kingdom before it was mopped up in the summer and the nobles brought to heel. At last, the king's ordinances became the law of the land.

Siege of Pontoise, 1441

The English were in no position to take advantage of the Praguerie. Normandy had been without a permanent commander since Warwick had died in Rouen in April 1439. The duke of York finally agreed to return to France, but he insisted on having the full powers Bedford had once held there, in addition to promises that substantial resources would be put at his disposal.

When York finally arrived in June 1441, the focus of military attention in Normandy had fallen on Pontoise, the location of a major bridge over the River Oise, roughly in the same spot where the D14 crosses today. The town itself sat on the west end of this bridge, overlooked by a castle on the heights. This was the last English stronghold on the Île-de-France, guarding the last approach that the English had to Paris. The French were desperate to possess it. By the time York reached the town, Charles was in possession of the east bank. The English tried to convince him to engage in a pitched battle, but the king very wisely did not take the bait.

Who came up with the plan that the English now put into action isn't known, but York and Talbot were the men who pulled it off. They marched north under cover of night, portaging boats that they used to cross the Oise about 15 miles upstream near Viarmes. Crossing unseen, they rushed down the east bank of the river at the completely unprepared French army.

It was a brilliant action, and it set the French to flight. The English took control of the east bank, repairing and refortifying the gatehouse on the east end of Pontoise's bridge over the course of several days. Then Talbot and York set off in pursuit of Charles, who had hurried over the Seine to Poissy. This plan appears to have been all Talbot: he would march down the Seine in order to cross at Mantes, then march back up to surround Poissy from the south; York would in the meantime cut off Poissy from the north on the other side of the river. Talbot so thoroughly surprised the positions at Poissy that the king's bed was said to be still warm when his men reached it. But York had meanwhile left his position – he blamed a lack of supplies – giving Charles the chance to double back over the Seine and retreat to Saint-Denis.

After regrouping, Charles was back at Pontoise by mid-August. The English did what they could, but within a month the French bombards were knocking holes in the walls. On 19 September, the French assaulted the town through multiple breaches. Hundreds of English were killed. Hundreds more were captured.

English setbacks were proliferating, and not just in Normandy. The landscape of the war was broadening, which only further debilitated England's chances.

Gascony in Peril, 1442–43

Gascony had sat at the heart of the Two Hundred Years War from the beginning. It was the question of its sovereignty – made personal in the act of homage – that had set the machine of war in motion after an otherwise inconsequential murder in 1292. It's something of a historical oddity, then, that for more than a generation Gascony had been relatively untouched by fighting. Henry's conquest of Normandy had completely shifted the axis of the war, and with both sides suffering from the limitations of money and manpower, all their chips had been played upon that landscape.

But the situation abruptly changed. In 1438 Charles II of Albret had made a minor incursion into Gascony that had seized the castle of Tartas. This was not, in and of itself, a disaster. But the local Anglo-Gascon forces had laid siege to Tartas and in 1441 Sir Thomas Rempston – the man who in 1426 had held Saint-James de Beuvron against Richemont – cut a deal with Albret that the castle would be handed over to the English if Charles VII did not personally relieve him by the middle of 1442. What's more, Albret would give his son over to the English cause. By these terms, it wasn't just Tartas that was at stake: the deal could potentially move Albret's lands from French to English control.

Charles marched to Tartas with an army said to be well over 10,000 strong. It was overkill – Rempston had perhaps a tenth as many men – and after relieving Tartas the French overran garrison after garrison, raising concerns that Charles could take the great ports of Bayonne or Bordeaux. Winter blunted his momentum, but he'd significantly reduced the areas under Anglo-Gascon control.

England was already overstretched trying to defend the collapsing front in Normandy. Desperate to save Gascony, though, the crown raised a substantial army – much of it paid for by Cardinal Beaufort, who was about the only source of money left in a war-impoverished England. The cardinal's nephew, John Beaufort, the earl of Somerset, was given command – as well as a commission that effectively pushed the duke of York aside in France. To be sure that York could not counter him, Somerset also demanded to be made a duke.

Somerset's plan to save Gascony was to avoid the perils of the sea by landing in Normandy. He would then conduct a fiery march through French lands, cross the Loire and bring Charles to battle. By the time Somerset disembarked on the Cotentin in the summer of 1443, however, Charles had returned from Gascony to again threaten Normandy. The new duke proceeded to march towards Anjou and Maine, but it was an expedition with no real strategic aim. About the only thing he managed was to piss off the duke of Brittany – with whom a peace treaty was in place. He was shunned upon his return to England, and likely committed suicide in 1444. The damage he'd done by alienating York would cost many, many more lives in the years to come.

Treaty of Tours, 1444–49

Around the same time that York and Talbot were making their daring crossing of the Oise in 1441, a massive scandal was unfolding back in England. Two astrologers had predicted Henry VI was soon to die, then claimed that they'd been asked to divine that future by Eleanor Cobham – the wife of the king's heir presumptive, the duke of Gloucester. The whole affair went to an ecclesiastical trial, at which Eleanor admitted acquiring potions for the purpose of conceiving a child. When the court found her guilty of dabbling in sorcery, her marriage to Gloucester was annulled, and she was sentenced to life in prison.

Though he was never tied to the scandal, Gloucester's reputation was shattered and his influence at court erased. He had been the most powerful voice against peace. With his removal, there was renewed hope that a deal between England and France could be reached. The combination of the events in Gascony and the farce of Somerset's expedition now pressed home the urgency of making it happen.

A new peace conference was established, but the hopes for permanent settlement broke against the same rocks that had caused the war: sovereignty. Henry would not do homage to Charles. Even if they were willing to give up their king's claim to the French throne – a potential compromise now actively being considered – the English demanded to have their lands in France free and clear of the French king. But this flew in the face of the unified France that Charles was fighting to preserve.

The best that could be managed was a truce, established as the Treaty of Tours, which was agreed to on 28 May 1444. It gave the English a 21-month cessation of fighting and the hand of Margaret of Anjou – the daughter of Charles's brother-in-law. Margaret and Henry were wed by proxy in France, after which she sailed for England. Henry met her upon arrival, and they were married in person on 22 April 1445.

The truce was meant to buy time to resolve the thorny issues that obstructed a permanent peace, which now included a power imbalance between the two sides. The French knew they were in a better position, and the time of the truce only widened the gap. It was across this time that the promise of the *compagnies d'ordonnance* became a reality. Most of the mercenary companies were folded into a new army with systems of training and advancement. It was the first standing army in Europe since the time of Rome, a force of professionals that needed little time to spin up. Even with the cost of maintaining and training this army, the kingdom's treasuries began to fill up. The people of France, freed from the onslaught of both the predatory companies and the enemy English, had peace and a growing prosperity.

England had none of this. Its treasuries were stuffed with promissory notes. The lands in Normandy that it had fought so hard to maintain had been ravaged by war, and exported little more than unrest.

So when the truce neared its end, the French were in a position to drive a hard bargain. To reset the clock, Henry quietly agreed to hand Maine over to Charles. When this concession became public, many in England were infuriated. And England's subsequent foot-dragging with the handover infuriated many in France. Tensions were rising once again. Peace might still have won the day, if not for a calamitous mistake by the English that would bring about not just a final French victory, but a culmination of France's remarkable transformation after two centuries of war with England.

The Years of the End, 1449–92

*Reconquest of Normandy | Formigny | Rebellion and
Normandy's Fall | Gascony's Fall | Last Gasp | Castillon |
Another Mad King | A New France | Treaty of Picquigny |
Burgundy and Brittany Fall | Peace of Étaples*

The tricky part was the ladders.

François de Surienne, an Aragonese soldier of fortune, had taken his share of fortifications fighting for the English over the years. His booted feet had kicked the bark of countless rungs as he'd clambered up, sword in hand, to assault and kill whatever defenders had been placed atop whatever walls stood between him and his goal. It was dangerous work.

But the real problem, he knew, was that long before the ladders could be climbed, they needed to be built, transported and then put into place before anyone inside the walls knew what was happening. Everything had to be kept as quiet and as hidden as possible before the final push.

Some days earlier, he and his small army of around 600 men had left the castle of Condé-sur-Noireau – it belonged to the English leader John Fastolf – and travelled down into the large forest of Fougères. There, in the thick woods, they'd used axes to cut down the tallest, stoutest, straightest trees they could find, then hacked them clean of branches. Wedges were hammered down the lengths of the logs, splitting each one into paired rails. Rungs, cut and trimmed from straight branches and smaller trees, were shoved into matching holes bored into the rails before even thicker framing rungs were pinned through the rails at the top and bottom to hold the whole thing together. Iron spikes were driven into the rail bottoms, creating spiked feet that could bite into the earth and keep the ladder from kicking out. Near the top of the ladder, hooks were driven into the rails. Threaded with rope, these could be used to lash the ladder to the wall.

It was exhausting work, and it had to be done quickly. Even with the woods as cover, Surienne knew they couldn't hide so close to their target for ever. He also knew that darkness was their natural ally. So the attack was meticulously timed: ladders in hand, they needed to leave the forest in the hours after midnight on 24 March 1449, the night of the new moon.

Amazingly, they'd pulled it off. The assault was running on schedule.

Around two in the morning he and his men hurried out of the trees in the black night with only the stars to light their way. They moved as carefully as silence would allow, following the routes that their scouts had reconnoitred while the rest of them were preparing. The ladders were heavy, but no one complained, and no one made a sound.

Fougères was a prosperous and well-populated town, nestled at a crossroads in the valley of the River Nançon where two Roman roads met. At its heart, rising on a rock amid marshes and the turns of the river, was a formidable castle, the latest in a line of fortifications that had stood there for at least half a millennium.

The castle had a sizable garrison. But the guards didn't know what was happening until it was too late. The ladders were hustled to the walls. Their iron feet plunged into the earth. Their heads reached up to the wall tops. And the men, taking the rungs at something close to a run, rushed up and over.

Surienne and his men achieved perfect surprise. It's unclear if anyone in the garrison was even able to arm themselves before the attackers were let loose on the town. A French chronicle claims they killed many, imprisoned the rest, and 'violated churches and women, stole all the goods that were there, and did every evil they could think of'.[1]

Fougères was not a target because of its riches, however. It was targeted because it was one of the most important fortresses on the Breton frontier with Normandy, and the English had a bone to pick with the duke of Brittany.

Francis I had become duke after the death of John V in 1442. Though in practice he'd remained fairly neutral in his early years, he was theoretically an English ally. All that changed in 1446, however, when he discovered that his younger brother, Gilles, had secretly been forging an alliance with England. When Francis imprisoned him, Gilles called upon the English for help. Francis, in turn, moved closer to Charles VII and the French. Surienne had been sent by the English to capture Fougères as a bargaining chip that could be exchanged for the release of Gilles, with Somerset and Suffolk thinking this would have no greater diplomatic repercussions.[2]

The English had made an astounding misjudgement. For the French, the capture of Fougères was nothing less than a blatant and aggressive violation of the truce of Tours. After several abortive attempts to restore the tenuous balance of peace, the French king decided he'd had enough.

On 31 July, the French court declared that the truce was dead. The English cause was deeply, perilously wounded, and there'd be no time to staunch the bleeding now. The Two Hundred Years War had entered the endgame.

The Reconquest of Normandy, 1449–50

The English had not meant to break the truce, so they were completely unprepared for the consequences. By the end of the year multiple French armies were on the march in Normandy. Unleashed against an ill-prepared foe and focused in their leadership, these forces reconquered lands with stunning efficiency. By the end of August, they already had taken Pont-de-l'Arche, Verneuil, Pont-Audemer, Pont-l'Évêque, Lisieux, Mantes and a long list of other territories. Many of these were handed over without a fight as the inhabitants welcomed the liberating armies of Charles.

At the beginning of October, the French king reached Rouen. The English had a garrison of over 1,000 men, with Talbot in command under Somerset. The city's walls were strong, but its supplies were not. It was in no way ready for the siege that everyone must have known was inevitable.

The people of Rouen knew the truth of it, and they made several attempts to seize the gates and let Charles in. The besiegers, hearing the pleas of the populace, agreed to terms, provided the city was handed over by 20 October, but Talbot and Somerset insisted that Rouen would hold out. The day before the deadline, knowing their fate if the city was taken by storm, the populace rose up against the English, who were forced into a handful of fortifications. The gates were flung open. The French came in. On 29 October, a trapped Somerset agreed not only to surrender his remaining forces in the city, but to surrender five other key fortresses, too: Arques, Caudebec, Honfleur, Montivilliers and Tancarville. Talbot and other officers were handed over as hostages to ensure compliance. When the men in charge of Honfleur refused to hand the town over, Talbot was made a prisoner of war.

By the end of the year, Harfleur fell. Despite its efforts, Honfleur submitted in January. So did Fresnoy. Back in England, the attempts to raise a relief army were stymied not only by the usual problems of money but by the new problems of blame. Everyone was pointing fingers at everyone else for what was happening in Normandy. Aside from the actual facts of the case – which provided plenty of blame to go around – the disaster was fast becoming a powerful cudgel to be wielded for political gain.

Battle of Formigny, 1450

By March, England clung to a fragment of lower Normandy. The scraps of its administration held on in Caen, where Somerset had fled after the debacle at Rouen. They held only a single friendly port, Cherbourg, at the tip of the Cotentin peninsula, not far from where Edward III had first landed in 1346. It was here that a relief army finally landed.

The army was under the command of Sir Thomas Kyriell, who'd fought under both Henry V and Talbot in Normandy. He was hardly an inspiring choice to lead the force, but it may well be that he was one of the only men of any rank willing to do it.

Anyone with sense knew that Normandy was a lost cause. Most were jockeying to be in the best position to survive the fallout.

Kyriell's orders were to rush to Somerset's side in Caen and then make plans for an offensive, but he decided first to attack nearby French-held Valognes. The decision was one he would be blamed for, but in all likelihood he was genuinely concerned about securing the roads between Cherbourg and Caen. Whatever was going to happen, the English would need that artery open. It was their only lifeline to England.

Hearing that Kyriell had stopped, Somerset sent all the men he could spare marching north to meet him. This probably gave Kyriell some 6,000 men on the Cotentin, a truly formidable force. After Valognes fell, the English marched south towards Caen.

The French forces in the Cotentin had coalesced in Carentan after Kyriell's landing. By the time the English marched past them, they numbered a few thousand men, all under the command of the count of Clermont, the 24-year-old son of the duke of Bourbon. Clermont's scouts followed Kyriell's army, while other French riders made contact with the nearest additional army in the region: another few thousand men who were marching up from Dol-de-Bretagne under the command of Richemont and the Marshal Laval. The decision was made to try to pin the English down in the field before they could reach Bayeux. The English were following the main road, which the D613 generally tracks today. The two French armies hoped to catch them where this crossed the River Aure, a place called Vieux-Pont.

On 14 April, the English camped beside a small stream, near the town of Formigny – soon to be called Formigny La Bataille – about two and a half miles shy of the Aure. They knew that Clermont was to their rear and was preparing to march out after them, but they also knew they had a significant numerical advantage. Full of confidence, they settled in and prepared to take him on.

They did *not* know about the other French army, which had crossed the base of the Cotentin through Saint-Lô and was making for the village of Trévières, less than two miles to their south.

On 15 April, Clermont marched straight for Formigny along the road, and around midday he found the English arrayed in front of him on the ridgeline, the stream at their backs. They'd used their swords and daggers to dig trenches across the road and in the fields on either side of it. They'd planted sharpened stakes. Kyriell's men were arranged behind this much as the English were at Agincourt. Clermont arrayed his men out into a wide line facing them, about 600 yards away, well out of bow range.

The two lines faced each other. This appears to have been Clermont's first significant field command, and he was wisely playing it safe. He could see the English had at least half again as many men as he did, and they were in a strong defensive position. He wasn't going to charge recklessly, especially when he didn't know the whereabouts of Richemont and Laval.

Two field guns had been brought up from Carentan, and Clermont decided to open the fighting with them. The shots would have been cracks of thunder over the fields. The balls crashed holes in the enemy lines. The English didn't want to leave their prepared position, but they also didn't want to be pounded into the dirt. Some 500 archers rushed out, charging for the guns, taking quick stands to launch arrows the moment they came into range. The French gunners fled, and the archers began to pull the abandoned artillery back to their lines. Clermont's lines wavered from the attack. Had Kyriell ordered a general charge at this point, it seems likely that the French would have routed.

It wasn't to be.

The firing of the guns had not just pulled the English into action. It had also informed the approaching Richemont and Laval that the battle had begun and exactly where it was happening. They shot up the road from the south, their mounted vanguard churning up dust.

It's hard to imagine the shock that must have gone through the English lines when they saw the clouds that signalled the arrival of the second French army. The position Kyriell had taken was entirely focused on attack from the west. The roads that Richemont and Laval had at their disposal led directly into him from the south and east.

Kyriell did what he could, pulling the southern end of his line backwards towards the village of Formigny, bending his position into an arc that could defend against both armies. This was a difficult and dangerous manoeuvre to conduct under pressure, but he managed it. Had things gone differently in the next minutes, it might well have been remembered as a triumph of English command and control.

Instead, it would be a triumph of French coordination. Though their commanders lacked the benefit of immediate two-way communications, the two armies acted as one. Kyriell's lines were destroyed by the onslaught. Men tried to flee in panic, but beset on three sides – with the sea only a couple of miles away on the fourth – there was nowhere for them to go. A scant number made it out. Over a thousand surrendered, including Kyriell. According to French heralds, 3,774 English lay dead in the field.

Rebellion and Normandy's Fall, 1450

In England, news of the disintegration of Kyriell's army was at first met with despair and panic. Rumours spread that a French invasion was imminent. The mood, as it often does in such times, coalesced into vicious anger. *Someone* needed to pay for the years of wallet-crushing expenses and bone-crushing defeats.

The nobility settled on blaming Suffolk, who was exiled to Burgundy. On the way there, his ship was waylaid; his decapitated corpse washed up on a Dover beach. Pretty much everyone else settled on blaming the nobility. As it was with the Peasants' Revolt in 1381, a wide variety of grievances came together in Jack Cade's Rebellion, so named after the man who came to lead it. The rebels marched on London in May. In the tumult of the following weeks, many were seized and killed.

On 8 July, Cade was forced into a fight on London Bridge, where only a few years before Henry VI had been greeted by a man-made giant proclaiming his power. The rebels lost. Hundreds died. Cade fled, but he was caught and killed four days later. The rebellion petered out, but it had destroyed any desperate chance to shore up the English foothold in Normandy. On 5 June, the French followed up their victory by investing Caen in a siege. Somerset held out longer than he did at Rouen, but he was still forced to surrender on 1 July. French forces wasted no time marching up the Cotentin peninsula and putting Cherbourg under siege on 6 July.

Despair was easily the most formidable weapon in the long line of French conquests across Normandy. The defenders of Cherbourg had no hope of victory and little chance of rescue. For many, their core aim was to survive, and to do so with dignity and honour intact. Their sense of doom was born of the disintegrating English position, of course, but it was also propelled by a changed enemy. In the decades after Joan of Arc's death, the rising fortunes of the French army were paralleled by the rise in the ranks of Jean and Gaspard Bureau. The two brothers were neither noble nor born to the military life. They were instead resourceful men who, as the sons of a merchant, had a sense for recognizing and capitalizing on innovations in the marketplace. In fifteenth-century France, the market was war, and the innovation was gunpowder. The Bureau brothers became experts in artillery, developing new ways to make their guns more reliable, more accurate and more powerful. Under their direction, France built the most feared artillery in Europe.

The brothers were a key part of most of the successful sieges of this period. The siege of Cherbourg was one more instance of their ingenuity. Recognizing that the sea provided ideal firing locations against the otherwise stout walls, the master gunners moved cannons out onto rocks that were exposed at low tide. When the tide came in, the cannons were secured against the salt and the surf. When it went back out again, the gunners would return and continue their work of pummelling Cherbourg's defences.

Though it was the last bastion of England in Normandy, with a large garrison in place, Cherbourg lasted just over a month under Bureau's punishing fire. On 12 August, it surrendered.

Some of the English who'd been born or moved to Normandy over the years decided to swear oaths to Charles and stay. Most did not. They swarmed over the Channel to England. Few of them had anything but what they could carry. In many cases, those in England treated them as foreigners, as potential spies and enemy collaborators. The refugee crisis only worsened the many resentments that had given rise to Cade's Rebellion – which had been put down but not extinguished.

The duke of York had been serving the crown in Ireland since 1447. He'd been a vocal critic of the king's peace efforts, and the foreign appointment had been at least partially aimed at removing him from the centres of power. Now, in the midst of this growing tempest in England, he abruptly returned.

He'd come, he said, to defend himself against accusations of treason. Suffolk's death had done nothing to restore Normandy, nor had it satisfied the need to pin blame for its loss. Some of the fingers were now turning to point at him, and that could not be allowed to stand. But almost as soon as he stepped off his ship York also made himself the magnet for those who wanted reform at the highest levels. There were whispers that the time had come to end Lancastrian rule of the kingdom, that York, who arguably had a better claim, would be a better king than Henry ever could.

York marched on London and arrived on 27 September. At this point thousands had gathered behind him. He presented the king with an outline of reform that would, he was certain, resolve the kingdom's woes. It would include the expulsion of traitors in the government, whom York would root out himself. These were un-named, but York's experience in Normandy had given him a long list of grudges. Somerset's name was undoubtedly at the top of the list.

Mobs were soon chanting in the streets. Weapons were gathered and sharpened. The king announced some reforms to try to defuse the situation, but it didn't work. Many were shouting for York to at least be made the heir to the throne for the still childless Henry. Somerset found refuge in the Tower of London after vigilantes made attempts on his life.

England wasn't just falling apart on the Continent. Losses in the war over the sea were bringing losses at home, and the kingdom itself seemed at risk of fracture.

Gascony's Fall, 1450–51

The fall of Cherbourg was as sad a moment in the reign of Henry VI as it was happy for Charles VII. With Normandy fallen, he could turn his attention to Gascony, which had only barely survived the last invasion in 1442. Although the king still had to assign a great many men to the pacification of his newly acquired lands – and their protection, should the English somehow perform a miracle and reinvade – he was still able to spare a few thousand to march southwest. By coincidence, they crossed the border at nearly the same time that York was marching into London.

The Anglo-Gascons had done even less than Normandy to prepare for the inevitable. The English possessions on the Continent were continually hampered by a lack of funding, and most of that had gone to Normandy and Calais, where the need had been most desperate. Gascony had also been relegated to an afterthought in matters of leadership. Long gone were the heady days of the Black Prince and his magnificent court in Bordeaux. In his place was Gadifer Shorthose, the mayor of the city, whose oversight of the duchy was confined to his ability to influence its various economic and political players. For the most part, Gascony was holding together because this loose assemblage of men thought it was in their interests that it do so. It could hardly have been less ready for the organized effort that war would require.

The end of the truce of Tours had already opened the gates for some French incursions, which had led to a string of successes. The new army was able to capitalize on these by marching almost directly on Bergerac, a key position on the River Dordogne. Jean Bureau had come with his guns and, perhaps more importantly, his reputation. Bergerac surrendered.

The French pushed down the valley, encountering so little resistance that the army separated into smaller units to make its sweep more efficient. Within weeks, one of them had arrived outside the walls of the capital. They set up an encampment on the banks of the Jalle, probably near Blanquefort.

Inside the walls of Bordeaux, Shorthose doubtless recognized that his best chance was to defeat the invaders before they could gather back up into a single force. On 1 November he marched out with almost every fighter who could be found. The majority were militia.

Exactly where the Battle of the Bad Day occurred is uncertain.

It is sometimes associated with Jallepont, where the road out of Bordeaux crossed the Jalle – essentially where the D1 bridges it today – but the action was clearly wide-ranging on a landscape that has been much changed by modern drainage and the growth of the suburbs. What's very clear, though, is that Shorthose was obliterated despite a substantial advantage in numbers. The French force, organized and disciplined, simply outclassed their hastily assembled opponents. Very likely, they led Shorthose into a trap. The mayor fled on horseback. His militia were left behind, like lambs among wolves. A couple of thousand may have died.

Despite the victory on the field, the French had neither the weapons nor the men to conduct a siege against Bordeaux's fortifications. The city was safe for the moment, and there'd be a respite for the winter. But no one in Gascony was sleeping easy.

Shorthose and what was left of his army tried to make a stand against the French spring offensive, but most of them were captured at Blaye after Jean Bureau's guns made ruins of its walls in May 1451. There was almost nothing left to protect Bordeaux, which promised to surrender if it was not relieved from England by 23 June. No relief came. The gates of the proud city were opened. In August, after a short siege, Bayonne's gates opened, too.

The Last Gasp, 1452

After a winter and spring of recriminations and domestic peril, the English decided to assemble a new army, sail to France and reverse the defeats that threatened to rupture the kingdom. The English commander, Talbot, was one of the few veteran military leaders whose reputations had survived Normandy unscathed.

The French thought Talbot was headed for Normandy. They knew that its loss had stung English pride more than any other, and it was a target that made logistical sense given its proximity to English ports. They prepared accordingly.

Instead, Talbot dropped anchor in Gascony. The French military had left few men to occupy Bordeaux, and many of its citizens were more than ready to give them up. On 23 October, Talbot retook the city. He then made quick work of expanding his area of control around the city.

Over the winter, both sides readied for a showdown. The English sent more money and more men to support Talbot. The French readied their own forces to take him out. But though they moved with impressive speed, the bulk of the English reinforcements had much further to go to get to Gascony. It was no surprise that the French showed up first.

In June 1453, four French armies descended on Gascony. Leaving nothing to chance, Charles himself rode at the head of one of them. Talbot's situation was not unlike that which Shorthose had faced the year before. If he allowed the separate French forces to converge, he was doomed. His only hope would be to confront them one by one.

On 14 July, Talbot received word that two of the invading armies had locked down into sieges. One was at Castelnau-de-Médoc, northwest of Bordeaux, about 20 miles up the road from where the Battle of the Bad Day had occurred. The other was in almost the opposite direction outside today's town of Castillon-la-Bataille, about 30 miles east of Bordeaux. If he was going to defeat the French in detail, he now knew where to find two of his targets.

We don't know why Talbot decided to strike the more distant target first. It may be that many of his men were fearful of heading up the road that had so recently seen many of their numbers killed in what may have been a trap. Just as easily, it could be that Talbot recognized the fall of Castillon as a bigger threat. The town controlled a vital bridge over the Dordogne. The artillery train of the brothers Bureau was at that moment preparing to reduce the meagre fortifications at Castillon to dust. Once they did so, the French would be one step closer to bringing those same guns against Bordeaux. So began what is traditionally regarded as the final fight of the Hundred Years War.

Battle of Castillon, 1453

The French had come to Castillon down the valley of the Dordogne, along the road that still underlies the D936 today. Immediately east of the town, it runs between the foot of a wooded ridge and the Lidoire, a smaller river that winds around the high ground to join with the Dordogne a half-mile east of where the medieval castle once stood.

Encampments were often made close to or upon main roads, but Bureau and the other French commanders decided not to do so at Castillon. They were in hostile territory, and they wisely viewed the treed heights above it as a potential source of danger. Instead, they decided to move to the other side of the Lidoire, whose waters could protect them from any threat in the woods. This put them on a wedge of fertile farmland extending out from Castillon, bounded to the north and west by the Lidoire and to the south by the Dordogne. They placed their encampment at the northern edge of this space, alongside the Lidoire, on the opposite bank from the main road. The water protected the northern side of the position, and a winding, older channel of the river provided dry-ditch protection to the remaining sides. The French very likely further fortified the position by digging dirt out of the bottom of this channel and piling it on the camp side. Hammering cut stakes into this would have created a simple wooden palisade.

The French had at least two additional positions. The first was a group of Breton cavalry on the forested heights somewhere to the north of the encampment. This was a protective watch, but if any English tried to approach the French encampment via the main road, the cavalry could attack them from behind.

The second additional position was the priory of Saint-Laurent (sometimes called Florent). It stood on the other side of the Lidoire close to where the main road entered the town. For the French, its walled enclosure served as a forward operations base for the siege, while also providing a watch over the approaches from the west – the direction from which any reinforcements were likely to come. Up to a thousand French archers were stationed there.

Having crossed the Dordogne at Libourne, Talbot was indeed approaching from the west with just over 4,000 men. The old leader had a trick or two up his sleeve, however. He made his final approach on Castillon at night – similar to what he'd done so well at Pontoise in 1441 – and it appears that at least some components of his vanguard swung north to connect with another road leading into the town from that direction. This allowed them to stay partially hidden from view using the wooded heights.

Talbot's men would have been exhausted. He'd covered more than 30 miles in 24 hours. But his plan had worked. His advanced force caught the men at the priory by surprise. They swooped in. After heavy losses, the French survivors hurried away towards the main encampment to the east.

At this point, events get fuzzy. And, frustratingly, it's in this fog of war that the most crucial and confounding decisions were made. We know Talbot attacked the main French encampment. He rode against the fortified position, straight into the fire of Bureau's several hundred pieces of artillery. He did this without the whole of his army behind him, though they seem to have entered the battle piecemeal as they subsequently arrived upon the field. The English got the worst of a barrage of gunfire, but bravely fought on, sending wave after wave forward in what many have called a 'reverse Crécy'. A few English may have reached the palisade, but it can only have been a handful, and they were cut down as quickly as they came. For an hour the carnage continued. Then, without warning, the Breton cavalry – no doubt alerted by the artillery fire – appeared at the English flank and trampled whatever was left. Survivors drowned trying to get away. The lucky ones made it to the temporary safety of Castillon – which within days was pummelled into submission by those same guns.

As for Talbot himself, a ball struck his horse in the fierce fighting. Mount and rider tumbled. The horse's weight shattered the earl's leg and pinned him to the ground. Seeing him go down, French soldiers rushed in, cutting through his guard to surround him. He had no means to defend himself, and his head was caved in. When his tomb was opened in 1874, a surgeon examined the massive vertical blow to the back of his head and determined it was from an axe.[3]

Why, then, did Talbot attack the encampment, setting himself, his army and the last hopes for English Gascony on the path towards annihilation? Some historians have suggested that the

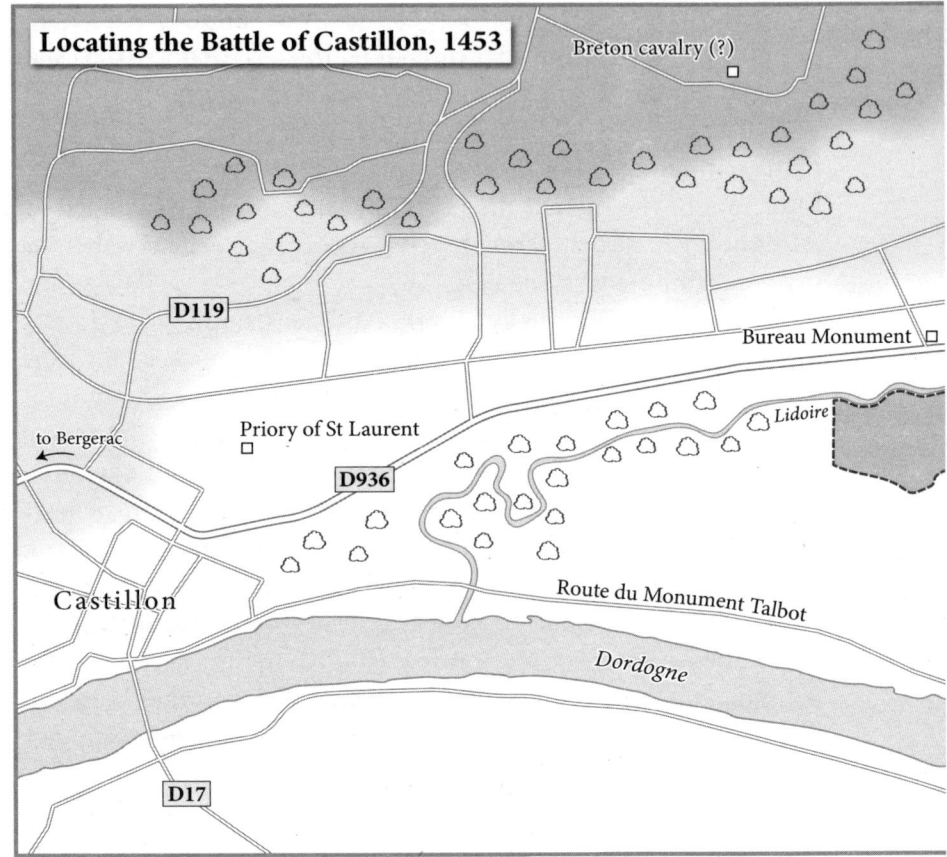

Locating the Battle of Castillon, 1453

Breton cavalry (?)

D119

Bureau Monument

to Bergerac

Priory of St Laurent

D936

Lidoire

Castillon

Route du Monument Talbot

Dordogne

D17

garrison at Castillon 'did not notice' the construction of the encampment one mile to their east. Seeing the dust raised from the fleeing men of the priory, the earl 'believed that he had the whole French army on the run'. He didn't hesitate to grab this advantage. Without waiting for the rest of his army, he pursued the men in flight, right over the Lidoire and straight against the main force in its fortified encampment. At that point, 'possessed by the *élan* of the attack', he refused to pull back. In 'reckless aggression' he rushed in and died.[4]

I doubt this. Talbot certainly knew the encampment was there. The French had built it over several days. Its location, size and strength would all be known to both the garrison in Castillon

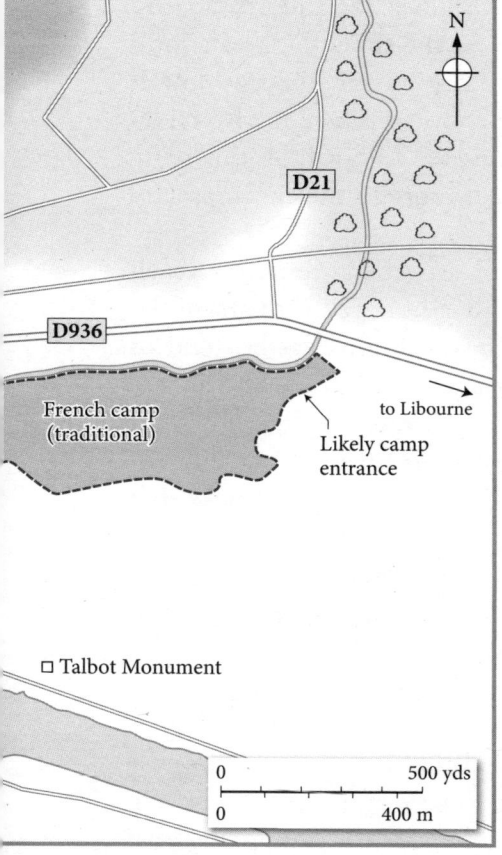

D21

D936

French camp
(traditional)

to Libourne

Likely camp
entrance

□ Talbot Monument

| 0 | | 500 yds |
| 0 | | 400 m |

and the local populace in a region that had been under English rule for generations. Given that we know Talbot was in communication with Castillon regarding its French presence – it's why he'd come, and it's also why he'd made an indirect approach on the priory – it's inconceivable that he didn't have access to such basic intelligence.

As an experienced commander, Talbot would also have recognized that the force he'd routed at the priory was not the whole of the French army. He would have seen that they were not fleeing via the main road, but were instead crossing it to take a less travelled, less convenient and certainly less likely path down by the river. Veterans know that men on the run tend to follow the path of least resistance or greatest safety – the men were running to the safety of the larger, main French force.

Talbot knew that riding down the men fleeing would not be worth the cost of riding straight into the strength of a large, dug-in encampment on a wedge of ground that, once entered, was not easily escaped.

So why did he make the attack? His actions may seem foolish in hindsight, but at the point of decision we must assume they seemed sensible. The key to unlocking what Talbot did at Castillon is to understand what Bureau and the French had already done.

As we know, the encampment was in the wedge formed by

the Lidoire and Dordogne rivers. Talbot entered this wedge at its pointed end, via a small bridge or ford over the Lidoire close to its confluence with the Dordogne. At the time, this was a local track along the embankment of the larger river. Then, as now, it accessed farms and fields. It was more or less where the Route du Monument Talbot runs today. Knowing Talbot took this path, scholars have assumed that it was *the* route to the encampment.

It was not.

The road that the French had marched down to reach Castillon crosses the Lidoire roughly a hundred yards from the encampment that Bureau built. It was at this eastern end of the wedge that the French had peeled off into it, and it was here that the French would have subsequently brought their guns in and out. The idea that they would forego the main road and instead move their artillery along a mile of dirt tracks that funnelled through a vulnerable wet-gap crossing at the feet of an enemy garrison… well, Bureau wasn't a fool, either. And if the front of it faced east, then Talbot was attacking the *rear* of the French position. This would not be foolish. To the contrary, it would be a very, very good idea.

Talbot knew about Bureau's main encampment. He knew it faced east. But he quickly recognized that just getting into position to attack that side was going to be awful work. He would have to march down the main road opposite the camp's northern edge, and the majority of Bureau's guns would be placed to cover that, ready to unload over the Lidoire. It would be a thousand-yard gauntlet of fire. And at the end – assuming he survived – he'd have to fight across the bridge over the Lidoire, make a U-turn and then drive into the defended front of the camp. It was a hellish prospect. To have any chance of success he would need his whole army and a brilliant plan.

So after taking the priory, Talbot stopped to regroup. While the men with him feasted on the supplies left behind by the French, he prepared to hear mass in the priory chapel. But at this moment the garrison of Castillon sent him a message. They told him, according to the chronicler Jean Chartier, that if he 'advanced easily and rapidly, the French would flee'.[5] These locals knew about the 'back door' approach to the encampment via the farm track. If Talbot used it quickly, before the French could organize a response, then he could strike the camp where it was least expected. This would not be 'an instant attack and pursuit' of the fleeing priory remnants, as is so often imagined,[6] but a bold move to steamroll a surprised enemy from behind.

Talbot quickly rallied his men. They raced out, hurtling over the Lidoire and into the fields beyond. Talbot expected to see an easy path into the back of the encampment. 'But when he came there,' Chartier tells us, 'he was very astonished to see things were quite the contrary, and the magnificent fortifications that the French had made of ditches, artillery and other things.' The English nevertheless charged in, hoping to blast through, but they were stopped by a line of 'valiant skirmishers, highly experienced in the arts of war'. These held off the initial English charge. Talbot withdrew, unfurled his banners and organized his men into battle lines. The rest of his army was streaming up. He still thought he could win.

But Bureau was hauling his guns off their prepared positions facing north and east, weaving them through the tents and wagons and all the other detritus of the camp to reposition them facing south and west. When they were ready, there was 'such a terrible, rattling storm' of gunfire 'that it was a marvel to hear it'. Bodies were blown apart. Whole lines of English were shattered in the thunder. And then the Breton cavalry, having crossed the bridge over the Lidoire that they'd expected the English to attempt, swung around onto the field from the east. They charged over the farms and plunged into the English flank.

Thousands died with Talbot, whose monument stands on the southern edge of the battlefield where tradition says his body was found. A monument to Bureau stands almost due north, along the main road beside the Lidoire. It is far less visited.

Another Mad King, 1453–55

Within three days, Castillon surrendered to Bureau's guns. On 1 August, the siege of Bordeaux began. On 19 October, it, too, gave up. Gascony, which had been in English hands for three centuries, was lost. All that was left of the once vast English lands in France was Calais.

For most scholars, this marks the end of the so-called Hundred Years War. Yet no one at the time thought the war was over. There were no proclamations of peace, nor had any claims been relinquished. The king of England still thought himself the king of France, and soon enough an English army would indeed return to fight for his claim. It would just take more than two decades before it showed up.

For years now, it had been difficult for England to scrounge the money and men needed for overseas expeditions. These troubles were still there, but the far graver problem was the complete breakdown of civil order.

The seeds of the Wars of the Roses are many, but the fertile soils in which they took root were the losses in France. The tax base overseas had crumbled. The tax base at home was hollowed out. Trade was disrupted. Domestic economics quaked. Refugees destabilized communities. Order broke down. The question of hereditary right brought on by Henry IV's Lancastrian usurpation had been an afterthought during the glory days of Henry V, but the string of losses after his death convinced many to support Richard of York's claim to the throne.

All of it might have been managed by a greater king, one who could deftly steer the kingdom through its many crises and into a new stability. But England's king was not a great one, and he was himself anything but stable.

It was a medieval commonplace to liken rulers to the head of a human body. As the poet John Gower wrote, on the occasion of Henry IV's coronation after deposing Richard II: 'When the head is sick, the limbs ache.'[7] France had suffered under a mad king a generation earlier when, in 1392, Charles V's sanity cracked in the wake of the assassination attempt on Clisson. It had opened up political fractures that resulted in civil war. England would now experience the same horror: in 1453, Henry VI's sanity cracked in the wake of the loss of Gascony.

There were hints of mental illness before this. He might always have had some debilitation. But there's no question that something broke in him now. He went silent, staring blankly. He reportedly had to be fed with a spoon. The question of who should rule in his name left open rifts. That he was childless only made it worse: his most likely heir was York, the man who many thought had a better claim to the throne in the first place.

The Wars of the Roses began in earnest in 1455. England, still at war with France, was now at war with itself, too. This civil war was disastrous for any attempt to return to France, but that doesn't mean the desire to do so had vanished. On 1 March 1460, during a festive entry that the king made into London during a momentary lull in the fighting, an English parson from Calais presented Henry with a poetic modernization of a Roman military manual. In it, the churchman called for England to unify and return to Normandy and France, 'until none are alive who lack true faith' in the English cause there.[8]

A New France, 1455–75

As England descended into a civil war, the French continued the hard work of healing the fractures that the English had left behind. Mopping-up operations sought out anyone still loyal to the old regimes in Normandy and Gascony. Administrative courts were rebuilt and tasked with figuring out how to handle questions of rights and taxation as exiles tried to reclaim property that had not been theirs for a generation. Defences were strengthened so that the surprise of Talbot's invasion could not be repeated.

The French went on the offensive, too: at sea, fleets allied to France conducted a pirate war against English shipping that looked very much like the fighting at the start of the war. As before, these successes encouraged raids on the coasts. The biggest of these occurred in 1457, when a French fleet from Honfleur landed at least 1,600 men – in some tellings it was 4,000 – at Sandwich. The fight to expel them was hard and bloody, costing the mayor his life.

For the most part, though, Charles VI's preoccupations, now that he had pushed the English out of France, looked inward.

As it was with his formation of the *compagnies d'ordonnance*, he was slowly but surely dismantling old social systems and replacing them with new models of authority centralized upon a king whose right to rule was, more than ever, derived directly from God.

For many reasons, this programme meant looking anew at Joan of Arc. There was no question that she'd been integral to France's resurgence and his own coronation, but the inescapable fact that the church had labelled her a heretic undercut his message of unity and divine purpose. The work of resolving this problem began shortly after Rouen was seized in 1450, with Charles ordering an inquest to determine whether her trial and execution had been just. After a series of escalating investigations, the pope agreed to a rehabilitation trial that began in 1455. Its verdict, handed down on 7 July 1456, nullified the verdict against her. Nothing could bring the teenager back to life, but her reputation had been restored – and by no coincidence that of her king, too.

Many nobles were understandably furious at the increases in the king's power – so many of which were at their expense. The Praguerie had exposed these fault lines, and they continued to widen. The Dauphin had participated in that revolt, drawn by his own lack of power under the rule of his father. His failure to get what he wanted hadn't stopped him from wanting it. The king was forced to send him into unofficial exile in the southeastern province of the Dauphiné, but Louis continued to scheme against him from afar. When Charles sent an armed force to put his son to rights in August 1456, the Dauphin fled for the court of Burgundy. Though it infuriated Charles, Philippe the Good gave him sanctuary – the duke, too, was worried about the threat of the king's growing power.

Charles VII died in 1461. Though he repeatedly called for his son to return to his side before the end, the Dauphin refused. He instead rode for Reims, where he was crowned Louis XI. Though he'd presented himself as a champion for the disaffected nobles when it might give him more power, Louis reversed course now that he had the crown.

In 1465, the fight of the Praguerie was renewed in what came to be called the War of the Public Weal. Among its leaders was the son and heir of Philippe the Good, who would come to be known as Charles the Bold. He was integral in helping the noble leaders get enough of an upper hand that they received concessions from the king. It looked like a victory, helping to check the power of the French monarchy.

Louis was not one to forgive and forget. He was especially furious that at least some of those standing against him were in communication with Edward IV: the son of Richard, the duke of York, Edward had taken up the Yorkist claim when his father was killed at the Battle of Wakefield on 30 December 1460, and been made king himself after his victories at Mortimer's Cross and Towton.

When Philippe the Good died in 1467, Charles the Bold became the new duke of Burgundy. He immediately began a new campaign to solidify his authority as a counterbalance to the French king. In July 1468, the duke married Margaret of York, the English king's sister. During the build-up to the event, Edward's chancellor addressed Parliament to condemn the lack of justice the kingdom had previously experienced at home and abroad: England, he said, had been despoiled of the crown of France and its duchies of Normandy, Gascony and Guyenne, and at every turn confronted with 'oure old and auncient Ennemyes of Fraunce'.[9] The message was clear: England had not given up the fight.

Each for their own reasons, Charles and Edward were attempting to recreate the Anglo-Burgundian alliance of old. They roped the duke of Brittany in, too. For a moment, it seemed France would be a battleground once again.

Louis struck first. His army rushed Brittany, forcing its duke to submit, and then Charles had to make a temporary peace with him, too. As if that wasn't enough, Edward was forced to flee when the Wars of the Roses reignited and Henry VI was reinstalled on the throne in 1470. It took Edward a year – and the support of Burgundy – to reclaim the crown. Henry died, likely on the order of Edward, on 21 May 1471.

King once more, Edward now openly eyed a return to the Continent. As Henry V had proved, going to war abroad could be a good way of solidifying support at home – support that he needed very badly.

Treaty of Picquigny, 1475

In 1474, Edward and Charles signed the Treaty of London. It created a new Anglo-Burgundian alliance. Charles agreed to support an English invasion of France and to recognize Edward as the king of France.

While Edward prepared for an invasion the following year, Charles looked to his own borders. For years he had been working to expand them – not just against France, but against his other neighbours as well. Just four days after signing the treaty with England, the duke of Burgundy began a siege of Neuss, an imperial city near Düsseldorf in modern Germany.

On 4 July 1475, Edward landed in Calais at the head of at least 10,000 men. It was an army that hearkened back to the great invasions of Edward III in 1346 and Henry V in 1415. Burgundy, though, didn't hold up his end of the bargain. Exactly one week earlier his siege of Neuss had failed. It was the first of a chain of losses in what would be called the Burgundian Wars.

Louis offered talks with Edward immediately. Philippe de Commines, a trusted courtier of the French king, wrote in his memoirs that they believed France 'was in great danger'. North of Amiens, representatives of the two kings met. The initial demand from the English, 'according to their custom, was the crown of France', Commines reports, but it reduced quickly to the re-establishment of English Normandy and Gascony: 'yet, from the very first day... there was great prospect of accommodation'. Quickly, they reached an agreement.

To sign off on it, the two kings would meet at Picquigny, a small castle on the Somme less than ten miles from Amiens. A bridge was hastily constructed, with 'a strong wooden lattice' barrier at its midpoint over the river. A roof was built over the top, 'to keep off the rain', and the sides of the bridge were barred. All of this, it seems clear, was done with the assassination of John the Fearless at Montereau in mind. The two kings would be able to speak to one another, but neither would be in any danger. The river was even cleared of traffic, so that only 'one little boat rowed by two men' was on the water, there for the purpose of ferrying anyone across who might be needed in the negotiations. Only twelve men from each side would be allowed upon the bridge.

The agreement was already in hand when the two kings made their way up to the barrier on 29 August. The Treaty of Picquigny, which they now swore upon the Bible and relics of the True Cross to uphold, was a broad and comprehensive agreement. It established a seven-year truce between England and France. In return for an initial payment of 75,000 crowns, Edward would return to England. Thereafter, he would receive a yearly payment of 50,000 crowns. Another 50,000 crowns would ransom Henry VI's French wife and return her to France. It was a staggering sum, but Louis thought it would be worth it: 'The king declared he would do anything in the world to get the King of England out of France,' Commines says, 'except putting any of his towns into his possession.' There was a pact of mutual defence – aimed at Burgundy – and an agreement to put the English claim to the throne to arbitration.

When they'd both assented, Louis joked that Edward – who was known to be a womanizer – ought to come to Paris: 'and if he would come and divert himself with the ladies, he [the king of France] would assign him the cardinal of Bourbon for his confessor, who he knew would willingly absolve him, if he should commit any sin by way of love and gallantry'.

The pact being made, the kings went to Amiens to celebrate. Edward did not, in the end, go to Paris to be entertained. Louis admitted to Commines that he was very relieved.[10]

Burgundy and Brittany Fall, 1475–91

England's attacks on France dominate the story of the Two Hundred Years War. But, as I said at the outset, we ought to see the conflict the other way around. The English were attacking France because the French were pushing England out. The French monarchy was centralizing power while extending the reach of that power to borders more or less recognizable as France today.

While the Treaty of Picquigny could be said to mark the end of England's threat to France – the seven-year truce lasted far longer – it doesn't quite conclude France's work of internal consolidation. Edward had tried to ally with Burgundy and Brittany. Louis had removed one from play, but the other two remained.

The king would come to be called Louis the Prudent, something shown in his dealings with Edward. He knew that renewed bloodshed would cost him enormous amounts of money and wreck the realm. It was a road they'd been down before. So instead he spent those enormous amounts on peace, which spared him all the other costs. Whatever else he was, Louis was both smart and, as it turned out, incredibly lucky. Charles the Bold's failure to seize Neuss and his subsequent loss of Edward as an ally was the beginning of his end. He was defeated three times in battle against the Swiss confederation in less than a year: at the Battle of Grandson on 2 March 1476, at the Battle of Morat on 22 June and finally at the Battle of Nancy on 5 January 1477. At the last of these, Charles was killed. Louis pounced. He seized the core of the duchy of Burgundy and other lands along his border while trying to force Charles's nineteen-year-old heir, Mary, to wed his son and make the annexation official. Instead, she chose to marry Maximilian of Austria, a decision that would lead to a political rivalry between France and the Habsburgs that would last until the First World War.

In 1482, tragedy struck. While on a hunt, Mary's horse stumbled and fell. It landed atop her and shattered her back. In weeks, she was dead. Her husband Maximilian was shattered. Louis pounced, forcing the bereft man to submit to the Treaty of Arras on 23 December. The peace carved Burgundy up, bringing the old duchy under direct French control at last.

That same year, the truce of Picquigny ended, but England was in no position to do anything about it. Their Burgundian allies were no more, and events at home were spiralling into the next phase of the Wars of the Roses: Edward IV died in 1483. His brother Richard, tasked with protecting Edward's children – the Princes in the Tower – saw them declared illegitimate. He was then crowned as Richard III. The children disappeared, their fates unknown.

Louis didn't have long to enjoy his victory over Burgundy. He died in 1483, and the crown fell to his son, Charles VIII, who was thirteen – only one year older than the boy who would have become Edward V had he not disappeared from history. There was a struggle over who would hold regency for the king-to-be, and the victor was his older sister, Anne.

The struggle, and the sudden uncertainty over France's future, allowed old grievances to resurface. Over the course of three years, Anne successfully defeated a group of rebel lords that stood against the crown in what is called the Mad War. What's more, she was able to use that fight as a pretext to invade a weakened Brittany. On 28 July 1488, the royal army met its duke, Francis II, in the Battle of Saint-Aubin-du-Cormier. The Bretons were routed, and Francis submitted. He signed the Treaty of Le Verger, which ceded to France the lands it had already conquered, agreed that the duke would do homage to Charles and also stated that the French king could veto any possible marriage of Francis's daughter and heir, Anne of Brittany. Step by methodical step, the crown of France was securing its borders and strengthening its throne.

Peace of Étaples, 1492

In England, Richard III was defeated and killed at the Battle of Bosworth Field on 22 August 1485, by the exile army of Henry Tudor. He took the crown as Henry VII, the first of the Tudor monarchs who would hold the throne until 1603. His claim to the throne was not a strong one, and like many of the kings before him he looked to war with France to stabilize his position.

He got his opening in late 1488, when Francis of Brittany died. Henry and his family had been sheltered in Brittany during their long exile. They made quick work of connecting with Anne, the eleven-year-old who was now duchess and a much sought-after bride. In yet another attempt to stave off the growing power of the French monarchy, Henry became part of a coalition that included Mary of Burgundy's widower Maximilian, now king of the Romans, and Ferdinand and Isabella, the first rulers of a united Spain. All of them would support Anne. In early 1489, Henry sent

7,400 men into Brittany.[11] The struggle would eventually see Anne of Brittany married by proxy to Maximilian to shore up their positions. Brittany fell into a rough stalemate.

Charles VIII, though, would have none of it. In 1491, the same year that he ended the regency and took up the kingship in his own name, he was ready to end Brittany for good. Henry's men were by then less than 3,000. When the French showed up with far greater numbers, and neither Henry nor her distant betrothed showed up with more to defend her, Anne relented to the French king. Charles had her marriage to the Habsburg prince annulled on the grounds that it was illegal because he'd not given his consent to it. He forced her to marry him instead.

At the beginning of this book we talked about the marriage of Philippe IV to Jeanne, the heiress of Navarre. Though I may date the start of the Two Hundred Years War to the murder on Quéménès in 1292, that earlier marriage was indeed a sign of where things were headed: the centuries of conflict to create the state of France more or less as we know it today. It might be thought fitting that it was a marriage that brought the French monarchy to the conclusion of its great enterprise. Brittany's incorporation into the borders of France did not become official until the Edict of Union in 1532, but the marriage of Charles and Anne made it inevitable.

All that remained now was the renewed threat of England. The next year, Henry made his long-expected invasion of France. At the head of perhaps 12,000 troops, he marched out from Calais and began a siege of nearby Boulogne on 18 October 1492.

Both kings knew what had happened at Picquigny in 1475. A repeat of it seems very much to have been on Henry's mind: even before the fight in Brittany he had been in negotiations with the French crown. His invasion now was a show of force to bring Charles to a final agreement. It worked. As was the case before, the negotiations were quick and apparently easy.

The Peace of Étaples, signed on 3 November, more than reimbursed Henry for all the expenses he'd occurred against France. Charles also agreed to cease his support for Perkin Warbeck, a man who had claimed to be Richard of Shrewsbury, the younger of the missing Princes in the Tower, and was gathering support for Henry's overthrow. In return, Henry acknowledged France's takeover of Brittany.

The English went home. Brittany and Burgundy were formally subsumed by France, the kingdom's borders at last close to those familiar today.

And while Henry didn't agree to relinquish any claim he had to the crown of France, his acceptance of France's rights in Brittany were a tacit acceptance that England's territorial claims were gone and never coming back. It was no real threat to the French crown.

Two centuries after a man was murdered on the isle of Quéménès, France had beaten England and redefined itself in the process. The war was over.

Conclusion:
The Wars After the War

Wins and Losses | Birth of a New World

On 8 June 1520, Giovanni Gioacchino di Passano sat down in his lodgings at Ardres to write a letter to the governor of Genoa about what he'd just seen. An Italian resident in the court of the French King Francis I, he'd spent the previous days on what would be remembered as the Field of the Cloth of Gold.[1]

The occasion was a meeting, arranged by Cardinal Thomas Wolsey, between Francis and his English counterpart, Henry VIII. It was an attempt to bring the two kings and their kingdoms into greater friendship.

Between Ardres and Guînes in the Pale of Calais, a massive field had been constructed. It measured 400 paces by 200 paces, and it was surrounded by earthen slopes and two high, wooden stages from which spectators could watch the celebratory pageantry of the coming days. Some 220 men-at-arms from both sides were coming to joust for their respective honour. Ornate entrances on either end of this field led out to the tents of the two kings, which Wolsey had levelled in order to give them even ground: as equals, neither would stand above the other.

This was only the beginning of Passano's wonderment.

Equals they might be, friends they might become, but the two kings had spared no expense in trying to outdo each other with the opulence of their temporary lodgings. Passano reports that Henry

VIII's pavilion used 6,000 yards of cloth of gold – a fabric woven of silk threads that have been individually wrapped in fine gold, it was (and remains) obscenely expensive. This was all incorporated into the English king's 'palace', which was square, each side measuring 328 feet, with walls 50 feet high: the first 15 feet were brick, but the rest of its height was made of wood and painted canvas, with tall glass windows rising up to a slanted cloth roof painted to look like lead shingles. Inside were stairs and halls, tapestries and tiled floors, kitchens and cellars. Gold shone everywhere. Out front, two fountains provided ready flows of wine where the guests could fill cups and pitchers.

Francis was no less a show-off. His foundation might be equal to Henry's, but his roofline would not be: 'From the ground to its summit, on which is a gigantic St. Michael, it measures 60 paces', Passano writes, a height managed by lashing ship masts together. All his interior walls were gold brocade and azure velvet. Everything was splendour.

The tents were expected to be used for only a few days.

Passano also tells us this: as the two kings formally met amid the grandeur, Wolsey read out the articles of agreement and friendship that had been made between them. It was customary, in such instances, to begin with an introduction of each man's titles. 'Henry, king of England and of France', the cardinal began.

Henry stopped him with laughter. 'Expunge this title,' he said. Then he turned to his counterpart and smiled. 'They are titles given me which are good for nothing.'[2]

Wins and Losses

England, like all countries, has defined itself through its myths. Few of those myths have been more constant and more powerful than those attached to the Hundred Years War. They are those battles I mentioned in the first lines of this book. Agincourt. Crécy. Poitiers. They were such extraordinary wins, so overflowing in glory, that it might be a surprise to learn that England lost the war.

At the same time, though, we should not measure any conflict by wins and losses alone – especially one so long-lasting and wide-ranging as this. And in any case it would be wrong to attribute kingdom-sized conclusions to the people of the kingdoms on either side. No one who'd been there at the beginning was there at the end, but it's doubtful that the majority of lives were generally improved by the conflict, whether their ruling class won or not. For most, war was simply hell.

At least in France, a general economic recovery began around the same time as the expulsion of England from Normandy and Gascony. Some of this had nothing to do with the war: better weather brought better crops, and fewer plagues brought booming populations. But crops cannot be grown or traded in a war zone. And a population boom requires more than a lack of sickness: it needs optimism for the future. Safer roads and better security bound it all together, and these positive trend lines were further stimulated by the recovery of international commercial activity following the Treaty of Picquigny in 1475 – 'the Merchants' Peace', as many called it. England's recovery might have been less smooth, hampered as it was by the Wars of the Roses, but here, too, the end of the fighting was a good thing for the kingdom and its people.

Whether for good or ill, the war altered the course of history for the combatants. The end in 1492 may seem a whimper compared to much of the battle roar in the preceding two centuries, but this doesn't diminish the impact of what the Two Hundred Years War had done. Henry VIII laughing off his title to France was hardly what Edward III had in mind when he'd first claimed it. And that might have been the least of the changes brought about by the Two Hundred Years War.

New systems of taxation were formulated, and the need to collect, organize and spend that money meant the formation of new administrative bureaucracies and legal codes. Formal financial systems greatly swelled the royal coffers, widening the gap between the haves and the have-nots – as the grandeur of the Field of the Cloth of Gold makes abundantly clear.

New tax bases led to the creation of new, permanent standing armies across Europe, radically changing how future wars would be fought. Prosecuting the war might have begun as a hereditary responsibility in a feudal world, but by the end of the age the need to *win* the war had raised a generation of leaders who were not born into command but earned it as professionals. This was especially so in France, where the Battle of Castillon was won by the brothers Bureau – whose rise was due to merit, not birth.

The armies were different, too, with new organizational structures, new tactics and new technologies. As the Bureaus had so effectively shown, terms on the field of battle would be increasingly dictated by the advance of gunpowder weapons – an Asian import perfected in the abattoir of late-medieval siege warfare.

Economic shifts dramatically altered culture and society – in the arts, in trade, in power. Political systems changed accordingly, sometimes with dramatic results. Seeds of a constitutional government were sown in England as Parliament grew in power and influence throughout the long years of the war. Religious and philosophical revolutions were begun, most of them responding directly or indirectly to failures on the battlefield. These reactionary movements spawned conservative efforts in turn. Many of the political reformist movements in late medieval England, for example, became bound up with religious reform – Lollardy in particular – to the point that separating them is at times impossible. The English law of censorship that threatened heretics with the stake – *De heretico comburendo* [*On the Burning of Heretics*] – was an Act of Parliament, not a decree from the church, and it was passed in the wake of Henry IV's usurpation of the throne.

No ruling house survived the war unscathed. Every kingdom and duchy in western Europe saw its line of rulers broken, ended or utterly transformed by the conflict. Some dominions disappeared entirely. Others burst into new life.

Out of successes and failures, national myths were formed. In France, the desperation of disunity during the worst moments wrought a new nationalism, tied to the land, that overtook the crown and infused it with new meaning and power. Its ultimate success built a myth of French dominion, of how they had taken back what had always been their rightful share of old Francia.

In England, the desperation of territorial losses, as it shrank from a Continental power to an insular one, wrought a nationalism tied to the politics of language. Its memories of great success

– at Crécy, at Agincourt – became inspirations for future endeavours in the name of Englishness, not the lands upon which they were achieved.

The Birth of a New World

In ways big and small, the maps were being completely redrawn.

Portugal, left relatively untouched by the war after the failure of John of Gaunt's attempts to claim Castile, turned to the sea for its future. Among the children born to Gaunt's daughter and João I was Henrique, better known as Prince Henry the Navigator. Before his death in 1460 he had done perhaps more than anyone else to bring about what we today call the Age of Discovery. One of Prince Henry's captains had a daughter named Filipa Moniz Perestrelo, who married a young sailor in 1479 and gave him her late father's charts. Her husband's name was Christopher Columbus.

What Columbus and the many other exploratory mariners before and after him discovered changed the map of the world. The European encounter with the New World, Africa and Asia opened up vistas unimaginable during the Middle Ages – and provided a new stage for new, imperial wars.

France and England would repeatedly fight each other across that global landscape. Though he said its title meant nothing to him, Henry himself tried several invasions of his southern neighbour – in 1512, 1513, 1522 and 1544. None were successful. None were aimed at a true reopening of the old war and its old claims. They were instead built around an idea that having possessions on the Continent would, like boulevards before the walls of a medieval city, serve to protect the vital heart of England: they would make any fight between the powers happen over the sea and not at home.

Henry II of France finally responded to these provocations by attacking Calais on New Year's Day 1558. Such was the dilapidated state of its defences that the great jewel of Edward III's success – the city he'd spent nearly a year besieging – fell in a week.

The English made an unsuccessful attempt to reclaim Calais under Queen Elizabeth I, but the war between England and France was shifting more and more to the seas, the Americas and elsewhere. As one historian has put it, thinking of how England came out of the so-called Hundred Years War, 'The Angevin Empire had been lost, irrevocably; the search for a new empire would begin.'[3]

And so it was. The globalization of England and France – and all that this wrought – was due largely to the end of the Two Hundred Years War. Both stable in what they were, the two realms were forced to look elsewhere to dream of what they could become.

Thus the Two Hundred Years War did more than give birth to England and France as we know them.

It gave birth to our world.

Acknowledgements

I have elsewhere termed Jonathan Sumption's five-volume history of the Hundred Years War both monumental and generational, and I stand by those words. There are few corners of the conflict that he does not touch, so most pages in this book could easily contain a note to the effect of 'For more information, see Sumption.' Such is his erudition that when I found myself disagreeing with his scholarship, my starting assumption was that the error was mine. I have, in the end, found reasons to stand by many differences, but it is always with the utmost respect for what he has done… and we agree far more often than we do not. I thank him here, truly, for what he has gifted the world.

For what it is worth, I would not have written this book had it not been for a shared conversation I enjoyed with Dan Jones in the shade of trees beside the Blanchetaque. He told me to do this, and I hope the result meets with his approval.

So many colleagues have played roles in helping shape this book. Myke Cole lent his keen editorial eye to my drafts. More than simply saving me from errors and typos, he tightened my prose while making it stronger – and he was unwavering in his personal support all the while. Kelly DeVries was likewise generous in sharing his thoughts on the manuscript, thereby saving me from more than one misstep. Robert Woosnam-Savage taught me much about medieval arms and armour that helped make this a better book, and he was essential in helping me sort my thoughts about the rarely discussed wounds of Joan of Arc. Clifford Rogers, John Hosler, Dan Franke, Trevor Russell Smith, and so many others have also been generous in letting me bend their ears on one point or another. I thank them all.

My agent, Georgina Capel, welcomed my plan to attempt a one-volume history of the Hundred Years War and found a wonderful home for it. My thanks, too, to the extraordinary teams on the publishing side of things: Nicolas Cheetham, Richard Millbank, Brandon Proia, Ellie Jardine, and so many others. You've all been so wonderful to work with!

I dedicate this book to my wife, Kayla, who let me read it in pieces to her night by night. That she fell asleep on every occasion was, she assures me, an indictment of the hour and not the work. I love you.

Notes

PREFACE

1 Chrysanthe Ovide Desmichels, *Tableau chronologique de l'histoire du Moyen Âge* (Paris, 1823), p. 130.

2 Quoted by Michael Prestwich, *A Short History of the Hundred Years War* (I.B. Tauris, 2018), p. 1. This is one of several excellent short introductions to the period. Another is Christopher Allmand, *The Hundred Years War: England and France at War, c.1300–c.1450* (Cambridge University Press, 1989).

3 My translation, from Dante, *Purgatorio*, VII.109–11.

4 Among the scholars to see powerful connections between what was happening in the 1290s and the more famous later events in the 1330s is Malcolm Vale, whose book *The Angevin Legacy and the Hundred Years War, 1250–1340* (Basil Blackwell, 1990) is an excellent study of Gascony's importance to our understanding of what was happening between England and France from the outset of the conflict.

5 A good example of a very different approach is David Green's *The Hundred Years War: A People's History* (Yale University Press, 2014).

INTRODUCTION

1 The traditional date of this event is 496, following the chronology of Gregory of Tours. I follow here the alternative argued by Danuta Shanzer, 'Dating the Baptism of Clovis: The Bishop of Vienne vs the Bishop of Tours', *Early Medieval Europe* 7 (1998), 29–57.

2 The clothing described here matches that in which his father, Childeric, was buried in Tournai: his tomb was discovered in 1683. Though most of his remarkable grave goods were stolen in 1831 and never recovered, we are fortunate to have drawings and many descriptions of the artefacts.

3 Ralph W. Mathisen, 'Clovis, Anastasius, and the Political Status, 508 CE: The Frankish Aftermath of the Battle of Vouillé', in *The Battle of Vouillé, 507 CE: Where France Began*, ed. Mathisen and Danuta Shanzer (Water de Gruyter, 2012), p. 88.

4 For a recent popular history of this calamitous period, see Matthew Gabriele and David M. Perry, *Oathbreakers: The War of Brothers that Shattered an Empire and Made Medieval Europe* (Harper, 2024).

5 For a classic overview of this history, see Rosamond McKitterick, *Frankish Kingdoms under the Carolingians, 751–987* (Longman, 1983).

6 Translation my own, from Dudo, *De Moribus et Actis Primorum Normanniae Ducum*, ed. Jules Lair (F. le Blanc-Hardel, 1865), p. 169.

7 John France, *Medieval France at War: A Military History of the French Monarchy, 885–1305* (ARC Humanities Press, 2022), p. 35.

8 For a terrific history of their main line, running from 987 to 1328, see Justine Firnhaber-Baker, *House of Lilies: The Dynasty that Made Medieval France* (Basic Books, 2024).

9 For a look at the places and events surrounding the momentous Battle of Hastings, see Livingston and Kelly

DeVries, *1066: A Guide to the Battles and the Campaigns* (Pen and Sword, 2021).

10 This and the following translations mine, from Suger, *Oeuvres complètes de Suger*, ed. A. Lecoy de La Marche (J. Renouard, 1867), pp. 116, 120–21. On the question of just what Suger meant by 'France', see Charles T. Wood, '*Regnum Francie*: A Problem in Capetian Administrative Usage', *Traditio* 23 (1967), 117–47.

11 For a full accounting of the siege, see John D. Hosler, *The Siege of Acre 1189–91: Saladin, Richard the Lionheart, and the Battle that Decided the Third Crusade* (Yale University Press, 2018).

12 For an excellent overview of the deteriorating relationship between the two kings, see Catherine Hanley, *Two Houses, Two Kingdoms: A History of France and England 1100–1300* (Yale University Press, 2022), pp. 127–33.

13 Roger of Howden, *The Annals of Roger of Hoveden, Volume 2*, trans. Henry T. Riley (Bohn, 1853), p. 297.

14 On the wound, see John Gillingham, 'The Unromantic Death of Richard I', *Speculum* 54 (1979), 8–41.

15 The standard account of the battle, which I have gratefully followed, is John France, 'The Battle of Bouvines 27 July 2014', in *The Medieval Way of War: Studies in Medieval Military History in Honor of Bernard S. Bachrach*, ed. Gregory L. Halfond (Ashgate, 2015), pp. 251–72. But see also his more recent account of the fight in France, *Medieval France at War*, pp. 135–46. For a terrific look at how Bouvines reveals the limitations of a pre-modern field commander's tactical control from the front lines, see Laurence W. Marvin, 'Philip II's "Eye of Command" and the Battle of Bouvines', *Journal of Medieval Military History* 21 (2023), 129–45.

16 N. P. Milner, trans., *Vegetius: Epitome of Military Science* (Liverpool University Press, 1993), 3.7.

17 My translation, from *Oeuvres de Rigord et de Guillaume le Breton*, ed. Henri-François Delaborde (Librairie Renouard, 1882), 1.283.

18 See Georges Duby, *The Legend of Bouvines: War, Religion, and Culture in the Middle Ages*, trans. Catherine Tihanyi (University of California Press, 1992), p. 197.

19 Matthew Paris, *English History from the Year 1235 to 1273, Volume 3*, trans. J. A. Giles (Bohn, 1854), pp. 283, 291.

20 Joinville, *The Life of Saint Louis*, in Joinville and Villehardouin, *Chronicles of the Crusades*, trans. M. R. B. Shaw (Penguin, 1963), p. 334.

21 Elizabeth M. Hallam, *Capetian France, 987–1328* (Longman, 1980), p. 267.

22 Malcom Vale, *The Angevin Legacy and the Hundred Years War, 1250–1340* (Basil Blackwell, 1990), p. 14.

CHAPTER ONE

1 One of the few extended examinations of this incident and the immediate conflict that followed is that of Thomas K. Heebøll-Holm, in his *Ports, Piracy, and Maritime War* (Brill, 2013), pp. 83–125. I am pleased to acknowledge following his findings in my outline of these events.

2 Ibid., p. 86.

3 Among those who have taken it quite seriously indeed, see Malcom Vale, *The Angevin Legacy and the Hundred Years War, 1250–1340* (Basil Blackwell, 1990), pp. 175–215.

4 This and the following quotes from Guiart are my translation, from *Collection des chroniques nationales françaises*, vol. 7, ed. J.-A. Buchon (Paris, 1828), pp. 145–49.

5 My translation, from *Annales Monastici*, vol. 3, ed. Henry Richards Luard, Rolls Series (London, 1866), p. 385; see also Walter of Hemingburgh, *Chronicon*, ed. H. C. Hamilton (London, 1849), 2.42–45; *Chronicles of the Reigns of Edward I and II*, ed. W. Stubbs, Rolls Series (London, 1882–83), 2.101.

6 My translation, from *Les Olim II*, ed. Beugnot (Imprimerie Royale, 1842), p. 3.

7 Heebøll-Holm, *Ports, Piracy, and Maritime War*, p. 96.

8 Vale, *Angevin Legacy*, p. 194. The question of who was initially driving this antagonism is a difficult one – Vale argues for Charles of Valois and Robert II, count of Artois, as likely suspects

(pp. 196–201) – but in the end the actions taken were those of the king.

9   For this and a discussion of the surrounding issues of vassalage and lordship under the king, see J. R. Strayer, *The Reign of Philip the Fair* (Princeton University Press, 1980), pp. 381–82, 389–90.

10   Einhard and Notker the Stammerer, *Two Lives of Charlemagne*, trans. Lewis Thorpe (Penguin, 1969), p. 78.

11   In particular, it appears that the stones in question were quern-stones; see Meinrad Pohl, 'Quern-Stones and Tuff as Indicators of Medieval European Trade Patterns', *Papers from the Institute of Archaeology* 20 (2010), 148–53.

12   Translation my own, from 'Alcuini sive Albini Epistolae', in *Epistolae Ævi Karolini II*, ed. Ernst Dümmler, Monumenta Germaniae Historica IV (Berlin, 1895; rpt. Hanover, 1994), letter 100.

13   *Calendar of Documents Relating to Scotland*, ed. Joseph Bain (Edinburgh, 1881), vol. 2.

14   For an excellent look at this battle, see Murray Cook's *Bannockburn and Stirling Bridge: Exploring Scotland's Two Greatest Battles* (Extremis, 2021).

15   Vale, *Angevin Legacy*, p. 176.

16   The best study of the battle, still unmatched over two decades later, is Jan F. Verbruggen's *The Battle of the Golden Spurs: Courtrai, 11 July 1302*, ed. Kelly DeVries, trans. David Richard Ferguson (Boydell Press, 2002).

CHAPTER TWO

1   The best edition of the poem, from which my following translations come, is in *Recueil des historiens des Gaules et de la France*, vol. 22, ed. N. de Wailly and L. Delisle (Paris, 1865). This particular story appears in lines 19876–916. On the sources utilized by Guiart, see R. D. A. Crafter, 'Materials for the Study of the Sources of Guillaume Guiart's *La Branche des royaus lingnages*', *Medium Ævum* 26 (1957), 1–16.

2   My translation, from *Recueil des historiens des Gaules et de la France*, vol.

22, ed. de Wailly and Delisle, lines 17556–70.

3   For an extended translation of these portions of Guiart, from which this and the following excerpts are taken, see Livingston, 'An Army on the March and in Camp: Guillaume Guiart's *Branche des royaus lingnages*', *Journal of Medieval Military History* 17 (2019), 259–72.

4   For a look at the complexities of these negotiations, see Elizabeth A. R. Brown, 'The Political Repercussions of Family Ties in the Early Fourteenth Century: The Marriage of Edward II of England and Isabelle of France', *Speculum* 63.3 (1988), 573–95.

5   My translation, from *Histoire du différend d'entre le pape Boniface VIII et Philippes le Bel*, ed. Pierre Dupuy (Paris, 1655), p. 56.

6   Boniface actually echoes an earlier statement by Thomas Aquinas in his *Contra errores Graecorum*, ch. 38: 'subjection to the Roman Pontiff is necessary for salvation' (my translation).

7   Translations my own, from the surviving text as printed in J. R. S. Phillips, *Aymer de Valence, Earl of Pembroke, 1307–1324: Baronial Politics in the Reign of Edward II* (Oxford University Press, 1972), p. 316; for an examination of the document, see also his discussion on pp. 25–28.

8   On the evidence that these rumours were true, see J. S. Hamilton, 'Piers Gaveston and the Royal Treasure', *Albion* 23.2 (1991), 201–07.

9   Paul Doherty, *Isabella and the Strange Death of Edward II* (Carroll and Graf, 2003), pp. 57–59.

10   I here accept the dating of events, and Isabella's involvement in them, as presented by Elizabeth A. R. Brown, 'Philip the Fair of France and His Family's Disgrace: The Adultery Scandal of 1314 Revealed, Recounted, Reimagined, and Redated', *Mediaevistik* 32 (2019), 71–103.

11   Michael Prestwich, *The Three Edwards: War and State in England, 1272–1377* (Weidenfeld & Nicolson, 1980), p. 50.

12   At present, the best published reconstruction of the battle is that found

in Murray Cook's *Bannockburn and Stirling Bridge: Exploring Scotland's Two Greatest Battles* (Extremis, 2021). I was pleased to find this, as it matched my independent conclusions almost entirely.

13   *Registrum Monasterii S. Marie de Cambuskenneth, A. D. 1147–1535*, ed. Sir William Fraser (The Grampian Club, 1872), charter 104, pp. 136–37.

14   James Ronald, *Landmarks of Old Stirling* (Eneas Mackay, 1899), p. 115.

CHAPTER THREE

1   My translation, from André-François-Victoire-Henri Carrion-Nisas, *La Loi Salique traduite en français* (Paris, 1820), pp. 31–32. That legal codes varied widely in medieval France is most humorously shown by the complaint of Archbishop Agobard of Lyon in 817 that 'it often happens that five men walk or sit together, and none of them has a common law with the others' (my translation, from Monumenta Germaniae Historica, *Epistolarum V: Karolini Aevi III* [Berlin, 1899], p. 159).

2   A terrific, potentially first-hand account of the tense few days surrounding the homage was located by E. Pole Stuart and published as 'The Interview between Philip V and Edward II at Amiens in 1320', *English Historical Review* 41 (1926), 412–15.

3   My translation, from *Archives nationales*, J 624, no. 18, as printed in F. Funck-Brentano, *De exercituum commeatibus: tertio decimo et quarto decimo saeculis post christum natum* (Librairie Honoré Champion, 1897), pp. 60–63. It is likely that an undated royal order demanding aid in the war against England should also be assigned to this same period; this order is printed in Joseph Petit, *Essai de restitution des plus anciens mémoriaux de la Chambres des comptes des Paris* (Bailliere, 1899), pp. 203–04.

4   My translation, from Jusselin, 'Comment la France sa préparait à la guerre de cent ans', *Bibliothèque de l'École des Chartes* 73 (1912), 220–22.

5   Exactly what constitutes 'men-at-arms' depends on who is referring to them and when. For an overview within English contexts relevant to Agincourt, see Adrian R. Bell, Anne Curry, Andy King and David Simpkin, *The Soldier in Later Medieval England* (Oxford University Press, 2013), pp. 95–138.

6   Malcolm Vale, *The Angevin Legacy and the Hundred Years War, 1250–1340* (Basil Blackwell, 1990), p. 247.

7   Jean le Bel, *The True Chronicles of Jean le Bel, 1290–1360*, trans. Nigel Bryant (Boydell Press, 2011), p. 31.

8   Adam Murimuth, *Continuatio Chronicarum*, ed. Edward Maude Thompson, Rolls Series 93 (Eyre and Spottiswoode, 1889), p. 51.

9   Le Bel, *True Chronicles*, trans. Bryant, pp. 39–40.

10   For an excellent look at the logistics involved, see Craig Lambert, 'Taking the War to Scotland and France: The Supply and Transportation of English Armies by Sea, 1320–60', PhD Dissertation, University of Hull, 2009, pp. 87–97.

11   Ian Mortimer, *The Greatest Traitor: The Life of Roger Mortimer, First Earl of March, Ruler of England, 1327–30* (Jonathan Cape, 2003), p. 178.

12   Le Bel, *True Chronicles*, trans. Bryant, p. 46.

13   Ibid., p. 47.

14   The best book on the subject to date is that of William H. TeBrake, *A Plague of Insurrection: Popular Politics and Peasant Revolt in Flanders, 1323–1328* (University of Pennsylvania Press, 1993).

15   Ibid., pp. 139–41.

16   On the dating, see Jusselin, 'Comment la France sa préparait', pp. 214–15; the document itself is on pp. 222–26. Compared to the 1327 estimate, this document provides less detail on the supplies, transport and other necessaries of the expected campaign – but it spends a great deal of time getting into the fascinating particulars of how the cost might be borne.

17   Paris, Archives Nationale, MS J 918, no. 20.

18   *Chronographia regum Francorum*, ed. Henri Moranvillé. Société de l'histoire de France (Librairie Renouard, 1891), 2.12.

CHAPTER FOUR

1 My translation, from Thomas Rymer, ed., *Foedera, conventiones, litterae, et cujuscunque generis acta publica*, 20 vols. (London, 1704–35), 2.2.61.

2 It is possible that the English had earlier planned to utilize something like these tactics – what many historians would call the 'English system' – during the Weardale campaign in 1327, but because the Scots refused to give battle we can't know exactly what it would have looked like at that time. See Michael Prestwich, *Armies and Warfare in the Middle Ages: The English Experience* (Yale University Press, 1996), p. 318.

3 My translation, from *Chronicon de Lanercost*, ed. Joseph Stevenson (Edinburgh, 1839), p. 268.

4 This and the following translations mine, from *The Brut, or The Chronicles of England*, ed. Friedrich W. D. Brie (Kegan Paul, Trench, Trübner & Co., 1906), pp. 278–79.

5 For the text of the letter, see Eugène Déprez, *Les Préliminaires de la guerre de Cent ans: la papauté, la France et l'Angleterre (1328–1342)* (Megariotis, 1902), pp. 414–15.

6 For the letter, see Maurice Jusselin, 'Comment la France se préparait à la guerre de cent ans', *Bibliothèque de l'École des Chartes* 73 (1912), 233–34.

7 *Calendar of Patent Rolls of Edward III, 1338–40 (London, 1898)*, p. 286. Such was the destruction that as late as 4 December 1342 the area was being given tax relief to help it recover.

8 For a recent overview of the economics of the period, see Tony K. Moore and Adrian R. Bell, 'Financing the Hundred Years War', in *The Hundred Years War Revisited*, ed. Anne Curry (Red Globe, 2019), pp. 57–84.

9 Rymer, *Foedera*, 2.1080. There is good reason, in fact, to think the king had already defaulted on at least some of his loans.

10 *Chronographia regum Francorum*, ed. Henri Moranvillé, Société de l'histoire de France (Librairie Renouard, 1891–97), vol. 2, pp. 80–81.

11 For Sluys and Tournai, see the examinations by Kelly DeVries: 'God,

Admirals, Archery, and Flemings: Perceptions of Victory and Defeat at the Battle of Sluys, 1340', *American Neptune* 55 (1995), 223–42, and 'Contemporary Views of Edward III's Failure at the Siege of Tournai, 1340', *Nottingham Medieval Studies* 39 (1995), 70–105.

12 Jean le Bel, *The True Chronicles of Jean le Bel, 1290–1360*, trans. Nigel Bryant (Boydell Press, 2011), p. 109.

13 Ibid., p. 131.

14 My translation, from Gilles li Muisit, *Chronique et annales de Gilles le Muisit, abbé de Saint-Martin de Tournai (1272–1352)*, ed. Henri Lemaître (Librairie Renouard, 1906), p. 295.

15 One explanation offered in Continental chronicles is that Edward III had raped the wife of one of his earls, and in the fallout the earl passed incriminating evidence about Clisson to Philippe. The story is almost assuredly French war propaganda. See Antonia Gransden, 'The Alleged Rape by Edward III of the Countess of Salisbury', *The English Historical Review* 87 (1972), 333–44.

16 The Order of the Round Table is often confused with the longer-lasting Order of the Garter, which Edward founded four years later. On the history of the Order of the Round Table and its conflation with the later Order of the Garter, see Christopher Berard's 'Edward III's Abandoned Order of the Round Table', *Arthurian Literature* 29 (2012), 1–40, and 'Edward III's Abandoned Order of the Round Table Revisited: Political Arthurianism After Poitiers', *Arthurian Literature* 33 (2016), 70–109.

17 The finest historical study of Arthur's origins to date is Nicholas J. Higham, *King Arthur: The Making of a Legend* (Yale University Press, 2018).

18 My translation, from Thomas Walsingham, *Historia Anglicana*, ed. H. T. Riley, Rolls Series 28 (London, 1863–64), 1.263.

19 Among the best studies on the subject is Richard W. Kaeuper, *Chivalry and Violence in Medieval Europe* (Oxford University Press, 1999).

20 E. Kennedy, 'The Knight as Reader of Arthurian Romance', in *Culture and the*

King: The Social Implications of Arthurian Legend, ed. M. B. Shichtman and J. P. Carley (State University of New York, 1994), pp. 81–82. See also Richard Kaeuper, 'Chivalry and the "Civilizing Process"', in Violence in Medieval Society, ed. Kaeuper (Boydell Press, 2000), pp. 21–35.

21   On this construction, see Julian Munby, 'The Round Table Building: The Windsor Building Accounts', in Munby, Richard Barber and Richard Brown, Edward III's Round Table at Windsor (Boydell Press, 2007), pp. 44–52.

22   The indenture, E 159/123, m. 254d, is helpfully transcribed and published as Appendix A in Nicholas A. Gribit, Henry of Lancaster's Expedition to Aquitaine, 1345–1346 (Boydell Press, 2016), p. 251.

23   My translation, from Chronique des quatre premiers Valois (1327–1393), ed. Siméon Luce (Paris, 1862), p. 12. For a terrific study of just one sequence in his career, see Clifford J. Rogers, 'The Bergerac Campaign (1345) and the Generalship of Henry of Lancaster', Journal of Medieval Military History 2 (2004), 89–110.

24   Those readers wanting an even more in-depth look at Crécy are advised to examine Livingston, Crécy: Battle of Five Kings (Osprey, 2022), from which much of what follows is compressed.

25   The Battle of Crécy: A Casebook, ed. Livingston and Kelly DeVries (Liverpool University Press, 2015), pp. 20–23.

26   These are the numbers resolved by Andrew Ayton, which subsequent research has appeared to confirm; see Battle of Crécy: A Casebook, ed. Livingston and DeVries, p. 6.

27   The battle is traditionally located north of the town of Crécy-en-Ponthieu, but in Livingston, Crécy: Battle of Five Kings I go through the evidence that points instead to a rise beside the forest of Crécy roughly four miles southeast. The brief account of the battle given here follows my larger reconstruction of the conflict in that book.

28   Walter of Hemingburgh, Chronicon, ed. H. C. Hamilton (1948–49), 2.422–23;

trans. Sumption, Trial by Battle, p. 504.

CHAPTER FIVE

1   Monica H. Green and André Filipe Oliveira da Silva, 'Shifting Paradigms in Black Death Chronologies', 22 March 2023, https://urbrel.hypotheses.org/5550

2   My translation, from Boccaccio, Decameron, First Day, Introduction, https://www.brown.edu/Departments/Italian_Studies/dweb/

3   Geoffrey le Baker, Chronicon, trans. Trevor Russell Smith, in Kelly DeVries and Livingston, Medieval Warfare: A Reader (University of Toronto Press, 2019), pp. 192–93.

4   Jean le Bel, The True Chronicles of Jean le Bel, 1290–1360, trans. Nigel Bryant (Boydell Press, 2011), p. 215.

5   Sumption, Trial by Fire, pp. 71–72.

6   See Clifford J. Rogers, 'The Symbolic Meaning of Edward III's Garter Badge', in Gary Baker, Craig Lambert and David Simpkin, eds., Military Communities in Late Medieval England: Essays in Honour of Andrew Ayton (Boydell Press, 2018), pp. 125–46.

7   Ian Wilson and Nigel Bryant, The Book of Geoffroi de Charny with the Livre Charny (Boydell Press, 2021), pp. 114, 127.

8   Les Grandes Chroniques de France: Chronique des règnes de Jean II et de Charles V, ed. Roland Delachenal (Société de l'histoire de France, 1910–20), 1.37–38.

9   My translation, from Chronique des quatre premiers Valois (1327–1393), ed. Siméon Luce (Paris, 1862), pp. 27–28.

10   Translation by Sumption, Trial by Fire, p. 125.

11   Ibid., p. 185.

12   Le Bel, True Chronicles, trans. Bryant, p. 223.

13   These and the following translations from Villani are mine, from Matteo Villani, Cronica, ed. Giammaria Mazzuchelli (Milan, 1834), pp. 207–12.

14   All quotations from the Black Prince's letter are from Richard Barber, The Life and Campaigns of the Black Prince: From Contemporary Letters,

Diaries and Chronicles, Including Chandos Herald's Life of the Black Prince (Boydell Press, 1979), p. 58.

15 This and subsequent quotations from Geoffrey le Baker are mine, from his *Chronicon*, ed. Edward Maunde Thompson (Clarendon Press, 1889), pp. 146–55.

16 A good translation of the letter can be found in Clifford J. Rogers, *The Wars of Edward III: Sources and Interpretations* (Boydell Press, 1999), pp. 163–64.

17 Peter Hoskins, *In the Steps of the Black Prince: The Road to Poitiers, 1355–1356* (Boydell Press, 2011), p. 162. Though I have several disagreements with Hoskins's reconstructions of the action from this point, the book is a terrific and thoughtful study of the engagement.

18 My translation, from *Petite chronique françoise de l'an 1270 à l'an 1356*, ed. M. Douet d'Arcq (Société des Bibliophiles, 1866), pp. 27–29.

19 This and the following quotes from Chandos Herald are from *Life and Campaigns of the Black Prince*, trans. Richard Barber, pp. 95–99.

20 Le Bel, *True Chronicles*, trans. Bryant, pp. 226–27.

21 Sumption, *Trial by Fire*, p. 236. This would track the information back to someone in the cardinal's party moving back and forth between the armies and explain why, as Sumption says, Villani is 'the most reliable account' on the lead-up to the fight, but not for the battle itself – the cardinal had at that point left the area.

22 My translation, from John of Fordun, *Chronica Gentis Scotorum*, ed. W. F. Skene (Edinburgh, 1872), 1.375–77.

23 Hoskins (*In the Steps of the Black Prince*, p. 189), suggests this flanking manoeuvre was executed instead via another ford just west of the Gué de l'Omme. However, this route is very narrow and suitable for only a couple of horses abreast. It also leads to ground that was surely on the English left flank above Les Bordes. There's no way to reconcile this with our specific description of the attack coming out at the same place the French had come from.

24 I use here the translation of Sumption, *Trial by Fire*, p. 244 – because it is magnificent.

25 *The Black Prince's Register*, Part IV (London: H. M. Stationery Office, 1933), p. 339.

26 Wilson and Bryant, *Book of Geoffroi de Charny*, p. 113.

27 Jean Froissart, *Chronicles*, trans. Geoffrey Brereton (Penguin Books, 1978), p. 143.

28 My translation, from Thomas Rymer's *Foedera, conventiones, litterae, et cujuscunque generis acta publica*, 20 vols. (London, 1704–35), 3.1, p. 129.

29 For a terrific study of these cases, see Chris Given-Wilson and Françoise Bériac, 'Edward III's Prisoners of War: The Battle of Poitiers and Its Context', *English Historical Review* 116 (2001), 802–33, as well as their *Les Prisonniers de la Bataille de Poitiers* (Librairie Honoré Champion, 2002).

30 On the financial systems of the period, the standard work remains John Bell Henneman, *Royal Taxation in Fourteenth Century France: The Development of War Financing, 1322–1356* (Princeton University Press, 1971).

31 Le Bel, *True Chronicles*, trans. Bryant, pp. 235–36.

32 Justine Firnhaber-Baker, 'The Social Constituency of the Jacquerie Revolt of 1358', *Speculum* 95 (2020), 689–715; the finest account of the revolt entire is her *The Jacquerie of 1358: A French Peasants' Revolt* (Oxford University Press, 2021).

33 My translation, from *Chronique dite de Jean de Venette*, ed. Colette Beaune (Librairie Générale Française, 2011), p. 234.

34 Le Bel, *True Chronicles*, trans. Bryant, p. 257.

35 Clifford J. Rogers, 'By Fire and Sword: *Bellum Hostile* and Civilians in the Hundred Years War', in *Civilians in the Path of War*, ed. Mark Grimsley and Clifford J. Rogers (University of Nebraska Press, 2002), pp. 48–49. This source is reprinted in *Medieval Warfare: A Reader*, ed. Kelly DeVries and Livingston (University of Toronto Press, 2019), pp. 16–17.

36   My translation, from Petrarch, *Epistole de Rebus Familiaribus*, 22.14.

CHAPTER SIX

1   These stories come from, in order: Froissart (*Chroniques*, ed. Siméon Luce, 11 vols. [Librairie Renouard, 1869–99], 6.102–04); Cuvelier's almost hagiographic poetic biography of du Guesclin, *La Chanson de Bertrand du Guesclin de Cuvelier*, ed. Jean-Claude Faucon (Éditions Universitaires du Sud, 1990–93); and the *Chronique des quatres premiers Valois*, ed. Siméon Luce (Paris, 1862), 1.139–40. The historian in question is Richard Vernier, *The Flower of Chivalry: Bertrand du Guesclin and the Hundred Years War* (D. S. Brewer, 2003), p. 69; this remains the best study of du Guesclin in English.

2   This and the following are my translation from Froissart, *Chroniques*, ed. Luce, 6.117–19, 123–24.

3   This and the following translations are mine, from *Chronique des quatre premiers Valois*, ed. Luce , pp. 160–62.

4   My translation, from Thomas Rymer's *Foedera, litterae, et cujuscunque generis acta publica*, 20 vols. (London, 1704–35), 3.39–40.

5   Excellent work has been published on its more exact route, including its descent south: see Joan Mari Martínez Txoperena and Rafael Zubiria Mujika, 'La vía de Hispania a Aquitania en el paso del Pirineo por Ibañeta: resultado de la investigación sobre la calzada romana desde Campo Real-Fillera a Donezaharre / Saint-Jean-Le-Vieux', *Jornadas sobre las calzadas romanas en la Antigüedad* (2017), 151–204.

6   The finest study of the campaign and battle is that of L. J. Andrew Villalon and Donald J. Kagay, *To Win and Lose a Medieval Battle: Nájera (April 3, 1367), a Pyrrhic Victory for the Black Prince* (Brill, 2017). Importantly, Villalon and Kagay provide translations to all the primary sources, which are utilized here unless otherwise noted.

7   Seeing it as a flanking movement, for instance, is P. E. Russell, *The English Intervention in Spain and Portugal in the Time of Edward III and Richard II*

(Clarendon Press, 1955), p. 87, and Sumption, *Trial by Fire*, p. 551. Villalon and Kagay specifically take this interpretation apart in *To Win and Lose a Medieval Battle*, pp. 190–96.

8   For a discussion of these options and the meagre evidence, see Villalon and Kagay, *To Win and Lose a Medieval Battle*, pp. 211–15.

9   Sumption, *Trial by Fire*, p. 552; his reconstruction appears to follow Villalon and Kagay, *To Win and Lose a Medieval Battle*, pp. 238–39. I am aware that I disagree with these scholars at my peril.

10   This seems to be the ultimate position of Villalon and Kagay, and Sumption not only takes it as a given, but further suggests that the Black Prince 'skilfully fed these fears' in order to achieve his own ends (*Trial by Fire*, p. 552).

11   This, according to the Chandos Herald, in Richard Barber, *The Life and Campaigns of the Black Prince: From Contemporary Letters, Diaries and Chronicles, Including Chandos Herald's Life of the Black Prince* (Boydell Press, 1979).

12   My translation, from *Political Poems and Songs Relating to English History Composed During the Period from the Accession of Edward III to that of Richard III*, ed. Thomas Wright, Rolls Series (Longman, Green, Longman, and Roberts, 1859), 1.119–20.

13   Sumption is spot on in his observation that 'there could hardly have been a better illustration of how developed the hunt for prisoners had become in fourteenth-century warfare than the scale of the slaughter at Nájera combined with the almost complete survival of the rich and ransomable' (*Trial by Fire*, p. 555).

14   For a recent summation of the evidence on the prince's failing health, see Guilhem Pépin, 'The Sack of the "City" of Limoges (1370) Reconsidered in the Light of an Unknown Letter of the Black Prince', *Journal of Medieval Military History* 21 (2023), 164, n 7.

15 Jean Froissart, *Chronicles*, trans. Geoffrey Brereton (Penguin Books, 1978), pp. 177–78.
16 Pépin, 'Sack of the "City" of Limoges', p. 170.
17 The text is printed in Charles Mill, *History of Chivalry* (H. C. Carey and Lea, 1826), 1.116–17.
18 My translation, from *Chronique des quatre premiers Valois*, ed. Luce, pp. 233–34.
19 This and the following quotation are from Froissart, *Chronicles*, trans. Brereton, pp. 189–90.
20 Clifford J. Rogers, *The Wars of Edward III: Sources and Interpretations* (Boydell Press, 1999), p. 201.
21 *Anglo-French Negotiations at Bruges, 1374–1377*, ed. Eduoard Perroy (Offices of the Royal Historical Society, 1952), pp. 53–66. Sumption provides an excellent narrative of these proceedings and the events that followed in *Divided Houses*, pp. 212–80.
22 My translation, from *Les Grandes Chroniques de France: chronique des règnes de Jean II et de Charles V*, ed. Roland Delachenal (Société de l'histoire de France, 1910–20), 2.183–84.

CHAPTER SEVEN

1 Christine de Pisan, *Le Livre de l'advision Christine*, ed. Christine Reno and Liliane Dulac (Librairie Honoré Champion, 2001), p. 98; this translation from Sumption, *Divided Houses*, p. 390.
2 *The Chivalric Biography of Boucicaut, Jean II Le Meingre*, trans. Craig Taylor and Jane H. M. Taylor (Boydell Press, 2016), p. 36.
3 Ibid., pp. 30–31.
4 Jean Froissart, *Chronicles*, trans. Geoffrey Brereton (Penguin Books, 1978), p. 249.
5 These numbers are improbable. Pitti's account is translated by Julia Martines in *Two Memoirs of Renaissance Florence: The Diaries of Buonaccorso Pitti and Gregorio Dati*, ed. Gene Brucker (Harper and Row, 1967), p. 38.
6 Froissart, *Chronicles*, trans. Brereton, p. 250.

7 For a look at the conditions that led to the Despenser Crusade, see Kelly DeVries, 'The Reasons for the Bishop of Norwich's Attack on Flanders in 1383', in *Fourteenth Century England III*, ed. W. M. Ormrod (Boydell Press, 2004), pp. 155–65.
8 We know disappointingly little about these talks, which Sumption rightly calls 'the most important since the proceedings at Bruges in the 1370s' (*Divided Houses*, p. 515).
9 Fernão Lopes, *Crónica del rei dom João I da boa memória*, ed. Anselmo Braamcamp Freire, Luís F. Lindley Cintra and William J. Entwistle (Imprensa Nacional-Casa da Moeda, 1977), 2.183–84.
10 My translation, from *Chronique du religieux de Saint-Denys, contenant le régne de Charles VI, de 1380 à 1422, publiée en latin pour la première fois et traduite*, ed. Louis François Bellaguet (Imprimerie de Crapelet, 1839–52), 1.428–30.
11 For an excellent look at the relationship between Richard II and Bolingbroke, see Helen Castor, *The Eagle and the Hart: The Tragedy of Richard II and Henry IV* (Simon and Schuster, 2024).
12 For Froissart's description of this event, see his 'Peace-time Jousts at Saint-Inglevert', in *Medieval Warfare: A Reader*, ed. Kelly DeVries and Livingston (University of Toronto, 2019), pp. 49–61.
13 My translation, from Geoffrey Chaucer, *The Riverside Chaucer*, 3rd edn, ed. Larry D. Benson (Houghton Mifflin, 1987), section 17.
14 My translation, from Jean Juvenal des Ursins, *Histoire de Charles VI, Roy de France* (A. Desrez, 1841), p. 377.
15 *Medieval Warfare*, ed. DeVries and Livingston, pp. 30–33.
16 Quoted in Sumption, *Divided Houses*, p. 864.
17 On Owain's claim, see John K. Bollard, 'Owain Glyndŵr, *Princeps Wallie*', in *Owain Glyndŵr: A Casebook*, ed. Livingston and Bollard (Liverpool University Press, 2013), pp. 425–30.

18 For an examination of what is known and not known about this battle – including the question of whether it ever happened at all – see Livingston, 'The Battle of Hyddgen, 1401: Owain Glyndŵr's Victory Reconsidered', *Journal of Medieval Military History* 13 (2015), 167–78.

19 Adam of Usk, 'Chronicle, Part 2', in *Owain Glyndŵr: A Casebook*, ed. Livingston and Bollard, pp. 65–67.

20 I have elsewhere attempted a reconstruction based on the traditional site, but until archaeological confirmation can be found this must remain tenuous at best; see Livingston, 'The Battle of Bryn Glas, 1402', in *Owain Glyndŵr: A Casebook*, ed. Livingston and Bollard, pp. 451–72.

21 My translation, from Prince Henry, 'Razing of Owain's Homes', in *Owain Glyndŵr: A Casebook*, ed. Livingston and Bollard, p. 82.

22 On this battle, this wound and the remarkable operation that saved the young prince, see Livingston, *Agincourt: Battle of the Scarred King* (Osprey, 2023), pp. 26–33.

23 Quoted in Sumption, *Cursed Kings*, p. 83.

24 Among the duties keeping him busy was active military engagement in other directions; see Kelly DeVries, 'John the Fearless' Way of War', in *Reputation and Representation in Fifteenth Century Europe*, ed. Douglas L. Biggs, Sharon D. Michalove and Albert C. Reeves (Brill, 2004), pp. 39–55.

25 For texts of all these agreements, see *Owain Glyndŵr: A Casebook*, ed. Livingston and Bollard, pp. 104–13.

26 Livingston, 'Owain Glyndŵr's Grand Design: The Tripartite Indenture and the Vision of a New Wales', *Proceedings of the Harvard Celtic Colloquium* 33 (2014), 145–68.

27 'Battle of Grosmont', in *Owain Glyndŵr: A Casebook*, ed. Livingston and Bollard, p. 117.

28 Adam of Usk, *Chronicle, Part 3*, in *Owain Glyndŵr: A Casebook*, ed. Livingston and Bollard, p. 149.

29 Pintoin, *Chronicle of Charles VI*, and Thomas Walsingham, *St. Alban's Chronicle*, in *Owain Glyndŵr: A Casebook*, ed. Livingston and Bollard, pp. 155 and 165, respectively.

30 Henry IV, 'Resisting the French Invasion', in *Owain Glyndŵr: A Casebook*, ed. Livingston and Bollard, pp. 119–21.

31 The remainder of this chapter is adapted from Livingston, *Agincourt*, pp. 99–110.

32 For a fantastic popular account of the murder and the remarkable investigation that followed, I highly recommend Eric Jager's *Blood Royal: A True Tale of Crime and Detection in Medieval Paris* (Little, Brown, 2014).

33 Sumption, *Cursed Kings*, p. 366.

34 My translation, from *Le Procès de Maître Jean Fusoris*, ed. Léon Mirot (Paris, 1900), p. 244.

35 Sumption neatly lays out what little we know about the letters in *Cursed Kings*, pp. 374–76.

36 John Strecche, a canon of Kenilworth Priory during the king's life, tells a similar tale of frustrated French negotiators saying that they would send such a gift. See E. F. Jacob, *Henry V and the Invasion of France* (English Universities Press, 1947).

37 *Issues of the Exchequer, Being a Collection of Payments Made Out of His Majesty's Revenue, from King Henry III to King Henry IV Inclusive*, ed. Frederick Devon (John Murray, 1837), p. 327.

38 I'm pleased to acknowledge my debt to Sumption's marvellous account of this entire embassy in *Cursed Kings*, pp. 423–28.

39 Henry V, 'Licence to Treat with Owain', in *Owain Glyndŵr: A Casebook*, ed. Livingston and Bollard, p. 151.

40 My translation, from *Mémoires de la Société de l'histoire de Paris et de l'Ile-de-France* (Paris, 1900), pp. 248–49.

CHAPTER EIGHT

1 For details on these numbers, see Livingston, *Agincourt: Battle of the Scarred King* (Osprey, 2023), pp. 115–17 and notes.

2   All quotes from the *Gesta* and other Agincourt sources are from Anne Curry's indispensable *Agincourt: Sources and Interpretations* (Boydell Press, 2000).

3   The reconstruction here follows that in Livingston, *Agincourt*, pp. 167–284, which builds on the suggestion of a southern location first proposed by Tim Sutherland, 'The Battlefield', in *The Battle of Agincourt*, ed. Anne Curry and Malcolm Mercer (Yale University Press, 2005), pp. 196–98.

4   Clifford J. Rogers, 'The Battle of Agincourt', in *The Hundred Years War, Part II: Different Vistas*, ed. Andrew Villalon and Donald Kagay (Brill, 2008), p. 83. Rogers presents the best reconstruction utilizing the traditional site of the engagement.

5   My translation, from *Chronique du religieux de Saint-Denys: contenant le règne de Charles VI, de 1380 à 1422, publiée en latin pour la première fois et traduite*, ed. Louis François Bellaguet (Imprimerie de Crapelet, 1839–52), 6.100–02.

6   For a study of this artillery – both before and after Jean the Fearless – see Robert Douglas Smith and Kelly DeVries, *The Artillery of the Dukes of Burgundy, 1363–1477* (Boydell Press, 2005).

7   Sumption rightly notes the ways in which this battle plan appears to show 'that John the Fearless had studied the battle of Agincourt and absorbed its lessons' (*Cursed Kings*, p. 538).

8   This comes from the official account of the government that September, published in *Ordonnances des roys de France de la troisième race*, ed. Denis-François Secousse, 21 vols. (Imprimerie royale, 1723–1849), 10.478–79. Chroniclers provide other numbers, up to 5,000.

9   For the following, I am indebted to Michael Sizer, 'The Calamity of Violence: Reading the Paris Massacres of 1418', *Journal of the Western Society for French History* 35 (2007), 19–39.

10   I adopt this understanding of France's political split from the work of Graeme Small, who builds on the 'men of the West' and 'men of the East' concept of Raymond Cazelles in 'French Politics During the Hundred Years War', in *The Hundred Years War*

Revisited, ed. Anne Curry (Red Globe Press, 2019), pp. 33–56.

11   My translation, from *Journal d'un Bourgeois de Paris, 1405–1449*, ed. Alexandre Tuetey (Librairie Honoré Champion, 1881), p. 91.

12   My translation, from Pierre de Versailles, 'Epître à Juvenal après le massacre de 1418', in *Thesaurus Novus Anecdotorum*, ed. Edmund Martène and Ursin Durand (Florentinus Delaulne, 1717), p. 1723.

13   This from the duke's secretary, who was on the bridge and testified to what he saw. Specifically, he describes the weapon as a large war axe without any point on the butt or spike on the head. As expected, there are a number of competing, propagandized narratives of the assassination. While the Armagnac retelling has been that most recounted by historians, I find the Burgundian accounts more convincing. These are helpfully collected in *Memoires pour servir à l'histoire de France et de Bourgogne, contenant un journal de Paris, sous les regnes de Charles VI et de Charles VII* (Paris, 1729), 1.271–89. That Sumption likewise follows the Burgundian side is encouraging (*Cursed Kings*, pp. 651–54, 668–69 and 833 n 53).

14   *Calendar of Close Rolls, Henry VI: Volume 1, 1422–29*, ed. A. E. Stamp (Public Record Office, 1933), p. 46.

15   Dan Jones, *Henry V: The Astonishing Triumph of England's Greatest Warrior King* (Viking, 2024), p. xxii.

CHAPTER NINE

1   For a recent, excellent description of these events, see Chris Given-Wilson, 'The Funeral of Henry V', in *The Funeral Achievements of Henry V at Westminster Abbey: The Arms and Armour of Death*, ed. Anne Curry and Susan Jenkins (Boydell Press, 2022), pp. 32–43; the other essays in this collection are likewise superb.

2   *A Book of London English 1384–1425*, ed. R. W. Chambers and M. Daunt (Clarendon Press, 1931), p. 146; I follow here the suggestion of Given-Wilson, 'The Funeral of Henry V', that the rituals described in the 1448 *Liber Regie*

Capelle also generally correspond to the events of Henry's funeral.

3 Sumption, *Cursed Kings*, pp. 751–52, 767.

4 Sumption, *Triumph and Illusion*, pp. 6–7.

5 This second treaty was long understood to undermine the Treaty of Amiens, but for the corrective view followed here that it was instead a supplement to it, see Clifford J. Rogers, 'The Anglo-Burgundian Alliance in the Hundred Years War', in *Grand Strategy and Military Alliances*, ed. P. R. Mansoor and W. Murray (Cambridge University Press, 2016), pp. 232–33. For a succinct look at the wider importance of the Treaty of Amiens itself, see Aleksandr Lobanov, 'The Treaty of Amiens (1423): Towards a Reconsideration', *Proslogion: Studies in Medieval and Early Modern Social History and Culture* 14 (2016), 242–61.

6 Sumption, *Triumph and Illusion*, p. 94; this otherwise solid account makes the assumption (p. 98) that the medieval bridge was of the same stone design as that built in the early eighteenth century. I am less certain.

7 Alfred H. Burne, *The Agincourt War* (Eyre and Spottiswoode, 1956), p. 185.

8 Translation my own, from 'Le Livre de trahisons de France', in *Chroniques relatives à l'histoire de la Belgique sous la domination des ducs de Bourgogne*, ed. Kervyn de Lettenhove (Brussels, 1873), p. 170.

9 *A Parisian Journal, 1405–1449*, trans. Janet Shirley (Clarendon Press, 1968), p. 189.

10 Ibid., p. 191.

11 Jean de Waurin, *Recueil des croniques et anchiennes istories de la Grant Bretaigne, à présent nommé Engleterre*, ed. William Hardy (Longman, 1879), 3.22–23.

12 On the numbers, see Richard Wadge's discussion in *The Battle of Verneuil, 1424* (History Press, 2015), pp. 227–28. Of the available accounts of the battle, this is among the best.

13 Burne, *Agincourt War*, pp. 200–01. Burne's account of the battle is, like many of his reconstructions, saddled

by his determinist readings of history. For a point-by-point rebuttal of Burne, see Michael K. Jones, 'The Battle of Verneuil (17 August 1424): Towards a History of Courage', *War in History* 9 (2004), 375–411.

14 Sumption, for reasons that are not clear, mistakenly places the battle due east of Verneuil, along the road to Nonancourt, which follows the bank of the Avre (*Triumph and Illusion*, pp. 131 and 134). This changes his construction of the battle considerably.

15 Wadge, *Battle of Verneuil*, p. 158.

16 This and the subsequent translations from Waurin are mine, from *Recueil des croniques*, ed. Hardy, 3.111–12, 114.

17 Thomas Basin, *Histoire de Charles VII*, ed. C. Samaran (Paris, 1933), p. 93.

18 Sumption, *Triumph and Illusion*, p. 135.

19 Basin, *Histoire de Charles VII*, ed. Samaran. p. 95.

20 The siege of Orléans is among the most studied engagements of the period, but for this and for Joan's career in general I am particularly indebted to Kelly DeVries's *Joan of Arc: A Military Leader* (Sutton, 1999).

21 *A Soldiers' Chronicle of the Hundred Years War: College of Arms Manuscript M9*, ed. Anne Curry and Rémy Ambuhl (D. S. Brewer, 2022), p. 366. For an interesting look at part of the afterlife of this passage, see Scott Lucas's essay in this same volume, '"In the Mids of his Glory": the M9 Chronicle, "A Mirror for Magistrates", and the Tragedy of English Imperialism', pp. 165–74.

22 DeVries (*Joan of Arc*, p. 66) presents it as the Bastard's idea, but the fingerprints on the operation seem more in keeping with La Hire, as Sumption suggests (*Triumph and Illusion*, p. 246).

23 *Soldiers' Chronicle of the Hundred Years War*, ed. Curry and Ambuhl, p. 368. The use of Janville before the battle indicates that it took place near Rouvray-Sainte-Croix rather than (as tradition would have it) Rouvray-Saint-Denis; first to note this was Stephen Cooper, *The Real Falstaff: Sir John Fastolf*

and the Hundred Years War (Pen and Sword, 2010), pp. 53–55.

24 I quote here Burne (*Agincourt War*, p. 235), but the sentiment appears universal. Most recently, see Sumption, *Triumph and Illusion*, p. 246.

25 Kelly DeVries and Livingston, *Medieval Warfare: A Reader* (University of Toronto Press, 2019), p. 140.

26 DeVries, *Joan of Arc*, p. 116.

27 Translation my own, from Christine de Pisan, *Le Ditié de Jehanne d'Arc*, ed. A. J. Kennedy and K. Varty (Society for the Study of Medieval Languages and Literature, 1977), stanzas 28, 34–36.

28 DeVries presents an excellent summary of the basic arguments in *Joan of Arc*, pp. 173–81.

29 My translation, from Pierre Champion, *Procès de condamnation de Jeanne d'Arc* (Librairie Honoré Champion, 1920), I.220–21. A more recent edition of the trial transcript has since appeared by Yvonne Landers and Pierre Tissot (Klincksieck, 1960), but it is more difficult to find.

30 *The Trial of Jeanne d'Arc*, trans. W. P. Barrett (Gotham House, 1932), p. 112.

31 Scott Manning, '3000 Miles to Rouen: Joan of Arc on Horseback', in *Saints and Sinners on Horseback*, ed. Miriam A. Bibby (Trivent, 2023).

32 Sumption, *Triumph and Illusion*, p. 366.

33 My translation, from Champion, *Procès de condamnation de Jeanne d'Arc*, I.375–76.

CHAPTER TEN

1 My translation, from John Lydgate, 'Henry VI's Triumphal Entry into London', in *Mummings and Entertainments*, ed. Claire Sponsler (Medieval Institute Publications, 2010), lines 73–98, 510–23.

2 Sumption, *Triumph and Illusion*, pp. 418–19.

3 On the implications of Carpenter's juxtaposition of these materials, see Kristin Bourassa, 'The Royal Entries of Henry VI in a London Civic Manuscript', *Journal of Medieval History* 42 (2016), 479–93.

4 Translation my own, from *Collection générale des documents français qui se trouvent en Angleterre*, ed. Jules Delpit (Paris, 1847), pp. 238–39.

5 The standard study of Calais at this point is David Grummitt, *The Calais Garrison: War and Military Service in England, 1436–1558* (Boydell and Brewer, 2008).

6 For a study of these weapons – many of which still survive – see Robert D. Smith and Kelly DeVries, *The Artillery of the Dukes of Burgundy, 1363–1477* (Boydell and Brewer, 2005).

7 An interesting snapshot of the conditions left behind is a surviving list of provisions brought to the militia positioned on the dunes outside Ostend in expectation of an English attack; see Kelly DeVries and Livingston, *Medieval Warfare: A Reader* (University of Toronto Press), p. 72.

8 A significant part of this power struggle involved the Douglases and the Livingstons – the latter of whom may well have arranged the infamous 'Black Dinner' at Edinburgh Castle. And no, I don't know if I'm related to them or not!

CHAPTER ELEVEN

1 My translation, from Jean Chartier, *Chronique de Charles VII, roi de France*, ed. Auguste Vallet de Viriville (P. Jannet, 1858), 2.61.

2 On the English rationale, see Craig Taylor, 'Brittany and the French Crown: The Legacy of the English Attack upon Fougères (1449)', in *The Medieval State: Essays Presented to James Campbell*, ed. J. R. Maddicott and D. M. Palser (Hambledon Press, 2000), pp. 243–57.

3 Of trivial interest, a mouse was found to have taken residency in the skull. The surgeon suggested that the mouse was French. The church rector insisted it was English. In any case, the mummified rodent was itself interred, with a poem composed in its honour; it ends thus: 'The skull which once upreared great Talbot's crest / Gashed by a foeman, gave this mouse a rest.' See David Jenkins, *Parish Church of S. Alkmund Whitchurch, Shropshire:*

A Short History & Guide (Porter Printing Services, 1978), p. 5.

4 Sumption, *Triumph and Illusion*, pp. 744, 746.

5 My translation, from Chartier, *Chronique de Charles VII*, 3.4.

6 Alfred H. Burne, *Agincourt War* (Eyre and Spottiswoode, 1956), pp. 337–38.

7 My translation, from John Gower, *In Praise of Peace*, line 260, in *The Minor Latin Works with In Praise of Peace*, ed. and trans. R. F. Yeager and Livingston (Medieval Institute Publications, 2005).

8 My translation, from *Of Knyghthode and Bataile*, ed. Trevor Russell Smith and Livingston (Medieval Institute Publications, 2021), lines 2233–37.

9 *Rotuli Parliamentorum* (London, 1755), 5.622.

10 *The Memoirs of Philip de Commines, Lord of Argenton*, trans. Andrews R. Scoble (London, 1877), 1.262–64, 273, 276.

11 John M. Currin, '"The King's Army into the Partes of Bretaigne": Henry VII and the Breton Wars, 1489–1491', *War in History* 7 (2000), 387.

CONCLUSION

1 The best attempt at reconstructing the landscape of the event is Julian Munby, 'The Field of Cloth of Gold: Guînes and the Calais Pale Revisited', *English Heritage Historical Review* 9 (2014), 30–63.

2 *Calendar of State Papers and Manuscripts Relating to English Affairs Existing in the Archives and Collections of Venice, and in Other Libraries of Northern Italy*, ed. Rawdon Brown (London, 1869), 3.39–45.

3 David Green, *The Hundred Years War: A People's History* (Yale University Press, 2014), p. 249.

Bibliography

A full research bibliography of two hundred years of European history would be a book itself, and a 'greatest hits' bibliography of the period would present its own set of subjective issues. But for the ease of those wanting to check my work, the following titles are those either specifically cited within this book or particularly influential upon it.

Adams, Tracy. *Christine de Pizan and the Fight for France.* Pennsylvania State University Press, 2014.

Allmand, Christopher. *The Hundred Years War: England and France at War c.1300– c.1400.* Cambridge University Press, 1989.

Anglo-French Negotiations at Bruges, 1374–1377. Ed. Eduoard Perroy. Offices of the Royal Historical Society, 1952.

Annals of Dunstable Abbey. Annales Monastici, vol. 3. Ed. Henry Richards Luard. London, 1866.

Araguas, Philippe. *Bordeaux au Moyen Age: la ville et ses monuments.* Les Éditions de l'Entre-deux-Mers, 2022.

Barber, Richard. *Edward, Prince of Wales and Aquitaine: A Biography of the Black Prince.* Boydell Press, 1978.

———. *The Life and Campaigns of the Black Prince: From Contemporary Letters, Diaries and Chronicles, Including Chandos Herald's Life of the Black Prince.* Boydell Press, 1979.

Bell, Adrian R., Anne Curry, Andy King and David Simpkin. *The Soldier in Later Medieval England.* Oxford University Press, 2013.

Berard, Christopher. 'Edward III's Abandoned Order of the Round Table'. *Arthurian Literature* 29 (2012), 1–40.

———. 'Edward III's Abandoned Order of the Round Table Revisited: Political Arthurianism After Poitiers'. *Arthurian Literature* 33 (2016), 70–109.

The Black Prince's Register, Part IV. H. M. Stationery Office, 1933.

A Book of London English 1384–1425. Ed. R. W. Chambers and M. Daunt. Oxford University Press, 1931.

Bourassa, Kristin. 'The Royal Entries of Henry VI in a London Civic Manuscript'. *Journal of Medieval History 42* (2016): 479–93.

Brown, Elizabeth A. R. 'The Political Repercussions of Family Ties in the Early Fourteenth Century: The Marriage of Edward II of England and Isabelle of France'. *Speculum* 63.3 (1988), 573–95.

————. 'Philip the Fair of France and His Family's Disgrace: The Adultery Scandal of 1314 Revealed, Recounted, Reimagined, and Redated'. *Mediaevistik* 32 (2019), 71–103.

The Brut, or The Chronicles of England. Ed. Friedrich W. D. Brie. Kegan Paul, Trench, Trübner & Co., 1906.

Burne, Alfred H. *The Crecy War: A Military History of the Hundred Years War from 1337 to the Peace of Bretigny, 1360*. Eyre and Spottiswoode, 1955.

————. *The Agincourt War*. Eyre and Spottiswoode, 1956.

Calendar of Close Rolls, Henry VI: Volume 1, 1422–29. Ed. A. E. Stamp. Public Record Office, 1933.

Calendar of Documents Relating to Scotland. Ed. Joseph Bain. Edinburgh, 1881.

Calendar of Patent Rolls of Edward III, 1338–40. London, 1898.

Carrion-Nisas, André-François-Victoire-Henri. *La Loi Salique traduite en français*. Paris, 1820.

Castor, Helen. *The Eagle and the Hart: The Tragedy of Richard II and Henry IV*. Simon and Schuster, 2024.

Chaucer, Geoffrey. *The Riverside Chaucer*. Third Edition. Ed. Larry D. Benson. Houghton Mifflin, 1987.

The Chivalric Biography of Boucicaut, Jean II Le Meingre. Trans. Craig Taylor and Jane H. M. Taylor. Boydell Press, 2016.

Christine de Pisan. Le Ditié de Jehanne d'Arc. Ed. A. J. Kennedy and K. Varty. Oxford, 1977.

Christine de Pisan. Le Livre de l'advision Christine. Ed. Christine Reno and Liliane Dulac. Librairie Honoré Champion, 2001.

Chronicles of the Reigns of Edward I and II. Ed. W. Stubbs. London, 1882–83.

Chronicon de Lanercost. Ed. Joseph Stevenson. Edinburgh, 1839.

Chronique des quatre premiers Valois (1327–1393). Ed. Siméon Luce. Paris, 1862.

Chronique du religieux de Saint-Denys, contenant le régne de Charles VI, de 1380 à 1422, publiée en latin pour la première fois et traduite. Ed. Louis François Bellaguet. Imprimerie de Crapelet, 1839–52.

Chroniques relatives à l'histoire de la Belgique sous la domination des ducs de Bourgogne. Ed. Kervyn de Lettenhove. F. Hayez, 1970.

Chronographia regum Francorum. Ed. Henri Moranvillé. Société de l'histoire de France. Librairie Renouard, 1891–97.

Cook, Murray. *Bannockburn and Stirling Bridge: Exploring Scotland's Two Greatest Battles*. Extremis, 2021.

Cooper, Stephen. *The Real Falstaff: Sir John Fastolf and the Hundred Years War*. Pen and Sword, 2010.

Crafter, R. D. A. 'Materials for the Study of the Sources of Guillaume Guiart's *La Branche des Royaus Lingnages*'. *Medium Ævum* 26 (1957), 1–16.

Currin, John M. '"The King's Army into the Partes of Bretaigne": Henry VII and the Breton Wars, 1489–1491'. *War in History* 7 (2000): 379–412.

Curry, Anne. *The Hundred Years War, 1337–1453*. Osprey, 1992.

————. *Agincourt: Sources and Interpretations*. Boydell Press, 2000.

————, ed. *The Hundred Years War Revisited*. Red Globe Press, 2019.

Curry, Anne, and Rémy Ambuhl, eds. *A Soldiers' Chronicle of the Hundred Years War: College of Arms Manuscript M 9* D. S. Brewer, 2022.

Curry, Anne, and Susan Jenkins, eds. *The Funeral Achievements of Henry V at Westminster Abbey: The Arms and Armour of Death*. Boydell, 2022.

Davies, R. R. *The Revolt of Owain Glyn Dŵr*. Oxford University Press, 1995.

Delpit, Jules, ed. *Collection générale des documents français qui se trouvent en Angleterre*. Paris, 1847.

Déprez, Eugène. *Les Préliminaires de la guerre de cent ans: la papauté, la France et l'Angleterre (1328–1342)*. Megariotis, 1902.

Desmichels, Chrysanthe Ovide. *Tableau chronologique de l'histoire du Moyen Âge*. Paris, 1823.

DeVries, Kelly. 'Contemporary Views of Edward III's Failure at the Siege of Tournai, 1340'. *Nottingham Medieval Studies* 39 (1995), 70–105.

———. 'God, Admirals, Archery, and Flemings: Perceptions of Victory and Defeat at the Battle of Sluys, 1340'. *American Neptune* 55 (1995), 223–42.

———. *Joan of Arc: A Military Leader*. Sutton, 1999.

———. 'John the Fearless' Way of War'. In *Reputation and Representation in Fifteenth Century Europe*. Ed. Douglas L. Biggs, Sharon D. Michalove and Albert C. Reeves. Brill, 2004. Pp. 39–55.

———. 'The Reasons for the Bishop of Norwich's Attack on Flanders in 1383'. In *Fourteenth Century England III*. Ed. W. M. Ormrod. Boydell Press, 2004. Pp. 155–65.

DeVries, Kelly, and Michael Livingston. *Medieval Warfare: A Reader*. University of Toronto Press, 2019.

Doherty, Paul. *Isabella and the Strange Death of Edward II*. Carroll and Graf, 2003.

Duby, Georges. *The Legend of Bouvines: War, Religion, and Culture in the Middle Ages*. Trans. Catherine Tihanyi. University of California Press, 1990.

Dudo. *De Moribus et Actis Primorum Normanniae Ducum*. Ed. Jules Lair. F. le Blanc-Hardel, 1865.

Einhard and Notker the Stammerer. *Two Lives of Charlemagne*. Trans. Lewis Thorpe. Penguin, 1969.

Epistolae Ævi Karolini II. Ed. Ernst Dümmler. Monumenta Germaniae Historica. Berlin, 1895.

Epistolarum V: Karolini Aevi III. Ed. Ernst Dümmler. Monumenta Germaniae Historica. Berlin, 1899.

Firnhaber-Baker, Justine. 'The Social Constituency of the Jacquerie Revolt of 1358'. *Speculum* 95 (2020), 689–715.

———. *The Jacquerie of 1358: A French Peasants' Revolt*. Oxford University Press, 2021.

———. *House of Lilies: The Dynasty that Made Medieval France*. Basic Books, 2024.

France, John. 'The Battle of Bouvines 27 July 2014'. In *The Medieval Way of War: Studies in Medieval Military History in Honor of Bernard S. Bachrach*. Ed. Gregory L. Halfond. Ashgate, 2015. Pp. 251–72.

———. *Medieval France at War: A Military History of the French Monarchy, 885–1305*. ARC Humanities Press, 2022.

Froissart, Jean. *Chroniques*. Ed. Siméon Luce. 11 vols. Librairie Renouard, 1869–99.

———. *Chronicles*. Trans. Geoffrey Brereton. Penguin Books, 1978.

———. 'Peace-Time Jousts at Saint-Inglevert'. In *Medieval Warfare: A Reader*, Ed. Kelly DeVries and Michael Livingston. University of Toronto Press, 2019.

Funck-Brentano, F. *De exercituum commeatibus: tertio decimo et quarto decimo saeculis post christum natum*. Librairie Honoré Champion, 1897.

Gabriele, Matthew, and David M. Perry. *Oathbreakers: The War of Brothers That Shattered an Empire and Made Medieval Europe*. Harper, 2024.

Geoffrey le Baker. *Chronicon*. Ed. Edward Maunde Thompson. Clarendon Press, 1889.

Gilles li Muisit. *Chronique et annales de Gilles le Muisit, abbé de Saint-Martin de Tournai (1272–1352)*. Ed. Henri Lemaître. Librairie Renouard, 1906.

Gillingham, John. 'The Unromantic Death of Richard I'. *Speculum* 54 (1979), 8–41.

Given-Wilson, Chris. 'The Funeral of Henry V'. In *The Funeral Achievements of Henry V at Westminster Abbey: The Arms and Armour of Death*. Ed. Anne Curry and Susan Jenkins. Boydell Press, 2022. Pp. 32–43.

Given-Wilson, Chris, and Françoise Bériac. 'Edward III's Prisoners of War: The Battle of Poitiers and Its Context'. *English Historical Review* 116 (2001), 802–33.

———. *Les Prisonniers de la Bataille de Poitiers*. Librairie Honoré Champion, 2002.

Goodman, Anthony. *John of Gaunt: The Exercise of Princely Power in Fourteenth-Century Europe*. St Martin's Press, 1992.

Gower, John. *In Praise of Peace*. In *The Minor Latin Works with 'In Praise of Peace'*. Ed. and trans. R. F. Yeager and Michael Livingston. Medieval Institute Publications, 2005.

Les Grandes Chroniques de France: chronique des règnes de Jean II et de Charles V. Ed. Roland Delachenal. Société de l'histoire de France, 1910–20.

Gransden, Antonia. 'The Alleged Rape by Edward III of the Countess of Salisbury'. *The English Historical Review* 87 (1972), 333–44.

Green, David. *The Battle of Poitiers, 1356*. Tempus, 2002.

———. *Edward the Black Prince: Power in Medieval Europe*. Pearson, 2007.

———. *The Hundred Years War: A People's History*. Yale University Press, 2014.

Green, Monica H., and André Filipe Oliveira da Silva. 'Shifting Paradigms in Black Death Chronologies'. *Hypotheses*, 22 March 2023, https://urbrel.hypotheses.org/5550

Gribit, Nicholas A. *Henry of Lancaster's Expedition to Aquitaine, 1345–1346*. Boydell Press, 2016.

Grummitt, David. *The Calais Garrison: War and Military Service in England, 1436–1558*. Boydell and Brewer, 2008.

Guiart, Guillaume. *Branche des royaux lignages*. In *Collection des chroniques nationales françaises*, vol. 7. Ed. J.-A. Buchon. Paris, 1828.

———. *Branche des royaux lignages*. In *Recueil des historiens des Gaules et de la France*, vol. 22. Ed. N. de Wailly and L. Delisle. Paris, 1865.

Hallam, Elizabeth M. *Capetian France, 987–1328*. Longman, 1980.

Hamilton, J. S. 'Piers Gaveston and the Royal Treasure'. *Albion* 23.2 (1991), 201–07.

Hanley, Catherine. *Two Houses, Two Kingdoms: A History of France and England 1100–1300*. Yale University Press, 2022.

Heebøll-Holm, Thomas K. *Ports, Piracy, and Maritime War: Piracy in the English Channel and the Atlantic, c. 1280–c. 1330*. Brill, 2013.

Henneman, John Bell. *Royal Taxation in Fourteenth Century France: The Development of War Financing, 1322–1356*. Princeton University Press, 1971.

Higham, Nicholas J. *King Arthur: The Making of a Legend*. Yale University Press, 2018.

Histoire du différend d'entre le pape Boniface VIII et Philippes le Bel. Ed. Pierre Dupuy. Paris, 1655.

Hoskins, Peter. *In the Steps of the Black Prince: The Road to Poitiers, 1355–1356*. Boydell Press, 2011.

Hosler, John D. *The Siege of Acre 1189–91: Saladin, Richard the Lionheart, and the Battle that Decided the Third Crusade*. Yale University Press, 2018.

Issues of the Exchequer, Being a Collection of Payments Made Out of His Majesty's Revenue, from King Henry III to King Henry IV Inclusive. Ed. Frederick Devon. John Murray, 1837.

Jacob, E. F. *Henry V and the Invasion of France*. English Universities Press, 1947.

Jager, Eric. *Blood Royal: A True Tale of Crime and Detection in Medieval Paris*. Little, Brown, 2014.

James, Edward. *The Origins of France: From Clovis to the Capetians, 500–1000*. Macmillan, 1982.

Jean de Venette. *Chronique dite de Jean de Venette*. Ed. Colette Beaune. Librairie Générale Française, 2011.

Jean de Waurin. *Recueil des croniques et anchiennes istories de la Grant Bretaigne, à présent nommé Engleterre*. Ed. William Hardy. Longman, 1879.

Jean Júvenal des Ursins. *Histoire de Charles VI, Roy de France*. A. Desrez, 1841.

Jean le Bel. *The True Chronicles of Jean le Bel, 1290–1360*. Trans. Nigel Bryant. Boydell Press, 2011.

Jenkins, David. *Parish Church of S. Alkmund Whitchurch, Shropshire: A Short History & Guide*. Porter Printing Services, 1978.

John of Fordun. *Chronica Gentis Scotorum*. Ed. W. F. Skene. Edinburgh, 1872.

Jean de Joinville. *The Life of Saint Louis*. In *Chronicles of the Crusades*. Trans. M. R. B. Shaw. Penguin, 1963. Pp. 163–353.

Jones, Dan. *Henry V: The Astonishing Triumph of England's Greatest Warrior King*. Viking, 2024.

Jones, Michael. *The Black Prince: England's Greatest Medieval Warrior*. Pegasus, 2018.

Jones, Michael K. 'The Battle of Verneuil (17 August 1424): Towards a History of Courage'. *War in History* 9 (2004): 375–411.

Journal d'un Bourgeois de Paris, 1405–1449. Ed. Alexandre Tuetey. Librairie Honoré Champion, 1881.

Jusselin, Maurice. 'Comment la France se préparait à la guerre de cent ans'. *Bibliothèque de l'École des Chartes* 73 (1912), 209–36.

Kaeuper, Richard W. *Chivalry and Violence in Medieval Europe*. Oxford University Press, 1999.

———. 'Chivalry and the "Civilizing Process"'. In *Violence in Medieval Society*. Ed. Kaeuper. Boydell and Brewer, 2000. Pp. 21–35.

Kennedy, Elspeth. 'The Knight as Reader of Arthurian Romance'. In *Culture and the King: The Social Implications of Arthurian Legend*. Ed. Martin B. Shichtman and James P. Carley. State University of New York Press, 1994. Pp. 70–90.

La Chanson de Bertrand du Guesclin de Cuvelier. Ed. Jean-Claude Faucon. Éditions Universitaires du Sud, 1990–93.

Lambert, Craig. 'Taking the War to Scotland and France: The Supply and Transportation of English Armies by Sea, 1320–60'. PhD Dissertation: University of Hull, 2009.

Livingston, Michael. 'Owain Glyndŵr's Grand Design: The Tripartite Indenture and the Vision of a New Wales'. *Proceedings of the Harvard Celtic Colloquium* 33 (2014), 145–68.

———. 'The Battle of Hyddgen, 1401: Owain Glyndŵr's Victory Reconsidered'. *Journal of Medieval Military History* 13 (2015), 167–78.

———. 'An Army on the March and in Camp: Guillaume Guiart's *Branche des royaux lignages*'. *Journal of Medieval Military History* 17 (2019), 259–72.

———. *Crécy: Battle of Five Kings*. Osprey, 2022.

———. *Agincourt: Battle of the Scarred King*. Osprey, 2023.

Livingston, Michael, and John K. Bollard, eds. *Owain Glyndŵr: A Casebook*. Liverpool University Press, 2013.

Livingston, Michael, and Kelly DeVries, eds. *The Battle of Crécy: A Casebook*. Liverpool University Press. 2015.

———. *1066: A Guide to the Battles and the Campaigns*. Pen and Sword, 2021.

Livingstone, Marilyn, and Morgen Witzel. *The Black Prince and the Capture of a King: Poitiers, 1356*. Casemate, 2018.

Lobanov, Aleksandr. 'The Treaty of Amiens (1423): Towards a Reconsideration'. *Proslogion: Studies in Medieval and Early Modern Social History and Culture* 14 (2016), 242–61.

Lopes, Fernão. *Crónica del rei dom João I da boa memória*. Ed. Anselmo Braamcamp Freire, Luís F. Lindley Cintra and William J. Entwistle. Imprimerie Nacional-Casa da Moeda, 1977.

Lydgate, John. 'Henry VI's Triumphal Entry into London'. In *Mummings and Entertainments*. Ed. Claire Sponsler. Medieval Institute Publications, 2010.

Manning, Scott. '3000 Miles to Rouen: Joan of Arc on Horseback'. In *Saints and Sinners on Horseback*. Ed. Miriam A. Bibby. Trivent, 2023.

Marvin, Laurence W. 'Philip II's "Eye of Command" and the Battle of Bouvines'. *Journal of Medieval Military History* 21 (2023), 129–45.

Mathisen, Ralph W. 'Clovis, Anastasius, and the Political Status, 508 CE: The Frankish Aftermath of the Battle of Vouillé'. In *The Battle of Vouillé, 507 CE: Where France Began*. Ed. Mathisen and Danuta Shanzer. Water de Gruyter, 2012. Pp. 79–110.

Matteo Villani. *Cronica*. Ed. Giammaria Mazzuchelli. Milan, 1834.

McKitterick, Rosamund. *Frankish Kingdoms under the Carolingians, 751–987*. Longman, 1983.

Mémoires de la Société de l'histoire de Paris et de l'Île-de-France. Paris, 1900.

Mémoires pour servir à l'histoire de France et de Bourgogne, contenant un journal de Paris, sous les regnes de Charles VI et de Charles VII. Paris, 1729.

Mill, Charles. *History of Chivalry*. H. C. Carey and Lea, 1826.

Mondschein, Ken. *The Knightly Art of Battle*. Getty Publications, 2011.

Moore, Tony K., and Adrian R. Bell. 'Financing the Hundred Years War'. In *The Hundred Years War Revisited*. Ed. Anne Curry. Pp. 57–84.

Mortimer, Ian. *The Greatest Traitor: The Life of Roger Mortimer, First Earl of March, Ruler of England, 1327–30*. Pimlico, 2003.

Munby, Julian. 'The Field of Cloth of Gold: Guînes and the Calais Pale Revisited'. *English Heritage Historical Review* 9 (2014): 30–63.

———. 'The Round Table Building: The Windsor Building Accounts'. In *Edward III's Round Table at Windsor*. Ed. Munby, Richard Barber and Richard Brown. Boydell Press, 2007. Pp. 44–52.

Murimuth, Adam. *Continuatio Chronicarum*. Ed. Edward Maude Thompson. Rolls Series 93. Eyre and Spottiswoode, 1889.

Nicolle, David. *Poitiers 1356: The Capture of a King*. Osprey, 2004.

Oeuvres de Rigord et de Guillaume le Breton. Ed. Henri-François Delaborde. Librairie Renouard, 1882.

Les Olim, ou registres des arrets rendus par la Cour du Roi sous les règnes de Saint Louis, de Philippe Le Hardi, de Philippe Le Bel, de Louis Le Hutin at de Philippe Le Long. Ed. Auguste-Arthur Beugnot. 3 vols. Imprimerie royale, 1839–48.

Ordonnances des roys de France de la troisième race. Ed. Denis-François Secousse. 21 vols. Imprimerie royale, 1723–1849.

Paris, Matthew. *English History from the Year 1235 to 1273, Volume 3*. Trans. J. A. Giles. Bohn, 1854.

Pépin, Guilhem. 'The Sack of the "City" of Limoges (1370) Reconsidered in the Light of an Unknown Letter of the Black Prince'. *Journal of Medieval Military History* 21 (2023), 161–80.

Petit, Joseph. *Essai de restitution des plus anciens mémoriaux de la Chambres des comptes des Paris*. Bailliere, 1899.

Petite chronique françoise de l'an 1270 à l'an 1356. Ed. M. Douet d'Arcq. Société des Bibliophiles, 1866.

Philip de Commines. *The Memoirs of Philip de Commines, Lord of Argenton*. Trans. Andrews R. Scoble. London, 1877.

Phillips, J. R. S. *Aymer de Valence, Earl of Pembroke, 1307–1324: Baronial Politics in the Reign of Edward II*. Oxford University Press, 1972.

Pierre de Versailles. 'Epître à Juvenal après le massacre de 1418'. In *Thesaurus Novus Anecdotorum*. Ed. Edmund Martène and Ursin Durand. Florentinus Delaulne, 1717.

Pohl, Meinrad. 'Quern-Stones and Tuff as Indicators of Medieval European Trade Patterns'. *Papers from the Institute of Archaeology* 20 (2010), 148–53.

Political Poems and Songs Relating to English History Composed During the Period from the Accession of Edward III to that of Richard III. Ed. Thomas Wright. Rolls Series. Longman, Green, Longman, and Roberts, 1859.

Pollard, A. J. *John Talbot and the War in France 1427–1453*. Pen and Sword, 2006.

Prestwich, Michael. *The Three Edwards: War and State in England, 1272–1377*. Weidenfeld & Nicolson, 1980.

———. *Armies and Warfare in the Middle Ages: The English Experience*. Yale University Press, 1996.

———. *A Short History of the Hundred Years War*. I.B. Tauris, 2018.

Le Procès de Maître Jean Fusoris. Ed. Léon Mirot. Paris, 1900.

Registrum Monasterii S. Marie de Cambuskenneth, A. D. 1147–1535. Ed. Sir William Fraser. The Grampian Club, 1872.

Richardson, Thom. *The Tower Armoury in the Fourteenth Century*. Royal Armouries, 2016.

Roger of Howden. *The Annals of Roger of Hoveden, Vol, 2*. Trans. Henry T. Riley. Bohn, 1853.

Rogers, Clifford J. *The Wars of Edward III: Sources and Interpretations*. Boydell Press, 1999.

———. 'By Fire and Sword: *Bellum Hostile* and Civilians in the Hundred Years War'. In *Civilians in the Path of War*. Ed. Mark Grimsley and Clifford J. Rogers. University of Nebraska Press, 2002. Pp. 33–78.

———. 'The Bergerac Campaign (1345) and the Generalship of Henry of Lancaster'. *Journal of Medieval Military History* 2 (2004), 89–110.

———. 'The Battle of Agincourt'. In *The Hundred Years War, Part II: Different Vistas*. Ed. L. J. Andrew Villalon and Donald J. Kagay. Brill, 2008. Pp. 35–132.

———. 'The Anglo-Burgundian Alliance in the Hundred Years War'. In *Grand Strategy and Military Alliances*. Ed. P. R. Mansoor and W. Murray. Cambridge University Press, 2016. Pp. 216–53.

———. 'The Symbolic Meaning of Edward III's Garter Badge'. In *Military Communities in Late Medieval England: Essays in Honour of Andrew Ayton*. Ed. Gary Baker, Craig Lambert and David Simpkin. Boydell Press, 2018. Pp. 125–46.

Ronald, James. *Landmarks of Old Stirling*. Eneas Mackay, 1899.

Rose, Susan. *Calais: An English Town in France, 1347–1558*. Boydell Press, 2008.

Russell, P. E. *The English Intervention in Spain and Portugal in the Time of Edward III and Richard II*. Clarendon Press, 1955.

Rymer, Thomas, ed. *Foedera, conventiones, litterae, et cujuscunque generis acta publica*. 20 vols. London, 1704–35.

Shanzer, Danuta. 'Dating the Baptism of Clovis: The Bishop of Vienne vs the Bishop of Tours'. *Early Medieval Europe* 7 (1998), 29–57.

Shirley, Janet, trans. *A Parisian Journal, 1405–1449*. Clarendon Press, 1968.

Sizer, Michael. 'The Calamity of Violence: Reading the Paris Massacres of 1418'. *Journal of the Western Society for French History* 35 (2007), 19–39.

Small, Graeme. 'French Politics During the Hundred Years War'. In *The Hundred Years War Revisited*. Ed. Anne Curry. Pp. 33–56.

Smith, Robert Douglas, and Kelly DeVries. *The Artillery of the Dukes of Burgundy, 1363–1477*. Boydell Press, 2005.

Smith, Trevor Russell, and Livingston, Michael, eds. *Of Knyghthode and Bataile*. Medieval Institute Publications, 2021.

Strayer, J. R. *The Reign of Philip the Fair*. Princeton University Press, 1980.

Strohm, Paul. *England's Empty Throne: Usurpation and the Language of Legitimation, 1399–1422*. Yale University Press, 1998.

Stuart, E. Pole. 'The Interview between Philip V and Edward II at Amiens in 1320'. *English Historical Review* 41 (1926), 412–15.

Suger. *Oeuvres complètes de Suger*. Ed. A. Lecoy de La Marche. J. Renouard, 1867.

Sumption, Jonathan. *The Hundred Years War, Volume 1: Trial by Battle*. University of Pennsylvania Press, 1990.

———. *The Hundred Years War, Volume 2: Trial by Fire*. University of Pennsylvania Press, 1999.

———. *The Hundred Years War, Volume 3: Divided Houses*. University of Pennsylvania Press, 2009.

————. *The Hundred Years War, Volume 4: Cursed Kings*. University of Pennsylvania Press, 2015.

————. *The Hundred Years War, Volume 5: Triumph and Illusion*. University of Pennsylvania Press, 2023.

Sutherland, Tim. 'The Battlefield'. In *The Battle of Agincourt*. Ed. Anne Curry and Malcolm Mercer. Yale University Press, 2015. Pp. 190–201.

Taylor, Craig. 'Brittany and the French Crown: The Legacy of the English Attack upon Fougères (1449)'. In *The Medieval State: Essays Presented to James Campbell*. Ed. J. R. Maddicott and D. M. Palser. Hambledon Press, 2000.

TeBrake, William H. *A Plague of Insurrection: Popular Politics and Peasant Revolt in Flanders, 1323–1328*. University of Pennsylvania Press, 1993.

Two Memoirs of Renaissance Florence: The Diaries of Buonaccorso Pitti and Gregorio Dati. Ed. Gene Brucker. Harper and Row, 1967.

Txoperena, Joan Mari Martínez, and Rafael Zubiria Mujika. 'La vía de Hispania a Aquitania en el paso del Pirineo por Ibañeta: resultado de la investigación sobre la calzada romana desde Campo Real-Fillera a Donezaharre / Saint-Jean-Le-Vieux'. *Jornadas sobre las calzadas romanas en la Antigüedad* (2017), 151–204.

Vale, Malcolm. *The Angevin Legacy and the Hundred Years War, 1250–1340*. Basil Blackwell, 1990.

Vegetius. *Vegetius: Epitome of Military Science*. Trans. N. P. Milner. Liverpool University Press, 1993.

Verbruggen, Jan F. *The Battle of the Golden Spurs: Courtrai, 11 July 1302*. Ed. Kelly DeVries. Trans. David Richard Ferguson. Boydell Press, 2002.

Vernier, Richard. *The Flower of Chivalry: Bertrand du Guesclin and the Hundred Years War*. D. S. Brewer, 2003.

Villalon, L. J. Andrew, and Donald J. Kagay. *To Win and Lose a Medieval Battle: Nájera (April 3, 1367), a Pyrrhic Victory for the Black Prince*. Brill, 2017.

Wadge, Richard. *The Battle of Verneuil, 1424*. History Press, 2015.

Walsingham, Thomas. *Historia Anglicana*. Ed. H. T. Riley. Rolls Series 28. London, 1863–64.

Walter of Hemingburgh. *Chronicon*. Ed. H. C. Hamilton. London, 1848–49.

Warner, Michael P. *The Agincourt Campaign of 1415: The Retinues of the Dukes of Clarence and Gloucester*. Boydell Press, 2021.

Wilson, Ian, and Nigel Bryant. *The Book of Geoffroi de Charny with the Livre Charny*. Boydell Press, 2021.

Woosnam-Savage, Robert C. *Arms and Armour of Late Medieval Europe*. Royal Armouries, 2017.

Wood, Charles T. '*Regnum Francie*: A Problem in Capetian Administrative Usage'. *Traditio* 23 (1967), 117–47.

Image Credits

1. Charlemagne, Pictures from History / Getty Images
2. Tomb of Eleanor of Aquitaine, Author's Photo
3. Philippe II at Bouvines, API / Getty Images
4. Quemenes, Jean-Luc Luyssen / Getty Images
5. Edward I Does Homage, API / Getty Images
6. Treaty of Paris, Archives Nationales / Wikimedia Commons
7. Battle of Golden Spurs, 1302, Photo Josse / Leemage / Getty Images
8. Edward III Does Homage, Photo Josse / Leemage / Getty Images
9. Battle of Sluys, 1340, Universal History Archive / Contributor / Getty Images
10. Edward III Coat of Arms Partitioned, Author's Photo
11. Battle of Crecy, Photo 12 / Getty Images
12. Death Strangling a Plague Victim, Heritage Images / Getty Images
13. Burghers of Calais, PjrStatues / Alamy Stock Photo
14. Jean II of France, Photo Josse / Leemage / Getty Images
15. Jacquerie Defeated, Heritage Images / Getty Images
16. Poitiers, Author's Photo
17. Najera, Geography Photos / Getty Images
18. Black Prince Effigy, Epics / Getty Images
19. Du Guesclin and Charles V, Photo 12 / Getty Images
20. Tomb of Edward III, Angelo Hornak / Getty Images
21. The Madness of Charles VI, Heritage Images / Getty Images
22. Shrewsbury Beauchamp Pageant (Colorized), duncan1890 / Getty Images
23. Assassination of Louis of Orleans, Nastasic / Getty Images
24. Portrait of Henry V, Art Images / Getty Images
25. Looking North Towards Maisoncelle, Author's Photo
26. MS Battle with Mud, Heritage Images / Getty Images
27. Siege of Rouen, Print Collector / Getty Images
28. Assassination of Jean the Fearless, Photo 12 / Getty Images
29. Joan of Arc at the Stake, Photo Josse / Leemage / Getty Images
30. Joan of Arc, Pictures from History / Getty Images
31. Castillon, Author's Photo
32. Field of the Cloth of Gold, Photo Josse / Leemage / Getty Images

Index

About the Author

Dr Michael Livingston is Citadel Distinguished Professor and teaches the military and cultural history of the Middle Ages at The Citadel, the Military College of South Carolina. In 2024 he was shortlisted for the Crown Award for *Agincourt: Battle of the Scarred King*. He co-authored the textbook reader *Medieval Warfare*, winner of the 2020 Distinguished Book Prize. These add to previous books *The Battle of Crécy: A Casebook*, winner of the 2017 Distinguished Book Award from the Society for Military History, *Never Greater Slaughter: Brunanburh and the Birth of England* (2021), and *Crécy: Battle of Five Kings* (2022). He is an elected Fellow of the Royal Historical Society and former Secretary-General for the United States Commission on Military History.